THE WRITER'S GIFT OR THE PATRON'S PLEASURE?

The Literary Economy in Late Medieval France

DEBORAH MCGRADY

The Writer's Gift or the Patron's Pleasure?

The Literary Economy in Late Medieval France

UNIVERSITY OF TORONTO PRESS
Toronto Buffalo London

Toronto Buffalo London
utorontopress.com

ISBN 978-1-4875-0365-9

Library and Archives Canada Cataloguing in Publication

McGrady, Deborah L., 1967–, author
The writer's gift or the patron's pleasure? : the literary economy in late medieval France / Deborah McGrady.

Includes bibliographical references and index.
ISBN 978-1-4875-0365-9 (hardcover)

1. Authors and patrons – France – History – To 1500. 2. Charles V, King of France, 1338–1380 – Art patronage. 3. Art commissions – France – History – To 1500. 4. France – Intellectual life – To 1500. 5. French literature – To 1500. I. Title.

PQ193.M34 2019 840.9'001 C2018-903181-6

University of Toronto Press acknowledges the financial assistance to its publishing program of the Canada Council for the Arts and the Ontario Arts Council, an agency of the Government of Ontario.

Canada Council for the Arts Conseil des Arts du Canada

Funded by the Government of Canada | Financé par le gouvernement du Canada | Canada

To my three "boyz"

Contents

Illustrations

Acknowledgments

This book has resulted from a luxury that my medieval counterparts passionately lobbied to realize – an intellectual community that fostered my efforts and institutions that respected my scholarship and sponsored my pursuits.

Over the years, colleagues have generously provided me opportunities to share my work, and I am especially grateful to audiences at the University of Michigan, NYU, Princeton, UCLA, Oxford, and Dalhousie University who contributed in key ways to the development of my ideas. I owe a great debt to those who have talked with me about this project and read portions over the years, including Andrea Tarnowski, Helen Swift, Tracy Adams, Peggy McCracken, Lawrence Earp, Daisy Delogu, Jennifer Bain, Sylvie Lefèvre, Nancy Regalado, Zrinka Stahuljak, Noah Guynn, Christine Reno, and Helen Solterer, as well as colleagues past and present at UVa, especially John D. Lyons, Bonnie Gordon, Claire Waters, Bruce Holsinger, and Elizabeth Fowler. I want to thank especially my eternal colleague and friend, A.C. (Tony) Spearing, who regularly found time to talk about my project over lunch and who, more than once, reignited my enthusiasm for the project with his insightful questions. Above all, I want to thank Cynthia J. Brown who set me on this path when I was assigned a presentation on medieval patronage in my first medieval course. I thank all of you for valuable input and I hope I did justice to the goodwill you showed me.

This project required numerous travels to libraries and took (far too many) years to complete, but I never wanted for support. I am grateful to the University of Virginia French Department, the Buckner W. Clay Dean of Arts and Letters, and the Vice President for Research as well as the National Humanities Center for much-needed financial support and precious writing time to realize this project. I owe a particular debt to the Bibliothèque nationale de France, the Bibliothèque royale de Belgique, the Château de Chantilly library, the British Library, and the Hague for allowing me access to so many beautiful manuscripts.

When this project seemed too large to handle, I always found myself buoyed by those dearest to me. Thanks to Anne McCall and Sir John McCall for unrelenting enthusiasm and frequent scotches for good measure, to Francesca Calamita for our Sunday morning tea breaks, to Bernadette Luciano who accompanied me on the final stretch and who generously awaited a daily progress update, to my mother who fought to live and who, for the last four years, has spent much of her precious time encouraging me, but most of all, thanks to Terry, the most amazing husband, who can explain my project better than I can, who filled my glass with champagne at even the smallest milestone, who listened intently on endless hikes about my new ideas or patiently waited for me to work through a problem, and who was always eager to plan a working holiday or a great escape – you made even the low points happy moments.

Abbreviations

Advision Christine de Pizan, *Le livre de l'advision Cristine*
Apparicion Honorat Bovet, *Apparicion Maistre Jehan de Meun*
Charles V Christine de Pizan, *Le livre des fais et de bonnes meurs du sage roy Charles V*
Chemin Christine de Pizan, *Le livre du chemin de longue étude*
Cité Raoul de Presles, *La cité de Dieu*
Confort Guillaume de Machaut, *Le confort d'ami*
Deux amans Christine de Pizan, *Le débat de deux amans*
Ethiques Nicole Oresme, *Le livre des ethiques d'Aristote*
Fonteinne Guillaume de Machaut, *Le dit de la Fonteinne amoureuse*
Fragilité Eustache Deschamps, *Double lay de la fragilité humaine*
Mutacion Christine de Pizan, *Le livre de la mutacion de la Fortune*
Navarre Guillaume de Machaut, *Le jugement dou roy de Navarre contre le jugement de Behaigne*
Othéa Christine de Pizan, *Epistre Othéa*
Paix Christine de Pizan, *Le livre de Paix*
Policratique Denis Foulechat, *Le policratique de Jean de Salisbury*
Prod'hommie Christine de Pizan, *Le livre de la Prod'hommie*
Racional Jean Golein, *Le "racional des divins offices" de Guillaume Durand*
Rose Christine de Pizan, *Dit de la rose*
Vergier Evrart de Trémaugon, *Songe du vergier*

THE WRITER'S GIFT OR THE PATRON'S PLEASURE?

Introduction

Rethinking Literary Patronage in a Medieval Context

The mystique of patronage continues to pull at the heart and, more recently, purse strings of French society. In 2011, Christie's auction house contacted the Bibliothèque nationale de France (BnF) with the news of the impending sale of the privately owned *Livre d'heures de Jeanne de France*. The symbolic value alone of this fifteenth-century book of hours named after its first owner justified its presence in the national library. After all, the core BnF collection dates back to Jeanne of France's great grandfather, the Wise King Charles V, revered bibliophile and avid supporter of French writing. Given this fact, we ought not be surprised that once alerted to the impending auction, the French Minister of Culture and Communication Frédéric Mitterrand immediately responded by classifying the book as a national treasure, a move that forestalled possible private purchase of the book. The minister's actions also afforded the national library much needed time to devise its first campaign for public patronage or "mécénat populaire." The library's campaign was a staggering success. One hundred directly solicited donors covered 75 per cent of the manuscript cost, while 1,600 additional donors, over the brief period of three months, answered a public call to supply the remaining funds.[1] The significance of this donor campaign for collective sponsorship in France cannot be overstated. Since at least the creation of the ministry of culture at the founding of the Fifth Republic, France rigorously favoured state sponsorship of the arts over individual involvement. When the first French minister of culture, André Malraux, proposed in a 1965 speech that France imitate American patrons of contemporary European art so as "to provoke in France a true culture of patronage" ("provoquer en France un véritable mécénat culturel"),[2] his own cabinet rejected the idea and claimed a unique form of French exceptionalism. A report authored by cabinet member Michel Pomey claimed state sponsorship of the arts as a fundamental legacy that bound the Republic to the nation's past. For Pomey, it was government's exclusive right and responsibility to perpetuate the royal tradition of artistic patronage: "The State," he intoned, "had inherited the artistic responsibilities of the princes of yesteryear" ("l'État a hérité des responsabilités artistiques des princes d'hier").[3] Until recently, Pomey's assertion has reigned in France. With the French tax code providing breaks for individual giving only in 2003 and with a continued popular stance that the state is responsible for supporting the arts, the French are still far behind their American counterparts when it comes to individual or corporate sponsorship of creative activity.[4]

It might seem strange to begin a book on medieval literary exchange during the reigns of Charles V and Charles VI of France with discussion of modern donor practices, but I want to use this incident to draw attention to the complex history surrounding the sponsorship of arts and letters in France, a history that can be traced directly back to Charles V's involvement in vernacular book culture. There is good reason to argue that this quickly mythologized moment in patronage history survives in the BnF advertising campaign that inspired thousands of citizens to become art donors in 2012. To persuade the average citizen to participate in the still-novel practice of collective patronage, the BnF *Jeanne de France* donor campaign needed to reeducate the public about artistic sponsorship so as to entice them into adopting new behaviours. The campaign's advertisement sought to create what Pierre Bourdieu refers to as a "vision, both enchanted and mystifying, of human behavior" ("vision enchantée, et mystificatrice, des conduites humaines").[5] As with the "enchanted visions" enveloping the various institutions or *champs* studied by Bourdieu, so too does patronage possess its own seductive narrative in which a nostalgic desire for an intimacy that "never was" (as is the case with all products of nostalgia) casts an aura of selfless giving over acts influenced by personal ambitions. The *Jeanne de France* donor campaign promoted such feelings about artistic patronage through an evocative image extracted from deep within the codex in which the Virgin Mary with child sits before a kneeling angel with harp. This scene offers a studied meditation on the sanctity of artistic exchange by masterfully conflating Annunciation iconography centred on God's ultimate gift with an iconic artistic donation scene that promises to honour the event in song (Figure 0.1: Advertisement for the BnF *Livre d'heures de Jeanne de France* campaign). Entangling art and religion, this reproduced scene provided an especially seductive "enchanted vision" for both France's Catholic population and its secular citizenry, educated

Figure 0.1: Advertisement for the Bibliothèque nationale de France public campaign to purchase the *Livre d'heures de Jeanne de France*.

since the Revolution to venerate the arts in place of religion.[6] The poster ingeniously casts the scene in its own aura by capturing the sparkle of the elaborate gold leaf borders, a strategy that also flaunts the extravagance of this coveted object. This none-too-subtle allusion to the book's opulence serves as a reminder that what has assured this book's survival and its modern price tag of 100,000 euros is its status as a luxury object far more than its religious use or value. This book has always circulated as a high-end commodity intended to symbolize the power, wealth, moral qualities, and taste of those who possessed it.

Advertising, however, rarely counts on viewers' ability to decipher complex messaging, and the BnF poster campaign proved no different. To make legible for its modern viewers the messaging of this imagery, the advertisement compresses into the right column a single narrative that shepherds viewers through the long and thorny history of patronage in France. Flanking the title of the coveted book that advertises its religious and royal ties, four pronouncements travel across time, passing from the medieval period to revolutionary France to arrive in the present. At the top of the column, an unpunctuated command relocates viewers in a distant past, where they are called upon to perform as a noble patron: "Devenez mécène" (Become a patron). In direct opposition to Pomey's 1965 argument for the exclusive patronage rights of the French state, this first declaration calls on viewers to perpetuate an ancient aristocratic gesture. The next command in slightly larger font counters the first through reference to France's Republican ideals. The call to participate in acquiring a "national treasure" recalls the argument of the great preservationist of the French Revolution, Abbé Grégoire, who urged his fellow citizens in 1793 to cease viewing books, jewels, furniture, art objects, and monuments formerly possessed by the nobility as symbols of aristocratic excess and, instead, to claim these art objects as national "property" ("propriété").[7] In ever shrinking font, the poster follows these two historically inspired appeals with acknowledgment of contemporary economic realities governing giving. At the bottom of the poster, an invitation to citizens to send a "gift" of financial support leads to a reminder that such acts of financial generosity come with tax breaks: "les dons donnent droit à une déduction fiscal de 66%" (donations afford the right to a fiscal deduction of 66 per cent). The persistent use of gift language in this final statement ("votre don," "les dons," "donnent") softens the financial details while the font size reduces the economic advantage to a footnote with little bearing on the revival of the illustrious and ancient act of artistic patronage. Yes, the donor will benefit financially from the transaction, but what is most valued is the transformation of an everyday citizen into a patron of the arts and, through this act, that citizen's entry into an elite community united by the belief that the arts and letters are to be treasured and protected. Key to cultivating this sentiment is the maintenance of an aura around the work of art that substantiates its status as a gift rather than a commodity, hence the advertisement's masterful visual subordination of the personal economic advantages of giving to a mythical scene in which the humble Virgin acquires a divine gift of inestimable value.

The Writer's Gift or the Patron's Pleasure examines the long history of this competing philosophy of sponsorship by returning to a pivotal moment when writers and artists responded to the Valois dynasty's unprecedented investment in the book arts. This royal interest in the book world coincided with an urgent need for the struggling Valois dynasty to bolster its claim to the French throne. The first Valois kings viewed books as tools of power and as expressions of their will, but their rationale clashed with the learned community's vision of texts as inestimable treasures to be shared only with those who valued knowledge above all other riches. For the learned, the price of access to books first required acceptance of one's duty to invest in and protect the production and circulation of truth and knowledge. The third Valois king, Charles V (1360–84), would become associated with this viewpoint and he would be memorialized thereafter as the quintessential patron. How he achieved this position as a sovereign who valued learned gifts rather than pursuit of his pleasure is a complex history that remains unexplored.[8]

It is surprising that given the status afforded Charles V in the history of patronage and given the immediate use of his legacy to urge his extended family to invest in letters, there has been scant critical attention given to what his status as a paragon tells us about the literary economy before and after his reign. To be sure, beginning with Léopold Delisle's foundational work on Charles V's library, there has been a tradition of recognizing the king's investment in texts and his crucial role in the legitimization of vernacular writing as unprecedented.[9] So too, the groundbreaking work of Claire Richter Sherman on the Wise King's portraits in his commissioned books has made clear the role artists had in fashioning a new royal identity in which books became influential symbols of power.[10] Yet, as to whether Charles V stood out because of his faithfulness to an established model of the literary benefactor, because of his introduction of new practices, or because of an ideal ascribed to him by the book community is a topic that has failed to spark scholarly interest. Part of the reason for the lack of critical engagement with this issue stems, I believe, from a tendency to identify literary patronage as a universal paradigm immune to cultural, social, or historic mutations.[11] Silent accord with this view permeates the language and frameworks used to discuss medieval literary exchange between a writer or artist and a noble recipient. In the absence of medieval terminology, anglophone and French scholars regularly adopt the descriptors "patronage" and "mécénat" to identify these literary exchanges without acknowledging that, as anachronistic constructs, these words carry cultural baggage.[12] Some scholars have, however, recently noted that understanding premodern textual and artistic exchange is hampered precisely by a lack precise terminology appropriate to the period.[13] The problem with applying frameworks promoted by scholars of later periods to medieval cases should be obvious. When these frameworks derive from study of sixteenth-century cases, the looming problem centres on claims that the Renaissance motivation behind patronage of arts and letters stemmed from a sense of obligation to foster intellectual and creative pursuits.[14] While, as this study will show, fostering the production and circulation of knowledge was an ideal promoted by the medieval intellectual community, there is scant evidence that the nobility supported artists and writers for purely intellectual reasons and virtually no indication that medieval patrons sought to foster creativity. As regards creativity, Corine Schleif has rightly highlighted the problem with retrofitting the model of patronage promoted by Renaissance scholars to medieval cases of aristocratic investment in arts since medievalists deal with patronage of "art before art."[15] On this point, Schleif follows Malcolm Vale, who has stated that medieval aristocratic investment in what we now identify as the arts and letters was never driven by the notion of "art for art's sake."[16]

Scholarship on medieval literary exchange also suffers from the longstanding practice of assigning limited agency to the book community (understood here as including the learned, who read and authored texts, as well as book artisans, librarians, and booksellers, who saw to the production and acquisition of manuscripts). In early influential studies of aristocratic involvement in letters, writers are, at best, cast as calculating players whose desire for fame and fortune lead them to submit without reservation to the patron's will.[17] Even later arguments that identify late-medieval writers as responsible for educating, informing, and bolstering leadership still cast authors as subservient and accommodating participants.[18] Studies of the textual and visual manipulation of literary exchange in medieval works addressed to women have provided the most productive challenge to this scholarly penchant for assigning a passive role to the writing community; in these cases, the book community is shown to have regularly disputed the authority of a female patron.[19] This recognition of the book community as an active agent – for better or worse – in constructing the literary relationship has deeply influenced my interest in the way the book community used text and image to engage with the moral and philosophical underpinnings of literary exchange. In this regard, I take up Jill Caskey's recent call for medievalists to consider the viewpoint of artistic creators and to rethink how they "conceptualized, represented, attributed, and understood" the creative partnerships they forged with the powerful.[20]

To bring attention to the involvement of late-medieval writers and artists in shaping literary dynamics, I first address the disconnect between the historical reality of the literary economy and the narratives of literary exchange as detailed most extensively in the framing matter of works commissioned by or addressed to members of the Valois court. Rather than approach textual and visual depictions of literary dealings as transparent testimonials of lived transactions, I recognize them as creative sites where social realities and philosophical ideals intersect. I approach these sites as textual "biographies" in light of Arjun Appadurai's discussion of the "social lives" of objects as created via "their forms, their uses, their trajectories."[21] Book-presentation scenes and dedicatory addresses breathe life into a work by moving beyond the moment of inception to imagine a book's future reception, whether in terms of its uses or the trajectories it might follow. As narratives that anticipate a future not yet realized (the hoped-for moment when the recipient will accept the work is a key example),[22] they necessarily function as sites of negotiation. Nowhere is this function more apparent than in late-medieval Valois texts in which we frequently discover writers and artists attempting to harmonize the ruling class's view of books as expressions of power and prestige with the intellectual ideals of texts as sources of knowledge and truth. For those individuals who were commissioned to satisfy the "patron's pleasure" by providing vernacular writings, the paratext became a site for articulating a competing philosophy centred on the concept of the "writer's gift." At play in this exchange was far more than a rhetorical game that temporarily destabilized power dynamics by turning an order into a gift. By replacing a royal claim for goods with a philosophy of intellectual giving, authors and bookmakers defined their relationship with the political elite as a partnership built on the free circulation of intellectual riches intended for the common good. This philosophy set the stage for vernacular authors to conceive of their writing activity as a distinctive, valuable, and rare talent that would subsequently justify writers' claims of membership in the emerging field of letters.[23]

The works to be examined here create a tight network of texts produced for a Valois audience during the reigns of Charles V (1364–80) and Charles VI (1380–1422). In a fifty-year timeframe that extends from Charles V's coronation to Christine de Pizan's final discussion of Charles V in her 1414 *Livre de Paix*, we witness the introduction of an unprecedented campaign to foster writing through royal commissions in the French territories followed by a series of authors who relentlessly promoted the king's literary activity as crucial to the survival of the Valois dynasty. In so doing, I stretch the normal perimeters of study of Charles V's patronage of letters so as to place in dialogue the learned translators whose services he solicited (with close attention given to Denis Foulechat, Raoul de Presles, and Nicole Oresme) with learned authors of didactic works geared towards Valois princes (e.g., Philippe de Mézières, Evrart de Trémaugon, Jacques Legrand, and Honorat Bovet) and canonical French writers often categorized as "court poets" because of their focus on an aristocratic audience (e.g., Guillaume de Machaut, Eustache Deschamps, and Christine de Pizan). These last two categories of writers were, for the most part, not commissioned writers, yet they positioned their works in relation to the literary economy detailed by the Wise King's commissioned translators and they pitched their works to an audience who had good reason to have intimate familiarity with Charles V's practices and who were expected to perpetuate his legacy, specifically, two of the king's brothers, Duke John of Berry and Duke Philip of Burgundy; his sons, Charles VI and Duke Louis of Orléans; and his grandson, Louis of Guyenne. Following Charles V's death in 1380, these men were all addressed as potential successors to the Wise King's distinctive legacy.[24] To better appreciate the expectations placed on the king's family members, it is first important to address briefly Charles V's literary dealings in terms of their historical and conceptual uniqueness. Only then do we have the tools to appreciate the active role of writers and artists in shaping the ideal, if not the actual practices, of literary exchange.

The Valois Dynasty and the Transformation of the Vernacular Literary Landscape

Several European rulers had shown interest in book collecting and even a keen awareness of the way books might contribute to royal self-fashioning leading up to Charles V's reign, but no one – not even Alfred the Great,

Charlemagne, or Alfonse X – launched a literary program comparable to the Wise King's ambitious, expensive, and innovative investment in book culture.[25] During his brief sixteen-year reign, Charles V secured the participation of at least seventeen learned authors who were joined by scribes and artists to provide him with new vernacular works. Charles V's literary vision was, however, unquestionably influenced by his immediate predecessors' dependence on the book community to endorse the contentious rise of the Valois dynasty. When the last Capetian king, Charles IV of France, died in 1328 with no male heir, Philip VI of Valois emerged as the victor among the three contenders. Philip's claim to the French throne led to a protracted war with the English, retrospectively and erroneously named the Hundred Years War. Beyond this Anglo-French conflict, the French crown would subsequently endure internal political uprisings and a civil war pitting Valois cousins in a destructive battle for the throne. At every stage, these conflicts played themselves out as much in writing as on the battlefield.

On one hand, it can be argued that the early Valois rulers' reliance on writers to promote their authority differed little from regional lords and their Capetian royal predecessors who attracted writers willing to produce chronicles and treatises celebrating their houses.[26] On the other hand, the distinctive testimony of the translator Jean de Vignay establishes the first Valois royal couple as unmatched in their enthusiasm for vernacular works. Vignay repeatedly linked his extensive corpus to the first Valois couple, especially Queen Jeanne of Burgundy, who was credited with having inspired most of his translations. Vignay also praised the precocious book interests of the dauphin, the future John the Good. In his translation of the *Echecs moralisés*, Vignay claims that the work was inspired by the dauphin's desire for books containing "des choses prouffitables et honnestes" (profitable and honest things) and "information des bonnes meurs" (information on good behaviour).[27] Vignay's early praise was confirmed later when King John commissioned a translation of Livy, a new vernacular Bible, and a new edition of the *Grandes chroniques*.[28] If not captured at the Battle of Poitiers in 1356, King John's support of learned vernacular writings would have surely continued to mark his reign. Instead, it would be the third Valois king who would confirm royal investment in letters as a Valois dynastic tradition by, in François Avril's modest assessment, "amplifying" the practices of his predecessors.[29]

Charles V provided, in fact, a new blueprint that redefined the vernacular literary community both in terms of membership and the works produced. The sheer size of the writing community Charles V gathered already signalled a dramatic shift in the literary landscape. In comparison to the seven translators identified by Serge Lusignan as having served French kings from Philip IV (1268–1314) through John the Good (1354–64), twice as many translators are now linked to Charles V alone.[30] To these fourteen translators, we can add three authors who produced original vernacular works for the king: Evrart de Trémaugon, presumed author of the *Songe du vergier*; Pierre d'Orgemont who provided a crucial continuation to the *Grandes chroniques*; and the anonymous author of the king's distinctive version of the *Livre du sacre des rois de France*. Over the Wise King's brief sixteen-year reign, these seventeen men composed in his name at least thirty-five works. The unique qualifications that these writers brought to the job also signal an important shift in the perception of the vernacular writer. Charles V appears to have bypassed the celebrated contemporary vernacular poets in his midst – specifically, Guillaume de Machaut and Eustache Deschamps – to solicit new vernacular works from university-trained men who often held important positions in ecclesiastic or royal circles. The fact is that few members of the king's coterie of commissioned writers had established reputations as vernacular writers before receiving a royal commission.[31] In place of an established vernacular reputation, the king apparently prioritized Latin learning. The translators were eager to confirm this distinction in their dedicatory addresses, where they asserted that their extensive familiarity with Latin uniquely equipped them to oversee the transference of knowledge from learned circles to the laity. To prove this point, several of the king's translators spoke of coining new vernacular terms to address the lofty philosophical, theological, and political topics they introduced.[32] Although never openly stated, these learned men also profoundly influenced vernacular writing through their exclusive privileging of a Latinate vernacular prose over verse.[33] The commissioned writers, however, repeatedly credited Charles V with both the choice of subject matter and language. The king's controlling hand is even visible in the well-established *Grandes chroniques* tradition, where, as Anne D. Hedeman observes, Charles V played an instrumental role in assuring the inclusion of the Valois dynasty in the updated version produced during his reign.[34] Likewise, the *Livre du sacre des rois de France* assured that a centuries-long coronation tradition became part of Charles V's legacy by presenting his coronation as the standard.[35] The commissioned writers were also unified in stating that it was the king's vision of intellectual improvement that drove the royal commissions; the king desired to educate himself and his people on the principles of good leadership by securing vernacular translations of learned and devotional writings.

Both Charles V and the learned coterie he organized made certain that the king was identified as the primary agent responsible for the positive advancements in vernacular literature. He loomed large for multiple unique reasons, ranging from his uncommon appreciation for learned men to his intimate familiarity with the foundational texts of medieval society to his determination to make this knowledge available to a non-university trained audience. Four decades later, Christine de Pizan's biography of the Wise King would emphatically identify the king as the mastermind who engineered the transfer of knowledge to the laity:

> Pour la grant amour qu'il avoit à ses successeurs, que, au temps à venir, les voult pourveoir d'enseignemens et sciences introduisables à toutes vertus [...] fist par solempnelz maistres, souffisans en toutes les sciences et ars, translater de latin en françois tous les plus notables livres.
>
> (Because of the great love he had for his successors, because, in future times, he wanted them to have access to the teachings and sciences linked to all virtues [...], he had translated from Latin into French by learned masters, competent in all sciences and arts, all of the most important books.)[36]

For Christine, the king's literary commissions promised an everlasting partnership between the learned and the ruling class.

Christine's praise for Charles V's pursuit of the very best scholars to produce the works he desired signals the most significant paradigm shift wielded by the king. The traditional circuit of literary exchange had long favoured the unsolicited offering.[37] In contrast, Charles V took control of literary production when he solicited specific thinkers who were expected to accept pre-chosen literary assignments. This extreme oversight of the initial stages of production identifies the Wise King as a paradigmatic patron; for, as Helen Swift reminds us, patronage is a system "predicated upon a culture of bespoke literary production."[38] If a recipient's direct participation in the initial stages of the creative process cannot be confirmed, the title of patron cannot be applied. Thus, Vignay's multiple claims that he composed works for the Valois dynasty because he was convinced that they would be appreciated differs substantially from the many writers who declared that they wrote and translated because Charles V ordered them to do so. There is corroborative evidence for the dramatic shift in the literary paradigm orchestrated by Charles V. Beyond authorial testimonials, archival evidence confirms the king's commanding role in his literary dealings. To be discussed later in this study are official financial contractual agreements, sometimes bearing the king's personal signature, that testify to a practice not witnessed prior to Charles V's reign in which the king solicited specific literary services from individuals. These author contracts constitute the most distinctive component of Charles V's literary investment practices because they detail a pension program for writers that promised financial support during the many years presumed necessary to complete a commissioned work (sometimes involving up to eight years). Nor does the king's oversight appear to have ceased with the production of the translations. Artisans closely associated with the royal family transcribed and decorated luxury copies of the commissioned texts, which were then displayed in the royal library attached to the king's private chambers in the renovated Louvre palace.[39] For Marie-Hélène Tesnière, the king's motivations were far from altruistic, as the king gathered these luxury copies to create a "bibliothèque d'une famille royale" (library of a royal family);[40] that is, a collection that self-consciously celebrated a dynastic commitment to literary activity. The inventory of the king's library completed after his death endorses the views that the royal court recognized books as a unique form of wealth and an expression of dynastic power. Breaking with the earlier tradition in which household inventories usually referenced manuscripts only if they possessed bejewelled bindings and thus merited being included alongside precious jewels, wrought metals, dinnerware, bedding, and other miscellaneous objects of material worth, the 1380 Louvre library inventory provided an exhaustive list of the king's books that afforded equal value to both luxury books and modest or damaged codices.[41] Yet in spite of this archival evidence confirming the king's clear role as literary patron in its strictest sense and even in spite of writers' confirmation of this arrangement, these same writers, along with miniaturists, persisted in using archaic gifting language and iconography that packaged the king's ordered books as freely offered gifts. This discrepancy between archival evidence and textual and visual narratives of the transaction points to underlying tensions concerning the competing economies linked to solicited and unsolicited texts.

Clientelism and the Literary Commission

This quick overview of literary exchange during Charles V's reign makes apparent that there were two distinct economies that have been traditionally lumped together under the nebulous term of literary patronage.[42] Marcel Mauss's watershed study of archaic gifting provides a helpful model for understanding the offering of an unsolicited text to a chosen recipient as an arrangement in which the exchanged object must at least assume the pretense of an unsolicited offering.[43] Gift theory fails, however, to capture the particularities of the commissioned event. When the text-object is explicitly positioned as a solicited or "bespoke" text, clientelism provides a more apt framework.

In her study of the patronage system as a political and social phenomenon, Verena Burkolter provides a concise definition of clientelism that centres on the patron's interests, to which both the exchanged object and its human agent are subordinated:

> The patron grants favours, protection and help in various circumstances, in return for small pieces of material assistance, services, loyalty, and political allegiance from the side of the client. Such a reciprocal relationship may be expressed in terms of a formal contract or in less formal relations.[44]

In Burkolter's classic definition, clientelism institutes a preordained agreement in which the patron's expressed needs and desires constitute an order for specific services. It is clear that this act of soliciting goods or services overturns gifting patterns from the outset by usurping the inaugural gesture reserved for the donor – the possessor of the exchanged object – to allow the recipient the right to initiate the exchange and, in so doing, assume a new overarching role in the transaction. In clientelism, the patron initiates exchange through a twofold gesture: there is both a promise of favour and the request for a favour. Through this inaugural gesture, the client takes shape when responding favourably to the patron with a matching twofold response: commitment to answer the order and final satisfaction of the order. In archaic gifting, reciprocation by the recipient is encouraged but not required, whereas clientelism is a closed system built on this two-part transaction in which the patron's reciprocation is promised from the outset: once the patron receives the desired services and fulfils the initial contractual promise to reward those services, the transaction is completed.

Several scholars have detected important shifts in artistic and literary exchange dynamics in the premodern era that reflect clientelistic practices. Dale Kent's insightful work on the role of Renaissance art patrons is a case in point, even though she is adamant that applying modern socio-economic frameworks to premodern artistic exchange is an anachronism best avoided.[45] Kent argues in her study of commissioned Italian Renaissance art that bespoke works are best understood as constitutive of the "patron's oeuvre" (as opposed to the "artist's oeuvre") since they are expected to embody the tastes, intentions, and desires of the patron. Douglas Kelly makes a complementary claim when arguing that late-medieval francophone literature most often served to communicate the "genius of the prince" rather than the creative enterprise of the author.[46] Likewise, scholarship on conspicuous consumption patterns shaping literary and artistic transactions in the later Middle Ages emphasizes that a desire for symbols of personal power triggered aristocratic interest in creative works. For Malcolm Vale,

> patronage and acquisition of 'cultural' artefacts and objects in a court context was ... a facet of consumption which could carry social, political, and religious meanings. The meaningful use of these artefacts and objects was both mental and material, and could reflect the identities of the status-groups that consumed them in distinctive ways. Consumption was accompanied by investment in cultural artefacts of many kinds. But to invest implies a hope of gaining a return on that investment.[47]

Corine Schleif insists to an even greater degree on the careful management of this exchange by the ruling class when contending that the art objects collected or commissioned by wealthy individuals or organizations in the Middle Ages were "the stage sets and the costumes, the containers and the scripts, the abbreviations and the visual embellishments, or perhaps even the signage and advertising" that "constructed the patrons as persons of substantial means, devotional largesse, and pious privilege."[48]

What we now categorize as medieval art began with the belief that investment in aesthetic objects confirmed the power, wealth, and moral stature of their owners. The medieval economic historian John Day endorses this point when noting that conspicuous consumption not only fuelled the production and purchase of luxury clothing, but also led to "investments in humanist culture."[49] It should be noted, however, that recent work has shown the extent to which the Valois consumption-driven desire for these perceived luxury items required careful management of appearances: studies of both the language adopted in court treasury records and the reintroduction of gifting rituals at Valois courts testify to conscious manipulation of the language and rituals of exchange to disguise questionable consumption behaviour as expressions of largesse and to divert attention from the economic transformations that threatened the ruling class's dominance.[50] Disguising clientelistic transactions motivated by self-interest as altruistic acts through the use of gifting language and rituals points to what C.A. Gregory defines as an "ambiguous economy": that is, a system in which an exchanged object functions simultaneously as gift and commodity or exhibits the clear capacity to change status based on the prescribed transaction.[51] In the case of texts circulating in late-medieval society as solicited objects that are nonetheless staged as gifts, there is suggestive evidence to consider these texts as commodities rather than as gifts. For, as Gregory states, a commodity is fundamentally "a socially desirable thing with a use-value and an exchange-value."[52] Moreover, the solicited text can be said to constitute a commodity because it is first secured by a contractual speech act that commits the speaker to answer receipt of the desired object with a promised reward.[53]

In spite of the striking differences between archaic gifting and clientelism detailed here, clientelism is commonly recognized as an offshoot of archaic gifting, in part because it relies heavily on gifting rhetoric and rituals to articulate exchange.[54] This association of gifting and clientelism, however, fails to capture the distinctiveness of these two economies. Rather than a natural extension – an arboristic outgrowth, if you will, of archaic gifting – clientelism is best likened to grafting. Consider the following comment by Burkolter regarding the capacity for clientelism to harmonize archaic and modern worlds:

> In many societies undergoing speedy processes of modernization, the old relationships of patronage have revealed great flexibility and capability of change, which made it possible for the old particularistic interpersonal relationships to adapt to the new conditions, needs and political structure.[55]

In short, clientelism is a system that adapts the "old particularlistic interpersonal relationships" of gifting to new realities.

Burkolter's nuanced understanding of clientelism is particularly informative when applied to the late-medieval literary economy. Whereas it is common to locate unsolicited and solicited texts in an archaic gifting framework, Burkolter helps us appreciate that the solicited text is, in fact, the product of a new dynamic in which archaic practices were grafted onto a new literary economy deeply influenced by contemporary conspicuous-consumption practices and by an emerging consumerism.[56] This grafting process has a long and troubled history when it comes to the arts and it has long inspired an enduring ideology about creative work, one that Lewis Hyde summed up at the outset of *The Gift: Imagination and the Erotic Life of Property* when declaring that "a work of art is a gift, not a commodity," adding for emphasis, "a work of art can survive without the market, but where there is no gift there is no art."[57]

Intellectual and Literary Views on Exchange

Whereas the nobility is said to have disguised their conspicuous consumption practices behind the language and rituals of gifting, Charles V's commissioned writers reveal a keen interest in repackaging the king's command as the writer's gift. To achieve this outcome, the artistic community responded to royal consumption practices with its own distinctive grafting of the commission onto an archaic gifting model. In fact, a striking disconnect is revealed between historical record and the narrative accounts authored by Charles V's commissioned writers. Contrary to archival evidence that testifies to royal pensions for authors, not a single commissioned writer spoke of such lucrative arrangements in writing. This detail is all the more noteworthy because commissioned texts systematically begin with the genesis of the work. Albeit quick to acknowledge that the king ordered the work, commissioned writers, nonetheless, avoided open discussion of promises or monetary rewards received in advance of writing. More common was an elaborate rhetorical masquerade intended to discourage any belief that authors profited financially from royal dealings by presenting instead their work as a disinterested gift freely offered to Charles V. In dedicatory addresses, the commissioned writers disassociated their work from the logic of the commission to assert instead that the product of their intellectual labour issued from a natural response to the king's esteem for knowledge. Court artists frequently reinforced this message of giving with frontispieces heading the king's personal copies of commissioned works, where they spotlighted the transference of the work from writer to sovereign instead of the inaugural transaction of the commission.[58]

If our first reaction is to read commissioned writers' silence about the material benefits they reaped from their royal literary dealings as motivated by an interest to disguise their involvement in an emerging consumer culture, there is good reason to consider more carefully intellectual traditions specific to the learned community that might also have informed their silence. Longstanding debates regarding the role of money on the circulation of knowledge likely played a major role in the commissioned writers' desire to distance themselves from the clientelistic relations with the king that, at least in some documented cases, resulted in lucrative arrangements for the writer-clients. Profiting from one's knowledge was the topic of a protracted, centuries-long university debate concerning the potentially irreparable contamination of knowledge once economic gain was introduced into the exchange.[59] Sensitive to this debate and potentially seeking a pre-emptive defence against accusations that they had profited from their royal dealings, Charles V's commissioned writers repeatedly asserted that their fulfilment of a royal commission hinged not on profit but on the intellectual tradition that recognized knowledge as a gift to be shared with worthy members of the learned community. As keepers and mediators of this knowledge, they followed Aristotle's writings and Scripture, both of which called for a learned sodality centred on promoting, enhancing, sharing, and preserving knowledge as a treasure that surpassed earthly riches.[60]

Identification of texts as gift-offerings in Charles V's commissioned works provides an important bridge between twelfth-century vernacular poets who promoted the archaic gifting ideal as a framework for literary exchange and late-medieval writers' celebration of the writer's gift. Scholars recognize the gifting discourse adopted by twelfth-century writers as serving to produce a closed, mutual-reciprocation dynamic between a donor and donnee (as opposed to between client and patron). This "system of constraints," nevertheless, presented the gift-text as a "don contraignant" that obliged the recipient to reciprocate.[61] This system echoes the main tenets of Maussian gifting, which is built around three interlocking and interdependent acts: the obligation to give, to receive, and to reciprocate.[62] Mauss specified, however, that in spite of the obligatory nature of the process, the transaction must appear "free and disinterested" even though it was, in fact, "constrained and self-interested."[63] According to William Burgwinkle, the troubadour poets were already aware of the breakdown of this arrangement in light of an aristocracy that skirted its obligation to writers and an emerging market economy; they responded with a "rhetoric of negotiation and exchange" that emphasized the metaphorical value of poetic texts.[64] Jacqueline Cerquiglini-Toulet identifies a continued frustration with aristocratic stinginess in late-medieval French poetry and she too finds that it led poets to negotiate; here, however, she speaks of a negotiation between a nostalgic longing for the golden age of noble magnificence and emerging mercantile realities. In contrast to Burgwinkle's troubadours, Cerquiglini-Toulet believes that late-medieval poets abandoned the gifting ideal and adapted to consumer demand by "stockpile[ing]" their poetry so that they could provide it on demand.[65] I believe, however, that we can read the market metaphors studied by Cerquiglini-Toulet as a continuation of the earlier negotiations detailed by Burgwinkle rather than as evidence of poets' acquiescence to a consumer-driven economy. Writing on the other side of Charles V's commissioning practices, these late-medieval writers found in the works of the king's commissioned writers a unique strategy for converting a demand into a gift, and they did so by imagining scenarios in which they held on to their works until their gift was solicited. It would, in fact, be the late-medieval vernacular poets whose services were not solicited by Charles V who would articulate most fully a philosophy already taking shape in twelfth-century troubadour poetry that insisted on this concept of the writer's gift as an invaluable good.

When drawing inspiration from narratives of literary exchange developed at Charles V's court, later vernacular writers enhanced this tradition of valuing poetry with new arguments for the intellectual worth of vernacular writing. Adrian Armstrong and Sarah Kay's argument that the late Middle Ages witnessed a revival of and renewed appreciation for verse as a "medium of reflection and enlightenment"[66] is, I believe, deeply indebted to the promotion of vernacular intellectual thought during Charles V's reign. For it was thanks to the commissioned writers that we see some of the most influential arguments for what Armstrong and Kay refer to as medieval French poets' belief in their "powers of mediation" as well as the view that poetry was "caught up in history rather than abstracted from it."[67] The fact that Charles V's commissioned texts were presented and revered as intellectual treasures fuelled contemporary arguments for poetic talent as a divine gift. It would be, in fact, the commissioned writers' contemporary, the celebrated poet and composer Machaut, who, in the prologue to his collected works, would most explicitly challenge the commission by reasserting an earlier vernacular poetic tradition. Machaut's Prologue provided the late-medieval literary community with an unprecedented complex and fertile meditation on the "writer's gift" as entailing poetic skill and talent – unique gifts, in addition to knowledge, that were reserved for a select few. This daring manifesto on the singularity of the poet who figures as the wealthiest of souls because both Nature and the God of Love bestowed on him the gift of verse would have a powerful effect on his self-declared protégée, Deschamps. Deschamps would state even more explicitly at the outset of his *Art de dictier* that verse depended on God-given talents conferred on a privileged few. This tripartite treatment of writing as a gift – one that demands reward at the same time that it represents an inestimable treasure first conferred on the writer and then shared with society – would inspire fifteenth-century French writers to claim for themselves and their work a central role in society. No author more vividly captures this shift than Christine de Pizan, who would first secure her fame through poetry focused on the sentimental world and verse that advertised its worth as "jeux à vendre"[68] before shifting to lengthy, politically engaged writings that called on the ruling class to take seriously their obligation to better society. That these later developments occurred during the troubled reign of Charles VI is crucial. As a period defined not only by the king's struggles with severe mental illness and internecine conflict that led to a civil war, it was also a time when the ruling class resisted invitations to view writers as partners or to consider literary activity as more than a form of entertainment that reflected aristocratic prerogatives.[69] Nowhere are the repercussions of the aristocratic "divestment" in writing more manifest than in the works of Deschamps and Christine, both of whom would give expression to a growing nostalgia for Charles V's mythologized engagement with the book community to counter the practices of contemporary Valois princes who sought to impose a culture of literary subservience on writers whose talents were expected to confirm the power and prestige of the ruling class.

Promoting the Writer's Gift in Text and Image

For many of the late-medieval francophone writers studied here, the dynamics and conditions of exchange mattered as much as the knowledge they communicated. Both Charles V's commissioned writers and the book community that produced works for Valois consumption carefully encased texts in a meta-reflective paratextual frame that envisioned the literary economy as stretching from creative inception to consumption. These metatextual reflections have long been mined as rich resources for discussion of literary dynamics.[70] Rare, however, are studies of this material that venture beyond a flattened analysis of the recycling of gifting models and feudal rituals to describe literary exchange. This resistance is all the more surprising given the rich scholarship and intellectual inquiry that has followed in the wake of Marcel Mauss's study of archaic gifting. I have found especially valuable for investigating the manipulation of consumption patterns by the late-medieval book community four avenues of inquiry into gifting that extend Mauss's work: 1) research into the performance of gifting, 2) the inalienable status of certain gifts that forever binds them to the giver, 3) the effect of timing of reciprocation on power dynamics, and 4) the concept of sacrifice as a radical form of gifting. In the first instance, the ritual of exchange plays a central role in realizing a gifting event. If not carefully managed, the performance itself could communicate conflicting motivations, thereby failing to protect, for instance, the transferred object from being identified as a commodity. Gadi Algazi has noted that "practices of representation are an integral part of gifting" because in distinguishing the exchange from "other transaction modes," the performance confers on the object "particular value and efficacy," and in cases in which the status of the object is difficult to discern easily, "the more labor such would-be presents require of givers, recipients, and their audience: minute symbolic distinctions, studied ignorance, and strained belief are often at play."[71] Add to the role performance plays in articulating the value of an exchanged object the fact that every culture distinguishes certain gifts as more valuable than others. For Annette B. Weiner, these "inalienable possessions" are "imbued with the intrinsic and ineffable identities of their owners."[72] Weiner's central interest in inalienable possessions was the role women played as producers and givers of these specially endowed objects and how these objects confirmed kinship and conferred authority on the community that formed around them. The relevancy of her work to medieval literary exchange dynamics even when women do not play a direct role is made apparent in her pairing of artistic creations (e.g., myths, songs, and dances) alongside more obvious symbols of authority (e.g., crowns, fine fabrics, land, and genealogies) as possessing a similar power. For Weiner, all these objects share in common their capacity not only to confer power on the recipient and the recipient's descendants but also to represent for the giver "vehicles for political autonomy."[73] For this reason, Weiner refers to the art of offering such objects to another as an exchange centred on "keeping-while-giving." These unique gifts bind givers and recipients in a closed, intimate community in which all participating parties are expected to promote and protect these inalienable possessions while they afford both parties a unique form of power. Also crucial are Pierre Bourdieu's reflections on destabilizing power dynamics through manipulation of the time lapse between the act of offering and the act of reciprocating. As first noted by Mauss, the timing of reciprocation opens up space for critical recalibration of power dynamics. Reciprocating too soon suggests premeditation, whereas delay causes the donee-turned-donor to occupy indefinitely the vulnerable state of recipient rather than advance immediately to the role of master of the giving act. For Bourdieu, the dangerous space that opens between the gift and the counter-gift is one in which the initial giver assumes temporary power, thereby dramatically altering the hieratic structure of gifting.[74] Finally, Georges Bataille's identification of sacrifice as the ultimate gift is crucial because of his claim that this extreme form of gifting, which inevitably requires the destruction of a work, serves to restore intimacy where it has been lost.[75]

Drawing on these theoretical elaborations on Mauss's early work can elucidate the complexity and the messaging of literary exchange by the late-medieval book community. For instance, Algazi's work in light of Weiner and Bourdieu's studies encourages us to linger on the function of the presentation scenes that head many luxury codices. The vast majority of these images privilege the moment of the book presentation, and thus the viewer's first encounter with the book halts time to allow for sustained reflection on the power dynamics surrounding this stage of the transaction. Given that these opening scenes often depict the book suspended between the two participants, it is worth considering that it is the instability rather than the maintenance of power structures that is put on display. For, in truth, these scenes create uncertainty around the actors whose roles waver between that of donor or client and donnee or patron. This insight sheds new light on commissioned writers' reluctance to discuss anticipated reward, illustrators' privileging of the book transfer over visual accounts of the commission, and vernacular writers' frequent identification of the offering as the crux of exchange in dedications and in fictional accounts, even when a commission preceded this event. To be developed in the opening chapters, Charles V's commissioned writers identified their texts as inalienable goods that may have been requested by the king with the goal of confirming his authority, but they were depicted as a shared wealth that bound the sovereign to the book community. Machaut would take another angle when professing that the writer's gift conferred power on the author himself. Christine de Pizan who transformed an abandoned commissioned text into a spiritual offering to the long-deceased Charles V countered Machaut's aggressive appropriation of his gift with the ultimate sacrificial writing act. Christine wrote for a patron who could not reciprocate, and yet this extreme form of literary giving anticipates Bataille's claim that the sacrifice restores intimacy because she used her orphaned text to connect with the deceased king she so admired.[76] So too, the inalienability of gifts demands that we think differently about threats by a writer like Deschamps who claimed the right to use his poetry to destroy the ruling class's legacy either by excluding its members from his poetry or by exposing their shortfallings in verse. These observations will be more fully developed in subsequent chapters as we examine how vernacular writers' engagement with past ideals informed their response to the contemporary literary economy. Rather than bend to social pressure that frequently identified its works as luxury commodities, the late-medieval writing community developed a nuanced philosophy that asserted the inestimable value of the knowledge and talents its members possessed. It is crucial to recognize this shift as a response to Charles V's application of clientelism to the literary economy.

Plotting the New Literary Terrain

Studying the literary exchange dynamics of the reigns of Charles V and Charles VI requires that we first reassess literary dealings at the court of Charles V and investigate more deeply the competing logics briefly mentioned that distinguished the sovereign's practices and ambitions from the philosophy of intellectual giving promoted by the commissioned writers. Chapter 1 identifies Charles V's signature commissioning practices as an expression of clientelism and argues that this approach found justification in Mirrors of Princes. This medieval advice literature for princes promoted large-scale artistic projects – *granz euvres*, as they were termed at the time – as valued expressions of sovereign power. Charles V inaugurated his own large-scale project – which I identify as the *Sapientia* project – that was to reflect his newly fashioned identity as a wise and learned ruler. We shall examine here key components of this project, namely the construction of the first French royal library – attached, no less, to the king's private chambers at the new Louvre residence; royal financial contractual agreements with intellectuals to produce texts for this library; and, finally, the acquisition of luxury copies of these works to display in this newly conceived treasure house of knowledge. This multi-pronged project reflects the patron's pleasure or what Kent refers to as the "patron's oeuvre"; Charles V enlisted the services of a large clientele to realize an oeuvre intended as an immediate reflection of his power and authority and a lasting testimony to Valois sovereignty. To end the story here, as is common, would be to ignore evidence that the literary and artistic community performed as an active agent in the service of the king. Chapter 2 turns full attention to the ways in which the textual and visual accounts of the royal commissioning program as detailed in the king's own books engaged with the king's clientelism. Instead of rehearsing the king's clientelistic practices, writers revived archaic gifting ideals that they then grafted onto the realities of their royal dealings. The commissioned writers provided uncommonly elaborate paratextual testimonials that redefined their service to the king's *Sapientia* project as a partnership through a carefully articulated politics of gifting. It is important to emphasize that the commissioned writers were not interested in destabilizing power dynamics by raising themselves to the status of their king; rather, working in collaboration with the king's illustrators, they sought to reposition the king as an elite member of their learned sodality. With this realignment of the royal literary deal, the commissioned work came to represent an intellectual gift freely offered to their learned sovereign reader. To explore these ideas, three commissioned translations are privileged: Denis Foulechat's *Policratique* (1372), Raoul de Presles's *Cité de Dieu* (1375), and Nicole Oresme's *Ethiques d'Aristote* (1376).

It would be to a separate albeit intersecting group of vernacular authors associated with the Valois court to negotiate the nuanced account of literary dynamics expressed in these highly influential commissioned works. Chapters 3 through 6 widen our view of the writing community born out of Charles V's *Sapientia* project by turning to vernacular authors of original works whose own relations with the Valois dynasty were profoundly shaped by the legacy of the king's commissions. Three authors are privileged in these chapters: Guillaume de Machaut (c. 1300–77), Eustache Deschamps (c. 1340–c. 1404), and Christine de Pizan (1364–c. 1430). For all three writers, literary exchange dynamics constituted a pressing literary subject. Each writer weighed the advantages and risks associated with the commission, spoke of the Valois responsibility to perpetuate the Wise King's legacy, lectured on the value of the knowledge they possessed, openly acknowledged their unique talents to communicate wisdom, and reiterated their willingness to partner with the ruling class to make the French kingdom a stronger and more unified nation.

Guillaume de Machaut merits an important role in this study because of his "fictions of engagement" in which aristocratic involvement in the arts came under scrutiny, and particularly crucial is the fact that Machaut's fictional treatment of literary exchange coincided with the implementation of Charles V's *Sapientia* project and his establishment as the model royal patron. The poet's scepticism about noble readers who played too active a role in poetic creation elucidates reservations lurking in the writings of Charles V's commissioned writers. Machaut's *Jugement de Navarre* (c. 1355), the *Confort d'ami* (1357), the *Fonteinne amoureuse* (1362), and the Prologue to his collected works (1370s) develop the author's reservations concerning the value of commissions. In these texts, patrons' desires and commands are repeatedly presented as threats to the literary enterprise. The author responded to this threat with his own unique form of rhetorical violence by introducing unworthy patron-figures, by imagining fantastical arrangements in which a prince might cede power to a poet in exchange for a text, and by asserting the unique ability of verse to communicate learning, cultivate introspection, and offer comfort. In his final composition, the Prologue to his collected works, Machaut supplanted the disappointing terrestrial patron-figures of his earlier works with divine sponsors who, in lieu of demands, offered the poet the "gift" of poetic talent. In these works, timing in the Bourdesian sense is everything: we repeatedly witness the poet stalling exchange to assert authorial control of the poetic gift. Extant manuscript copies of Machaut's works allow us to consider how Machaut's unconventional accounts of poet-prince relations were received in Valois circles. In the final decade of Machaut's life through the 1390s, Charles V's favoured miniaturists were regularly enlisted to decorate several copies of his writings destined for members of the Valois circle. These visual treatments of Machaut's writings testify to artists' attempts to negotiate the philosophical divide that pitted the poet's antagonistic treatment of literary clientelism against both the idealized account of exchange portrayed in the king's commissioned works and the changing views on poet-prince relations that emerged following the Wise King's death.

The challenge faced by writers in the wake of the Wise King's unexpected death in 1380 was immediately expressed through their swift disappearance from the royal court. Chapter 4 opens with discussion of this sudden vanishing of Charles V's writers as well as the immediate abandonment of the *Sapientia* project by the newly formed court. Against this backdrop, Deschamps stands out as a lone voice militating for Charles V's legacy at the French royal court. This chapter begins with an argument for acknowledging Deschamps as a yet-unrecognized contributor to Charles V's *Sapientia* project, given that he surely composed the *Double lai de la fragilité* to answer the Wise King's desire for vernacular translations. Had Charles V lived long enough to receive Deschamps's daring and ambitious translation and had he appreciated the work, the *Lai* would stand as the only known contemporary vernacular-verse-translation contribution to the *Sapientia* project. Instead, the partially completed copy of the *Lai* would bear witness to the abrupt end of the *Sapientia* project, in spite of efforts by men like Deschamps to persuade the young Charles VI of the inestimable value of knowledge. Faced with the young king's indifference to this arrangement, which was only exacerbated by his descent into madness, Deschamps progressively reworked the literary model of the past to institute a radical dynamic in which gifting language was repurposed to speak of dues, debts, and curses. This repurposing is especially apparent in a series of poems from 1396 in which Deschamps announced his decision to abandon a work undertaken to celebrate the Valois dynasty on the basis that the royal family was not worthy of inclusion in the learned sodality once fostered by Charles V. In this regard, Deschamps presents a radical departure from Weiner's concept of keeping-while-giving because he keeps what he ought to give; nonetheless, the result is that the poet's inalienable gift gives him "political autonomy," but at the king's expense.

One poet stands out during this period of crisis for her relentless efforts to revive the ideal of intellectual exchange previously promoted at the court of Charles V. As part of her pursuit of this ideal, Christine de Pizan turned her literary focus on Charles V's second son, Louis of Orléans (1364–1407), who, in the wake of his royal brother's early struggle with mental illness, sought to position himself as a worthy inheritor of the throne. Chapter 5 argues that an important part of Louis's political self-fashioning involved efforts to revive his father's *Sapientia* project and that Christine emerged as one of the prince's most vocal supporters of his claims to his father's learned legacy. Christine would stipulate in her writings, however, that for Louis to assume completely his father's seat, he needed to commission new learned works that reflected a royal ideal rather than accept what she perceived as the more passive role of the donnee who was satisfied simply with textual offerings from his learned servants. Duke Louis never committed to the role Christine proposed and, ultimately, she would look elsewhere for a worthy continuator of Charles V's legacy. Duke Philip of Burgundy, Charles V's youngest living brother (1342–1404) would come to fill that role. In 1404 the duke commissioned from the author a work certain to revive the Wise King's literary practices and to bind this legacy to himself rather than his nephew Louis. The closing chapter focuses on Duke Philip's commissioned biography, the *Livre des fais et bonnes meurs du sage roy Charles V*. Conceived of as a revival of the intimate partnership Christine imagined between Charles V and his learned servants, this biography had the opposite effect and ultimately exposed the risks linked to clientelism, here triggered by the duke of Burgundy's sudden death only a few months after Christine had accepted the assignment. Christine responded to this double tragedy of the duke's death and the collapse of the commission by introducing the most extreme form of giving, that of sacrificial giving. Faced with a text cursed to remain orphaned, Christine ultimately transformed the commissioned text into a sacrificial offering. In the final part of her three-part biography, Christine turned to the deceased Charles V to whom she humbly offered the abandoned commissioned biography as a gift-text. This literary act, however, does not correspond to Christine's actual treatment of the biography; in fact, she struggled throughout the biography, as testified in several metatextual asides, with the reception of her work by the living and she further oversaw production of multiple copies of the biography that she then distributed as her "oeuvre."[77] The chapter closes with a study of these manuscript copies and Christine's treatment of the biography in later works.

As we saw with the modern BnF campaign to acquire the *Livre d'heures de Jeanne de France* through public patronage, efforts to reshape literary dynamics are complex. This study exposes long-ignored evidence that late-medieval vernacular writers were deeply attuned to their own participation in promoting and shaping the ideal of an intimate partnership that continues to inform modern discussions of artistic and literary patronage. When we apply the same critical gaze afforded the BnF *Jeanne de France* donor advertisement to the paratextual material framing Charles V's commissioned texts and those many unsolicited works offered to later Valois princes, we discover literary accounts that often require reading between the lines and looking past the standard images to consider the cultural and historical particularities as well as the enduring nostalgic drive for an intimate partnership forged between artists and supporters that influenced this messaging. Just as we find in the BnF *Jeanne de France* advertisement a careful management of the traditions and expectations of modern-day sponsorship of the arts, so too medieval accounts of literary exchange functioned as sites of complex negotiations that involved manipulation of language and imagery, attentiveness to cultural sensitivities, staged re-enactments of ritualized performances, and concerted efforts to transform a nostalgic ideal into real action. This approach to the textual, visual, and material treatment of the economic and interpersonal dealings framing medieval artistic creation reveals that at the core of the history of patronage of letters, there has always been a competing discourse authored by the beneficiaries of this sponsorship that concerns the rules, purpose, parameters, and risks associated with the benefactor's investment in intellectual activity. The complex messaging witnessed in these late-medieval texts furnishes good reason recognize the iconic patron-figure, whether represented by the Virgin Mary, Jeanne de France, or Charles V, as a creative construction that reveals more about the hopes of the literary community than about lived reality. In the BnF *Jeanne de France* donor poster, the artist is depicted as a heavenly angel in possession of the divine gift of music, and in the works studied here, we shall discover writers who recognized their knowledge and their literary talents also as divine gifts. When it came to literary exchange, they were keen to articulate the product of their intellectual labour as the writer's gift to give or to withhold rather than the patron's pleasure to demand at will.

Chapter One

King Charles V's *Sapientia* Project: From the Construction of the Louvre Library to the Books He Commissioned

During the reign of Charles V of France from 1364 to 1380, the textual arts enjoyed unprecedented royal support. By the time of the king's death, the royal book collection consisted of between 1,200 and 1,300 manuscripts.[1] By some estimates, this number registers a 40 per cent increase in holdings dating to the last seven years of the king's reign.[2] It is commonly accepted that Charles V's unparalleled bibliophilia had an immediate impact on the field of letters. Scholars link Charles V's sustained royal sponsorship of the textual arts to the rise of the vernacular,[3] the emergence of an early French humanist movement,[4] and the creation of a new royal identity grounded in book learning.[5] Add to this already impressive list the fact that his investment in letters resulted in dramatic structural, administrative, and financial changes at the French royal court. Only a few days after his coronation, plans to relocate the royal family from the Palais de la Cité to the Louvre were announced. The king had ordered a major renovation of the northwest wing of the Louvre that included the creation of a new repository for what would become the largest personal library in Europe. Treasury accounts document substantial sums related to this library, ranging from funds reserved for its construction and furbishing to money allotted for book preservation, to gratifications, salaries, and fixed pensions offered to the artists and intellectuals who filled the royal shelves with new works. Once the books previously housed at the Palais arrived at the Louvre in 1368, the king promptly named Gilles Malet as the first royal librarian responsible for inventorying the collection, assuring book preservation, and securing new worthy acquisitions.[6] These new additions to the collection arrived through various channels: as gifts from peers, courtiers, and authors; as purchases from merchants, *libraires*, and the occasional entrepreneur; and as appropriations acquired through estate liquidations. The most coveted works, however, resulted from direct royal commission. The number of works recognized as having been commissioned by Charles V is now thirty-five. They range from overt political commemorations, such as the *Livre du sacre des rois* and the continuation of the *Grandes chroniques*, to translations of ancient philosophy, Scripture, theological and devotional writings, to at least two original vernacular compositions completed during the king's lifetime: Jean de Brie's *Vray regime et gouvernement des bergers et bergeres* and Evrart de Trémaugon's *Songe du vergier.*[7]

For Léopold Délisle, author of the essential study on Charles V's library, the king's ambitions for this collection distinguished him from his royal predecessors:

> Les prédécesseurs de Charles V avaient possedé des livres; la plupart d'entre eux, et notamment le roi Jean, son père, avaient encouragé la culture des lettres, subventionné les auteurs et fait executer par d'habiles artistes des livres de grand luxe. Mais aucun n'avait songé à créer ce que nous appellerions aujourd'hui un établissement d'utilité publique, destiné à survivre au fondateur.[8]

> (Charles V's predecessors had owned books; most of them, most notably his father King John, had encouraged a culture of letters, subventioned authors and had produced by skilled artists luxury books. But none among them had thought to create what we would refer to today as an institution dedicated to the public good that was intended to survive its founder.)

Jean Devaux underscores the link between Charles V's investment in letters and the practices of the modern French state by referring to this activity as an early expression of a "politique culturelle" (cultural policy).[9]

This scholarship on Charles V's investment in book culture has secured for him the role of the quintessential patron of letters, a role first attributed to him by the late-medieval book community. Authors, artists, and book merchants alike nourished his desire for books and praised his learned interests. In spite of this long history of praise for Charles V's literary patronage, scant attention has been paid either to the clientelistic mechanisms of his sponsorship or to the effect of the king's investment in letters on the literary economy. To be certain, Charles V is frequently acknowledged as having influenced vernacular writers' shift away from chivalric adventures and other forms of casual entertainment towards more serious matters,[10] but still to be examined is the dramatic reconceptualization of literary dynamics sparked by Charles V's wide-ranging investment in letters. To shed light on this matter, this chapter first briefly reviews previous French kings' investment in books and then considers how princely advice literature provided important justification for the king's activity. Charles V's commissioned writers turned to these Mirrors of Princes to privilege especially two concepts related to the king's large-scale investment in books. First, they recalled the aphorism that knowledge was an inestimable treasure that surpassed worldly riches, and second, they revived the argument that princes were obliged to invest in large-scale projects or "granz euvres" (great works) to benefit the community.[11] Together, these two principles provide important context for understanding how the support, collection, and preservation of books came to be identified as central to dynastic legacy.

Hereafter, these initiatives are referred to as components of the king's *Sapientia* project, a "great works" project centred on investment in book culture as a means of establishing his legacy while also promoting knowledge within the kingdom. The *Sapientia* project entailed a set of interlocking initiatives that began with the creation of a physical monument to learning (the private royal library in the renovated Louvre palace), which then prompted rapid acquisition of materials (from parchment to completed books) and the convening of highly skilled clients who made commitments to the king to produce new works (from university-trained scholars to bookmakers). Special attention is afforded in the final section of this chapter to the royal literary commissions that proved central to the realization of the *Sapientia* project. In favouring solicited works over unsolicited offerings, Charles V recast royal literary engagement as a clientelistic arrangement that broke with the traditional gifting model that had long regulated the circulation of literature and knowledge. In the next chapter, we turn to the responses of his commissioned writers to this shift in the literary exchange paradigm.

Past Models of Literary Engagement and the New "Law of Letters"

By the time Charles V ascended to the throne, royal investment in book culture had been firmly established as a Valois family affair.[12] In fact, as the first reigning couple of the Valois dynasty, Philip VI and Jeanne de Bourgogne stand out for the eleven vernacular translations of Latin works that Jean de Vignay dedicated to them. In particular, the queen was singled out as the inspiration for most of the translator's work, including his influential multivolume *Miroir historial*, *La légende dorée*, *Épistres et Évangiles*, *Chronique de Primat*, and *Ysopet et Avienet*.[13] When Jeanne died from the plague in

1349, it would be to Philip VI's new queen, Blanche de Navarre, to continue this practice. By the end of her extraordinarily long life, which covered the reign of the first four Valois kings, Blanche had acquired the sobriquet "la belle sagesse," which was, at least in part, surely inspired by the forty manuscripts she had collected and that were listed in her final testament.[14]

The first two Valois queens' investment in book culture had an obvious impact on subsequent French rulers. As already noted, at an early age, the future John the Good had been identified by Vignay as sharing his parents' interests in book culture, and upon ascending to the throne in 1350, King John quickly revealed his personal passion for book collecting by commissioning a number of translations and new writings. Archival evidence suggests that John the Good went even further than his predecessors when expanding his support of translators to encompass book artisans as well. King John conferred on numerous illuminators, including Jean de Bruges, Girard d'Orléans, and Jean d'Orléans, the title of *pictor regis*, along with a fixed salary.[15] In addition, Jean Lavenant was a salaried scribe for King John (Lavenant would have to wait, however, until Charles V's reign to be given the newly created title of "écrivain du roi" or royal scribe).[16] During his time as a prisoner in England, King John continued to invest in books, ranging from purchases of both devotional writings and romances from local *libraires* to a commission addressed to his chaplain and fellow prisoner, Gace de la Buigne, asking that he write the *Déduits de la chasse* for Philip the Bold, the king's youngest son, who remained alongside his father in England.[17]

Back at the French court, first as dauphin and then king, Charles V also had as models two of the most avid female book collectors, Blanche de Navarre and her royal cousin Jeanne d'Evreux, last wife of the last Capetian king Charles IV. Both matriarchs maintained a strong presence at Charles V's court throughout their lives. Beyond symbolizing a harmonious transition of dynastic power, Jeanne d'Evreux's presence also assured a dynastic genealogy for Charles V's *Sapientia* program. Providing physical confirmation of this association is the presence in the 1380 library inventory of nine books linked to Jeanne d'Evreux, including the *Heures de Jeanne d'Evreux*, which she bequeathed to Charles V in 1371.[18] Charles V's queen, Jeanne de Bourbon, was an equally important contributor to the royal book collection: her dowry added twenty-two works to library.[19] In this respect, Charles V's own bibliophilia reflects an obvious continuation of a multigenerational Valois passion for books. That said, justification for his heightened interest in books also owed a great deal to arguments developed in writings geared to the aristocracy.

Jean Devaux argues that Mirrors of Princes dating from the reigns of the first three Valois kings testify to a shift away from a theological vision of sovereignty in favour of a more practical and political understanding of leadership.[20] Charles V surrounded himself with these writings and filled his library with Mirrors old and new. One of the most striking examples of the value placed on these earlier writings dates to 1372, when a compendium of Mirrors entered the king's library. This compendium, Besançon Bibliothèque municipale MS 434, provided the king with new copies of Mirrors that could be traced back to previous reigns stretching from Philip IV to John the Good. The codex includes such titles as *Le gouvernement des roys et des princes*, *Moralitez des philosophes*, and *Enseignements des princes*.[21] Several illuminations in MS 434 reinforce the bond these works cultivated between the learned community and the sovereign through scenes depicting sovereigns listening to clerics' instruction or receiving a book offering from the author.[22] The king's library likewise contained a translation of Vincent of Beauvais's *De regimine principum puerorum nobelium*, dedicated to Louis IX; the minstrel Watriquet de Couvin's vernacular contributions to this genre – the "Miroir du prince" and "Li enseignement du jone fil de prince"; and even a now lost *Miroir aux dames*, which the 1380 inventory identifies as a text commissioned by Jeanne d'Evreux.[23] Around the same time frame, the king commissioned other works intimately related to the Mirror genre. For instance, he commissioned Nicole Oresme to translate Aristotle's *Ethics*, *Politics*, and *Economics* (1371–7), while Jean Golein agreed to translate the *Liber de informatione principum* (1379). This latter commission was likely inspired by Golein's own earlier contribution to the Mirror tradition that headed his *Racional des divins offices* (1372).[24]

In the same year that MS 434 and Golein's *Racional* entered the royal library, Denis Foulechat completed at the king's command a translation of the quintessential example of Mirror literature, John of Salisbury's *Policraticus*. To a large extent, John of Salisbury's work set the tone of Charles V's reign. For Michel Sennelart, John of Salisbury's famous declaration that "the illiterate king is like a crowned ass" augured a shift from the ancient model of the *rex sapiens* to the clerically inspired *rex litteratus*.[25] According to Salisbury, wisdom was not simply imparted by God; rather, it was incumbent on the prince to hone this virtue through study. In Jacques Krynen's words, thereafter, "le prince pour être sage se doit aussi d'être cultivé" (to be wise, the prince must also be cultivated).[26] In other words, *sagesse* became a direct product of *savoir*. This classic pronouncement came both to validate Charles V's support of letters and to empower the learned community with the responsibility of articulating a new royal identity focused on the sobriquet Charles would quickly acquire, that of the Wise King. For Jeannine Quillet, the collaboration between the learned community and the king reflected a "prise de possession par le roi et son entourage d'un savoir" (a taking of possession by the king and his entourage of a knowledge) once controlled exclusively by the learned masters.[27]

The learned coterie that encircled Charles V drew from this Mirror tradition to author a powerful defence for the king's privileging of learning over might. Golein, for example, declared at the outset of his *Racional* that the recent royal reacquisition of territories from the English resulted from Charles V's "estude et sapience" (study and wisdom)[28] rather than from physical feats on the battlefield. Likewise, in the prologue to his *Policratique*, Foulechat explained Charles V's recent military successes as resulting from the same strategies of past military heroes who conquered their enemies through "wise" leadership:

> Dont sont venues les nobles victoires de grans roys, les multiplicacions de biens, les accroissemens de terres aus seigneurs fors par vraie sapience et par bon gouvernement selon philosophie … ?[29]
>
> (From whence came the noble victories of great kings, the increase of goods, the growth of lands for lords if not from true wisdom and good government according to philosophy?)

Foulechat reinforced this point deep in his translation through the addition of an otherwise rare gloss to Salisbury's pronouncement that the prince "doit estre endoctriné es lettres" (the king must be educated in letters) in which the translator claimed a sovereign's success as dependent on his respect of the "law of letters": "Et qui vivent du tout selon la doctrine des lettres … ses besoignes viegnnent à bonne fin et grant profite" (and those who live above all according to the law of letters … their needs will be achieved and at great profit).[30]

It is common to find the commissioned writers constructing a revered genealogy for Charles V that associated him with great sovereigns known for their extensive learning. Charles V often found himself in the company of a respected list of ancient and biblical models of appropriate conduct, including Alexander the Great as well as David and other kings of the Old Testament. Charles V's namesake, Charlemagne, now factored into this illustrious gathering as a means of more firmly linking the king to this learned tradition.

Golein provides a representative example in the *Racional* when praising King Salomon and the other great leaders for their desire to read and collect books:

> Trouvons nous en pluseurs escriptures que non mie tant seulement le roy Salemon enqueroit a savoir de toutes choses sagement, mais trouvons que les roys qui ont tenu les nobles monarchies des grans empires et nobles royaumes ont enquis et encerchié sagement de toutes choses, et lisoient et enqueroient les livres et les escriptures diverses, si comme il appert des Rommains et empereurs paiens, de Ptholomee et les Egypciens, du grant Caan et les Tartariens, de Salemon et les Juifs sachans, de Alixandre et les Grejoys puissans, du noble Charlemain et les crestiens vaillans.[31]
>
> (We find in several writings that not only did King Salomon inquired to know all things wisely, but we find that kings who reigned over the noble monarchies of great empires and noble kingdoms inquired and sought out wisely all things, and they read and inquired into books and various writings, so it seems to be the case with the Romans and pagan emperors, for Ptolemy and the Egyptians, for the Great Khan and the Tartans, for Solomon and the wise Jews, for Alexander and the mighty Greeks, and for Charlemagne and the valiant Christians.)

Later, in the same text, Golein singled out Ptolemy and the Grand Khan to praise their commitment to creating large libraries, an act that provided precedence for his king's own *Sapientia* project.[32]

The most overt and most developed argument in support of Charles V's learning, however, takes shape in Evrart de Trémaugon's *Songe du vergier* (1378). The *Vergier* stands out as both the only original fictional vernacular work among Charles V's commissions and the most direct in defending the king's promotion of a royal identity centred on learning. In his opening address to the king, Trémaugon praises his sovereign for his dedication to the learned (clers), which is manifested through his efforts to assure their "promotion" at court: "tu lez avances et leur portes honeur et reverance, et lez as en remembrance, en lez promouvent de ton propre emouvement" (you see to their advancement and extend to them honour and respect, and you honour them when you promote them by your own will).[33] When establishing the king's investment in the learned community as key to his sovereign identity, Trémaugon evokes an established royal tradition. After all, Gerald of Wales also praised Louis VII for his "generous support of learned labors" ("liberales et largos ad remunerandum litterati labores ingenii").[34] Trémaugon thereafter links the king's concern for the learned community to other examples of royal investment in large-scale projects undertaken on behalf of the people. These projects are referred to as "le grant tresor" (the great treasure) the king assembled as well as the "edifices de palais et de chastiaux ... de plus grant magnificence" (palaces and castles ... of the greatest magnificence) he had built (*Vergier*, 1:6.15). In pairing the king's investment in intellectual activity with architectural structures and the accumulation of wealth, Trémaugon provides the most explicit effort to associate the king's interest in books to the tradition of what Gilles de Rome referred to in *De regimine principum* as "granz euvres."[35] The most obvious expressions of such projects involved major contributions to churches and religious activities, although gifts intended for the community – including offerings to honour the meritorious, establishment of castle and home for the prince, and hosting celebrations such as weddings and tournaments – also figured among Gilles's examples.[36] In the most generous sense, "granz euvres" were understood as visible and public accounts of royal power and magnificence undertaken with the principal intention of "doing good" ("en entention de bien").[37] For Trémaugon, Charles V's acts of royal magnificence set him above even Alexander the Great: "Alixandre, conme seigneur de tout le monde, ne fust onques de plus grant magnificence que tu soies come roy de France" (Alexander, as lord of the entire world, was never more magnificent than you are as king of France) (*Vergier*, 1:6.14). Yet, Trémaugon makes clear in the narrative itself that there was still a need to defend Charles V's practices.

The narrative centers on a debate the author recalled from an earlier dream in which a knight and a cleric discussed a number of pressing issues facing the kingdom. Among subjects treated, we discover, rather surprisingly, an extended discussion concerning the king's book interests. It is to the knight to defend the king's passion for learning, which he does by praising books for containing answers to all the questions a ruler might have, including

> se la chose publique doit estre gouvernee, se bataille doit estre ordenee, se chasteaulx sont a asieger, engyns a drecer, se la paix du peuple, se la franchise et la liberté devent estre gardees, se lez loys et lez constitucions essaucees, aliances estre acquises et fermees, tout ce nous est enseigné par lez livres. (*Vergier*, 1:223.5)

> (how the *res publica* is to be governed, how battles are to be organized, how castles are to be attacked, machines to be constructed, how the people's peace and if truth and liberty are to be protected, how the laws and constitutions upheld, alliances acquired and maintained, all of this is taught to us by books.)

The knight concludes here with an open reference to John of Salisbury's famous declaration, which he softens by replacing the comparison of a "roys sanz lattreüre" (a king without letters/learning) to an ass with the more palatable allusions to "une nef sanz avyrons et come oysel sanz elles" (a ship without sails, a bird without wings) (*Vergier*, 1:223.5). The knight's message, however, remains the same as Salisbury's: like the oars that move the ship and the wings that define the bird, so too book learning makes a king. This point had already made in the previous pages where it was argued that the king's daily practice of reading constituted the best remedy against tyranny:

> Se nous considerons parfaitement conment chascun jour il lit ou fait lire devant luy de Ethyques, de Pollitiques ou de Yconomiques, ou d'autres moralités, pour savoir que appartient au gouvernement de tout seigneur naturel, et conment il doit justement et virtusement vivre, et son peuple garder d'oppressions et deffendre, certes nous povons dire et maintenir que sa seignorie est vraye et naturele seignorie. (*Vergier*, 1:222.3)
>
> (If we think carefully how everyday he [Charles V] reads or has read before him the *Ethics*, the *Politics* or the *Economics*, or still other moral writings, so as to know the responsibilities of government of all natural lords, and how he must live justly and virtuously, and keep his people from oppression and defend them, certainly we are able to say and maintain that his rule is a true and natural sovereignty.)

Let us note that Trémaugon spotlights in this passage Aristotle's corpus, which Nicole Oresme had translated over the previous seven years at Charles V's request. Thus, Trémaugon discreetly acknowledges here that in addition to being an avid reader, the king was also responsible for the vernacular transference of this knowledge.

The two debaters dispute the value of these works before concluding that the library constitutes the learning contained within as the kingdom's greatest wealth. Playing the role of the devil's advocate, the cleric counsels that the royal family should stick to Scripture rather than read widely. It is hard to not hear a pointed critique of Charles V's own voluminous library in his next observation that "nous povons conclurre que ce n'est mie chose expedient, ne profitable, que lez enffens dez Roys soient enformés en plusieurs livres, ne que lez Roys aient plusieurs volumes de livres" (we can conclude that it is neither expedient nor profitable for the king's children to be informed by many books, nor that the king have many volumes of books) (*Vergier*, 1:226.2). It is to the knight to defend Charles V's book predilections. He counters that it is "profitable, *mesmement a un Roy*, avoir plusieurs livres, vieux et noveaux, pour y avoir recours en temps et en lieu, selon lez divers cas qui luy avienent de jour en jour; et *est biau tresor a un Roy avoir grant multitude de livres*" (profitable, *even for a king*, to have many books, old and new, to be able to reference them when necessary and according to the different issues that concern him daily; and *it is a great treasure for a king to have many books*) (*Vergier*, 1:228.9; emphasis added). In qualifying a book collection as a worthy treasure, the knight allows us to see clearly how Charles V's investment in books and learning could be interpreted as a form of magnificence. It is this very magnificence that will serve, once again, to place Charles V in the company of revered leaders. Here the king's generous treatment of the intellectual community is comparable to Emperor Titus's generous support of Pliny the Elder and Tacitus (*Vergier*, 2:269.15).

Others writers would associate the king's book collection with the philosophy of the "granz euvres" by arguing that the king invested in knowledge in the name of his people. Jean Corbechon observes in his *Livre des proprietés des choses* that the king's books constitute far more than a treasure trove of luxury items: the king's investment in the preservation and dissemination of learning reflects true princely magnificence that redounded to the kingdom:

> Cest desir de sapience, prince trés debonnaire, a Dieu fichié, planté et enraciné en vostre cuer trés fermement dés vostre jeunesce, si comme il appert manifestement en la grant et copieuse multitude de livres de diverses sciences que vous avez assemblez et assemblez chascun jour par vostre fervent diligence, esquelz livres vous puisiez la parfonde eaue de sapience, au seau de vostre vif entendement, pour la espandre aux conseilz et aux jugemens au prouffit du peuple que Dieu vous a mis a gouverner.[38]

> (This desire for wisdom, most debonair prince, God placed, planted, and rooted in your heart with great firmness since your youth, as it manifests itself in the great and copious multitude of books about various sciences that you assembled and collect each day due to your fervent diligence, through these books you delve into the deep waters of wisdom, to the abilities of your quick understanding, so as to share it through advice and judgment to the profit of the people that God has you govern.)

For Corbechon, the king's dedication to book learning extended to his willingness to enrich his people through the dissemination of knowledge via his own words and judgments. Nearly twenty-five years later, Christine de Pizan would be even more forceful in associating Charles V's *Sapientia* project with the "granz euvres" concept. In her biography of the Wise King, she followed a listing of the more typical "granz euvres" financed by Charles V, including new constructions and renovations of palaces, hotels, churches and bridges,[39] with discussion of his greatest edifice, one that had resulted from the "grant amour qu'il avoit à l'estude et à science" (great love he had for study and science) (*Charles V*, 2:42). Out of the king's personal intellectual interests, Christine identified a large-scale venture that included "la belle assemblée des notables livres et belle librairie" (the beautiful collection of noteworthy books and a beautiful library) (*Charles V*, 2:42). This edifice, she added, housed "tous les plus notables volumes" (all the most noteworthy volumes) thanks to the king's ability to gather "les meilleurs escripvains" (the best writers) and "solempnelz maistres" (serious masters) who were willing and able to assist him "en tel ouvrage" (in such an endeavour) (*Charles V*, 2:42–3). So successful was Charles V's refashioning of royal identity from warrior king to wise leader through his learned investments that Christine de Pizan would refer to him as a "vray disciple de sapience" (true disciple of wisdom) and "vray philosophe ameur de sapience" (a true philosopher, lover of wisdom) (*Charles V*, 2:12). She even identified him in her later work, *Livre de Paix*, as a "clerc" (cleric) because he "souverainement amoit livres, dont il avoit a merveilles grant quantité, et de toutes manieres" (deeply loved books, of which he had an extraordinarily large and diverse quantity).[40] For Christine and her public, Charles V and the learned books he commissioned had become one, and the royal library was the lasting mark of his magnificence. To pursue the language of the knight in Trémaugon's *Vergier*, Christine helps us appreciate that beyond gathering a treasure trove of books, Charles V constructed a physical space intended to promote, protect, and spotlight learned writings as central to the king's "oeuvre" and reflecting his pleasure. With the Louvre library looming over the Paris landscape as an extension of the king's private chambers, library visitors would have had visual evidence on a grand scale of the powerful role knowledge was afforded in the kingdom.

The Economics of the *Sapientia* Project

In the days following his coronation on 8 April 1364, Charles V freed up resources to fund the massive multi-year renovation of the Louvre that would transform Philip Augustus's *chateau fort* into a royal palace. At the same time, the new king made certain that an equal if not superior sum was reserved to finance his related investment in literary culture. As regards the Louvre building renovations, records show that Charles V reserved 55,000 *livres* (or 20 per cent) of his annual revenues to fund this ambitious renovation.[41] These renovations reflected changing practices in the fourteenth century that saw the *grande salle* fall out of favour as the receiving site for visitors, to be replaced by a new centre of court culture, the royal apartments.

The Louvre renovations focused precisely on the reconstruction of the north wing, the site of these lodgings. The new plans reserved the entire second floor for the queen's apartments, while a new top floor provided individual spaces for both the king and the dauphin. On 22 April 1364, Charles V designated as the architect-in-charge Raymond du Temple, who would acquire a series of titles over the next sixteen years of his service to the crown, including "sergent d'armes et maçon du roi" (sergeant-at-arms and the king's builder), "maître des oeuvres de maçonnerie" (master of works of construction) and "maître maçon des oeuvres" (master builder of works).[42] Raymond du Temple is most celebrated today for the long-ago destroyed Louvre spiral staircase, identified as the "grand viz," an expansive marble grand entryway into the palace that provided direct access to the individual receiving chambers of the king and queen.[43] An innovative structure for its time, the "grand viz" entailed a central staircase consisting of three flights of stairs of varying dimensions, with the widest steps believed to have designated the final ascent to the king's receiving room.[44] This staircase was deliberately imposing and was clearly intended to have a powerful effect on anyone heading to the royal apartments.

Another aspect of the north wing renovations for which Raymond du Temple ought to be celebrated concerns the creation of a library in the *tour de la fauconnerie* attached to the king's chambers. The three upper floors of this turret came to house the manuscript collection previously kept at the Palais de la Cité alongside the king's own personal acquisitions. So significant was the transformation of this tower into a library that it quickly acquired the new title of the *tour de la librairie*. Mary Whitely has provided the most comprehensive account of the creation of this extraordinarily symbolic space.[45] According to Whitely, the layout of the king's apartments likely afforded Charles direct access to the adjoining library from his *chambre du jour*, a symbolic arrangement that complemented the library's placement in the privileged architectural space of the tower. A further enhancement that should likely be credited to the architect concerns the stairway presumed to have connected the king's chambers to the library. All we know about this second staircase comes from court records indicating purchased materials to build a staircase leading to the tower. These materials consisted of forty-one marble steps, measuring 1.80 metres. The stature of this planned staircase baffled Whitely, who remarked that its anticipated dimensions suggested "une largeur surprenante pour un escalier intérieur"[46] (a surprising width for an interior staircase), and she further confessed in a footnote: "Je ne comprends pas la raison de cette singularité"[47] (I don't understand the reason for this peculiarity). Based on these albeit scant details, Whitely speculated that the chosen materials for the library staircase were expected to guarantee a strong visual and material link between the library staircase and the architect's imposing "grand viz," as both the quantity and dimensions of the library steps would have echoed the makeup of the first and smallest flight of the "grand viz" stairs.[48] These presumed visual associations led Marie-Hélène Tesnière to speculate that the library staircase linked the king's private chambers directly to the tower, thereby assuring that visitors fully appreciated the architectural nod.[49] If true, the effect that this second marble staircase would have had on visitors cannot be overstated. For the visitors who ascended to the king's new apartments via the grand staircase, another flight of white marble stairs in the corner of the royal chambers would have indicated the path to the "summit" of the king's private space and, as such, it would have provided a powerful architectural expression of the relationship between the Wise King's refashioned sovereign identity and his *Sapientia* project.

Upon entry into the library space, presumably via the forty-one marble stairs, the visitor would have encountered a well-appointed room worthy of housing a king's "biau tresor." Court accounts provide invaluable evidence indicating the particular care taken in creating a luxurious space that would magnify the grandeur represented by the book collection.[50] Thick wooden doors that were more than 2 metres high and approximately 1 metre large guarded the entryway to rooms that measured 4 to 4.5 metres in diameter. On the first floor of the library, visitors would have marvelled over walls panelled with high-quality Irish wood presented to the king for this purpose by the seneschal de Hainaut. If the visitors proceeded to the top two floors of the library, they would take in the high-vaulted windows that had been covered in iron and net to protect the books from birds and insects while letting in natural light. To furnish each level, the king enlisted the services of two woodcarvers, Jacques du Parvis and Jean Grosbois, who were hired to retrofit shelving, desks, and book-wheels taken from the Palais de la Cité. Instead, these men ultimately built new shelves and constructed new chairs because "les sieges [brought from the Palais de la Cité] estoient trop viez" (the seats were too old).[51] Finally, according to Henri Sauval, special lighting illuminated the space, which he interpreted as serving solely to encourage constant intellectual activity: "et afin qu'à toute heure on y put travailler, trente petits chandeliers et une lampe d'argent furent pendus à la voute, qu'on allumoit le soir et la nuit" (so that at all hours, one could work there, thirty small candelabras and a silver lamp were hung from the ceiling, which were lighted night and day).[52] While industriousness may have been the justification for the expense of lighting such a vast space, we should not ignore the added aura of luxury provided by the candles. Far from constituting a closed repository constructed to store away a king's private treasure, the layout and staging of the Louvre library anticipated bustling activity. At the same time that the library layout appears to have anticipated serious intellectual activity, court records make clear that the king went to great expense to assure that visitors appreciated the treasure represented by the intellectual wealth gathered within the library walls. Following the transfer of the Palais book collection to the Louvre in 1367–8, the court made several purchases of large swathes of silk in blue, green, and red to cover books in the collection.[53] As a result, when entering the first floor of the Louvre library, visitors would certainly have been dazzled by the multicoloured silk wrappings and the many silver manuscript clasps that glittered from panelled library recesses.[54] Perhaps some of the king's books were left open on the new shelving so that viewers could catch a glimpse of the even greater riches contained within.

Gilles Malet's 1380 inventory of the royal book collection provides us with a good idea of what visitors would have encountered upon entering the first level of the library. It has been argued that the distribution of codices reflected a prioritization of Latin learned texts because these writings were primarily stored in the upper chamber, while the first floor is said to have housed works relevant to good government, and the intermediate floor, with its preponderance of vernacular romances, is said to have reflected a typical aristocratic collection.[55] These conclusions, however, do not reflect faithfully Malet's inventory, nor do they speak to the shrewd display of the king's intellectual wealth. The 1380 inventory of the first-floor holdings lists a stunning variety of works that would have introduced the visitor, immediately upon arrival, to the collection's diversity and richness. Entering the Louvre library, the visitor would have been treated to several luxury codices among the nearly 300 works that made up the first-floor collection. These works ranged from learned writings to popular romance. Multiple Bibles described as "bien escript" (nicely written) and "bien hystoriée" (well illustrated) filled the first-floor shelves.[56] Luxury editions crowded the first floor, whereas lesser codices were typically relegated to the higher floors. For example, of the several *Roman de la Rose* copies housed in the Louvre library, Malet identified one on the first floor as "tres bien escript et ystorie" (very well written and decorated), whereas another copy of the romance described as "tres viel et mal escript" (very old and poorly written) was stored on the second level.[57] An intriguing exception to this practice concerns the presence among the first-floor holdings of an early version of Bersuire's translation of Livy.[58] That the luxury copy of this same translation produced for John the Good also figured on the first floor invites us to imagine that visitors had the occasion to compare the two versions.[59] Alongside King John's *Livy*, numerous books on the first floor testified to a dynastic legacy of book collecting. For immediate consultation upon entry into the library were copies of Vignay's works,[60] the *Miroir aux dames* linked to Jeanne d'Evreux, as well as a *Bible historiale* attributed to the same queen,[61] and an *Ovide* said to have been commissioned by Jeanne de Navarre, queen to Philippe le Bel.[62] Perhaps, one of the listed *Miracles de Notre Dame* by Gauthier de Coincy on this floor was King John's copy confiscated at Poitiers, which Charles had gone to great lengths to recuperate.[63] Further enhancing this well-established royal collection was evidence of King Charles's recent contributions to the library, such as luxury copies of the commissioned writings he solicited from Jean Golein, Nicole Oresme, Denis Foulechat, Raoul de Presles, Simon de Hesdin, and Evrart de Trémaugon.[64] So too, it is here that the *Grandes chroniques* and the *Livre du sacre des rois de France* were staged.[65] For Jean Corbechon, the translator commissioned by Charles to produce the *Livre des proprietés des choses*, the Louvre library displayed an inhuman overabundance of knowledge that was all the more impressive because it reflected the king's personal vision: "la vie d'un homme ne souffiroit mie pour lire les livres que vostre noble desir a assemblez" (a man's entire life would hardly suffice to read the books that your noble desire brought together).[66]

Corbechon's description of the library as resulting from the king's "noble desir" suggests that rather than reflecting the concept of the common good associated with the "granz euvres" ideal, this enterprise spoke to what I refer to as the patron's pleasure. Otherwise stated, the Louvre library as the centrepiece of the king's *Sapientia* project reflected Charles V's tastes, goals, and ambitions rather than represented the eclectic choices of individual artists and artisans. Pursuing Dale Kent's argument that in cases in which we are aware of an overarching vision provided by the patron, such as we have with Charles V's project, it follows that the modern scholarly practice of studying components of the project as reflecting a writer's, artist's, or architect's vision rather than the patron's pleasure would ignore the real purpose of the *Sapientia* project. Moreover, it is crucial to recognize that Charles V's *Sapientia* project depended heavily on a clientelistic approach to literary exchange.[67] Rather than rely on unsolicited book offerings to fill his library shelves, the king took the initiative and solicited the services of members of the intellectual community to satisfy his desires. In short, the commissioned writers were expected to express the patron's pleasure. How Charles V's clients responded to this new literary arrangement and the effect it had on the field of letters is at the heart of this study, but before considering the book community's responses to the king's commissioning activity, we need first to study the dynamics of this distinctive form of exchange, beginning with how a patron might go about securing the services of authors.

To realize the king's "noble desir" manifested in the *Sapientia* project, a new socio-economic framework was introduced that positioned the patron as the driving force behind writing and bookmaking. While unsolicited contributions to the project are registered – whether in the form of panelling for the first floor of the library that the seneschal of Hainaut offered the king or as expressed by the many gift-books that entered the collection offered by foreign nobility, family members, and courtiers – a large portion of materials and services related to the *Sapientia* project were acquired through clientelistic avenues. Whether performing as builder or architect, scribe or translator, contributors to the project were treated as clients whose skills were solicited in response to the patron's needs and desires. As discussed in the introduction to this study, clientelism represents a partnership initiated by a patron with a client in which the first promises a reward in exchange for the second's services, and, as Verena Burkolter notes, this arrangement "may be expressed in terms of a formal contract or in less formal relations."[68] As concerns the *Sapientia* project, a variety of financial models appear to have been adapted to the circumstances. Some clients were treated as labourers who received a set payment for services completed or necessary materials acquired. For example, the men responsible for the new Louvre furniture, Jacques du Parvis and Jean Grosbois, were rewarded 66 francs d'or (52 livres, 16 sous) at the end of their services, while Pierre l'Escot, responsible for creating the protective coverings for the library windows, received 18 francs d'or (13 livres, 8 sous), and the blacksmith who provided l'Escot with the iron-work received 24 livres, 4 sous.[69] Likewise, as regards the most fundamental components of book production, the court account books testify to merchants reimbursed for materials delivered to the court. For example, binding and protective coverings for around two dozen works contained in the Louvre library cost more than 200 francs, while just the parchment for a Bible could cost 250 francs.[70] We also know that the court supported a royal parchmenter, who may have provided this key material for the king's copies of his commissioned works.[71]

Treasury accounts are less informative on the subject of financing the artisanal aspect of book production. Neither the scribes nor illuminators at the king's court figure in the account books alongside carpenters and builders. Emilie Cottereau-Gabillet's recent research on Italian and French scribal contracts offers two economic models (fixed and long-term) that may have been adopted by Charles V's treasurer when dealing with skilled bookmakers.[72] A fixed contract typically concerned non-household book artisans who worked under contract with remuneration determined in advance, whereas a long-term contract, a contract "à la durée," according to Cottereau-Gabillet, assured food, lodging, and pre-determined remuneration for each assignment.[73] Turning to the artisans involved in Charles V's *Sapientia* project, it is noteworthy that several book artisans are believed to have worked exclusively for the royal court. For instance, the scribes Raoulet d'Orléans and Henri du Trevou, together, are credited with transcribing more than two dozen books in the king's library (including the three codices to be privileged in the next chapter) and are believed to have served the king exclusively in spite of their absence from the royal treasury records.[74] This constant service may indicate that they enjoyed the equivalent of Cottereau-Gabillet's long-term contracts. Raoulet d'Orléans, in particular, seemed confident in his familiarity with the king since he did not hesitate to advertise his services in the books he produced. For instance, in the king's private copy of Oresme's *Ethiques* (The Hague, Museum Meermanno-Westreenianum, MS 10 D-1), the scribe competed with the translator for the privileged role of royal client when identifying the codex with himself instead of the translator: "Ci fine le livre d'Ethiques, lequel fit faire très noble, très excellent et vray catholique prince Charles le quint, [...] et l'escripst Raoulet d'Orliens" (Here ends the book of *Ethics*, which the very noble, most excellent and true Catholic, Prince Charles V, had made [...] and Raoulet d'Orléans transcribed it).[75] As concerns the miniaturists who illustrated the king's books, we know little about the formal arrangements governing their activity, although here again there is circumstantial evidence pointing to a number of key illuminators working exclusively for the royal court and thus, similarly, likely beneficiaries of long-term contracts.[76] Although we have no evidence of the king's involvement in the aesthetic choices made concerning the luxury copies of his commissioned works, the fact that we recognize a tight-knit group of book artisans as responsible for these copies suggests a certain collective awareness of the king's aesthetic preferences.[77]

Moving further up the professional ladder, hybrid financial arrangements are evidenced for other contributors to the *Sapientia* project. In contrast to the fixed payments awarded for work accomplished and materials required for furnishing the library, Raymond du Temple, the architect in charge of the Louvre renovations (as well as other large-scale projects undertaken by Charles V), received a daily wage of 4 soldis parisis, for an annual income of 74 livres 8 sous.[78] As already mentioned, Raymond du Temple also benefited from increasingly more elevated titles that reflected his advancement at court. As regards the management and production of the book collection housed in the Louvre library by Gilles Malet, the financial arrangements are less transparent since there is no record of a salary linked to his position as *garde de la librairie du roy*, which he acquired around 1369 and held until his death in 1411.[79] Rather, it appears that the king rewarded Malet by offering him court positions. Malet would see himself progressively promoted to ever more lucrative positions during Charles V's reign. The librarian entered the court in 1364 as a simple *valet de chambre* and was ennobled around 1366, which led to the attainment ten years later of the title of squire. Over the years, Malet would incrementally purchase as many fiefs as were given to him by royal decree. He ended his life still holding the office of *libraire* and as a very wealthy man who was capable of securing burial monuments for himself and his wife. One might presume that the king's commissioned translators benefited from a similar reward system to that of Malet, but archival records suggest that this was at least not always the case. The king's arrangements with the commissioned writers appear in some known instances to have entailed formal contractual agreements in which writers were promised compensation not simply for the final text-product requested but also for the intellectual labour required to produce the work.

The Economics of Ordering Books

As the Palais library was being relocated to the Louvre in 1368, Charles V was seeking out and retaining the services of learned men who could fill the shelves of his new library with modern translations of canonical writings.[80] The king turned to the learned community to acquire these works rather than presume that his needs would be answered without his active intervention. That is, rather than expect writers to submit unsolicited works that matched his desires, the king sought out clients with the knowledge and skills required to contribute to his *Sapientia* project. He also appears to have appreciated the need for incentives. Archival evidence and author testimonials combined point to the implementation of an economic system influenced by fixed and long-term contracts commonly offered to book artisans. Rather than pay for services rendered or provide an annual salary to retain indefinitely the services of the writers, Charles V introduced a contractual agreement that promised to support in advance the intellectual work to be accomplished during a fixed time frame that presumably reflected what both parties believed to be necessary to complete the desired translation. Thus, to secure a writer's commitment to complete a desired book project, pre-emptive promises of financial reward were sometimes offered. In the two instances for which we have record of such contracts issued, the king proposed a fixed annual pension in exchange for the commissioned writer's intellectual services. Contractual agreements made with Nicole Oresme and Raoul de Presles testify to this practice. So valuable did the king believe the intellectual labour of these men to be that the annual pensions offered to them exceeded by four times Raymond du Temple's yearly income.

Oresme received regular payments from the royal treasury between 1371 and 1377 to support work on his translations of Aristotle's *Nicomachean Ethics*, *Politics*, *Economics*, and *On the Heavens*. His first payment of 100 gold francs was registered at the outset of the endeavour in December 1371 and was followed by a declaration of payment of 200 gold francs in May 1372.[81] In a letter the king signed, the agreement between the two parties is rehearsed. The king is said to have solicited two translations from Oresme, and in recognition of the "grant peine" (great effort) required to accomplish this commission, the king's treasurer was to provide immediately the indicated sum to the scholar:

> Nous faisons translater à nostre bien amé le doyen de Rouen, maistre Nicolle Oresme, deux livrez, lesquieux nous sont très necessaires et pour cause, c'est

> assavoir Polithiques et Yconomiques, et pour ce que nous savons que ledit maistre Nicolle a à ce faire grant peine et grant diligence, et que il convient que pour ce il delaisse toutes ses autres oeuvrez et besoignes quelconques, voulons que, pour sa dicte peine, et aussi pour ce que il y entende et laisse toutes autres besongnes, quelles que elles soient, vous li bailliez et delivrez tantost et sans nul delay la somme de deux cens franz d'or.[82]
>
> (We are having translated by our much loved deacon of Rouen, Master Nicole Oresme, two books that are very essential for us and for good reason, they are the *Politics* and *Economics*, and since we know that the said Master Nicole to do this will put forward great effort and practice great diligence, and because it would be appropriate for him to put to the side all other work and whatever other obligations, we desire, for his said efforts, and so that he understands he is to leave to the side all of his other obligations, whatever they may be, that you give him and deliver to him hereafter and with no delay the sum of 200 gold écus.)

One detects in this letter the negotiations that led to Oresme's pension. The king not only rehearses his commitment to the deacon, but also reiterates Oresme's obligation to dedicate himself exclusively to the imposed assignment. The king underscored the importance of this remuneration (and perhaps the novelty of the enterprise) when adding a postscript addressed to the treasurer in his own hand that warned that any delay in payment would provoke royal anger: "Gardez sur quanque vous douptez nous courouser" (Beware that on this matter you risk angering us).[83] A now lost letter dated to 5 February 1373 likely secured an additional payment of 200 grands écus for Oresme,[84] followed by a letter dated to 31 August 1374 that speaks again of 200 gold francs destined for Oresme. As late as 1377, we find record of the king according an additional 200 gold francs to Oresme in relation to his last commissioned translation for the king, the *Livre du ciel et du monde*.[85]

Charles V proved even more generous with Presles, who translated Augustine's *City of God*, than he was with Oresme. The seventeenth-century scholar Pierre Dupuy cites a now-lost treasury document from Charles V's reign in which the royal treasurer chronicled that the "mandement du [roi]" (king's command) for the translation of the *City of God* included a commitment to provide Presles with a pension of "400 frans d'or chascun an jusques à ce que la translacion soit faicte" (400 gold francs each year until the translation is completed).[86] Presles's pension, in fact, equalled the annual income of a parliamentary president.[87] At some point over the next four years, Presles's pension was raised to 600 gold francs.[88]

It may have very well been this contractual promise by the king that inspired Presles to conclude the king's luxury copy of the *Cité* with rubric confirming the years spent completing the king's commission:

> Ceste translacion et exposicion fu commenciee par maistre Raoul de Praelles à la Toussains l'an de grace mil CCC soixante et onze, et fu achevee le premier jour de septembre l'an de grace mil CCC soixante et quinze.[89]
>
> (This translation and exposition was begun by Master Raoul de Presles on All Saints' Day in the blessed year of 1371 and was completed the first day of September in the blessed year of 1375.)

It is important to recognize that the king relied heavily on an "ambiguous economy" that allowed him to mix pensions with court and ecclesiastic promotions to reward the commissioned writers.[90] Again, Presles stands out in this arena. Serious advancement at court had long been denied to him due to his status as an unrecognized bastard child. His fortunes changed when, two years after beginning work on the *Cité*, the king formally recognized his legitimate status as the descendant of Raoul de Presles, Sire de Lizy.[91] Having already experienced a round of promotions beginning in 1371 that saw Presles advance from simple "advocat" (lawyer) to "conseiller du roy" (adviser to the king) to "advocat général" (general lawyer), he rose to the position of "maître des requêtes" (master of petitions) in 1373 (a position previously denied him because of his illegitimacy), which was a salaried position that added 600 *livres* annually to his coffers.[92] The king intervened once more in Presles's personal matters when extending permission for the author to expand his study space in Paris to accommodate his growing personal library. This royal permission was justified with reference to Presles's intellectual obligations to the crown: "tant pour nous server en translacions et exposicions comme en autres choses dont nous l'avons chargie" (as much for his service on translations and expositions as for other things with which we have charged him).[93]

Regarding Oresme, Charles V also saw to the scholar's professional advancement by interceding on his behalf to assure Oresme the See of Lisieux in 1377. In an uncommon gesture among the commissioned writers, Oresme openly credited the king with this ascension in his final commissioned translation:

> Et ainsi à l'aide de Dieu je [ay] accompli le livre *Du ciel et du monde* au commandement de tres excellent prince Charles, quint de ce nom, par la grace de Dieu roy de France, leque en ce faisant m'a fait evesque de Lisieux.[94]

(And thus with the aid of God, I completed the book *Of the Sky and Earth* on the order of the very excellent Prince Charles, fifth of the name, by the grace of God, king of France, who in exchange made me Bishop of Lisieux.)

The king's dealings with Oresme also allow us to appreciate the extent to which both patron and client needed to negotiate outside demands to accommodate their uncommon partnership. The king intervened on several occasions on Oresme's behalf at his Rouen chapter, where he had been publically reprimanded on 1 September 1371 for his repeated absences. The king twice wrote directly to the Rouen chapter on the scholar's behalf. On 28 August 1372 and again on 21 December 1375, the king notified the chapter that Oresme's absences from Rouen were authorized due to his translation work for the crown.[95] As François Neveux notes, however, the king's justification appears to have had little effect on Oresme's dilemma since records show that his attendance at the chapter became increasingly regular in the months following the reprimand.[96] This incident, which placed the king and the church at odds over Oresme's responsibilities, points to both the struggles that translators could experience as they attempted to negotiate their professional obligations with their service to the king and the challenges that Charles V faced when recruiting the services of these men.

It is, in fact, likely that the personal situations of the commissioned writers often dictated the arrangements the king made with them. For instance, for neither Jean Golein, the most prolific of the king's translators, nor Denis Foulechat, responsible for the *Policratique*, do we have court documentation pointing to their receipt of financial reward. This fact very likely reflects their vows of poverty as a Carmelite and a Franciscan, respectively. That said, Foulechat alluded to Charles V's generosity when recalling "tant … de biens et d'onneurs" (so many kindnesses and honours) that he had received from the king (*Policratique*, 250.8). Perhaps the translator alludes here to a monetary award, but Foulechat would also identify his uncommon access to coveted books as the greatest wealth the king afforded him:

Lonc temps a que ce livre, du quel je ay veu et leu aucunes fois selon divers propos pluseurs auctorités alleguees, je ay desirré a veoir; et, se ce ne fust vostre commandement, onques ne l'eusse peu entierement veoir, si comme a l'aide nostre Seigneur par le vostre commandement le me faut visiter. (*Policratique*, 86.74–5)

(I had long desired to see this book of which I had seen and read several varied remarks elaborated on by several authorities, and, had it not been for your order, never would I have been able to see it in its entirety, and, as if guided by our Lord, your command made it necessary for me to consult it.)

To be developed in the next chapter, Foulechat, who had been reprimanded by the university and exiled from Paris, found that royal favour might not only secure his return to Paris but also assure his access to the university's library and, perhaps, the king's own "biau tresor." As for the Carmelite Jean Golein, who neither referred to royal reward nor was listed in the royal treasury accounts, he is nonetheless quoted in a later lawsuit as having received in exchange for a "certaine translation d'un livre" (certain translation of a book) a "certaine somme de florins" (certain sum of florins) from the king.[97]

Other commissioned writers allude to financial support for their intellectual labour. For instance, Corbechon thanked the king for the "grant magnificence" he showed when requesting the translation of *De proprietatibus rerum*, a euphemism that invites us to imagine that Corbechon also received a pension contract.[98] Jean Daudin appears slightly more forthcoming about having received reward in advance of his translation work. He identifies as his primary motivation for completing *Remèdes contre l'une et l'autre fortune* (1377) the receipt of significant reward from the king: "obligié et astraint, en especial par grans benefices" (obliged and obligated, in particular due to great benefices).[99] In addition to these references to royal support in advance of completion of the commissioned work, there is some evidence indicating that men linked to the *Sapientia* project received gratifications for book copies of new works once they were presented to the king. These financial rewards, in some cases, underscore yet again the presence of an ambiguous economy at work since they blur market transactions and the more common gifting model in which an individual presented the king with a book and was thereafter rewarded with a counter-gift. Thus, on one hand, in 1372, the king purchased from Jean Golein a two-volume Bible and two concordances for 500 francs.[100] On the other hand, in recognition of books offered to the king at New Year's gifting ceremonies in 1378, Malet was later paid 300 francs d'or for these books.[101] Even more ambiguous is the case of Daudin, who recognizes in his prologue to his translation of Petrarch's *De remediis utriusque fortunae* that rewards already received from the king inspired his work, although he is also on record as having received 200 livres from the king when he finally presented the book to him.[102] Similarly Corbechon, who had also praised the king's prior generosity, later received an undisclosed amount for a completed translation.[103]

It is crucial to underscore that references in the commissioned texts to royal benefits relied heavily on euphemism. Not a single writer named sums received, nor did Oresme and Presles acknowledge their pensions. Instead, the focus was on showing that the writer had satisfied the king's order. In the process, the king's commanding role as patron was detailed: he is routinely identified as having initiated the process by contacting the writer with a clear sense of the services he desired. In these accounts, Charles V is credited with having chosen the text to be translated, with securing the required materials to accomplish the commission, and even with a role in determining the adopted translation practices. Yet when it comes to open acknowledgment of his agreement to fund these services in advance, one needs to wait for 1404, when the commissioned writers' self-proclaimed protégée, Christine de Pizan, would praise Charles V for the "grans gaiges" (large wages) he afforded these men (*Charles V*, 1:44). What inspired their silence on these financial details is the subject of the next chapter.

Charles V's multifaceted *Sapientia* project depended on a highly efficient and flexible form of clientelism applied to every stage of the project, from the creation of the Louvre library to the acquisition of luxury books, to even the production of intellectual matter. Archival and authorial testimonials suggest that the same vision and economic methods that guided Charles V's renovation of the Louvre and directed the creation of a private library were applied to the literary arena. Charles V is shown to have sought out learned men who possessed the knowledge and talents necessary to take on the formidable task of translating into the vernacular the revered and complex writings he so coveted. Charles V committed to supporting intellectual labour, ostensibly from the early writing stage through the final commemoration of the work in the form of a luxury codex that would then enter the royal library. To achieve this, he first proposed lucrative arrangements intended to oblige intellectuals to serve at the patron's pleasure. It is crucial to underscore that although Charles V merits the title of patron, that title was not acquired through any precocious anticipation by him of the later ideal that patronage of the arts and letters resulted from a sense of obligation and responsibility to protect and nurture creative activity. Charles V neither sought to promote vernacular authorship nor intellectual authority when assuring the construction of a royal library, supporting the production of specified writings, or collecting luxury manuscripts. Rather, he sought to realize his *Sapientia* project, which was meant to articulate and promote his refashioned sovereign identity as the Wise King and to strengthen the Valois dynasty. The commissioned writings, as much as the library structure, were conceived of as a reflection of the patron's pleasure: that is, as instruments of royal power that signalled the king's magnificence and his learnedness. And yet his commissioned writers suggested otherwise: where the king assumed the role of the clientelistic patron, the writers assigned him the qualities and the vision that would inform future articulations of literary and artistic patronage as driven by altruistic intentions. As we shall see in the next chapter, Charles V's commissioned writers as well as the illuminators responsible for royal copies of these works may have acknowledged the text's status as a royal commission, but they made every effort to convert the ordered work into the writer's gift freely offered to his worthy sovereign. This conversion usually announces itself from the outset of the king's royal copies of his commissions, where the opening illumination most often depicts the book-presentation scene rather than the inaugural act of the commission. In these presentation scenes, the king's commissioned text functions as an offering presented by the genuflecting author. In spite of the subservient nature of this stance, the author's positioning serves less to confirm the king's actual role as the patron who commanded a client and instead confers on the king a new identity as a sovereign intellectual whose pursuit of knowledge and whose magnificence made him a worthy recipient of the writer's gift. To appreciate fully the complex messaging of the book presentation scene, we must turn our attention to the authors and artists who orchestrated the exchange event.

Chapter Two

The Writer's Work: Translating Charles V's Literary Clientelism into Learned Terms

Charles V's luxury copy of the commissioned *Policratique* introduces a novel image of royal power.[1] The frontispiece to BnF, MS fr. 24287 foregoes both the traditional frontal-facing representation of the seated sovereign and the common donation iconography that focused on book exchange (Figure 2.1: BnF, MS fr. 24287, fol. 2r). Instead, the *Master of the Policratique*, known to have illustrated several books in the royal library,[2] opens the codex with a three-quarter-profile portrait of the king reading in private the very book before us. Although the king dons a crown and the fleur-de-lis cloak, lacking are other expected royal accoutrements. Sceptre and throne give way to a lectern and a reading wheel overflowing with books – the new symbols of royal power. This learned rendition of kingship receives celestial approval from the divine hand that breaks through the rafters. The accompanying rubric, provided by Raoulet d'Orléans, another frequent contributor to the king's library collection, identifies the ensuing prologue as open praise for the king's commissioning of this work: "Prologue a la commendacion du livre et du tres noble roy qui le fist translater" (Prologue in praise of the book and the very noble king who had it translated).[3] With no visual reference to the translator Denis Foulechat, who completed the commission in 1372, the frontispiece appears to identify this book solely in relation to the king's *Sapientia* project detailed in the previous chapter and to confirm its function as (part of) the patron's pleasure.

As concerns the *Policratique*, first impressions are, however, deceiving: this codex will quickly insist on the translator's relationship to the text. The frontispiece itself prepares us for this alternative reading of the literary transaction through subtle challenges to the king's importance; even if Charles V enjoys the spotlight, his gloved hand redirects our attention

Figure 2.1: Frontispiece, *Policratique* translated by Denis Foulechat, Paris, Bibliothèque nationale de France, MS fr. 24287, fol. 2r.

to the material incarnation of this "oeuvre," whose proportions are nearly twice the size of the king's visage. In addition to his extended finger directing our gaze to the book, the entire royal body curves in towards it. Angled to facilitate our viewing, the book reproduced in the miniature entices us to imitate the king; we are pulled closer to the actual codex as we attempt to decipher the minuscule script of the reproduced book that reads "Beat[us] vir qui in[venit] sapiencia ..." (Blessed the man who finds wisdom...). At the same time that this variation of Proverbs 3:13 gives scriptural backing to the divine hand's endorsement of the king's learned predilections, it also anticipates the second appearance of Proverbs 3:13 in the second column of this folio. In this second instance, however, it is Foulechat's mediating role in our study of the text that takes precedence, since Latin recitation is immediately followed by, first, Foulechat's vernacular translation, then, his explanatory gloss. The translator's importance gains mythical weight thereafter when references to revered learned leaders are paired with the names of their intellectual partners – Alfred and Alcuin stand alongside Alexander and Aristotle. These references do far more than place Charles V in illustrious company: in evoking these renowned leaders along with their esteemed intellectual partners, Foulechat provides us with a framework for understanding his relationship with the king. We are reminded of an ancient tradition in which scholars freely shared their wisdom with learned sovereigns. By the end of Foulechat's address, the initial textual and visual depiction of the book as the sole possession and product of the royal patron is fully destabilized when the translator adopts conventional gifting discourse to address the king: "plaise a vostre tresparfaicte douceur a prendre en gré ce que je, la vostre povre creature, peut faire" (that it please you in your most perfect gentle way to accept willingly what I, your poor creature, am able to do) (*Policratique*, 86.85). With this final act, a patron-client relationship takes on the air of an intimate exchange between donor and donnee. With the goal of understanding the motivations that led a commissioned writer like Foulechat to reframe the king's commission as the writer's gift-offering, the present chapter sets out to examine how writers and artists who produced solicited works for royal consumption engaged with the new literary economy favoured by Charles V.

As detailed in the previous chapter, Charles V's solicitation of texts to fortify his *Sapientia* project bypassed the expected practice of depending on unsolicited book-offerings to fill his library and implemented instead a literary economy reminiscent of clientelism. The patron-king therefore sought out learned men as clients from whom he requested specified works for his collection. At least in some cases as seen in the previous chapter, pre-emptive contractual agreement promised these clients financial support during the writing period in exchange for the writers' agreement to produce a text for the king's pleasure. This financial commitment to intellectual labour *avant la lettre* could be combined with subsequent rewards upon receipt of the completed project – an indicator of the ambiguity and flexibility of this literary economy. The purpose of the king's patronage, to reiterate, did not reflect the concept of literary and artistic patronage we promote today; the king's intentions were not motivated by a desire to protect and promote creative activity but, rather, to acquire works that would substantiate his sovereign identity as the Wise King and confirm the power and prestige of the Valois dynasty. By favouring a clientelistic engagement at the outset, the king could impose his vision on the literary and intellectual realm by dictating subject matter, choosing participants, and establishing the value of the product. The situation appears clear-cut except for the fact that had we not the archival evidence of Charles V's contractual arrangements with some of his writers, we would never be the wiser about their existence, since the commissioned writers systematically described their relationship to the king in archaic gifting terms that emphasized their willingness to share their intellectual bounty with no view to personal gain. That the otherwise detailed accounts of their literary dealings with the king collectively avoided open discussion of the lucrative terms surrounding their work should make us suspicious. Although we may be tempted to write off these accounts as little more than a thoughtless rehearsal of the conventional book-transfer ritual, these accounts appear deliberate in their attempt to filter a patron-client relationship through the rhetoric and iconography of archaic gifting. Why were the commissioned writers eager to promote archaic gifting over clientelism? Why were they reluctant to speak openly of the lucrative royal pensions they received for their intellectual labour? What did they risk in acknowledging their works as solicited products, and conversely, what value was there in insisting that even a commissioned text ultimately circulated as a gift offered freely and without constraint? These questions require us to revisit with a more critical gaze the framing matter in which writers discuss their literary dealings.

Recent scholarship in the humanities and social sciences provides ample reason to approach the paratextual material so often framing medieval texts and frequently containing metatextual reflections on the work's genesis as more than redundant rhetorical flourishes, as was once claimed by Karl Julius Holznecht.[4] Ruth Evans best articulates the importance of this pivotal space when acknowledging in the case of prologues that they are far more than "repositories of information" since they represent "opaque entities, standing in a complex relation to the works they preface."[5] Expanding on Evans's observations, we can also recognize other forms of the paratext, including dedicatory addresses, frontispieces, and epilogues, as standing in complex relation to the social, political, and literary realities governing the existence of the books they frame. Christian Jouhaud and Hélène Merlin have demonstrated this point in their study of early modern dedicatory epistles, where they find that writers often used this space to reassess the patron's role in literary production.[6] Recent anthropological work on the ritualized gifting performance can also inform our study of paratextual accounts of literary transactions since this research recognizes that ritual acts constitute an opportunity to verbalize concerns inherent in exchange[7] as much as to "affirm the boundaries of exchange."[8] In the case of commissioned texts, accounts of a work's genesis merit recognition as performative scripts of ritualized exchange, especially presentation scenes and narrative accounts of that event, neither of which document lived events but, rather, provide a script for a desired future transaction. In this regard, literary and anthropological work on the narration and performance of exchange invites us to approach the paratext to medieval manuscripts as a creative space that allowed for critical engagement with traditions, contemporary realities, and future aspirations. This critical approach will inform my reading of the written and visual accounts of the literary-exchange performance framing Charles V's commissions. I shall approach accounts of textual genesis as exploratory compositions that register neither the lived past nor a certain future; rather, they will be studied as authors' and artists' thoughtful engagement with Charles V's literary practices.

This chapter turns to key representative cases of works commissioned by Charles V as part of his *Sapientia* project during the peak period of activity in the 1370s to examine how writers and artists managed the king's clientelism. In addition to the already mentioned Foulechat translation of *Policraticus* (1372), we shall also examine Raoul de Presles's translation of Augustine's *City of God* (1375) and Nicole Oresme's first instalment of a vernacular Aristotle, his glossed copy of the *Nicomachean Ethics* (1376). In the royal copies of these three works, metatextual reflections authored by the writers join with visual and scribal additions to generate textual biographies in which the king's clientelism was progressively converted into a vehicle for promoting a gifting philosophy based on intellectual ideals. In this carefully constructed narrative of exchange, texts did not circulate as ordered products transferred between client and patron as royal record suggests; instead, they functioned as a shared treasure freely offered to the king who figured as an intellectual partner. I begin with an assessment of the feudal discourse of duty and obligation adopted to justify the writer's agreement to fulfil the commission. This nuanced usage of archaic language served to reposition the solicited text as evidence of writers' willingness to serve their sovereign by sharing intellectual wealth. Particular concentration will be given to a set of interlocking intellectual concepts subsequently implemented to reconfigure the clientelistic model of exchange proposed by the royal court. First, the commissioned writers drew from intellectual ideals promoted in late medieval academic circles to justify the increasing vernacularisation of knowledge.[9] Then, in response to the king's ambitions of securing power and prestige through the accumulation of intellectual and cultural wealth, the commissioned writers countered with a new narrative that relocated king and writer in a learned sodality in which their mutual recognition of knowledge as a sacred treasure united them in intellectual friendship. In subsequent chapters, we shall consider the critical responses to this depiction of literary dynamics by contemporary vernacular writers who did not figure among the king's chosen coterie of supported authors, as well as later French writings composed after the Wise King's death that document a nostalgic longing for this model of exchange.

Claiming Intellectual Authority through Service to the King

I want to remain with Foulechat a bit longer to explore more extensively his stated relationship to the king and the reasons he gives for accepting a royal commission. While it becomes clear that Foulechat's situation was unique, his detailed account of literary dealings with Charles V helps us appreciate the incalculable benefits of receiving a royal commission and the extent to which a commission could profoundly alter an intellectual's social status, even without the benefit of court or ecclesiastic advances. It needs to be stated upfront that unlike the cases of Oresme and Presles who, as we have seen, received lucrative pensions to cover their intellectual labour and then enjoyed promotions clearly orchestrated by the king, Foulechat never appears in court records as having been paid for his services or having advanced in the ranks (even though he implies having received some form of royal reward prior to beginning the translation, as we shall see). Foulechat's absence in court records may be due to the translator's vow of poverty as a Franciscan as well as the fact that he never held a court position, or simply due to a loss of records over the centuries.

Fortunately for us, the translator spoke extensively about his royal dealings in paratextual additions to his *Policratique*, where we find him alluding, in an especially complex performative script that merits close scrutiny, to serious needs that only a king could satisfy. On one hand, Foulechat's portrayal of his relationship to the king follows convention: as is to be expected, he adopts the language of subservience common to the commissioned writers. Even Presles, whom the king clearly valued, would refer to himself as but a "humble serviteur et subget" (humble servant and subject) who was obligated to submit to the king's "commandement" (command).[10] Likewise, Jean Corbechon, also documented as having been financially rewarded for his translation of *De proprietatibus rerum*, identified himself as the king's "très humble et petit subget" (very humble and insignificant subject).[11] On the other hand, in the paratextual frame to the *Policratique*, Foulechat explains his inferiority not just in relation to his sovereign but also in relation to the intellectual community. His discussion of this issue is extensive since he broaches the topic not in one but two addresses to Charles V that frame the king's copy of the *Policratique*. That these two addresses have not attracted scholarly attention is surprising given that they clearly date to different stages in the translation project and provide a fascinating narrative detailing one writer's struggle, first with receiving a commission and, second, with completing the commission.

The first address, which opens the king's copy of the translation, is identified by its manuscript title of "premier prologue." The second address is identified here as the "addended address," given that it appears at the end of the codex (MS fr. 24287). Note, however, that the "premier prologue" appears to postdate the addended address.

Foulechat's two addresses to the king cover similar territory, but the addended earlier prologue, for instance, develops at greater length than the subsequent "premier prologue" the power dynamics associated with a royal commission. As a key example, one can compare Foulechat's description of his initial reluctance to accept the commission because of his own intellectual shortcomings. In the "premier prologue," Foulechat contrasts his own desire to refuse the commission with the political reality that requires him to obey his sovereign:

> Et en verité, tresexcellent, tressouverain et redoubté seigneur, veue la hautesce du livre, le tressoutil et ancien latin et la matiere estrange qui tout mon pouoir seurmonte, de ce grant fait je me deusse excuser et de fait ja m'en feusse excusé se ce ne feust la tressouveraine majesté royal, a qui tous doivent, et je par especial, en tous cas obeïr. (*Policratique*, 86.73)

(And in truth, very excellent, most sovereign, and feared lord, given the greatness of the book, the great subtlety of the ancient Latin and the complex material that exceeds my abilities, of this great deed, I ought to have excused myself and, in fact, I would have excused myself from this deed had it not issued from the most sovereign royal majesty whom all must, and myself most especially, obey in all matters.)

The si-clause construction combined with the imperfect subjunctive used to recount his predicament powerfully express the degree to which royal constraint imposed participation. As we shall see, Foulechat's syntax here is taken from the earlier "addended address," where he developed at far greater length the political pressures that forced him into the arrangement.

The addended address opens by paraphrasing John of Salisbury on the obedience owed a sovereign: "le roy est un ymage de divinité qui doit estre amé, servi et honnoré" (the king is a reflection of the divine who must be loved, served, and honoured) (*Policratique*, 250.2). Thereafter follows a summary of Salisbury's reflections on the obligations of all men to recognize the authority of their leader and to accommodate all his desires, provided they coincide with Christian doctrine. If some choose to behave otherwise, the culprits risk "diverses punicions" (various punishments) (*Policratique*, 250.5), ranging from being stripped of their wealth to public defamation and physical harm. Having thus evoked the sovereign's power and the dire consequences of disobedience, the addended address concludes that as "tous chevaliers et tous subgés doivent obeïr au prince et au duc" (all knights and all subjects must obey both princes and dukes) (*Policratique*, 250.7), so too Foulechat has no choice but to submit to his king:

Pour ceste cause, tres debonnaire et redoubté seigneur, je, le vostre povre petit orateur qui tant suy tenu a la vostre tres douce benignité et tant obligié a la vostre tres haute magesté et qui tant en ay recue de biens et d'onneurs que je ne le pourroie desservir de fait ne racompter de bouche et, se je valoie rien, je devroie mettre toute ma vie entierement et exposer pour le vostre plaisir, quant je os oÿ et entendu que il vous plaisoit et vouliés que je translatasse le livre qui est appelé *Policraticon* et le meisse de latin en romans, je n'osé pour rien contredire. (*Policratique*, 250.8)

(For this reason, most great and feared lord, I, your poor humble orator who is so greatly indebted to your most sweet kindness and greatly obliged to your very high majesty from whom I have received so many goods and honors for which I cannot do justice nor begin to recite, and even if I am worth

> nothing, I should give and dedicate my entire life to the realization of your pleasure. Thus once I had heard and understood that it was your desire and that you wanted me to translate the book entitled *Policraticus* and to put it in French from Latin, I did not dare contradict [you].)

As would be the case in the later "premier prologue," the conditional and the subjunctive serve here to express grammatically the constraints inherent in royal commissions. According to our "povre petit orateur," he is expected ("tenu") and required ("tant oblige") to dedicate his life ("mettre toute ma vie") to satisfying the king's pleasure ("pour le voste plaisir"). Under no circumstances would our translator "dare to contradict" ("osé pour rien contredire") the king's wishes. Moreover, Foulechat implies that his obligation to the king is even greater than that of other subjects because he is doubly indebted to the king as a result of rewards and honours ("de biens et d'onneurs") that he has already received from Charles V and that are too great to enumerate. Foulechat's subsequent claim that his only desire was to abide by the king's will – "le désir … de faire le vostre plaisir" (the desire … to please you) (*Policratique*, 250.9) rings off key since he has implied that his submission has less to do with the king's sovereign authority and more to do with satisfying an incurred debt. It is tempting to read these comments as signalling that Foulechat received a fixed pension during the writing of the text as we know Oresme and Presles did, but in the absence of archival support, one cannot know for sure. Regardless, in this scripted performance of exchange, Foulechat appears to have adopted what Webb Keane refers to as the conventional "boundaries of exchange."[12] Either he is referring euphemistically to a contractual arrangement with the king or he is simply grafting this literary transaction onto a well-established feudal framework. Whatever may be the case, as we advance in both addresses, we become aware of a distinctive new dynamic taking shape.

As we have already observed, in the "premier prologue," Foulechat speaks of his anxieties related to his intellectual shortcomings, which made him reluctant to accept the king's commission. It is an issue also treated in the addended address, although in this earlier version, Foulechat envisions himself as torn between the opposing forces of knowledge and royal authority:

> Je fus mis entre deux angoisses, dont je regardoie d'une part mon ignorance et la grant oeuvre … et de l'autre part je regardoie et consideroie la magesté royale, a qui tous doivent obeïr. (*Policratique*, 250.9)

(I was placed between two anxieties; on one hand, I examined my ignorance in face of this great work ... and on the other hand, I examined and considered your royal majesty, to whom all must obey.)

On one side, he confronts the assignment that exceeds his intellectual abilities; on the other, he confronts his sovereign, whom he must obey. Unlike in the "premier prologue," Foulechat recounts in the addended address how he resolves to remedy the situation given his obligation to accept the commission. He resolves that when he has questions about the meaning of a passage or his translation, he will turn to the intellectual community to consult "those more knowledgeable than [he]" ("pluseurs plus souffisans de [lui]," *Policratique*, 250.9). This plan is, however, quickly thwarted because, as Foulechat subsequently explains, his distance from Paris makes it impossible to consult either scholars or books. He hastens to add that his predicament might be remedied if permitted to return to Paris and, in that event, he would be able to complete his translation. For the time being, he informs the king that he can present only an incomplete work:

Et en pluseurs lieux, où je n'ay peu trouver conseil n'en livre n'en plus souffisans de moi, j'ay laissié les espaces en esperance de les corriger s'il plaisoit a Dieu que je retournasse a Paris, où je pourroie et par livres et par docteurs bien recouvrer de les amender. (*Policratique*, 250.12)

(And in many places where I was unable to find advice either in a book or from those more knowledgeable than I, I left blank spaces in hopes of correcting them, if, God willing, I return to Paris, where I would be able to address and correct the missing information through consultation of books and doctors.)

Foulechat appears to inform the king that he will discover actual empty spaces throughout the manuscript that can be filled only if the translator returns to Paris, where he can find answers. The translator apologizes for the state of his work – "se je l'eusse miex faire, je l'eusse fait" (if I could have done better, I would have) (*Policratique*, 251.16). The king's presumed copy of Foulechat's *Policratique* encourages us to believe that the king did, in fact, initially receive an unfinished text from the translator. It is clear that MS fr. 24287 initially contained blank spaces that were only later filled in with missing material.[13] It is based on these filled lacunae and the fact that the "premier prologue" makes no further mention of the translator's difficulties in completing the work that I argue for viewing the addended address as a precursor to the "premier prologue."

The "premier prologue" offers further support to this hypothesis since, here, Foulechat thanks the king for access to intellectual materials previously unavailable to him:

> Car lonc temps a que ce livre, du quel je ay veu et leu aucunes fois selon divers propos pluseurs auctorités alleguees, j'ay desirré a veoir; et, se ce ne fust vostre commandement, onques ne l'eusse peu entierement veoir, si comme a l'aide nostre Seigneur par le vostre commandement le me faut visiter. (*Policratique*, 86.74–5)
>
> (I had long desired to see this book of which I had seen and read several varied remarks elaborated on by several authorities, and, had it not been for your order, never would I have been able to see it in its entirety. And as it is with assistance from our Lord, by your command, I was required to consult it.)

We will consider later in the chapter the significance of Charles V's possible involvement in securing Foulechat's return to Paris and his access to learned matter. For the moment, what merits our attention is Foulechat's evolving self-portrait that begins with him as an intellectual outsider and ends with him, thanks to the king, accessing materials that make him an authority.

Foulechat makes it sound as if returning to Paris was a simple affair, when the truth is that in 1363, the University of Paris had condemned the translator, and this sentence meant that beyond being divorced from the intellectual community, Foulechat was likely exiled from the city itself.[14] When we factor into Foulechat's narrative the stripping of his intellectual rights and social identity by the university nearly a decade prior to the king's commission, his two addresses to the king included in the *Policratique* take on a very different tenor. In fact, what initially sounded like a subject's willing submission of his talents in honour of his king's authority now sounds like an opportunity for the subject to benefit from his sovereign's interest in him by carving out a new social identity for himself as an intellectual, in spite of the fact that the recognized institutional purveyor of knowledge had officially exiled him from the community. After all, what hope might a condemned scholar in the late Middle Ages have had for re-entering the intellectual fold other than through royal command? This logic appears to have driven Foulechat's thinking: in the earlier addended prologue, he proceeded to reclaim titles taken from him in 1363 through reference to his association with the king. For instance, Foulechat re-appropriated the title of *orator* by addressing himself to the king as "vostre petit orateur" (your humble cleric) (*Policratique*, 250.13).

Nonetheless, the translator seems to suggest that even if the king recognized him as a scholar, both he and the king suffered the consequences of the university's judgment against him as he was kept away from crucial resources available only in Paris.

Foulechat's dilemma speaks to the larger issue of the commissioned writers and their social status; Foulechat is not the only one who presented himself as an intellectual in spite of his separation from the university community. Raoul de Presles proved, in fact, even more adamant than Foulechat in identifying himself as an outsider in relation to the university community. Like Foulechat, Presles expressed surprise that the king chose him over an official member of the intellectual community to translate Augustine's *City of God*:

> Je doi estre esmerveillé, et non sans cause, de ce que, delaissiéz les souverains clers de vostre roiaume dont il en y a tant de si grans que en toute crestienté n'en a tant de telz, et ausquiex tele euvre appartenoit et leur estoit deuee à translater, il peut estre cheu en vostre pensee de le moy baillier, qui au regart de eulx ne suis que poudre et cendre. (*Cité*, 170.23–5 – 171.1–2)

> (I can only be stunned, and not without cause, by the fact that you rejected the sovereign clerics of your kingdom of whom there are so many great ones that in all Christianity there are none like them, to whom such a work belonged and was their right to translate, and that it came to you to give it to me, who, in their eyes, is but powder and ash.)

According to the translator, it was the "sovereign clerics," not he, who stood as the rightful proprietors and conveyers of St Augustine's knowledge. For this reason, they should have been the recipients of the king's commission – "such a work belonged" to them and "it was their right." Nonetheless, the king passed over the officially recognized *oratores* to favour Presles, a man whose humble intellect made him inconsequential – nothing more than "powder and ash." Presles goes even further in his address by identifying himself with the opposing camp, the humble *laboratores*. He professes to be a weak and inadequate labourer who is unable to perform even the simplest of duties: "vous avéz voulu, à moy qui sui de si feible entendement, baillier si fort fessel et à si petite main si grant mole à tourner" (you wanted to give to me who is of such weak understanding such a heavy load and to such a small hand, the task to turn such a great wheel) (*Cité*, 171.4). Notwithstanding his protestations, as we witnessed with Foulechat, at the same time that Presles speaks of his inadequacy to fill the intellectual role ordered by the king, he, too, uses the king's command to appropriate for himself a role normally controlled by the university. In this regard, both men signal the advantages they obtained when receiving and accepting a royal commission.

To appreciate the advantages involved in men like Foulechat and Presles appropriating the identity of an *orator* through direct association with the king, we need to take into account contemporary developments in the intellectual sphere linked to the migration of an ever-increasing number of university-trained men who assumed powerful (and lucrative) positions at court. In considering this angle, we can come to understand the advantages associated with Foulechat's and Presles's intentional disassociation from their university peers. Since the first edition of Jacques le Goff's *Les intellectuels au moyen âge* in 1957, important scholarship has tracked the spread in late-medieval France of intellectual thought beyond university walls. Beginning in the late thirteenth century, university-trained men exhibited a growing interest in introducing the laity to the "discipline de pensée" (discipline of thought),[15] a drive that led many among them to distance themselves from the university corporation.[16] According to Alain de Libera, intellectuals also maintained their distance from nobility, thereby staking claim to a space "entre le prince et l'évêque" (between the prince and the bishop).[17] By the end of the Middle Ages, according to Jacques Verger, the tide had changed, and medieval intellectuals sought to align themselves with nobility.[18] Surprisingly, scholarship on the medieval intellectual generally skips over the fourteenth century, and as a result, the influence of the royal commissioned writers on the development of intellectual identity as well as on the emergence of vernacular authorship has gone unexamined.[19] Serge Lusignan, however, has rightly pointed out that Charles V's commissioning of multiple translations represented far more than the transfer from the university to the court of knowledge; it simultaneously augured the transfer from the university to the court of intellectual activity.[20] In some cases, this migration involved members of the university, although the king also depended on men like Foulechat and Presles who were not recognized members of the university intellectual community to contribute to the effort. In this regard, the *Sapientia* project must be acknowledged as having played a key role in reimagining what it meant to be an intellectual and, specifically, the intellectual's role at court.[21]

To a certain extent, Charles V, when choosing his intellectual clients, was only following a trend already underway, since many of the commissioned writers were already important actors involved in the dissemination of knowledge beyond the university prior to participating in the king's *Sapientia* project.[22] Among those who already bridged university and court spheres, we can include Evrart de Trémaugon, advisor to the king and member of the law faculty; Evrart de Conti, royal physician and faculty in medicine; and Jean Corbechon of the St Augustin hermitage who served as both university chancellor and the king's confessor. Other commissioned writers used their university education in the exclusive service of the court, a shift that Verger associates with an increasing desire among the university elite to engage in political life as a means of positioning themselves within the noble class.[23] For instance, Presles was a court lawyer and, eventually, *maître des requêtes*,[24] while the translator Jacques Bauchant served his king as a sergeant-at-arms. Nonetheless, a few of the commissioned writers pursued predominantly ecclesiastic careers and became participants in the vernacularisation of knowledge only through their contributions to the king's *Sapientia* project: Daudin was a canon at St-Chapelle; Oresme, also a canon at St-Chapelle, served as dean of the Rouen Cathedral and eventually Bishop of Lisieux;[25] and Simon de Hesdin, a doctor in theology, headed two houses within the Order of Saint Jacques of Jerusalem. Likewise, the Carmelite monk Golein appears to have strayed from his university work as professor of theology only to answer the king's text commissions. We may want to include Foulechat in this last group, although by the time he received the king's translation, the university had publicly denounced and exiled him from the community.

To return to the adoption by both Foulechat and Presles of a subservient discourse to explain their acceptance of the king's commission for translated works, both men began their prologues by detailing their powerlessness to refuse royal order only to then emerge as newly empowered subjects thanks to their dealings with the king. Both men recognized the king's command as a recognition of their intellectual status, a status that had been stripped from Foulechat and one that had more than likely never been attributed to Presles, even though he had authored Latin texts and had used his university learning on behalf of the kingdom. Thanks to the king's commissions, these two men were able to lay claim to a new identity taking shape, that of the secular intellectual whose knowledge and talents identified them as essential members of the kingdom. While the king's commissioning practices identified them as clients who were expected to satisfy royal need and desire, the larger repercussions of the king's actions meant that men with university training and a talent for composing in the vernacular could claim intellectual affinity with their sovereign.

The Wise King among the Learned: Reimagining the Patron-Writer Relationship

At the same time that the commissioned writers used royal command to construct a new intellectual identity for themselves, they also sought to reimagine the king's role by positioning him as a member of a learned sodality. The king himself had already laid the groundwork by proclaiming his oversight of the university, which he referred to as "la fille aînée du roi" (the eldest daughter of the king).[26] The financial and material support that Charles V secured for his commissioned writers can be interpreted as an extension of his efforts to lay claim to the intellectual realm. As we have seen, Foulechat offered a compelling argument for believing that the king's authority in this arena was more than symbolic. After all, Foulechat gives us every reason to understand that the king not only orchestrated his return to Paris after he'd been banished by the university, but also secured the translator's access to the intellectual sources necessary to complete his translation of the *Policratique*. Other commissioned writers eagerly endorsed the king's authority over the intellectual realm. They did so in discreet ways: for example, by repeatedly comparing him favourably to Solomon and Alexander, whom the university had long singled out as the "grands ancêtres mythiques du savant" (the great mythic ancestors of the learned man).[27] They also regularly praised Charles V both for his personal commitment to learning and for his desire to share this knowledge with his subjects. In the prologue to his *Ethiques*, Oresme begins by reminding the king of that knowledge represents a unique treasure that multiplies and enriches an entire community: "l'estude de tous livres engenre et embat, ou acroist es cuers de ceuls qui y entendent, affeccion et amour au bien publique" (study of all books gives birth and encourages or makes grow in the hearts of those who understand it affection and love for the common good.)[28] Oresme then praises the king for supporting translations of learned writings in the name of "le bien commun" (the common good). For this reason above all, Oresme recognizes the king as worthy of a title that recognizes not just his dominion over an earthly kingdom but his possession of the greatest treasure of all, that of wisdom: "par quoy il appert clerement que nostre bon roy Charles puet estre dit Charles grant en sagesce" (for this [reason] it appears clear that our good King Charles can be named Charles great in wisdom) (*Ethiques*,100).

Artists responsible for decorating royal copies of Charles V's commissioned writings visually reinforced arguments for the king's close association with the intellectual community. In the frontispieces they created, the king's dress and posture associated sovereign power with the realm of learning. In the king's copy of Foulechat's *Policratique*, this point is underscored by the placement of the king at a lectern rather than enthroned and by the replacement of sceptre with learned writings. The presentation scene in the king's copy of Presles's *Cité* provides another representative example of this tactic; here the crowned king dons the cleric's robe (Figure 2.2: BnF, MS fr. 22912, fol. 3r). Claire Richter Sherman includes this frontispiece among a series of intimate royal portraits said to reveal artists' new efforts to privilege a "personal, humanized relationship between king and author."[29] As Sherman notes, this new visual account of literary exchange reconcieves the traditional hieratic scale that would have distinguished king and translator by systematically diminishing the distance between the two men, and by encouraging a sense of intimacy through, for example, shared attire.[30] Sherman's study focuses on the novel depiction of the sovereign, but she frequently acknowledges that the commissioned writers were also subject to new visual interpretation. For example, she identifies the MS fr. 22912 frontispiece as especially important to the development of royal portraiture but notes that this results from its privileging of the "personal communication" between the two men, and she further acknowledges that the *Master of the Coronation of Charles VI* took equal care in portraying the king as he did in depicting Presles, who is said to be distinguished through "individualized physiognomic traits."[31] Based on these observations, it is worth considering that the illuminator's shared interest in the king and the translator indicates that, in fact, it was the partnership rather than uniquely the king that captured his imagination.

The frontispiece to MS fr. 22912 deserves to be recognized as not only reconceiving the traditional role of the king but, more specifically, as visualizing the reimagined relationship between royalty and the intellectual community detailed in Presles's opening address to the king. The image deliberately destabilizes conventional power dynamics in its representation of both men. The king appears far less regal than expected, given his humble clerical attire, and his deferential posture, which has him leaning forward to accept the book rather than remaining erect and distant as expected of a sovereign. The miniaturist is even more inventive in his depiction of Presles, who while retaining the expected subservient posture of the author on bended knee, also maintains an upright torso that suggests his importance. Perhaps most striking is the insertion of St Augustine behind Presles, whose mere presence, not to mention the impression

Figure 2.2: Presentation scene, *Cité de Dieu* translated by Raoul de Presles, Paris, Bibliothèque nationale de France, MS fr. 22912, fol. 3r.

that he urges the translator forward, provides a powerful corrective to the translator's subsequent protests that he lacks the credentials of the "souverains clers." It is as if St Augustine personally selected Presles to translate his work. The church father's inclusion in this presentation scene also dramatically reworks the exchange by replacing a binary exchange with a triadic relationship in which Presles assumes a central role as mediator of the knowledge that passes from the *auctor* to the king. Finally, the open book held by Presles reinforces the translator's crucial position within this newly articulated learned community. Although located at the centre of the frame, the book nonetheless resides predominantly in the sphere shared by St Augustine and Presles. Thus, in MS fr. 22912, the king's act of reaching out to take the book held by Presles may have less to do with royal appropriation of knowledge and more to do with a visual account of the king's passage into a learned sodality, which is represented here by the learned trinity of the book, the translator, and St Augustine. Instead of visualizing the king's authority as resulting from his command for the work, the MS fr. 22912 frontispiece reinterprets this literary exchange as an invitation that the king assume his rightful place *within* the learned community. Through the *mise en scène* of the exchange, a new form of intellectual partnership takes shape. It is a partnership that equalizes the dynamics of patron and client through reference to their shared love of learning and removes literary exchange from the court setting to recast it in a learned sphere.

To measure the success of this revised account of literary exchange, consider Christine de Pizan's portrayal of the king as a learned man. When Christine composed her biography of Charles V in 1404, the private library or study as a space distinct from the university lecture hall where intellectual activity might flourish had been firmly established. For Christine, the king's library had long reflected this shift. It was a unique domain that put the king in direct association with learned writings and the learned men to whom he turned for new translations:

> Ne dirons nous encore de la sagece du roy Charles, la grant amour qu'il avoit à l'estude et à science: et qu'il soit ainsi bien le demoustroit par la belle assemblee des notables livres et belle librarie, qu'il avoit de tous les plus notable volumes [...]; et se son estude bel à devis estoit bien ordenné, comme il voulsist toutes ses choses belles et nettes, polies et ordennées, ne convient demander, car mieulz estre ne peust; mais non obstant que bien entendist le latin [...] pour la grant amour qu'il avoit à ses successeurs [...] fist par solempnelz maistres, souffisans en toutes les sciences et arts, translater de latin en françois tous les plus notables livres. (*Charles V*, 2:42–3)

> (Let us speak once more of King Charles's wisdom, the great love he had for study and science, which was clearly revealed in the beautiful assembly of notable books and the beautiful library, that he had all the most notable volumes [...], and that his well-appointed study was well ordered since he wanted all of his things beautiful and clean, polished and organized, there was no point in asking for more because it could not have been better; and even though he understood Latin [...], because of the great love he had for his successors [...], he had translated from Latin into French all of the most notable books by learned masters versed in all the sciences and arts.)

It should come as little surprise that Christine's enumeration of Charles V's most important commissioned translations included the three works privileged here and, in particular, the *Policratique*, whose frontispiece to the royal copy offers a powerful visual precursor to Christine's own textual description of the king's study (*Charles V*, 2:43–4).

Christine credited the king with carving out this hallowed space of learning that entailed a "belle assemblée" of both books and the learned. According to her, the king was at perfect ease in this space, where he shared with this elite coterie not just knowledge but also the language of learning, Latin. From this position of learned power, the king, as Christine would have it, worked to protect its practitioners and to assure that others had access to this knowledge.

"Je avoie assés labouré": The Commission as the Product of Intellectual Labour

Lest we imagine that the book community proposed an account of literary exchange with no footing in reality, it is important to recognize that its members appear to have tackled the issue that caused the most discomfort: receiving financial reward for work rendered. While it is true that not a single commissioned writer openly discussed his financial arrangements with the king, several do appear to have mounted pre-emptive defences for any reward they may have received. When negotiating their role on the fringes between the university and the court, many commissioned writers were compelled to bridge the relationship between a set of intellectual ideals and the reality of their contractual arrangements with the king. "Learned labour," a concept long debated within the university community, played a key role in justifying participation in the king's *Sapientia* project and, quite likely, in justifying acceptance of reward for intellectual activity.[32] Presles's opening address is a powerful case in point. As a reminder, Presles compares the commission to the physical demand required of the labourer to turn a grain wheel. Protesting that he is too weak to perform this duty, Presles uses this metaphor to speak of his intellectual weakness – "la foiblesse de mon engin" (the weakness of my thinking) – and then emphasizes the importance of the work itself – "la grandeur de l'euvre" (the greatness of the work) (*Cité*, 171.8–11). This conflation of intellectual work and physical labour prepares the way for the translator to then justify refusal of the commission because he has already laboured a lifetime on the king's behalf:

> Je avoie assés labouré en mon temps – tant à faire le livre qui se apele le *Compendieux moral de la chose publique* et le livre que se apele la *Muse*, laquele il vous plut à recevoir en gré pour ce que j'avoye intitulé à vouz comme les croniques en françois contemporisees ..., consideré encore la grant charge du fait de mon advocacie, qui est office publique, et qui requiert labour continuel. (*Cité*, 171.16-20–172.1-2)

> (I have laboured enough in my life – first in composing the book that is entitled *Moral Compendium of the Public Good* and the book entitled the *Muse*, which it pleased you to receive since I had addressed it to you as well as the chronicle of contemporary events in French ..., consider furthermore the great demand required of my work as a lawyer, which is a public office, and which requires endless labour.)

Presles's astute rhetoric links his paid legal services at court back to his earlier writings.[33] In this narrative arc covering a lifetime of work, Presles positions the commission as a bridge for these varied activities, all presented here as expressions of learned labour.

Presles's comparison of his intellectual activity in the secular realm with physical labour evokes a centuries-old debate surrounding questions of whether intellectual activity constituted work and if so, whether it merited financial recompense. These questions preoccupied the university community, where, since the twelfth century, its members had been divided on the issue of whether teachers ought to take payment from their students. The original stance was that university faculty should not receive compensation from their students for the knowledge they communicated.[34] Franciscan members of the university, in particular, regularly intoned Proverbs 23.23, "Noli vendere sapientiam, et doctrinam et intelligentiam," as a warning against accepting money from students; in contrast, for those who had not vowed a life of poverty, the need to secure a basic livelihood remained.[35] To get around this scriptural directive, medieval thinkers distinguished between knowledge that could not be bought and the labour required to master and to communicate knowledge, for which one could receive recompense. In 1245, Bartholomew of Brescia parsed out the situation as follows: "a master does not sell his *scientia*, since it cannot be valued in money; rather a recompense (*premium*) is offered to him for his labor" (Nec vendit magister scientiam, quia aestimari non potest sed pro labore suo promittitu ei premium").[36] Aristotle provided the ultimate justification for such a distinction since he had contended that all labour must be rewarded.[37] Aristotle also provided medieval thinkers with the language to distinguish between the competing economies governing the circulation of knowledge through his treatment of the teacher-student relationship. This relationship either proceeded on the grounds of stated conditions of reward – *per pactum et conventionem* – or by agreement among friends – *ratione amicitie*.[38] In the first instance, an agreement on financial recompense in exchange for knowledge was rendered at the outset. By the fourteenth century, this argument served to justify payment for the services of lawyers – Presles's own profession – and doctors, and also masters who requested remuneration from their students.[39] Likewise, by the late Middle Ages, university faculty relied less on payment from students because they now received pensions, salaries, and ecclesiastic benefices.[40] It is hard to read Presles's extended meditation at the outset of the *Cité* regarding the breadth and depth of his learned labour without thinking of the highly lucrative pension arrangements he enjoyed in exchange for committing to the *Cité* translation project. Moreover, it is striking that Oresme – the only other commissioned writer documented as having also enjoyed a royal pension – also openly identified his translation as the product of "[s]on labeur" (his labour) (*Ethiques*, 100).

"Doctrinam magis quam thesaurum eligite": Recognizing Learning as the Greatest of Treasures

In addition to valorizing their learned labour, the king's commissioned writers regularly identified knowledge as the learned man's treasure, a wealth that surpassed the riches of the wealthiest lord. Foulechat stands out for his savvy ability to valorize his work and his status through reference to this concept. While self-deprecating as we have seen, Foulechat, nonetheless, made clear that his work merited careful consideration when counselling the king to "considerer et estudier" (examine and study) (*Policratique*, 86.76) the work because it constitutes a unique treasure rarely possessed, even by "riches seigneurs qui en tout habondoient" (rich lords who had an abundance of everything) (*Policratique*, 86.78). He was also keen to not allow this treasure to be regarded as a good to be hoarded by the wealthy. Rather he wanted to maintain its status as a treasure unique to the learned community, and in asserting this point, Foulechat made certain that it not be severed from its maker. To this end, Foulechat's name was twice inserted into the fabric of the king's manuscript through anagrams, a technique that inscribed on the king's "oeuvre" the translator's signature.

In MS fr. 24287, inserted between the final book of the *Policratique* and the addended early address to the king, a fourteen-line poem discloses that Foulechat's name will be revealed if certain letters are manipulated. The coda merits full citation:

> Le translateur pas ne se nomme
> Car n'est pas amé de tout homme.
> Mais qui a l'arbre de science, come
> Dit est, retournera,
> Il en venra a congnoissance par
> Les rainsseaux qu'il trouvera.
> Prengne les chiefs par droite ligne
> Et les mette com dens de pigne.
> Il y venra par droite voie.
> Or li veulle Diex donner joie.
> Amen.
> Se le voulez plus clerement,
> Où son nom par les chiefs applique,
> Retournez au commencement
> Du livre de l'Eutetique. (*Policratique*, 22)

> (The translator does not name himself because he is not loved by all, but he who has the tree of science, as it is named, if he will return to it, he will know [his name] by the coloured letters that he will find. Take the letters in order and keep them like a row of teeth. It will come to you directly. Thus he wants to praise God. Amen. If you want it even clearer – where his name is exposed in letters – return to the beginning of the book of *Eutetique*.)

Up until this point in the translation, Foulechat has only been identified in relation to the book as "celui qui le translata" (he who translated it) (*Policratique*, 81.2). This coda, however, promises to name the "maker."

Even though the translator dare not speak his name, his identity can be discovered in the king's manuscript.

Léopold Delisle claimed to have cracked the code when identifying the beginning of John of Salisbury's "Euthetique" in the king's copy as the source of the solution. By piecing together the first letter of the first fourteen lines of the "Euthetique," we discover Foulechat's name.[41] Delisle's solution, however, speaks only to the instructions provided in the final four lines *after* "Amen" – in effect, a coda to the coda. Delisle, otherwise, ignored that the king's codex contains a second naming event. The coda's first ten lines direct the reader to return to the "tree of science," an allusion that points directly to John of Salisbury's own prologue, which followed the "Euthetique" and opened with reference to the "fruits of letters" – "le fruit de lectres" (*Policratique*, 94.1). To discover the translator's name here, the coda instructs us to seek out highlighted letters (les rainsseaux) and maintain their prescribed order (com dens de pigne). As a matter of fact, Foulechat's full name emerges when we lift from folios 9v–10v of MS fr. 24287 the first decorated letter and then the letters prefaced thereafter by red and blue paraph marks (excepting those distinguishing between "texte" and "glose").[42] These acrostics found in the opening folios of this codex, which are only acknowledged in the manuscript's closing folios, signal the combined efforts of the translator and the manuscript makers to temper claims that the work represented the patron's pleasure or "oeuvre" by simultaneously recognizing the translation as Foulechat's "oeuvre." The term "oeuvre" serves here not only to play against the concept of the commission as constituting exclusively the patron's pleasure, but also to insist on the double entendre that recognized the final product as a creative work resulting from the writer's labour. The king's personal copy of this "oeuvre" simultaneously identified the king and the translator as sharing this work. Where the king is depicted in possession of the work in the frontispiece, the translator's own "ownership" of the work emerges in the richly painted letters on the opening folios. Shared between the two men, the text constitutes an incomparable "tresor" (treasure) of intellectual wealth (*Policratique*, 86.81).

Oresme's first commissioned translation for the king makes this same point in an even more deliberate manner when the *Master of the Coronation of Charles VI*, the artist also responsible for the previously examined *Cité* frontispiece, inserted scriptural citations into the frontispiece of the king's private copy of the *Ethiques* (Figure 2.3: The Hague, Museum Meermanno-Westreenianum, MS 10 D-1).[43] Herein, Oresme orders the king to "Accipite disciplinam quam pecuniam, et doctrinam magis quam

Figure 2.3: Presentation scene, *Livre des éthiques d'Aristote* translated by Nicole Oresme, the Hague, Museum Meermanno-Westreenianum, MS 10 D-1, fol. 5r.

thesaurum eligite" (Choose learning rather than money and choose instruction more valuable than treasure). The reference to Proverbs 8:10 echoed the opinion of great thinkers, including Aristotle, who uniformly identified the intellectual as possessing the greatest wealth.

Both Oresme and Foulechat stand out for the presentation of their translations as treasures. When advertising their possession of this incomparable wealth, they drew from a learned tradition that countered both the feudalistic discourse adopted in royal addresses as well as the clientelistic practices implemented by the king to secure desired works. They did not, however, go as far as Boethius the Dane (d. c. 1284), who had proclaimed that the act of sharing knowledge placed the learned in the position of the ideal prince because it showed liberality, magnanimity, and magnificence.[44] In place of a hieratic exchange, the identification of knowledge as the greatest wealth enabled these men to balance out their relationship with the king.

This theme of equalizing the power of knowledge is most fully developed in the *Ethiques*, the first commissioned translation by Charles V's most celebrated commissioned writer. At the outset of his *Ethiques*, Oresme authored a nuanced narrative of what would entail a seven-year intellectual partnership with Charles V (1370–7) and that would result in the translation and glossing of four Aristotelian texts. After the *Ethiques* followed the *Politiques*, the *Yconomiques*, and the *Livre du ciel et du monde*. It is no exaggeration to claim for Oresme a far superior status to the king's other commissioned writers. By 1370, Oresme already enjoyed a strong scholarly reputation based on approximately a dozen datable works in which he treated such varied topics as mathematics, astrology, economics, law, and theology.[45] In fact, Charles V's interest in Oresme likely stemmed from the king's familiarity with the scholar's 1365 translation of his own Latin treatise on coin fluctuations, the *Traitié de la première invention des monnoies*, a work that engaged deeply with Aristotelian concepts and is considered to have had a profound effect on the king's economic policies.[46] It may be because Oresme already had a strong reputation as a formidable intellectual that he felt at ease to acknowledge openly the inestimable worth of the knowledge he provided the king. In fact, in the "proheme" (prologue) that introduced Oresme's *Ethiques*, the translation did not figure as much as a product of royal command as it did as a gift of great symbolic wealth that would enhance the king's status.

Oresme's repackaging of the commission as the writer's gift plays out most fully in the closing section of the "proheme," entitled "excusacion et (re)commendacion de ceste oeuvre" (explanation and praise for [recommendation of] this work) (*Ethiques*, 100).[47] Here, Oresme first focuses on his intellectual work. When reflecting on the challenge of translating Aristotle, the translator calls frequently on variations of the verb "bailler" (to offer, to give) to explain his activity. This term regularly figured in medieval dedications to describe exchange dynamics. Nonetheless, in this example, Oresme appropriates the term to describe his own linguistic work, thereby underscoring the generosity that undergirds his willingness to share his intellectual wealth with readers. Oresme uses versions of "bailler" five times in the closing paragraph to the "Excusacion" in reference to his learned labour. Observing that complex thought cannot be "bailliee en termes legiers a entendre" (expressed/given in terms easy to understand) (*Ethiques*, 100), Oresme assures his audience that he has made every effort to present this work in a clear French that might be further perfected by future translators:

> Mais se Dieux plaist, par mon labeur pourra estre mieulx entendue ceste noble science et ou temps avenir estre bailliee par autres en françois plus clerement et plus complectement. (*Ethiques*, 101)
>
> (But if it pleases God, by my labour, this noble science will be able to be better understood and in future times, be translated [given] by others in a French more concisely and more completely.)

By using the term "bailliee" to refer to translation, Oresme effectively reclassifies the king's ordered text as an expression of the translator's own intellectual generosity. The opening illustration to the Hague copy already spelled out that instruction was a treasure more valuable than money, but the "proheme" makes clear that the act of translating Aristotle is an expression of the intellectual's magnanimity.[48] Oresme pursues this line of thought immediately thereafter when declaring that

> translater telz livres en françois et baillier en françois les arts et les sciences est un labeur moult proffitable; car c'est un langage noble et commun a genz de grant engin et de bonne prudence. (*Ethiques*, 101)
>
> (to translate such books into French and render [give] in French the arts and sciences is a great and profitable labour; because it is a noble language and known by people of great wisdom and good prudence.)

Translating is a form of intellectual labour that Oresme believes valuable precisely because it assures the sharing of this inestimable knowledge within a community united in intellectual pursuit.

Serge Lusignan has already singled out Oresme among the king's translators for his unparalleled role in "transporting/translating" the intellectual power previously harnessed by the universities to the court when communicating this knowledge in the vernacular.[49] Oresme also diverges from fellow translators and intellectuals with his unabashed promotion of his intellectual "wealth." For Oresme, the "profit" his translation promised was shared between himself, his king, and other learned readers who might learn from or improve upon his work. In this regard, in Oresme's first commissioned translation, the king figured less as a benefactor than as a beneficiary. According to Oresme, the translation is neither an offering nor an ordered work; rather, it is the product of learned labour freely shared within the community of learned and wise men or "genz de grant engin et de bonne prudence." For Oresme, the king participated in this community as one of the intimates expected to "benefit" from the translation.

An Intellectual Friendship Centred on the Gift of Knowledge

The opening frontispiece to Charles V's personal copy of Oresme's *Ethiques* provides one of the most striking images of late-medieval literary exchange (Figure 2.3: The Hague, Museum Meermanno-Westreenianum, MS 10 D-1, fol. 5r). Its magisterial negotiation of traditional iconographies gives expression to a new, intimate form of literary exchange between king and scholar. In this two-register frontispiece, the top register depicts the presentation scene in which Oresme, identified as the "translateur" in the rubrics below, kneels before the enthroned king and offers him the gift-book.

Sherman has fully examined the extent to which artist and author collaborated to rework this traditional portrayal of the subservient author so as to confer on Oresme a "dominant role" in the transaction.[50] Sherman demonstrates that the hieratic dynamics on display in this frontispiece are immediately subject to aggressive visual and verbal mediation. Included among the recognized artistic manipulations of the relational dynamics in this frontispiece are the blurring of the king's and translator's spheres, the "direct confrontation of glance" between the two men, and the manipulation of scenery, vestiary items, and gestures, all of which serve to create a visual testimony of "a personal, humanized relationship between the king and author."[51] The previously mentioned inserted biblical citations, which Sherman argues were "undoubtedly chose[n]" by Oresme,[52] are key to understanding the reimagining of the relationship between the two men. The sacred wisdom inscribed on the banners issuing from their mouths counterbalances the hieratic iconography adopted in this scene. Addressing Oresme, the king cites a slightly adjusted version of Ecclesiastes 1:13 so that he "dedicates his heart" to "learning" (as opposed to the original term "prudentiam") and "instruction": "Dedi cor meum ut scirem disciplinam atque doctrinam" (I give my heart that I would know learning and instruction). The lexical alteration to Scripture assures perfect harmony between the king's scripted declaration and Oresme's paraphrase of Proverbs 8:10 to validate the king's commitment to learning and instruction: "Accipite disciplinam quam pecuniam, et doctrinam magis quam thesaurum eligite" (Choose learning rather than money and choose instruction more valuable than treasure). Sherman has argued that these verbal declarations "[confirm] the translator's position as moral and intellectual adviser to the king" while the "humbler tone of Charles V's declaration" reinforces the unexpected power Oresme's inscribed words afford him.[53]

Sherman's astute analysis of the Hague frontispiece opens the door to serious consideration of the impact of this scripted exchange on the larger commissioning narrative. In the Hague frontispiece, roles are reversed so that it is the king who "dedicates" himself to learning, while Oresme's recorded utterance, via the voice of God, issues a command that the king receive the intellectual wealth he possesses; that is, learning and instruction. In this illustration, the king's commission is pre-empted by a double reversal. First, the king's command for a text is supplanted by a royal promise to submit himself to instruction, a verbalized subordination to Oresme. Second, in place of the financial wealth secured for Oresme in advance of completing the translation (which is, once again, never mentioned by the author), the illustration presents the translator performing an intellectual form of magnificence when sharing freely his intellectual treasure with the king. What makes this frontispiece especially ingenious is that this new narrative of exchange grafts itself onto the conventional iconography of literary exchange. Rather than overturn the king's authority to attribute mastery to the translator, the image balances out competing claims of mastery to introduce a dialogue that points to intellectual friendship built on a mutual love for knowledge. That the lower register explicitly links back to the above dedication scene through a double of the exchanged book, now held by the enthroned "Félicité Humaine" (Human Happiness), further emphasizes that these men are united by intellectual love and friendship – the only path to true happiness according to Aristotle himself.

Scholars concur that Oresme's first commissioned translation for Charles V introduced radically new and far-reaching concepts central to the wedding of kingship and cultural production. As already indicated, Sherman demonstrates that the dedication image heading the king's private copy of the *Ethiques* introduced an unprecedented intimacy between writer and king that would profoundly influence future royal iconography.[54] For Lusignan, Oresme's translation documents an acute awareness that the French royal court could develop into a dominant cultural centre for intellectual pursuits.[55] Add to these scholarly observations Bénédicte Sère's claim that Oresme provided an unprecedented view of friendship for kings in his glosses that he then applied to his own intellectual partnership with Charles V.[56] The remainder of this section will examine how Oresme's treatment of royal friendship provided a foundation for redefining royal investment in vernacular learned writings as an exchange between learned friends that hinged on the writer's willingness to share freely his intellectual gifts with the king.

Oresme would deliberately and persuasively develop the notion that Charles V's investment in vernacular learned writing was a form of intellectual friendship through reference to the ancient tradition of the learned sodality. The Greeks conceived of learning as transpiring within an economy of friendship in which knowledge constituted a gift freely exchanged between friends. Aristotle dedicated Books VIII and IX of the *Nicomachean Ethics* to the question of friendship and the idea of intellectual exchange as the highest form of intimacy. Aristotle contended that, to achieve the highest form of friendship, partners had to be of equal standing. Book IX, chapter 1 thus categorized friendship of virtue as the exclusive pleasure of an elite category of men. As Aristotelian specialists are fond of noting, the philosopher's treatment of the highest form of friendship betrays much ambivalence; for it is a rare intimacy reserved for an elite few and specifically unattainable for men of power since they are considered superior to all others.[57] Oresme, like many commentators before and after him, was attracted to this problematic issue (surely more so given that his translation addressed the king). As Sère argues, Oresme debunked Aquinas's influential assessment that Aristotle revealed sovereign friendship to be "highly unlikely."[58] Oresme countered this established viewpoint with a methodic and subtle reworking of both Aristotle and the commentary tradition that led him to present his dealings with the king as an exchange between members of the learned sodality.

The descriptor used by Aristotle to define friends of virtue has a long history of perplexing translators. Aristotle's modern English editor,

Terence Irwin, translates the term as "those who have shared philosophy in common," which he then clarifies in a footnote as Aristotle's colleagues in the Academy.[59] Irwin follows here a long tradition already apparent in medieval commentary. Grosseteste's translation, which was Oresme's source (via Aquinas), identified these friends as members of a philosophical community (communicatione philosophiae).[60] Aquinas glossed this term with the example of "a master and a student" (magistrum et discipulum).[61] Oresme's own translation of this passage exposed his absorption of this multi-tiered tradition:

> Car tele amistié est selon vertu [...] Et ce doit estre gardé quant a ceuls qui communiquent et enseignent philosophie, car la dignité et la valeur de philosophie ne peut estre mesuree a pecunes, pour ce que l'en n'en pourroit faire pris equivalent. Mais par aventure, a ceuls qui ont enseigniee tele chose, l'en leur doit rendre ce qui souffist; si comme l'en fait as dieux et a ses parens. *Glose: c'est a savoir, honeur, service et aide selon sa possibilité, se ilz en ont mestier.* (*Ethiques*, 454 and 454n12)

> (For such friendship is built on virtue [...] and it must be reserved for those who share and teach philosophy, because the dignity and valour of philosophy cannot be measured in coin because one cannot establish an equivalent price. As such, in cases when one must give what is appropriate to those who teach such things, one ought to do as one does with gods and parents. *Gloss: that is to say, honour, service, and assistance according to his abilities if need be.*)

Oresme's translation of this passage blurs the master text and the commentary tradition. He fuses Grosseteste and Aquinas within the body of the master text to qualify virtuous friends as "ceuls qui communiquent et enseignent philosophie" (those who share and teach philosophy). In this manner, Oresme subtly expands this community outward to acknowledge students, such as the king himself, who appears at the outset of the translation promising to "dedicate himself" to learning. Oresme again intervenes in the main body of Aristotle's text to develop the philosopher's assertion that the superiority of the intellectual gift represents a degree of "the dignity and value" that "cannot be measured in coin." Oresme finally interrupts with a gloss in which he counsels that the gift of knowledge should be reciprocated with "honour, service, and assistance." This articulation of the highest form of friendship as built on mutual exchange in the realm of learning resonates with the visual depiction of exchange between the king and writer heading the Hague manuscript. It also surely would have provided a handy justification for Oresme's acceptance of financial support for sharing his intellectual wealth with the king.

It is in the first folios to the king's personal copy of the *Ethiques* where Oresme reflects on the king's commission that we discover what makes this glossed translation truly "inédites et originales" (novel and original)[62] to reappropriate Sère's assessment of Oresme's reworking of Aristotelian friendship. Here, Oresme discards the common rhetorical ploys of fellow translators who insist, at least initially, on their subservience. Instead, he explores intellectual friendship as a viable frame to accommodate royal sponsorship of learned vernacular writing. Oresme's address to Charles V begins as follows:

> En la confiance de l'aide de Nostre Seigneur Jhesu Crist, du commandement de tres noble et tres excellent prince Charles, par la grace de Dieu roy de France, je propose translater de latin en françois aucuns livres lesquelx fist Aristote le souverain philosophe, qui fu docteur et conseillier du grant roy Alexandre. (*Ethiques*, 97)

> (In the confidence of the assistance of Our Lord Jesus Christ, by the order of the very noble and very excellent Prince Charles, by the grace of God king of France, I propose to translate from Latin to French several books made by Aristotle, the sovereign philosopher who was doctor and advisor to the great king Alexander.)

In this novel account of the commission, Oresme rejects the submissive behaviour that commonly accompanied royal order. Instead, he refers to an exchange between the two men in which the king's command gave way to the scholar's proposal to translate multiple Aristotelian writings.[63] In this vein, Lusignan contends that Oresme's work "n'apparaît plus comme la résultante d'une seule volonté particulière, fut-elle royale" (no longer appears as the result of the unique willingness of an individual, even if royal); rather, it constitutes part of a larger philosophical goal.[64] It is, however, important to recognize that Oresme distinguishes himself from the other commissioned writers when he replaces royal decree with dialogue, as well as when he dismisses the subservient language and self-deprecation common in their writings and promotes instead a partnership explicitly linked here to the model provided by Alexander and Aristotle.

Oresme, of course, was not unique in turning to the famed partnership between Alexander and Aristotle to explain Charles V's commissioning practices, nor was he alone in using this ancient relationship to draw attention to the importance of the translator. Foulechat, for example, reminds the king of Aristotle's fundamental role in securing for Alexander his epithet:

> Qui esleva et acrust si grandement Alixandre de Macedoine que encore li demeure le nom de Alixandre le grant, fors le sage et subtil conseil du souverain philosophe Aristote ...? (*Policratique*, 83.41)
>
> (What raised and enriched so greatly Alexander of Macedonia whose name remains as Alexander the Great more than the wise and subtle advice of the sovereign philosopher Aristotle ...?)

Foulechat considers Alexander indebted to Aristotle for his sobriquet and his reputation, thereby implying that so too, Charles V is dependent on his commissioned writers to confer on him the title and legacy of Wise King. Oresme proposes a slightly different arrangement between king and intellectual than the one provided by Foulechat. Oresme announces that Aristotle did not compose his works as a result of royal decree but as part of his responsibilities as Alexander's advisor. Oresme discreetly extends this account of intellectual exchange to his own relationship with Charles V through syntagmatic manipulations that conflate the "roy de France" with the "grant roy Alexandre" and the translator "je" with the "souverain philosophe." Through this conflation of the four men and their intellectual relationships, once again we discover the hieratic relationship of the king's clientelism overturned to present literary exchange as an expression of intellectual friendship. It is in the spirit of intellectual friendship and exchange that Oresme permits himself to reimagine his benefactor as a beneficiary and a royal command as an opportunity for a public commendation of intellectual pursuits.[65]

Oresme further creatively engages with the king's "commandement" noted in the opening line of the prologue by balancing this order with his own "(re)commandacion" in the final section of the "prohème":

> Donques puis je bien encore conclurre que la consideracion et le propos de nostre bon roy Charles est a recommender, qui fait les bons livres et excellens translater en françois. (*Ethiques*, 101)
>
> (Thus I can easily conclude that consideration and the intentions of our good King Charles are to be recommended, he who has good and excellent books translated into French.)

Here, the king's command functions less as an order than as an intellectual act worthy of imitation. As Charles V worked with intellectuals to assure new texts in translation, so Oresme counsels future readers to follow the king's example and see to the "making" of new works. Otherwise stated, Oresme calls for future partnerships in which both parties will collaborate in the creation of knowledge.

Scholarship on Charles V's sponsorship of translated works has focused on the way this campaign refashioned kingship as well as the influence it had on the growth of the vernacular and in the development of a writing community. Charles V's reign also deserves attention, however, for its profound influence on the development of the enduring ideal of literary and artistic patronage, which is expressed in several ways: by the model of textual sponsorship developed to support his *Sapientia* project, the important shift in intellectual production resulting from the practice of commissioning new texts, and, most significantly, translators' treatment of the king's clientelism. The last point, furthermore, underscores that the Wise King's influence on literary dynamic was not uniquely linked to his actions. In fact, his greatest influence may derive from the traces left in the books he commissioned from the learned. This chapter has examined the astute negotiations by the commissioned writers and artists who revised a conventional narrative that emphasized the writer's subservience so as to assure that the commission would not devalue knowledge. Study of the paratextual treatment of the king's literary clientelism in the commissioned translations produced by Foulechat, Presles, and Oresme reveals translators and bookmakers recasting their relationship as an intimate partnership rather than a transaction intended to strengthen the patron's power and prestige. Instead, the commissioned writers, often with the help of miniaturists, provided a new script for literary exchange that survives in modern opinions on patronage of the arts and letters.

Given the importance of the king's investment in vernacular writings and the sustained popularity of these translations for generations to come, it is of little surprise that tales of Charles V's commissions influenced contemporary and later treatments of literary exchange authored by other Valois court-affiliated writers. Although there is evidence of only a few late-medieval francophone vernacular writers receiving commissions for their work from either the Wise King or his brothers and descendants, several celebrated authors of late-medieval French literature maintained an interest in this relationship. Guillaume de Machaut, Eustache Deschamps, and Christine de Pizan frequently referenced indirectly or explicitly Charles V's famed practices when discussing the economics of literary production and when seeking to insert themselves into the cultural and political landscape. In subsequent chapters, what these vernacular poets have to say about the commission will be examined. The next chapter studies the case of the vernacular poet and composer Guillaume de Machaut, contemporary to our three commissioned translators studied here and a familiar of the royal family. Machaut, however, stands in stark contrast to Foulechat, Presles, and Oresme, first on documentary grounds since there is no evidence that he ever answered a royal commission. Nonetheless, Machaut dealt extensively with commissioning dynamics in his fictional works. In a series of "fictions of engagement," Machaut's fictional doppelgängers provide the second distinguishing trait that separates this poet from the commissioned writers: namely, his strong critique of all forms of literary oversight by privileged readers, especially through the literary commission, which he presented as a direct threat to the writer's creative liberties.

Chapter Three

Guillaume de Machaut's Fictions of Engagement

Scholars have long maintained the belief that Guillaume de Machaut (c. 1300–77) had strong ties to the Valois dynasty, stretching from his early service as secretary to John of Luxembourg, king of Bohemia, who was Charles V's maternal grandfather, to the Wise King himself. Following the king of Bohemia's death at the 1346 Battle of Crécy, Machaut is believed to have composed numerous works for the king's daughter, Bonne of Luxembourg, who would briefly reign with John the Good over the French kingdom. It is speculated that Bonne inspired several of Machaut's powerful fictional female characters, that she was the intended recipient of an early manuscript *de luxe* of Machaut's collected works, and that her interest in her children's education led the poet to compose several didactic texts intended for them.[1] A prominent absence in this genealogy is John the Good, reigning king during Machaut's most productive years; the only possible link between these two men centres on speculation that the king acquired the luxury copy of the poet's works possibly destined for the queen, who died suddenly.[2] Consideration of the poet's direct association with King John's descendants also leads to an impasse. Even Duke John of Berry, the likely dedicatee of the *Dit de la fonteinne amoureuse*, appears to have taken an active interest in acquiring Machaut's writings only after the author's death, an interest which we now know spurred the production of four of the five single-author anthologies of Machaut's works.[3] As for Charles V, neither treasury records nor his library inventory provide sufficient evidence to buttress speculation that he supported Machaut.

Driving this present chapter is the manifest contradiction between scholarly assumptions that Charles V took an early interest in Machaut and the lack of historical and literary evidence to support this claim. Claims for this possible partnership are rooted in the citation in a seventeenth-century memoir of a now-lost medieval document that speaks of a royal visit in 1361 to Machaut's residence in Reims.[4] This unstable historical foundation has been bolstered by scholarly speculation that several of Machaut's works as well as manuscript copies of his complete works likely have ties to Charles V. For instance, scholars highlight references to Charles in two of Machaut's lengthier late works: in the *Voir dit*, Guillaume declares Charles, who was then the duke of Normandy, his "droit Signeur, quoy que nuls die" (liege lord no matter what others say),[5] and then in the *Prise d'Alixandre*, he praises Charles for having been a dauphin "tant nobles et fins" (so noble and pure).[6] In neither case, however, is the king declared the intended recipient of the work nor is he praised for his learned interests.[7] As regards Machaut's musical corpus, Anne W. Robertson has convincingly debunked the longstanding theory that the *Mass* was composed for Charles V's coronation.[8] Add to these points that in spite of conjecture that two manuscript copies of Machaut's works were in the king's possession, neither codex figures in the Louvre library inventory lists.[9] One Louvre library inventory entry, however, may signal that a multi-authored *chansonnier* in the collection opened with Machaut's Lai 10.[10] In sum, in spite of Machaut's collected works circulating during Charles V's reign, the author makes no reference to the king's active interest in his works nor does archival record confirm a royal commission. It is also noteworthy that Machaut never openly dedicated a work to Charles V, never claimed to have enjoyed royal support, nor did he join with contemporary intellectuals in praising the king's commitment to learning. These facts are less surprising when we consider that Charles V's commissioning record reveals a complete lack of interest in vernacular fiction.

This silence regarding royal Valois support, combined with Machaut's absence from royal archives, would serve as sufficient reason to exclude him from this study if it were not for the multiple and thought-provoking ways in which his writings intersect with the king's commissioning activity. First, in spite of the absence of evidence of Valois royal support for his writings, in the years leading up to Charles V's reign, Machaut produced numerous "fictions of engagement" in which he placed poet-prince(ss) relations in the realm of fantasy and approached literary exchange as a subject worthy of scrutiny and caution. Second, Machaut's early writings that predate the king's most active commissioning period anticipate the commissioned writers' savvy efforts to remediate the king's clientelism through reference to intellectual ideals. Third, in spite of Machaut's extensive criticism of literary sponsorship, several copies of his works were not only owned by important members of the ruling class but also illustrated by artists affiliated with the king's *Sapientia* project. What makes these manuscripts especially pertinent is that the illuminators drew on the visual vocabulary of royal literary exchange developed at Charles V's court to illustrate Machaut's works. As such, these artists negotiated a particularly complex set of issues that, on one hand, required resolving the divide between the poet's cynical take on literary exchange and the positive image of sponsorship portrayed in Charles V's commissioned books, and, on the other hand, the need to acknowledge important shifts in the literary landscape that quickly emerged in the immediate aftermath of the king's death. Regarding this final point, these illustrations allow us to detect the changing views on exchange dynamics in Valois circles over the next two decades, which will be developed in subsequent chapters. Finally, Machaut's fictions of engagement present an immediate challenge to the concept of the patron's pleasure that is crucial to his much-acclaimed novel conception of vernacular authorship and which profoundly influenced his successors. Machaut, in effect, countered Charles V's clientelism with an argument for recognizing texts as the writer's gift; that is, as a gift stemming from the writer's poetic labours and the lyric talents divinely awarded to him, a concept we have already witnessed in the writings of the king's commissioned translators.

This chapter considers four examples of Machaut's fictions of engagement, of which three were certainly composed before the reign of Charles V. These early works communicate, nonetheless, a strong critique of the literary commissioning practices that would be central to Charles V's *Sapientia* project. The *Navarre* (*terminus ante quem* 1355) is a pivotal work in Machaut's corpus that has already been recognized for its unprecedented treatment of authorship. It is additionally distinctive because of its sobering account of clientelistic exchange in which the poet endures threats of erasure, public humiliation, and legal punishment if he refuses to submit to Lady Bonneürté's literary demands. In subsequent years, Machaut composed the *Confort* (1357), which he directed to the ultimate judge of the previous debate, Charles of Navarre. This work offered a very different take on literary exchange by privileging unsolicited giving over the commission. This permutation of exchange practices would prove no easier to navigate, and paratextual additions to the *Confort* imply a breakdown in communication between poet and prince due to the king's unexpected ingratitude and insatiable need for the poet's services. On the heels of this work, Machaut wrote the *Fonteinne* (c. 1361), most likely for Charles V's younger brother, John of Berry. As Machaut's most extended meditation on literary exchange, the *Fonteinne* explores the purpose, the mechanics, and the risks associated with commissioned writings. Study of Machaut's writings closes with the Prologue to his collected works (c. 1372), which retrospectively presents his corpus as the result of a very different literary economy, one in which the focus is on the poet's receipt of divine gifts rather than the transfer of this gift to a privileged recipient. Both the presumed dating of the composition of this poem and its earliest copy (BnF, MS fr. 1584) place it during the peak period of Charles V's *Sapientia* project. This copy is also unique because of the stunning double frontispiece that is credited to one of Charles V's most accomplished illustrators, the *Master of the Bible de Jean de Sy*. This master's elaborate decoration of Machaut's Prologue will provide us the opportunity to examine fully how depictions of literary dynamics in the king's books were refracted in Machaut's collected works. For while one can only speculate that Machaut had Charles V's commissioning practices in mind when creating this novel account of the transfer of the literary gift, it is clear that this illustrator depended on the literary exchange iconography developed at the royal court when producing the double frontispiece. This chapter concludes with an analysis of subsequent copies of Machaut's collected work in which the visual apparatus attempts to return the author-figure to a more subservient role in literary exchange to better accommodate the literary views promoted by Charles V's brothers and heirs in the decades following the king's death.

The Patron-Function and Machaut

To appreciate Machaut's unconventional take on literary exchange, we need first to consider the many strategies commonly used in medieval texts and images to draw attention to the real or anticipated owners of these art objects. For Aden Kumler, a medieval patron is synonymous with "owner," and she explains that in the visual arts, we "know patrons or owners when we see them because we've come to know their favorite haunts ... and we've learned their customary postures, their signifying scale, and the often illustrious company they keep."[11] For the literary critic, the textual "haunts" that house patron-figures typically involve the paratext, where a privileged interlocutor often emerges as a primary player in literary creation. Such was the case in the previous chapter where we examined the accounts of literary dynamics registered in Charles V's commissioned works. Literary scholars, however, also frequently mine fictional re-enactments of literary exchange to uncover possible hidden allusions to living sponsors. In the end, it matters less where patron-figures lurk, since literary scholars identify them as such by their countenance and by the praise they enjoy. It is common practice to identify figures referenced in medieval texts as patrons when we read a testimonial to their interest in acquiring texts, when we discover references to their merits that justify honouring them in writing, or when we encounter praise for their role as generous supporters who provide encouragement or material and monetary assistance. Charles V's commissioned writers were keen to enlarge this list of expectations to include an abiding love for knowledge that associated the patron-figure with the learned community and that made it possible to imagine an intellectual friendship based on the inestimable treasure represented by exchanged knowledge.

When we seek out the patron-figure in Machaut's corpus, however, we encounter a very different arrangement. First, there is the issue of the predictable "haunts" of the medieval owner of books. Absent are transparent dedicatory addresses or re-enactments of historically grounded literary exchange in Machaut's works. Early *dits* dating from the 1330s and 1340s, including the *Dit dou vergier*, the *Dit de l'alérion*, and the *Dit du remède de Fortune*, for example, forego any overt staging of the extratextual events of writing and, instead, immediately enter into the matter of the narrative. When Machaut's *dits* include a frame, the work frequently opens on decidedly authorial spaces. The *Dit dou vergier* and the *Voir dit* privilege the *locus amoenus* of medieval authorship – the garden – while the paired judgment poems, the *Jugement dou roy de Behaingne* and the *Navarre* situate the poet in an open outdoor space that has more in common with the garden of creative inspiration than a controlled court environment. The *Dit dou lyon* opens on a springtime nature scene before turning to the author, who is confined to his bed, yet another privileged space of vernacular authorship that often demarcates entryway in the creative dreamworld. Likewise, the *Fonteinne* opens with the poet in bed, albeit in lodgings provided by the prince, and he spotlights this symbolic dream space at the end of the poem when he asks if "ce fut bien songé?" (was this well dreamed?).[12] A second characteristic of the distinctive treatment of the addressee in Machaut's writings concerns naming. Rather than openly identify a noble addressee, Machaut prefers to bury references in otherwise author-centric frames. Hovering behind the poet's words, a disembodied and dismembered addressee might be hidden in an anagram. If this anagram signals the poet's wish to honour the recipient, it does so by replacing the subservient discourse of a formal presentation with a provocative symbolic enactment of the recipient's subservience to the poet's words. These naming events, furthermore, play on ambiguity by deliberately blurring the boundaries of fact and fiction.[13] The final distinguishing characteristic of Machaut's treatment of literary exchange dynamics concerns the poet's frequent identification of a text's recipient as an anonymous beloved rather than a noble figure to whom he claims feudal allegiance. In both the *Confort* and the *Prise d'Alexandrie*, for example, anagrams embed the names of Charles of Navarre and Peter of Cyprus, respectively, as the princes who are honoured by the work, yet both are subordinated to the poet's beloved from the outset. In a similar vein, in the *Fonteinne*, although the prince whose name is communicated via an anagram is referenced as the recipient of the work, the poet's lady supersedes him as the person intended to be honoured by the work.[14] The fate of a female addressee is, however, no better, since she always remains anonymous (the most famous example being, of course, Toute-Belle in the *Voir dit*).

In spite of the difficulty in locating patron-figures in Machaut's writings, Douglas Kelly turns to Machaut's corpus to flesh out a working definition of medieval literary exchange dynamics. Kelly argues that the key distinction of medieval patronage is the patron's status as the mastermind and true author of literary creation. In his view, the medieval patron assumes the role of author because he provides the "genius" of a work, whereas the medieval writer merely provides the literary skills necessary to realize the patron's vision. In Kelly's account of medieval poet-prince relations, we hear strong echoes of Dale Kent's concept of the "patron's oeuvre."[15] Moreover, as I've argued in the case of Kent, so too, Kelly's account applies an unrecognized clientelistic drive to the relationship, one in which the patron seeks out clients with the requisite literary skills so as to answer stated needs or desires. Still yet, when defining the different potential roles assigned the patron in Machaut's work (e.g., donor, poet, master, pupil, or friend), Kelly systematically sidesteps evidence revealing Machaut's so-called patrons to be strikingly faulty models. Notwithstanding the fact that they answer to the roles Kelly generates, Machaut's patron-figures, nonetheless, sorely lack the qualities expected of a worthy addressee, such as generosity and gratitude, and they often lack even the essential qualifications of patron, namely, power, prestige, and wealth.

In Machaut's world, a curious crowd vies to occupy the patron role. Those candidates for the role of patron who are historically identified, few as they are, inevitably disappoint because of their problematic status, and their fictionalized doubles fare little better. If we accept the proposed solutions to the anagrams that identify the recipients of the *Confort* and the *Fonteinne* as Charles of Navarre and John of Berry, respectively, we must acknowledge that these men were deeply flawed candidates for the role of an actual patron. At the time of composition, both Charles and John were political prisoners who had been stripped of their power and had scarce means to fulfil the expected role of patron as someone who can promise material or financial reward in exchange for written matter. Yet another medieval ruler, Peter of Cyprus, who is identified by an anagram in the *Prise d'Alexandrie* as the prince intended to be honoured, wielded even less power to fulfil the role of patron since he died *before* Machaut composed the work and in a humiliating manner – he was brutally assassinated in 1369 by his angry subjects, a heinous crime detailed in the final section of the work. Similarly, while the king of Bohemia stands out in Machaut's corpus for the frequent and effusive praise he receives, most references to him are in works produced after his death.[16] In all these cases, to the extent that Machaut can be said to name a patron of a given work, he systematically selected men who were unable to participate as bona fide patrons because they had been stripped of power and possessions due to real-life imprisonment or death. The anonymous ladies who competed with men as privileged recipients of Machaut's works were equally problematic choices; unidentified, they were condemned to silence, and as women cast in an amorous role, any expression of stated desires or reciprocation would have led to a public stripping of their authority as women of the court (a fate that Toute-Belle claims to have endured in the *Voir dit*). These fictionalized patrons are, moreover, subject to the poet who controls dialogue. Thus, for example, Charles of Navarre's fictional double in the *Confort* speaks only through the poet's imagined conversations with him and then only to bewail his victimhood and powerlessness. John of Berry's fictional double in the *Fonteinne* first appears as a wailing phantom dependent on the poet to decipher his cries before emerging as a prisoner in transit. An important exception to this power vacuum occurs with Lady Bonneürté in the *Navarre*. Be that as it may, this allegorical female patron imposes her wishes only to be challenged by an increasingly petulant poet who fails to fulfil his court-ordered obligations to her. In short, Machaut's presumed patron-figures often entail imprisoned princes whose vulnerability and powerlessness are spotlighted or female readers who lack clear identification or certain authority. Only divine entities far removed from the terrestrial realm seem to perform as successful patrons and, in these cases, they prefigure the idealistic philosophy linked with the patronage of arts and letters that coincided with the coining of terms in the sixteenth century.[17] More immediately, however, they provide crucial fodder that allows Machaut to rewrite the exchange narrative that typically focuses on the transfer of the oeuvre to the patron so as to focus on the gifts received by the poet that allow him to create his oeuvre. In the Prologue to the collected works, Lady Nature and the God of Love insist that the poet must compose because he has received unique gifts, and the poet promises to obey their command to write poetry and compose music. In direct contrast to their stated expectations that he sing in their honour and according to their specifications, the poet reinterprets their command as a duty to share his poetry with a large audience.

To summarize, any attempt to read Machaut's writings as providing conventional models that reflect the literary dynamics formalized by accounts of Valois commissioning practices poses serious obstacles: (1) an absence of clear evidence regarding a Valois commission for an original text during his lifetime; (2) Machaut's failure to use spatial, rhetorical, and literary cues crucial to the patron-function to establish stable patron-figures; and (3) the problematic status of the potential candidates for the role of the patron embedded in his texts, most of whom lack the authority commonly assigned to a patron-figure or are divorced from reality by their allegorical status. Rather than promote (and define) patronage as Kelly might have it, Machaut's depictions of literary exchange between a poet and his privileged interlocutors repeatedly register a wariness that merits our attention.

The Commission as Punishment in the *Jugement de Navarre*

The *Navarre* marks an important stage in Machaut's treatment of literary exchange and is all the more striking for the way it anticipates Charles V's commissioning practices soon thereafter.[18] The *Jugement de Navarre contre le jugement de roy de Behaigne*, as it is titled in two Machaut manuscripts – BnF, MS fr. 1584 and BnF, MS fr. 22545 – presents a profoundly troubling, albeit fictionalized, account of a literary commission forced on a rebellious poet who refuses to submit to his would-be patron's desires. The work is presented as a continuation of a previous judgment poem. In Machaut's earlier *Jugement de roy de Behaigne*, the poet was a willing representative of his superiors, namely a lady and a knight who had arrived at a stalemate while attempting to determine who had suffered the greatest in love. The poet, who overheard their debate from behind the bushes where he hid, proposed to lead them to the king of Bohemia who would surely settle their dispute. The resulting text provided a record of these events. The later *Navarre* takes us further afield to detail the reception of the *Jugement de roy de Behaigne* by a female reader who attempts to impose her will on the unsuspecting poet. This reader is eventually identified as Lady Bonneürté, and we learn that she acquired a copy of the earlier judgment unbeknownst to the poet. Dissatisfied with the work, she orders Guillaume to reverse the judgment. Her demands eventually require a new legal proceeding in which Charles of Navarre will be called on to adjudicate the dispute caused by the poet's refusal to obey his would-be patron. The bulk of the lengthy poem records this trial, which culminates with the poet being sentenced to compose several new literary works in conformance with the lady's views. As it turns out, the poet fails to obey fully his superiors' commands.

A brief review of the mechanics of the literary commission can help clarify Machaut's distinctive treatment of the topic. As noted in the introduction, the commission respects the logic of clientelism rather than archaic gifting, the framework often adopted to speak of medieval literary exchange dynamics. For gifting to occur, according to Marcel Mauss, the object exchanged must take on the appearance of a "voluntary" act that is "free" (i.e., unsolicited) and "disinterested,"[19] while the exchanged object must function as an inalienable entity that emphasizes its eternal link to the giver.[20] In contrast, a commission represents a patron's command or order issued to skilled clients. Since a commission begins with a patron's expressed desire for a work, it represents the patron's alienable work, the patron's pleasure. As detailed in the previous chapter, Machaut's contemporaries, Denis Foulechat, Raoul de Presles, and Nicole Oresme, all of whom received commissions from Charles V, wrestled with the effect of the king's clientelism on intellectual ideals concerning the circulation of knowledge as an inalienable good to be shared among intellectual friends. The paratext of the king's commissioned works reveal numerous strategies adopted by writers and artists in an effort to rewrite the king's real-life clientelism to reflect an alternative model of exchange patterned on gifting ideals. Writing a few years in advance of these commissioned writers, Machaut exhibited a similar interest in promoting the text as a gift offered to worthy readers, although, in his case, the promotion of the gift-text was discussed against the backdrop of sinister accounts of meddling and ungrateful would-be patrons. Machaut is not approached here so much as an influence on the commissioned writers; rather he serves as a counterpoint, giving greater depth and insight into the concerns of a diverse literary community in late-medieval France regarding the influence of literary dynamics on the status and purpose of vernacular writing.

In his two judgment poems, Machaut played off the etymology of the commissioning lexicon that favours the "commandement" to insist on the legal and oppressive nature of being forced to submit to a superior's demands. In the *Navarre*, readers are made aware of Lady Bonneürté's intentions to make demands on the poet well before he even knows of her discontent. In fact, unbeknownst to Guillaume, he is observed from a distance and identified as the culprit by the lady's squire: "C'est la Guillaumes de Machau" (That's Guillaume de Machaut there).[21] Having spied him, the lady has him summoned without explanation. The squire who escorts Guillaume attempts to warn the poet of the lady's anger by advising the poet to prepare to defend himself (*Navarre*, lines 730–5). The poet remains deaf to these warnings as much as he will also prove impervious to the cause of Lady Bonneürté's displeasure. When the poet protests his ignorance, she commands him to consult his own works to figure out the source of her anger. In response, the poet expresses for the first of many times his refusal to submit to her order and he justifies his stance in a much-quoted and often misunderstood passage:

> J'ay bien de besongnes escriptes
> Devers moy, de pluseurs manieres,
> De moult de diverses matieres,
> Dont l'une l'autre ne ressamble.
> Consideré toutes ensamble,
> Et chascune bien mise a point,
> D'ordre en ordre et de point en point
> Dès le premier commencement
> Jusques au darrein finement
> Se tout vouloie regarder
> – Dont je me vorrai bien garder –
> Trop longuement y metteroie.

> (I've many written works/ In front of me, of various kinds,/ Concerning quite different matters,/ Each of which is unlike the other./ Considering all these together,/ And each one rather thoroughly,/ Section by section and sentence by sentence,/ From the beginning of the first/ To the very end of the last,/ That is if I wished to look through all of them/ – (Something I'd indeed like to avoid)/ I would spend too long in so doing.) (*Navarre*, lines 884–95)

At first glance, this passage reads as authorial bravado intended to draw attention to the richness of Machaut's corpus. It is true that Lady

Bonneürté's accusations present an opportunity for the poet to claim ownership of his poetic corpus, including, perhaps ironically, the work in question, whose official title identifies it as the property of a royal patron. Yet in the process, the poet not only dismisses her command but further intimates his unwillingness to serve her. He protests that even if he should obey the lady and dedicate himself to rereading his corpus, he would be no closer to knowing the source of her anger given his inability to access her "pensée invisible" (hidden thought) (*Navarre*, line 902).

The poet's professed inability to anticipate the lady's wishes matters little to Bonneürté since she proceeds to command not that he write on her behalf but that he destroy his earlier work: "Que ce jugement effacies" (erase this judgment) (*Navarre*, line 1032). The poet, once again, stubbornly refuses her order: "Pour nulle rien ne le feroie" (There is no way I'd do such a thing) (*Navarre*, line 1041, my translation). Faced with a stalemate, the two parties finally agree to submit their case to a worthy judge; in this instance, Charles of Navarre, and a jury made up of the Virtues. As the trial reaches its end, the king of Navarre sides with the lady and translates Lady Bonneürté's harsh directive into more lenient terms in which a literary commission will serve as the poet's sentence. The king orders Guillaume to compose three new lyric works on topics of interest to the court (*Navarre*, lines 4173–94). Instead of silencing the poet as the lady had desired, the king of Navarre orders the poet to speak in the name of his self-proclaimed patrons by composing a *lai*, a *rondeau*, and a *ballade*, all of which are to reflect the lady's opinion. The poet proves to be no happier with this sentence than with the lady's previous demands, a point evidenced when the king orders the poet to change his attitude – "Or n'en faites pas le malade" (Now don't act like you're sick about this) (*Navarre*, line 4190). Yet in spite of the king's admonishments, the poet will ultimately refuse to obey this final royal command.

The poet closes the *Navarre* by feigning acceptance of his literary sentence. He professes his desire to receive his lady's pardon and he does so by presenting the present work as a gift – "S'en feray ma dame present" (And I'll make my lady a present of it) (*Navarre*, line 4203) – and he further claims to have also composed this work "pour miex congnoistre mon meffait" (in order the better to understand my fault) (*Navarre*, line 4201). The judgment does, in fact, detail the poet's multiple errors, which range from his failure to anticipate how his work might offend ladies to the blunder of not recognizing Bonneürté as a privileged reader from the outset, to his persistent unwillingness to submit to her commands. At the same time, the *Navarre* registers his refusal to respect the lady's demands. Moreover, this new judgment only casts a larger spotlight on the earlier judgment through his extensive defence of it. In short, his "present" of the current judgment poem only underscores the inalienable nature of the previous judgment that he now accepts as his creation (rather than that of the Bohemian king) and that he alone is determined to defend and preserve. In contrast, regarding the three poems ordered by Charles of Navarre on behalf of the lady, the poet describes them as debts he must pay rather than as gifts:

> Mais pour ce que je ne vueil mie
> Que m'amende ne soit païe,
> Pour la paier vueil sans delay
> Commencier .i. amoureus lay

> (But because I don't want in any way/ that my debt not be paid,/ so as to pay it, I want without delay/ to begin a lay about love). (*Navarre*, lines 4209–12, translation altered)

In half of the eight copies of the *Navarre*, only one of these identified "debts" follows the judgment. In this addended work, the "Lay de plour," the poet revives and elaborates on the initial lament of the lady from the *Jugement de Behaigne*.

Sarah Kay has pointed out that the ordered lyric pieces scarcely answer Lady Bonneürté's demands, not to mention that in offering her the *Navarre*, he presents her with "the very work in which his lack of repentance is flaunted."[22] For Kay, the final literary product attests to the protagonist's "singularity" in relation to society,[23] but let it be noted that this singularity is precisely articulated through the poet's refusal to silence his own views in the name of the patron's pleasure. On trial due to his unwillingness to accommodate a would-be patron, Machaut enjoys the final laugh. In addition to retaining the unaltered first judgment as part of his corpus and parading his refusal to obey a powerful would-be patron in the second, he effectively unseats Lady Bonneürté when, in the closing lines, he replaces her ordered punishment with the presentation of a lyric "present." It is now he who forces her into an agreement since she is bound by ritual to receive the *Navarre* as a gift-text (which, to add injury to insult, he identifies as the king's property rather than hers) and the "Lai de plour" as no more than a debt he must repay. In his first extended treatment of a literary commission, Machaut presents the solicited work as a form of coercion and identifies it first as an unmerited punishment and then as an unjust debt he is obliged to satisfy. In response to this unfair punishment, he presents the inscribed would-be patron with an unwanted text that goes beyond simply communicating the opposite of the desired message to record instead the poet's rejection of patrons' authority. Machaut uses humour and fiction to make palatable this aggressive depiction of clientelism; from the outset, the poet appears as an absentminded and naive man whose ensuing obstinacy and misogyny cast him as the court fool in need of oversight. Even such a caricature, however, cannot disguise the poet's refusal to submit fully to the rules of the commission.

Soon after authoring this judgment, Machaut would again identify Charles of Navarre as a privileged reader. In 1357, when Machaut addressed the *Confort* to the king of Navarre, the intended recipient's situation had profoundly changed. No longer king, Charles had become a prisoner on King John the Good's order. Machaut presented the *Confort* as his personal attempt to console Charles in his time of crisis. Although now portrayed as a prisoner deprived of power and community, Charles is more directly implicated in the game of literary exchange in this work than in the previous *Navarre*. In this exchange scenario, we enter directly into an archaic arrangement that positions the poet as a donor intent on offering an unsolicited gift to his chosen recipient. As we shall see, the unsolicited gift carries its own troublesome baggage, and once again, the poet ends up with an unwanted commission. As with the previous judgment, Machaut's account of the patron-client relationship in the *Confort* presents a disturbing scenario; here, we discover an ungrateful recipient who responds to the poet's gift with more demands that reflect an insatiable desire for works that speak to his pleasure. That Charles of Navarre never figured again as a possible patron in Machaut's writings may be a telling indication of the real prince's failure to live up to the poet's expectations: in both fictions in which Charles appears, the king makes demands that the poet chooses to ignore.

The Ungrateful Patron in the *Confort d'ami*

The *Confort* stands out in Machaut's corpus as the work that comes closest to associating literary exchange with archaic gifting practices. The stated circumstances for composing the *Confort* could not be more different from those detailed in the *Navarre*. The poet introduces the text as an unsolicited gift intended for a friend in need of consolation:

Amis, a toy donner confort
Ay meintes fois pensé moult fort,
Et Diex scet que je le feroie,
Plus que ne di, se je pouoie,
De tres bon cuer et volentiers

(Friend, I've many times quite seriously/ Considered providing consolation for you,/ And God knows I'd do it,/ (And more than I can say) if I were able,/ Willingly, and with a happy heart)[24]

The opening two lines perfectly capture the essence of disinterested giving. The first word establishes an intimate bond that is further developed through the grammatical manipulations of these lines. Machaut reverses subject-object order to prioritize the friend's perceived needs and to underscore the willing subordination of both the poet's voice and thoughts in order to satisfy a self-imposed altruistic task. No sooner is the poet's willingness to comfort registered than doubts cloud his intentions. Disrupting the directness of his initial statement, Machaut transitions to the conditional in the third line, and the gifting scene previously set in motion comes to an abrupt halt. What first appears as a common dedication scene dissolves into an expression of regret and uncertainty as the poet enumerates obstacles that threaten the desired exchange. First, an insurmountable distance separating the men thwarts the poet's hopes of his verse reaching its destination:

Mais il n'est voie ne sentiers
Qui mon oueil peüst avoier
Que vers toy peüsse envoier.

(But there's no way or means/ Apparent to my eye/ For my message to reach you.) (*Confort*, lines 6–8)

Adding to this physical obstacle, the poet fears that his gift may be unwanted since the recipient is deemed wise enough to provide his own comfort:

... soies assez sages
pour toy garder sans mes messages
et sans mes confors recevoir.

(... you are wise enough/ To look after yourself without receiving/ A message or thoughts of consolation from me.) (*Confort*, lines 11–13)

With no certainty regarding the reception – either physically or psychologically – of his gift-text, the poet nonetheless proceeds with composing this consolation piece. He signals the presence of an anagram at the end of the text that promises to identify both poet and prince. Reference to the anagram also acknowledges the presence of other readers, but only so that Machaut might circumscribe their relationship to the text. These readers might benefit from the text, although they are not designated as recipients of the gift-text. In fact, he specifies what they might "take" from the text in terms of their involvement in deciphering the anagram. Even in this instance, he severely limits their freedoms: "que feme n'homs n'i porra riens oster ne mettre/ Qu'une sillabe et une lettre" (that no man or woman/ can remove from or add/ But a single letter and syllable) (*Confort*, lines 30–2, translation altered). Read in light of the *Navarre*, this warning appears to forbid another reader from appropriating the text, interpreting at will, or demanding changes (or worse) according to individual desires and needs as Lady Bonneürté endeavoured to do.

Machaut appears to have made every effort to assure that even without recourse to the deferred anagram, all readers would recognize this text as intended for Charles of Navarre. Details filtered throughout the work hint at Charles's identity. First, Machaut stages an array of Christian and pagan *exempla* that explore the unjust treatment of innocents as well as tales of repentant leaders who share in common with the intended reader unmerited captivity (*Confort*, lines 1652–3). In addition, the poet imagines the complaints his addressee might voice concerning his imprisonment and the effect it has on his honour and, most explicitly, he refers to the interlocutor's good fortune to have been in prison during the battle of Poitiers (*Confort*, lines 1793–8 and lines 2785–95). In subsequent sections, Machaut counsels his friend both on outwardly behaviour and psychological strategies that are intended to help him endure imprisonment. The final portion, which R. Barton Palmer likens to a *regimen principum*,[25] seeks to prepare the addressee for his imminent release and return to power. There can be no misunderstanding: this work represents a unique gift crafted for a chosen recipient, and future readers are constrained to see it in this context.[26]

The poem ends by recalling the gifting scene imagined in the opening lines. In the final lines, the poet adopts the rhetorical phrasing of the book presentation to conjure the image of the poet on bended knee before his sovereign. To his lord, he humbly presents his "ouvrage" (work) and hopes that it will be accepted: "Je te pri qu'en bon gré le pregnes" (I ask you to receive it in good grace) (*Confort*, lines 3946–7). To flesh out this imagined scene, the poet returns to the issue of the promised anagram. At the same time, the presentation scene becomes hazy in light of the poet's continued doubt surrounding the work's reception. The poet returns to the readers, whose freedom over the text he severely limited at the outset, to concede that they may be unwilling to follow his command to decipher the anagram. If they do refuse to solve it, the poet proclaims his indifference:

> Va y, qu'il y fait bon et chaut,
> Et s'aler n'i vues, ne m'en chaut.
>
> (Go to it while it is good and hot and if it is neither seen nor circulated, I could care less.) (*Confort*, lines 3977–8; my translation)

Although the direct reference of these final remarks concerns deciphering the anagram, they are sufficiently ambiguous to suggest reference to the fate of the text itself. That the poet now claims indifference regarding reception – whether understood in terms of the deciphering of the anagram or in terms of the circulation of the work – cannot disguise the undercurrent of anxiety expressed through this final homophonic play on Machaut's name. For inscribed within the poet's claim of indifference – "ne m'en chaut" – is a reminder of the very effacement he risked at the hands of his earlier resistant reader, Lady Bonneürté. In this instance, if the anagram/text is neither seen nor circulated, there is no Machaut. As such, Machaut's reflections on literary exchange in the *Confort* are no more reassuring than the message expressed in the *Navarre*. Regardless of the chosen register, clientelism or gifting, literary exchange with one's superiors proves problematic and threatening to both text and author should it not be correctly received. The commission risks silencing or effacing the poet because, as depicted in the *Navarre*, it demands that the poet submit his thoughts and abilities to the needs and desires of the patron. Gifting, however, proves no better because in offering an unsolicited text, as in the case of the *Confort*, the work must be accepted to exist. In either case, the poet and the text risk effacement.

The story does not end with the poet's uncertainty about the fate of his work, since a coda found in all extant copies of the *Confort* included in the single-author anthologies records a twenty-five–line octosyllabic response that appears to be in the voice of Charles of Navarre. It becomes clear that this prisoner has rejected the poet's gift of comfort and advice. Rather than accept with gratitude the poet's gift, the prisoner expresses insatiable need and ingratitude in the coda attached to the "explicit":

Explicit le Confort d'amy
Qui esveilla le cuer de my
Es tenebres ou il dormi,
Et au resveillier dist: "Aimy!
Que ne suis je partis par mi,
Quant j'ay si longuement gemi
Et tant plouré et tant fremi,
Que le gros de l'uef d'un fremi
N'ay receü, par saint Fremi,
De joie en plus d'an et demi!"

(Here ends Comfort for a Friend,/ Which awakened this heart of mine/ In those shadows where it slept,/ And in waking, it did say: "Alas!/ That I have not departed this place/ Since for so long I have sighed,/ Wept and shook so much,/ For in more than a year and a half/ I've not received, by saint Fremi,/ Joy equal to the yolk of an ant's egg!") (*Confort*, lines 3879–88)

Far from having been comforted by the poem, the coda's author claims that reading it caused great sorrow and awakened him to his powerlessness. In response to the poet's opening address intended to sooth his friend – "Amis, a toy donner confort" – the coda replies with a cry of anguish – "Aimy!" – followed by development of the speaker's discontent. The use of a single end-rhyme throughout – "mi" – maintains the speaker's suffering (and his demands) at the forefront of the coda and assures that subsequent readers never lose sight/sound of the speaker and his dissatisfaction.

As the coda continues, the failure of the poet's text to achieve its desired result becomes increasingly apparent. The speaker avows that the work made him realize that his enemies are numerous and stronger than ever. In addition to suffering emotionally at their hands, he also endures the destruction of his reputation since they portray him as "fol et esturmi,/ Com forsené et esrami" (foolish and excited/ As someone mad and provoked) (*Confort*, lines 3996–7). To counter this perception, the speaker solicits the poet's aid: "Amis, tu m'i/ Pues bien aidier" (Friend, you can/ Certainly help me here) (*Confort*, lines 3994–5). What the prisoner desires from the poet, however, proves perplexing, if only because it suggests that he is truly enraged (esrami):

Pour ce te require, alume y,
Car goute n'i voy; destumi
Mon triste cuer et desdormi,

> Et je te promet que tuit mi
> Annemi seront avec mi,
> Pour qui maint soupir ay vomi
>
> (And so I ask you, give me light,/ For I can hardly see; give life back/ To my sad heart and waken it,/ And I promise you that all/ My enemies will find themselves here with me,/ Those because of whom I've issued many a sigh) (*Confort*, lines 3999–4004)

Yet again, Machaut provides us a scenario in which a text written in good faith triggers yet another unexpected commission that openly overturns the poet's intentions. The prisoner declares at the outset of the coda that the poet's gift-text awakened his heart from the darkness in which it languished (*Confort*, lines 3880–1), which then ignited a desire for a new work that would give full expression to this anguish.[27] This "request" stands in direct contrast to the poet's initial desire to instruct his chosen reader on the power of the imagination to offer comfort[28] and instead the reader-turned-patron desires a text filled with anger. In this scenario, the poet's text is, once again, misread and discarded, leading to a commission for a work that would contradict the initial message. The poet's efforts to imagine an arrangement built on intimacy, mutual admiration, and the desire to comfort, spirals into a demand for a bellicose work that would enflame the prisoner and strike back at his enemies.

The ambiguity surrounding exchange relations in the *Confort* clearly captured the imagination of illustrators. MS fr. 1584 is often celebrated for its visual promotion of the author and its particular fidelity to his texts,[29] and it should thus not surprise us to discover that in privileging the metatextual context provided by the poet in the *Confort*, the author emerges in the MS fr. 1584 miniature cycle as a powerful figure. From the outset, the 1584 miniature cycle depicts an imprisoned king leaning out of a donjon window to receive counsel from the poet who towers over him. In addition to the surprising scale and proportions afforded the poet on folio 127r, there is also the king's posture, which implies his complete submission to the poet (Figure 3.1: BnF, MS fr. 1584, fol. 127r). Leaning towards the poet, the king's visage tilts upwards as if in deference, while his crossed hands further signal his submission. This unconventional portrait of the poet-prince relationship is slightly restabilized by the prisoner's gold crown against the backdrop of an otherwise muted *grisaille* drawing. MS fr. 1584 reserves for later, deep within the narrative, a

Figure 3.1: Poet addressing the imprisoned king, *Confort d'ami*, Paris, Bibliothèque nationale de France, MS fr. 1584, fol. 127r.

more destabilizing image of the imprisoned king that underscores to a far greater extent the poet's authority. Midway through the narrative, the miniature cycle breaks away from illustrating the stories recounted by the poet to recall the metatextual context. On folio 142v, we find our poet bending down to address the king, who is now depicted behind bars (Figure 3.2: MS fr. 1584, fol. 142v). The poet's stance suggests that he kneels before his king, although even this subservient gesture – no more than the gold crown still worn by the king – can soften this provocative scene of a royal prisoner behind bars. The smeared ink that blurs the king's crown in this illustration may reflect efforts to censor this humble image of nobility, a point reinforced by the fact that another late-medieval copy, Arsenal, MS 5203, reveals more explicit efforts to erase a similar illustration of an incarcerated king.[30] Later in this chapter, we will consider how copies of this work circulating

Figure 3.2: Poet addressing the imprisoned king, *Confort d'ami*, Paris, Bibliothèque nationale de France, MS fr. 1584, fol. 142v.

at the court of the duke of Berry bear witness to illuminators' interest in reconceiving this disturbing portrayal of royalty. For the moment, of value here is the extent to which the miniature cycle decorating the *Confort* visualizes authorial prerogative at the expense of the king, who is depicted in an uncommonly disempowering and vulnerable state. We could not be further from the depictions of Charles V in his commissioned books.

Orchestrating the Commission: The Case of the *Fonteinne amoureuse*

Approximately three years after completing the *Confort*, Machaut composed a new work directed to yet another prisoner-prince. This time, however, Machaut chose a Valois prince. The *Fonteinne* is believed to have been intended for the young Duke John of Berry, who was one of six princes called upon in 1360 to serve as exchange prisoners for the temporary return to France of King John the Good, who had been captured at Poitiers. Machaut opted, once again, to conceal the prince's name in an anagram rather than explicitly link a historical figure to the tale's generous young prince, who possesses extraordinary poetic talents and a deep appreciation for both love and the arts.[31] Machaut assumes, however, a more distant association with the young duke than the one he had adopted with the imprisoned king of Navarre. In fact, the opening line of the *Fonteinne* can be read as a dramatic rewrite of the first verse of the *Confort*. In place of identifying the desire to comfort the chosen recipient as he did in the *Confort* ("Amis, a toy donner confort," line 1), Machaut begins the *Fonteinne* with his own interests in mind: "Pour moy deduire et soulacier" (To delight and entertain myself).[32] He also chooses to defer acknowledging the intended recipient, "celui pour qui je fais ce livre" (the man for whom I'm making this book), until after fully developing his own poetic and amorous interests (*Fonteinne*, line 32), and then only in anagrammatic form. Moreover, the anagram itself is wedged between the poet's claims to have written the work in his lady's honour and to have done so by Love's command ("En l'onneur ma dame jolie," "And in the honor of my pretty lady," *Fonteinne*, line 8; "Que amours fine le me commande," "Because love commands it of me," *Fonteinne*, line 37, translation mine). Following after this peculiar presentation of the prince, Machaut qualifies the story as detailing his own "adventure":

> ... l'aventure
> Qui me fu diverse et obscure
> Au commencier et päoureuse,
> Mais a la fin me fu joieuse.
>
> (The adventure/ Which was to me strange and obscure/ At the outset, terrifying too,/ But happy in the end for me.) (*Fonteinne*, lines 57–60, translation altered)

Once again, the *Fonteinne* upends expectations regarding the presentation of literary exchange by emphasizing through the double presence of the self-referential indirect object in lines 58 and 60 that what follows is the poet's story.

As Machaut settles into this new fiction of engagement, the reader transitions from the pseudo-factual world of the opening lines to an ambiguous literary space. The poet occupies a space between real and imaginary worlds:

> En un lit ou pas ne dormoie
> Einsois faisoie la dorveille,
> Com cils qui dort et encore veille,
> Car j'aloie de dor en dor.
>
> (In a bed and not sleeping,/ But, rather, wakeful,/ Like a man who sleeps yet is awake,/ For I was tossing and turning.) (*Fonteinne*, lines 62–5)

In this realm, an unidentifiable and incomprehensible moaning startles the poet, causing "horreur et frëour" (fear and horror) (*Fonteinne*, line 75). He responds by hiding beneath his covers until he eventually recognizes the moans as stemming from a lover bewailing his predicament. In response to this realization, the poet installs himself at a desk and begins to transcribe the lover's lament. The lament continues into the early hours of dawn. Once silence falls, the poet marvels over the poetic artistry of the final product before heading out in search of the lover. Up until this point, we can easily recognize in this scenario Kelly's description of patronage as a division of labour wherein the prince provides the genius, and the poet, the skills. That said, what follows merits careful scrutiny because the story of the actual encounter of poet and prince turns on the poet first ascertaining whether the prince appreciates and respects the logic of archaic gifting before presenting him with this poetry.

After rereading the nocturnal transcription, the poet confesses to having a good idea of the lover's identity. Nonetheless he proceeds with great caution, opting first to observe the suspected lover from a distance before approaching him. Upon spying the prince, the poet praises the lover's physical beauty, which is matched by the generosity he shows a messenger who bears gifts from a neighbour. The lover's gratitude also leads to his recitation of the golden rule of gifting when declaring to the valet thereafter, "Vesci riche don./ Bien est dignes de guerredon" (What a rich present./ This certainly deserves recompense) (*Fonteinne*, lines 1143–4). The lover follows this statement with an appropriate gesture that has him reward 15 florins to the valet for having transported the gift. Thereafter, the lover shows even greater magnanimity when instructing one of his men to send the gifts on to his lady (*Fonteinne*, lines 1147–51). This stock performance of generosity does not fully satisfy the poet as one might expect; instead, the scene leads the poet to expound on the danger of putting too much credence in a staged scene: "Mais tels est riches de biauté/ Qui est povres de loiauté ..." (But some are rich in beauty/ Who are poor in loyalty) (*Fonteinne*, lines 1161–2). With this observation, the poet directly addresses all "riches hommes" (wealthy men) (*Fonteinne*, line 1169, my translation) to remind them of their obligation to imitate Alexander, noting in particular that they must "leur grant richesse despendre" (distribute their great wealth) (*Fonteinne*, line 1172, my translation).

Returning to the present situation, the poet acknowledges his own predicament: he knows no one at court and thus has no representative to present him officially to the prince. Our quick-thinking poet finds a solution by staging his own performance intended to attract the lover's attention. From his distant observation point, the poet drops to his knee and adopts the posture of a subservient subject. The gesture has its desired effect, and the prince interrupts his conversation to rush towards the poet:

Et quant il me vit en ce point,
De son bien il n'atendi point,
Einsois en laissa plus de vint
Et tout en l'eure vers moy vint
Et par la main destre me prist
Et moult durement me reprist
De ce qu'agelongniez m'estoie.

(And when he saw me thus,/ In his goodness he didn't delay at all,/ But left behind more than twenty of his company/ And at once came my way,/ Seized my right hand,/ And reproved me quite vigorously/ For kneeling there.) (*Fonteinne*, lines 1215–21)

Having thus gained the full attention of the lover, the poet declares that his love and admiration for the prince compelled him to visit court. Nevertheless, in a pattern that is all too common in Machaut's fictions of engagement, the poet destabilizes the very scene he has crafted by professing to have broken custom in arriving with no gift to offer his prince. He may be on bended knee, but he claims to be empty-handed. As a "povre homme" (a poor man) (twice stated, *Fonteinne*, lines 1262 and 1263), all he has to offer are his services and he urges the prince to command at will:

Mais ja soit ce que petit vail,
Cuer, corps entierement vous bail
Pour faire vo commandement.
Or commandez hardiement,
Car s'aucun don plus chier avoie,
Plus volentiers le vous donroie.

(Although of little value/ I give you all my heart and body/ to answer your order./ Now command in confidence,/ For if I had a more worthy gift,/ I would willingly give it to you.) (*Fonteinne*, lines 1265–70, translation mine)

The prince shows himself no less debonair with a pauper poet than with the messenger of a generous neighbour; indeed, he proves to be of discerning character when declaring the poet's offer of services as worthy of more than 2,000 silver marcs (*Fonteinne*, lines 1289–90). Although hyperbolic, this declaration will be confirmed to startling effect in the final moments of the tale. Of course, what strikes a curious cord in the poet's present performance is that he has not arrived empty-handed before the prince, since he carries with him the lyric lament that would make a worthy gift. Once more, Machaut stages a scene that recalls a conventional book-presentation scene, only to subvert the exchange process as it takes shape.

Gifting persists as a dominant theme as the two men walk through the prince's gardens. The prince leads the poet to the actual fountain of love, where he details its history. The fountain, according to the prince, was a commissioned work of art for which Jupiter and Venus presented

Pygmalion with the gold, marble, and ivory necessary to sculpt the fountain that was to commemorate their love. Thereafter, the prince confesses that his imminent departure causes him great sorrow because he must leave behind his beloved and, in the spirit of the artistic alliance he has just detailed, he requests of the poet a work about his love:

> Que de m'amour et de ma plainte
> Me faciés ou lay ou complainte.
>
> (That of my love and sorrow/ you compose a lay or complaint for me.) (*Fonteinne*, lines 1503–4, my translation)

With this request, the poet formally acknowledges the prince as the source of the nocturnal lament and presents his poem, declaring: "Sire, vostre requeste,/ Tenez; vesla ci toute preste" (Lord, your request/ here it is, right here all ready) (*Fonteinne*, lines 1519–20, my translation).

For Jacqueline Cerquiglini-Toulet, this exchange scene reveals a common late-medieval tactic in which the poet engages in lyric stockpiling so as to assure that any demand for verse can be immediately satisfied.[33] This poetic hoarding is said to reflect an "anxiety about poetic creation" stemming from the fear of missing opportunities to answer a patron's needs.[34] Machaut's drawn-out staging of this scene, however, suggests that the "anxiety" surrounding poetry concerns less the ability to compose or to deliver a desired text and relates more to an anxious desire to secure in advance the ideal circumstances for literary exchange. In the *Fonteinne*, the poet delays giving the text to the prince until the latter makes a formal request for it. In the interim, the poet has observed the prince practising appropriate generosity when receiving gifts, has heard him declare the poet's value in extravagant monetary terms as well as testify to an appreciation for the creative process that requires a skilled individual, whether Pygmalion or our poet, to realize the patron's desire. The poet's declaration when handing over the poem emphasizes the exchange system in which the work circulates. In declaring the poem "toute preste," that is, completed and ready, Machaut also hints at its function within an exchange system in which "preste" also signifies a loan. In this regard, the poem reflects the ties of exchange that ordain that a gift offered must be reciprocated.[35] Emblematic of this newly developed bond, the two men fall into a deep sleep with the prince's head on the poet's lap.

The symbolic harmony evoked through this pastoral scene of two men sharing a moment of rest will be immediately disrupted by the ensuing dream sequence. As the poem shifts to the dreamworld, only the poet "awakens" to this alternative universe, where he notices two beautiful women who turn out to be Venus and the prince's lady. The prince, in contrast, is described as remaining fast asleep (*Fonteinne*, line 2145). Venus's first words, nonetheless, are directed to the sleeping prince, whom she admonishes for not appreciating her powers. Rather than rouse the prince from his nap to present him with his lady, Venus turns her attention to the poet, who gazes with great interest upon the golden apple. The poet confesses both his ignorance regarding its significance and a great desire to understand the meaning of the words etched on its surface: "Donnee soit a la plus belle!" (Let it be given to the most beautiful woman!) (*Fonteinne*, line 1603). Venus entertains the poet's desire and proceeds to recount the tale of Paris and the golden apple to the poet "seulement" (alone) (*Fonteinne*, line 2638).

For Margaret Ehrhart, Machaut's placement of Paris's tale within the dream sequence of the *Fonteinne* allows the poet to take advantage of the "conventions established by the genre of the dream vision to create a landscape with profound moral tones" in which he might embed a critique concerning the prince's privileging of love over his duties as a ruler.[36] While Ehrhart has persuasively detailed the repeated use of this myth in medieval literature to achieve this type of critique, her overlaying of this reading on Machaut's use of the same myth ignores many curious factors specific to its retelling in the *Fonteinne*. Beyond the fact that the prince remains fast asleep during Venus's discussion of the golden apple, it is striking that the myth's retelling results from the poet's interest in the object itself. Machaut's Paris is also distinctive because of the emphasis placed on his desire to first learn what each goddess possesses as a potential reward ("de quoy chascune d'elles sert"; "what purpose each lady serves," *Fonteinne*, line 2010) before determining to whom he will offer the apple. This enhanced emphasis on the value of their purpose, which indicates their proposed (counter)gifts, is underscored by the repeated final argument of each goddess that Paris cede the apple because of the specific riches each promises. In this manner, the golden apple, which is inscribed with the obligation to give it to its most worthy recipient, functions here especially in terms of predetermined guarantees of recompense. Coming immediately after the poet's delay of delivering the lament to the prince until the prince himself detailed his wish for a poem and expressed his intention to respond with a hefty recompense, Paris's negotiations with the three goddesses establish a mythical precedence for the poet's own careful management of literary exchange achieved by fusing archaic gifting practices with a beneficial and desirable commission that he so carefully orchestrated.

It is upon awakening that the poet receives his due from the prince for the lyric gift. The prince spends his final hours on the continent preparing for departure, and the poet remains faithfully by his side until the very end. The prince's final gesture before handing himself over to his captors concerns the poet's reward. The poet announces that, at that time, the lover bequeathed to him all of his worldly goods:

> Tout son païs m'abandonna
> Et de ses joiaus me donna
> Liberalment et largement,
> Plus qu'a moy n'affiert vraiment.
>
> (He relinquished all his land to me/ And his jewels he gave me/ Liberally and generously/ Truly more than I had a right to have.) (*Fonteinne*, lines 2835–8, my translation)

As I discussed in an earlier treatment of this work, this gesture has a powerful effect on the poet-prince relationship because it radically reverses roles by stripping the prince of all signs of his political and social status for the poet's immediate benefit.[37] For Machaut, the poetic work that can provide comfort to a disempowered prisoner-prince merits a kingdom. This account of the patron's extreme generosity anticipates the more measured admonishments of Charles V's commissioned writers, such as Foulechat and Oresme, that the knowledge they offered their king constituted an inestimable treasure. Read through these more measured celebrations of the wealth represented by knowledge, Machaut does not so much strip the *Fonteinne* prince of his power as much as he provides him with a greater, albeit intangible, wealth in the form of the poetry and comfort he gives. The closing miniature in MS fr. 1584, however, insists on a dramatic role reversal when depicting the poet on horseback while the prince stands between his jailers on a boat headed out to sea.[38] Likely anticipating the shock that readers might experience in witnessing this topsy-turvy account of poet-prince relations in which the delivered commissioned text garners the prince's kingdom and material wealth, Machaut tempers the message in his final line when asking his readers, "dites moy, fu ce bien songié" (Tell me, was this well dreamed) (*Fonteinne*, line 2848). He thereby suggests that the entire *dit* transpired in the dream realm that would have had its starting point when the poet first placed his head on his pillow and heard the initial wailing of a prince in need of poetry.

This playful conclusion to the *Fonteinne* cannot mask the reality that this fiction of engagement offers yet another radical account of literary exchange. In the *Navarre*, Lady Bonneürté ordered the poet to suppress his views, while the judge commanded that he adopt her viewpoint. In the *Confort*, the poet's offering of a consolation poem prompted an unwanted and unacceptable demand for another consolation piece that was expected to strike a very different cord. Neither of these works resulted in the poet receiving a reward or positive recognition, but rather punishment. The *Fonteinne* changes this outcome. In this fiction of engagement, the would-be patron values above all else the poet and his talents. Yet in spite of this perfect ending, in its final moments, the *dit* casts the tale as a dream, as a fantasy narrative in which the actual hero is the poet.

Machaut's final and most extravagant account of literary engagement detailed in the Prologue to his collected works takes the fantasy even further. In Machaut's presumed final composition, nobility disappears entirely, and the poet takes centre stage in literary exchange as both recipient and donor of the gift of writing.

The Divine Commission and the Writer's Gift: The Prologue to Machaut's Collected Works

As Machaut took stock of his corpus in his final years, he chose to unite his collected works through the composition of a Prologue that heads four copies of his collected works.[39] It would be in the very years that Charles V was pursuing talented writers to contribute to his *Sapientia* project that Machaut, then living full-time in Reims, would present his writings as his own lifelong project, a project dedicated to proclaiming the incomparable gift of verse and music bestowed to him. In this final treatment of literary dynamics dictating poetic production, Machaut would appropriate for himself the role that commissioned writers as well as court artists and scribes afforded Charles V. That is, he imagined a form of divine commissioning in which instead of figuring as a client expected to produce on command, the writer emerged as the recipient of an inestimable gift. Poetic knowledge was a divine gift conferred on Machaut alone.

The language of the literary commission prefaces the Prologue in MS fr. 1584:

> Comment Nature [...] vient a Guillem de Machaut et li ordene et encharge a faire sur ce nouveaux dis amoureux et li baille pour li conseillier et aidier a ce faire trois de ses enfans, c'est asavoir Sens, Retorique, et Musique.
>
> (How Nature [...] comes to Guillaume de Machaut, orders and charges him to make new love poems and offers to him, for counsel and aid in doing this, three of her children, that is, Meaning, Rhetoric, and Music.)[40]

Playing off the language typical of the commission, the rubric positions Lady Nature as a patron who "orders and charges" Guillaume to write poetry in exchange for the gift of her children. The Prologue thereafter registers her command:

> Je, Nature, par qui tout est fourmé,
> Quanque a ça jus et sur terre et en mer,
> Vieng ci a toy, Guillem, qui fourmé
> T'ai a part pour faire par toi former
> Nouveaux dis amoureux plaisans.
> Pour ce te bail ci trois de mes enfans
> Qui t'en donront la pratique,
> Et, se tu n'es d'eulz troi bien cognoissans,
> Nommé sont Sens, Retorique, et Musique.
>
> (I, Nature, by whom all things took form,/ Whatever is above and on the earth, in the sea,/ Come here to you, Guillaume, a man/ I created especially to create/ New and pleasant poems about love./ And so I entrust you with three of my children/ Who will give you practical knowledge,/ And, if you do not recognize them readily,/ Their names are Meaning, Rhetoric, and Music.) (Prologue, lines 1–9)

Lady Nature assumes perfectly the patron-function within a clientelistic framework; she reigns over all men, exhibits both magnanimity and largess, and proves herself both in need of the poet and willing to nurture his abilities by presenting him with her greatest riches, her lyric offspring. The gift of her children will redound to the poet's credit since they will secure his unparalleled fame: "Ti fait seront plus qu'autres renommé" (your works will find more renown than others) (Prologue, line 19). In this instance, the patron-figure overturns the principal drive of the commission when promising the poet-client that acceptance of her command will be to his benefit, rather than hers. In response, the poet assumes the ritualistic posture of the subservient writer and adopts the feudalistic language of obligation and willing subordination to Lady Nature to craft his response:

> Riens ne me doit excuser ne deffendre
> Que ne face le bon commandement
> De vous, dame, se je vous say entendre,
> Par qui j'ay corps, vie, et entendement.
> Dont drois est, quant vous m'ordenez
> A faire diz amoureux ordenez,
> Qu'a ce faire je me soutive.
> Et je vueil bien estre a ce fait donnez,
> Tant qu'en ce mond vos plaira que je vive.
>
> (Nothing should either keep, prevent me from/ Obeying this excellent command/ Of yours, lady, if I understand you,/ To whom I owe body, life, and mind./ So you're right to command me/ To compose love poems in the proper form,/ And so I will apply myself./ And I'm willingly dedicated to this duty/ For as long as you please that I live in this world.) (Prologue, lines 28–36)

Yet again, the performance infuses the relationship with new meaning. Here, the poet blurs his promise of service with discussion of his own poetic powers. Lady Nature may "order" him to write, but he "orders" the poetry she desires. He even goes so far as to suggestively rework his expected subordination through reference to creative imagination. That is, rather than employ the expected term of "sou(bs)mettre" (to submit) to confirm his submission to Lady Nature, the poet employs the term "se soutiver," which conveys his willingness to "set his mind/apply himself" to making poetry.

The God of Love then arrives at the poet's domicile to present his own children to the poet to help with the writing task:

> Pour ce t'ameinne icy en pourvëance,
> Pour toy donner matere a ce parfaire,
> Mes trois enfans en douce contenance:
> C'est doulz Penser, Plaisance, et Esperance.
>
> (And so I bring you here to help,/ To provide you material to accomplish this,/ My three children of the sweet look:/ These are Sweet Thought, Pleasure, and Hope.) (Prologue, lines 61–4)

The God of Love's gifts are both chosen with awareness of the poet's needs (pourvëance) and as material freely given for the poet's use (toy donner matere). Thus, although the expected language of the literary commission filters throughout the Prologue, the exchange dynamics are dramatically reversed, and it is the poet who appears here as the recipient of great wealth rather than as the subordinate subject obligated to serve a powerful master.

This highly fictionalized account of the literary commission reveals important parallels with the more realistic declarations of Charles V's commissioned writers. As Foulechat acknowledged that the king furnished the learned matter necessary to complete his translation, so too Machaut identifies here the gifts offered to him by Lady Nature and the God of Love as allowing him to satisfy their command (Prologue, line 123). Machaut also expresses his willingness to accommodate their wishes – "Et ne doy mie desvoloir/ Leur plaisant gracious voloir" (And I ought in no way disdain/ Their pleasant, gracious will) (Prologue, lines 133–4) – and then adds that to contradict their requests would only lead to the unravelling of his work: "Certes mon oeuvre defferoie" (I would ruin my work for sure) (Prologue, line 156). Insisting on the harmony between their command and his interests, he concludes:

> Et quant Nature me commande
> Et li dieux d'Amours, que j'entende
> Aus choses dessus proposes
> Seur l'onneur des dames fondees,
> Bien est raison que je m'aplique
> A faire leur bon plaisir, si que
> Je n'i mesprengne ne mefface.
>
> (And since Nature commands me,/ And the God of love too, that I attend/ To those things proposed above/ Involving the honor of ladies,/ It's good sense for me to attempt/ Doing what would bring them evident pleasure,/ As long as I don't go wrong or fail.) (Prologue, lines 283–9)

Machaut's acceptance of the commission differs, nonetheless, in important ways from the declarations of the king's commissioned writers because the poet ingeniously disguises in words of subservience a resolve to satisfy his own interests. For the words chosen here to register the risk involved in the commission are rich with double meaning. Playing on the homophony that confuses "mefface" (fail/do incorrectly) with "m'efface" (erase myself) and "mesprengne" (go wrong) with "me prengne" (entrap myself), Machaut appears here to recall his abiding concern manifested in his earlier fictions of engagement. Specifically, we hear echoes of Lady Bonneürté's efforts to entrap the poet and to erase his words in the *Navarre* and of the risk linked to readers' rejection of either his intentions or his verse as seen in the *Confort*. In this final treatment of literary dynamics, Machaut implies that patronage arrangements ought to secure the poet's reputation and are thus worthy of accepting only if they allow for the author to express his wishes and desires rather than simply speak to a patron's declared pleasure. Machaut's identification of poetry as his inalienable good gives powerful expression to Annette Weiner's argument that inalienable possessions attribute an unparalleled degree of power to the beholder. Machaut seems to taunt his readers by "keeping-while-giving" his work.[41] His readers are allowed to enjoy his poetry but they are denied the right to view it as constituting the patron's pleasure.

Seeing Machaut's Fictions of Engagement through a Court Lens: The Illustrated Copies of Machaut's Complete Works Produced in Valois Circles

The novelty of Machaut's depiction of literary exchange dynamics in the Prologue was not lost on its early interpreters. The miniaturists responsible for illustrating Machaut's collected works manuscripts, most of whom had deep affiliations with the Valois courts,[42] necessarily came to his corpus with a received visual vocabulary prominently displayed in Charles V's books. Whether familiar with the contents and significance of Machaut's writings, simply obeying instructions of a superior, or assuming that Machaut employed common dedication strategies, the miniaturists adapted the presentation iconography of the king's recently commissioned works to Machaut's own fiction of engagement detailed in the Prologue. Nowhere is this more spectacularly developed than in MS fr. 1584. The richly decorated copy of the Prologue that was tipped into MS fr. 1584 has garnered much admiration. It is impossible to date with certainty either the illustration of this copy or its addition to MS fr. 1584, although François Avril speculates that the codex itself dates from the early 1370s and that the added Prologue was painted thereafter, possibly before Machaut's death in 1377. This double frontispiece to MS fr. 1584 stands out from the remaining illustrations not only because of its dimensions and the quality of the artistry, but specifically because of the royal miniaturist who designed it. In fact, Avril considers this work to represent the "chef-d'oeuvre" of the *Master of the Bible de Jean de Sy*.[43]

The *Master of the Bible de Jean de Sy* refers to an individual or a group of artists affiliated with several manuscripts produced for Valois princes during the second half of the fourteenth century.[44] Best known for his work on the unfinished *Bible historiale*, this master also participated in the decoration of the Bible offered by Jean de Vaudetor to Charles V (Museum Meermanno, The Hague, Museum Meermanno-Westreenianum, 10 B 23), as well as Charles V's commissioned copy of Evrart de Trémaugon's *Vergier* (British Library, Royal MS 19 C IV). Let us recall that this last work stands out in the king's commissioning history as the only known example of an original contemporary vernacular fiction to identify itself as resulting from royal commission. In addition to its fictional status, this illustrated *Vergier* shares in common with the tipped-in illustrated Prologue in MS fr. 1584 the fact that the master closely followed authorial accounts of literary creation over real-life circumstances. Both of these works stand out in fourteenth-century art for the highly original depictions of vernacular authorship that the *Master of the Bible de Jean de Sy* provided.

Dated to 1378 in a colophon signed by the king, the king's copy of the *Vergier* opens with two illustrations by the *Master of the Bible de Jean de Sy* that wed the fictional status of this new work with the dominant iconography of literary exchange decorating most of Charles V's commissioned works. Preceding the address to the king, a full-page visual rendering of poet-patron relations corresponds perfectly to details provided in the prologue (Figure 3.3: London, British Library, Royal 19. C. IV, fol. 1v). Alluding to the author's claim that a dream inspired his text, the illustration sets events in an enclosed garden. The master's true distinctiveness, however, appears in the "the peculiarly vigorous and dramatic narrative style"[45] that visualizes the author's account of creative inception. The poet takes position at the bottom-centre of a hierarchical triptych, where he adopts the authoritative role of the poet sleeping alongside a body of water, a frequent metaphor for creative inspiration. The poet's dream takes shape above him. At the nexus of the illustration, a debate scene between the cleric and a knight introduces the two principal interlocutors of the text/dream that follows. In the top tier of the vertical triptych, King Charles V sits in judgment over the debating figures. The allegorical judges from the text, Puissance spirituelle (Spiritual Power) and Puissance séculière (Secular Power), flank the king. The king's presence among these divine judges anticipates the author's claim in the prologue that his dream resulted both from his imagination and from discussions

Figure 3.3: Frontispiece, Evrart de Trémaugon's *Songe du vergier*, London, British Library, Royal 19. C. IV, fol. 1v.

that the king encouraged at court (*Vergier*, 1:4). The frontispiece's vertical visualization of the literary partnership reimagines the expected hieratic dynamics linking a royal patron and a writer-client and encourages instead the viewer to consider king and author as mutually responsible for one another's existence; the king's presence arises from the author's dream, and the author's dream appears sanctioned by the king's raised hand, which extends an imaginary line down the middle of the miniature to the sleeping poet. Lest the king be afforded too much control over the narrative, the scene transpires in a garden rather than court or castle, and by populating the scene with fictional characters from the text, the illustration appears to firmly locate the work and, by extension, the king within the writer's sphere of creative imagination as opposed to the regulated site of the royal chambers. The second illustration that heads the prologue on the facing page dialogues in provocative ways with this full-page oneiric vision by turning to the more conventional scene of the book transfer. This illustration, which spans the two columns and takes up approximately one-third of folio 2r, depicts what was, by 1378, common fare in the king's commissioned works (Figure 3.4: British Library, Royal 19. C. IV, fol. 2r). Wearing the same grey robe from folio 1v, the author now genuflects at the near-centre of the illumination with book in hand. His submissive posture is, nonetheless, counterbalanced by the king, who leans towards the author and who now dons the modest costume of a red robe and skull cap in place of the royal robe of the frontispiece. As was the case in the frontispieces to the three commissioned translations studied in the previous chapter, the artist uses posture and clothing to identify Charles V as a member of the learned sodality rather than as a distant overseer of the literary world. In this respect, both illustrations at the head of the *Vergier* invite viewers to see the king as inhabiting the creative and intellectual spheres of literary production.

As with the opening frontispiece to the *Vergier*, so too the *Master of the Bible of Jean de Sy* fully engaged with the originality of Machaut's Prologue to spotlight the creative sphere. In the Prologue, Machaut provided an unprecedented celebration of the vernacular writer that, as we have seen, depended heavily on an ingenious manipulation of commissioning conventions and dedication rhetoric. So too the illuminator reutilized standard presentation iconography to produce a new visual narrative of authorship that positioned Machaut at the heart of the literary system while effectively depicting the patron-figure as issuing from the sphere of creative imagination. Whether influenced by Machaut's verse or simply the descriptive rubrications that introduced each section of the Prologue,

Figure 3.4: Presentation scene, Evrart de Trémaugon's *Songe du vergier*, London, British Library, Royal 19. C. IV, fol. 2r.

the illuminator respected the textual account of literary creation and thus valourized creative inception in place of a more typical presentation scene. As noted, in the opening illustrations to the *Vergier*, the royal patron appears both as inspiration and as a product of the writer's imagination before assuming the role of recipient in the second illustration. In the illustrations to Machaut's Prologue, where the terrestrial patron has already been supplanted by divine inspiration within the text, the *Master of the Bible de Jean de Sy* visually proposed a new power dynamic that dramatically blurred oneiric and real-world accounts of the literary economy (Figure 3.5: BnF, MS fr. 1584, fol. D and Figure 3.6: BnF, MS fr. 1584, fol. E). Reinforcing Machaut's account, the illustrations encourage the viewer to approach Lady Nature and the God of Love as divine replacements for a royal patron. In the Prologue's double illustration (which was misordered when tipped in), these allegorical figures wear the crown typically reserved for royalty, and through the application of gold paint reserved for these patron-surrogates, they stand out against the partially coloured *grisaille* background. In spite of the authority afforded these surrogates, the *mise en scène* disrupts expectations. First, as was the case in the full-page illustration heading the king's copy of the *Vergier*, the master replaces the traditional court setting of the book presentation scene with a realistic nature landscape that strongly evokes the realm of poetic creation. Therein, he inserts objects that mark this space as the writer's realm. In the opening illustration depicting Lady Nature's arrival, the natural landscape includes a fountain at the centre, a clear allusion to creative imagination with an emphasis on the manmade artefact that contains the water source. In addition, the surrounding landscape bustles with activity often metaphorically linked with writing. In the upper portion of the MS fr. 1584 illustrations, we see visual allusions to Presles's own contemporary use of the labourer and the windmill to speak of his writing activities in his address to King Charles in the *Cité*, as discussed in the previous chapter. In MS fr. 1584, labourers carry heavy sacks, lead horses, and care for livestock, while the windmill on the horizon speaks to the unceasing labour of both field hands and writers. In this respect, the entire landscape can be interpreted as a symbolic celebration of the writing act linked to the author-figure prominently positioned in the lower right margin of this vibrant scene. The author stands on what appears to be a chair, a sure visual allusion to the writer's study contained within the architectural structure behind him. In this visualization of the Prologue, the poet neither seeks out the patron nor kneels in her presence. Instead, Lady Nature slightly bows before the poet to offer him her children. Tellingly, Sens appears here as a man of

Figure 3.5: Double frontispiece to the collected works of Guillaume de Machaut, Paris, Bibliothèque nationale de France, MS fr. 1584, fol. D.

Figure 3.6: Double frontispiece to the collected works of Guillaume de Machaut, Paris, Bibliothèque nationale de France, MS fr. 1584, fol. E.

learning, an *orator* who has come to serve the vernacular poet; an allusion that provides an intriguing alternative but complimentary scenario to the marginal positioning adopted by Foulechat and Presles vis-à-vis the learned community as discussed in the previous chapter. This scene is all the more important given that Machaut as a composer of fictional poetry rather than a recognized translator of learned matter receives an offer of the cleric's services. In the second illustration, the God of Love, depicted as a crowned, winged figure, slightly leans forward while presenting his own children dressed in costumes that link them to court society. By the time the God of Love appears in the second illustration, the poet has assumed the seat of learning. In this miniature, not only does the poet effectively assume the patronal seat, he also appears receiving gifts from his divine visitor.[46] Thus in multiple subtle ways the MS fr. 1584 double frontispiece expands on Machaut's celebration of vernacular authorship.

For Françoise Ferrand, the double frontispiece heading MS fr. 1584 is distinguished by its pivotal role in late-medieval author iconography since it functions here "que pour célébrer l'artiste" (only to celebrate the artist [i.e., the author]), and she adds that the author is portrayed "à l'égal des princes ses mécènes qui, eux, ont disparu de la scène ... laissant au seul artiste l'espace souverain et la gloire" (equal to his princely patrons who have disappeared from the scene ... leaving for the artist alone the sovereign space and glory).[47] Key to Ferrand's reading is the extent to which the miniaturist draws inspiration from conventional textual transmission scenes when placing the poet in a position of authority traditionally reserved either for the patron or the learned scholar.[48] Or, as was the case in the 1372 frontispiece of the king's copy of the *Policratique* (see Figure 2.1), a position occupied by the Wise King. In comparison to the *Policratique* frontispiece as well as the *Vergier* frontispiece, the Prologue's miniature cycle in MS fr. 1584 points to clear efforts to rework the developing iconography at the king's court to afford the vernacular writer and composer both the role of beneficiary and benefactor in a radically reconceived literary economy. This frontispiece replaces the intellectual's call to translate ancient works with a poet called upon to translate and shape emotions through verse. Affect replaces intellect; verse and music override prose translation. The double frontispiece further identifies poetry and music as divine callings that cause the patron-figures to express physically their reverent support for the author's efforts. This strong visual endorsement of a competing concept of literary creation found in the first two illuminations in MS fr. 1584 would not become the standard and, instead, miniatures decorating later copies of Machaut's Prologue would reserve a far more humble position for the poet.

Machaut's material legacy from the 1370s through the 1390s provides ample challenge to the promotion of authorship developed in the Prologue and the accompanying double frontispiece to MS fr. 1584. Artists responsible for later copies of Machaut's Prologue proposed complex visual narratives that reinserted the poet into a conventional patronage dynamic that would become the standard in books produced for Valois princes and their entourage. This fact is all the more relevant given that half the fourteen collected works listed by Lawrence Earp, including both extant and lost copies, are currently linked to the Valois dynasty and members of its immediate entourage.[49] In the case of the four extant collected works manuscripts now firmly linked to the duke of Berry's court, they are also linked to illustrators known to have worked on Charles V's commissioned books.[50] Given the *Master of the Bible de Jean de Sy*'s involvement in the Prologue to MS fr. 1584, we might add this copy to the list of works linked to the Valois dynasty.[51]

To appreciate the influence Valois-associated artists had on Machaut's visual legacy, a summary of the newly established historiography of Ferrell-Vogüé by Lawrence Earp and its relationship to the other three copies of Machaut's complete works manuscripts associated with the duke of Berry is in order.[52] We now know that in 1388–9, John of Berry was in possession of the Ferrell-Vogüé luxury codex containing solely Machaut's compositions. The duke decided to offer this codex to Gaston Fébus in hopes of securing a promise of marriage to the count's ward, Jeanne de Boulogne. Before sending the manuscript south, a rapid, undecorated paper copy of the codex was produced. That rough copy is identified today as BnF, MS fr. 1585. Thereafter, a new version of Machaut's collected works was produced for Duke John. This new version, BnF, MS fr. 9221, depended only partially on the MS fr. 1585 copy and distinguishes itself through the addition of Machauldian works not included in the Ferrell-Vogüé copy (including the Prologue and the *Voir dit*) and, in particular, through an innovative layout and an original miniature cycle. The fourth and final codex of Machaut's complete works linked to the court of Berry concerns BnF, MSS fr. 22545–6. It is now known that the duke of Berry's then father-in-law, Jehan, count of Boulogne and Auvergne, owned this two-volume codex, which dates to the 1390s.[53]

This new information regarding the duke of Berry's pronounced involvement in the preservation and dissemination of Machaut's works demands a radical rethinking of established views on the duke's book-collecting practices. Millard Meiss provided the first and still most exhaustive study of the duke's book-collecting practices, which he considered to have only become a serious preoccupation for the duke beginning in the first decade of the fifteenth century.[54] Up until now, Duke John has been portrayed as someone prone to reserve prodigious sums for luxury manuscripts. For example, the duke's secretary, Jean Flamel, estimated the worth of the duke's luxury copy of the *Grandes heures* at 4,000 livres, which Autrand confirms to be "un prix énorme" (an enormous price).[55] Likewise, Duke John showed particular generosity to the famed artist duo, the Limbourg brothers, who regularly received funds from him between 1413 and 1414, ranging from 6 écus to 100 écus, to precious jewels valued at 30 to 40 livres.[56] Little interest has been given to the less extravagant additions to his collection, especially his secular books, even though early on his collection included numerous vernacular writings. Duke John possessed copies of the *Roman de la rose* and a selection of popular romances.[57] New works by contemporary writers also figured in his collection, including the 1392 *Mélusine* by Jean d'Arras (which the author declares to be the result of a commission from the duke of Berry). To be treated more fully in the final chapters is the case of Christine de Pizan, who presented the duke with copies of her *Epistre Othéa*, the *Livre du chemin de longue étude*, and the *Livre de la mutacion de Fortune*, making her, according to Meiss, the most represented contemporary author in the duke's collection.[58] She would eventually receive from the duke a reward of 200 écus, although it is unclear if this sum was linked to a work already presented or a commission for a copy of her "livre de balades et dittiés" (a book of ballades and *dits*).[59] In later years, Laurent Premierfait dedicated to Duke John his translation of Boccaccio's *De casibus* and *Des cas des nobles hommes et femmes* (1411), Boccaccio's *Decameron* (1414), and Cicero's *De amicitia* (1416).[60]

To this received narrative, we must now acknowledge that the duke of Berry's book-collecting interests started much earlier than believed and that he played a formative role in shaping literary dynamics in the wake of his royal brother's passing. In fact, it now appears possible that in the last decade of the Wise King's life John of Berry emerged as a serious collector of vernacular writings, and he turned to the artists who served his brother to secure luxury copies of these works. In the specific case of Machaut, it is worth asking if Duke John deserves credit for orchestrating an important creative encounter that brought into dialogue Machaut's fictions of engagement with the presentation iconography introduced by Charles V's favoured illustrators. It is key, however, to note that the ensuing illustrations did not translate the intimate bond afforded the Wise King and his writers to Machaut's accounts of literary exchange. Instead, we discover in the miniature cycles of Machaut's collected works produced in the Berry circle a reinstatement of the strong hieratic dynamics common to stock images of literary transactions. What resulted from this encounter were visual correctives to Machaut's narratives that weakened the poet's promotion of vernacular authorship.

The illustrations decorating Machaut's *Confort* in the three decorated extant manuscripts linked to the duke of Berry's court provide a striking example of how the involvement of Charles V's favoured artists altered Machaut's account of literary dynamics in a manner that neither perpetuated the idealized visual accounts of exchange in the Wise King's commissioned books nor supported the alternative narrative of exchange dynamics in Machaut's works. For example, two of the three illustrated copies of the *Confort* included in the manuscripts linked to the Berry court overwrite the image of the powerless prince detailed by Machaut and portrayed in earlier copies of the work to provide instead a standard portrait of royal authority. In contrast to the depiction of the imprisoned king portrayed in the two manuscripts already examined, MS fr. 1584 and Arsenal 5203, the opening miniature to the *Confort* in Ferrell-Vogüé positions the kneeling poet before an enthroned king, while BnF, MS fr. 22545 depicts an enthroned king receiving a book from a messenger sent by the poet who appears on a distant shore, perhaps serving as a visual allusion to Charles of Navarre's imprisonment.[61] The final decorated manuscript linked to the duke of Berry, MS fr. 9221, completely occludes the uncomfortable prisoner status of Charles of Navarre by opening with an image of Susannah, whose story figures first among the *exempla* intended to comfort the addressee.

Of these illustrated manuscripts, the Ferrell-Vogüé copy deserves further attention because it includes a unique closing illustration to the *Confort*. This miniature precedes the coda with a visual portrait that appears to authorize the prince. Squeezed in as if an afterthought, the closing miniature to the Ferrell-Vogüé copy of the *Confort* depicts the king sitting up in bed with curtains pulled open. As such, it visualizes the coda's opening reference to the prisoner's arousal from a deep sleep.[62] The prisoner raises a clenched hand, a gesture that expresses the strife and sorrow articulated in the coda, and thus registers at the close of the *Confort* the king's dissatisfaction with the work. At the same time, his empty outstretched hand gestures to the absent text – the text he desires and has not received. The layout of the opening page of Ferrell-Vogüé, 196v–197r, encourages us to follow the king's outstretched hand to the facing page, where the *Fonteinne* begins. As already noted, the historical circumstances framing this second *dit* share much in common with the *Confort*, since we encounter another prisoner-prince in need of consolation. The prisoner's body in the final image decorating the *Confort* appears to direct our gaze to the facing page and to engage in a form of "reciprocal reading"[63] that would associate these two texts through their shared goals of comforting prisoners. The effect is otherwise, since in turning our gaze upon the *Fonteinne*, we encounter a poet in the opening miniature who literally turns his back on the ungrateful king of the previous work to record instead the laments of another prince who is depicted standing before him.[64] It is surely no small coincidence that this new prince may have been none other than the owner of the codex itself.

Whereas Ferrell-Vogüé does not include the Prologue, the other two decorated manuscripts linked to the court of Berry open with this work. That said, there is no reason to assume that the artists who decorated these two copies of the Prologue were familiar with the tipped-in version of the Prologue in MS fr. 1584. Still yet, it is enlightening to consider the strikingly different visual accounts provided in these later copies by masters who were also affiliated, along with the *Master of the Bible of Jean de Sy*, with Charles V's court. As the duke's replacement copy for the codex he sent to Gaston Fébus, MS fr. 9221 testifies to great effort and expense given to producing a manuscript that would be considered aesthetically superior to the previous copy. The miniature cycle of MS fr. 9221, however, shows little evidence of innovation and instead seems to announce a return to a more conservative tradition. Avril attributes the decoration of MS fr. 9221 to the *Master of the Policratique*, named for his work on the King Charles's copy of the *Policratique*, which we examined in the previous chapter.[65] In MS fr. 9221, a single condensed scene that exaggerates the writer's subordination to the allegorical patron-figures prefaces the Prologue. The opening miniature contains two joined scenes in a diptych that twice depicts the poet kneeling: on the left, the poet receives Lady Nature and her children and, on the right, he receives the God of Love and his children. Although there is no book in sight, the poet's positioning clearly aligns him with conventional scenes in which the author subordinates himself to his worldly superior. As a result, this rendition of the Prologue emphasizes the poet's promise to serve his divine patrons rather than his receipt of divine gifts and knowledge as was privileged in MS fr. 1584.[66] In MS fr. 22545, the Prologue is even more adamantly reinserted into a conventional patronage iconographic tradition by another Valois-affiliated artist, Perrin Rémiet, who presents four separate scenes depicting the poet genuflecting before Lady Nature and the God of

Love.[67] The first illustration dominates half of the page and insists on the poet's subordination both through posture and scale. Positioned against a flattened background, there is little to suggest that Lady Nature visits the poet. That the background bears the arms of the actual owner of this manuscript encourages us to imagine him in the space of the abstracted patron-figure.[68] By the time the poet is shown writing in the fifth image illustrating the MS fr. 22545 copy, the viewer appreciates that the present work results from the poet's acceptance "to work on the command of others" ("leur commande travaillier," Prologue, line 123), as it is declared only a few lines below this image. It is noteworthy that MS fr. 9221, similar to MSS fr. 22545–6, also prefaces Machaut's fictions of engagement with visual evidence of patronal ownership of the codices. Going even further than the placement of the owner's emblem in the background of several illustrations in MSS fr. 22545–6, MS fr. 9221 frames the codex with references to its ducal owner. The codex opens with a full-page, highly floral announcement by Flamel, Duke John's librarian, that claims the present manuscript as the property of the duke of Berry: "Ce livre de Machaut est a Jehan, filz dou roy de France, duc de Berry" (This book of Machaut belongs to Jean, son of the king of France, the duke of Berry) (folio Br). The codex also closes with the duke's own signature (folio 238v). The result of this oppressive visualization of Machaut's subordination to a clientelistic economy not only underscores the unconventionality of the poet's work, it also reveals how, with time and distance from Charles V's commissions, at least visual treatment of poet-prince relations had been flattened and stripped of the vibrancy with which writers and artists had dealt with the issue of literary dynamics. Illustrations for Machaut's Prologue MS fr. 9221 and MS fr. 22545 assign a submissiveness to the author that differs both from Machaut's fictional accounts of literary exchange as well as from the complex iconography displayed in Charles V's books, which Claire Richter Sherman has persuasively shown to have celebrated an uncommonly intimate and non-hieratic relationship between the king and his learned clients.[69] In these later copies of Machaut's works produced in the wake of Charles V's passing, the "poet's oeuvre" is displayed as the book owner's property. If Machaut's later manuscripts linked to the Valois dynasty provide any indication of evolving views regarding literary patronage, it is that the literary dynamics promoted in the Wise King's books were quickly replaced with an alternative account of poet-prince relations that reasserted a proprietary role for the book recipient and owner and the identification of luxury books as, once again, speaking to the patron's pleasure.

To be discussed in the remaining chapters are the poetic testimonials by Eustache Deschamps and Christine de Pizan that confirm this suspicion.

This chapter has taken a long view of literary exchange practices as detailed in Guillaume de Machaut's works, from early writings dating back to the 1350s through the composition of the Prologue in the 1370s to material traces of these writings in manuscripts produced after his death and as late as the last decade of the fourteenth century. The intention has been to recognize the presence of a counter narrative regarding the literary economy in Machaut's fictions of engagement that challenged the clientelistic practices undergirding Charles V's contemporary *Sapientia* project and that merits to be paired with the efforts of the king's commission writers to rework the king's practices to promote an intellectual ideal regarding the circulation of knowledge. Although we hear clear echoes between the negotiations of the learned men who answered Charles V's orders for learned works and Machaut's promotion of the vernacular writer, we detect important differences. Whereas the court-affiliated writers endorsed royal support of letters, Machaut repeatedly explored the dangerous repercussions commissioning practices could have on poetic creation. This brings us to another important distinction between Machaut and the king's commissioned writers. Whereas the king's writers were concerned with promoting intellectual labour and argued for the inestimable wealth of knowledge as a treasure to be circulated within the confines of a learned community, Machaut spotlighted poetic labour and the incalculable value of poetry as a source of wisdom and comfort to be shared among those who appreciated its power and recognized the talents required to produce it. As we shall see, both Deschamps and Christine shared with Machaut the belief that poetry was to be valued as much as prose; fiction as much as didactic or history writings. These two poets would play a crucial role in uniting Machaut's promotion of the lyric voice with the royal commissioned writers' idealized account of their dealings with the king. Both writers would use this material to call on Valois princes to perpetuate the legacy of the Wise King.

It is no small irony that by speaking out, albeit in veiled terms, about the dangers of the commission, Machaut ended up an author in high demand because he succeeded in convincing the ruling class that the gift of writing was to be esteemed above all others and that it was therefore to be treated as a treasure. Deschamps was so certain that the Valois princes would be among the mourners of Machaut's death that he singled out their suffering in his lyric lament for the poet: "Complains sera de princes et de roys" (There will be laments from princes and kings).[70] Deschamps's determination to link Machaut to the royal court through communal anguish over his passing provides a much-desired narrative linking the greatest francophone poet of the fourteenth century with those princes most often celebrated as the great medieval supporters of the book arts. Sadly, as will be pursued in the next chapter, such speculation seems to be borne out of nostalgia for a scenario that never was. For beyond the fact that Charles V left little evidence of an interest in original vernacular works, especially poetry, his brothers and descendants hardly showed a willingness to submit to poetic wisdom. As suggested by later copies of Machaut's works, it appears that Valois princes favoured the clientelistic approach to literature favoured by Charles V rather than the proposed model of exchange championed by writers and artists. To explore more closely what evidence there is for Valois support of new vernacular writings and, specifically, poetry spanning the reigns of Charles V and Charles VI, we shall now turn to Deschamps who provided an unparalleled testimonial detailing what it meant to be a vernacular poet at the royal court. Deschamps is clear on this matter: with the death of Charles V, court culture spiraled. Even a poet such as Machaut who expressed ambivalence regarding royal support of the poet would have certainly looked on in surprise and dismay as the status of writers dropped sharply with the passing of the Wise King and the arrival on the throne of a 12-year-old king who was scarcely interested in letters.

Chapter Four

Eustache Deschamps on the Duties and Dues of Poetry

The vast poetic corpus of Eustache Deschamps (c. 1340–c. 1404) reveals a wealth of insight into the changing views on literary exchange across the reigns of Charles V and Charles VI. Scholars have richly mined the notoriously unruly posthumous manuscript copy of Deschamps's writings for what it can tell us about the political and social upheaval that the poet witnessed firsthand.[1] Here, we shall approach the 82,000 lines of verse in BnF, MS fr. 840 as an invaluable resource for investigating the poet's literary dealings with the Valois dynasty.[2] In spite of the fact that historical record confirms Deschamps's official service to Charles V and Charles VI only as a sergeant-at-arms and not as a poet,[3] the author, nonetheless, merits recognition for his lifelong interest in the *Sapientia* project. In fact, Deschamps stands out from Charles V's known commissioned writers: first, because he is one of the few authors linked to Charles V who later regularly addressed works to Charles VI and his brother, Louis of Orléans; and second, because these later poems substantially contributed to the Wise King's learned legacy. During Charles VI's early regency followed by his declared independent rule in 1388, Deschamps used verse to urge the young king to model himself on his father, conveniently proposing his own writings as a resource for remembering the Wise King. Unfortunately for Deschamps and others, Charles VI showed scant interest in pursuing the Wise King's intellectual work, and Deschamps's poetry testifies to the general fall from grace of the book community following the Wise King's death. In light of these later dealings with the Wise King's descendants, who failed to live up to their father's ideal, Deschamps developed a radical new understanding of his responsibilities as a writer. In contrast to the models associated with Charles V's *Sapientia* project, Deschamps came to view poetry as neither a good to be freely offered nor something to be produced in response to royal desire; rather, it fulfilled a duty for the learned to speak the truth to the ruling class. Deschamps's account of his poetic responsibilities would become increasingly antagonistic over time, as seen in the later menacing warnings to the royal brothers of the poet's responsibility to mete out poetic justice and their obligation to abide by his shared wisdom or risk poetic wrath.

Deschamps's disappointment with the royal brothers was most fully expressed sixteen years into Charles VI's reign, at which time Deschamps brazenly announced his plans to abandon a thirty-two-year-long book project intended to honour Charles V:

> Je vueil cesser mon livre de memoire
> Ou j'ay escript depuis .xxxii. ans
> Du saige roy Charle le quint l'istoire.[4]
>
> (I want to cease writing my book of memory in which, for thirty-two years, I have written the history of the Wise King Charles V.)

In subsequent stanzas of this ballade, Deschamps provides further detail about the contents of this "book of memory" that makes clear its intended goal to celebrate also the Wise King's sons, had they not proved so disappointing. We learn that it covered the war with England, extending from Bertrand de Guesclin's glorious victories during the reign of Charles V to "the great misfortunes" ("les grans meschiez," B 1125, line 28) experienced by the Wise King's sons. It is only in the final stanza that Deschamps identifies what provoked him to abandon this project. He complains that since Charles VI's coronation in 1380, the royal brothers have remained distant, and as a result, the poet possesses scant knowledge of their activity:

> Puis son sacre me fut paine donnée
> Estans o eulx, d'encerchier et enquerre
> Et d'escripre leurs faiz par la contrée (B1125, lines 33–5)
>
> (Since his coronation, I have had great difficulty gaining access to them so as to seek out, inquire, and write about their accomplishments in the land)

Given that no trace remains of this "book of memory," we may conclude that Deschamps stuck to his word and abandoned the project.[5] Most important for this study is the poet's public declaration that such a project had been in the works, since it invites us to consider that this "book of memory" might have been a carryover of Charles V's *Sapientia* project. Ballade 1125 hints at the fate such a project would have faced; for whereas court-affiliated writers during Charles V's reign regularly celebrated royal investment in vernacular writing, this poem implicitly criticizes the Wise King's heirs for failing to perpetuate this practice and warns of the dire consequences of such inaction. This critique becomes clear in the suggestive declaration of the refrain: "Noble chose est de bon renom acquerre!" (It is a noble thing to acquire a good reputation!) (B1125, refrain). Implicit in this pronouncement is that if the poet ceased "to seek out, inquire, and write about their accomplishments," the royal brothers would be denied a legacy. By this stage, Deschamps had so thoroughly reworked conventional gifting dynamics applied to literary exchange that he would claim that by ceasing to write about the Valois dynasty, he presented the royal family with its rightful due.

To explore Deschamps's unique treatment of literary exchange dynamics, we will examine traces of his poetic engagement with Charles V and then turn to his writings addressed to Charles VI. Although most entries in MS fr. 840 are undated and organized by genre rather than by chronology, a few can be identified by reign. This study privileges a small segment of this poetic corpus according to three general time periods. The first group of poems dates from Charles V's reign (1364–80). Works to be considered from this period include examples of *poésie de circonstance* – poetry composed to publicize and commemorate events – and Deschamps's verse translation of sections of the *De miseria condicionis humane*, renamed the *Double lai de la fragilité*. In this last case, scholars have debated whether Charles V was the intended recipient of the only luxury copy of the work; this study argues that the translation itself was surely undertaken on behalf of the Wise King, who died before its completion, and the codex in question bears witness to the turmoil caused by his sudden passing. A second corpus of poems chronicle the first two decades of Charles VI's reign and includes brief didactic poems treating issues of sovereign duty, lengthier works that contrast the reigns of father and son, and a selection of Deschamps's so-called solicitation poetry, which demands financial recompense related to his official court duties. The final constellation of poems, all originating in 1396, returns us to Deschamps's "book of memory" to examine Deschamps's antagonistic form of literary circulation, which gained full expression in these works.

Deschamps at the Court of Charles V

Deschamps's poetry speaks of a lifetime of service to the Valois dynasty dating back to the reign of John the Good. In one of his earliest datable poems, Ballade 249, the poet promises his services to King John. The poem celebrates the marriage of Margaret of Flanders and the king's youngest son, the newly named Duke Philip of Burgundy, which had been announced in 1364 and finalized in 1369, but Deschamps took this opportunity to wed himself to the dynasty when vowing faithful service to "Jehan mon seigneur et ses enfans touz trois" (John my lord and all three of his children) (B249, line 22).[6] His status as a royal servant is officially documented, however, only with Charles V's ascent to the throne.[7] This fact is also confirmed by the poet in two poems addressed to Charles VI in which the poet refers to his earlier services to the Wise King, Ballades 250 and 1206. In particular, in Ballade 250, Deschamps refers to himself in the third person as having begun his service under the previous king: "il ait vostre pere servi,/ Huissier d'armes jadis treslonguement" (he served your father as sergeant-at-arms since long ago) (B250, lines 2–3). Ballade 1206 provides even greater precision by calculating the years of Deschamps's uninterrupted service to the crown:

> ... xx. et .viii. ans, sanz partir,
> A servi a royal lignie
> Vo pere et vous (B1206, lines 12–14)
>
> (Twenty-eight years without a break, I served the royal line, your father and you)

In contrast to these references to his official service to the Wise King, Deschamps's corpus contains only eight poems that can be linked with certainty to Charles V. This thin corpus consists primarily of *poèmes de circonstance*[8] in which the poet relayed royal news to the king's subjects and extended family members. For example, Ballade 55 announces to Charles V's brothers the birth of the future Louis of Orléans.[9] A few works address political events dating to 1379, including coverage of the king's tour of inspection in the Vermandois (B144 and CR393) and of the shift of allegiance of the people of Brittany to the king of England (B157). In Ballade 144, the poet communicates to the townsman the king's appreciation of the region, while Ballade 157, which presents to the people of Brittany the king's vow to reclaim the territory, includes the poet's partisan counsel that the "peuple ingrat" (ungrateful people) of Brittany (B 157, line 1) "vien au bon Roy" (come to the good king) (B157, line 24) and "com vray subject remet tout en sa main" (as a true subject, put everything back in his hands) (B157, line 26). Deschamps's poems commemorating the death of Bertrand de Guesclin in 1380 deserve inclusion in this cluster as well since they echo Charles V's own intense admiration for the constable (B206, B207, R652). This small lyric corpus adopts a consistent stance: avoiding directly addressing Charles V, the poet adopts a self-effacing role as the royal porte-parole.[10]

In spite of the clear propagandistic content of this poetry, the king's support of his sergeant-at-arms poetic talents remains a mystery. The fact that neither Deschamps's poetry nor any of his contemporary versifiers figured in the king's library strongly suggests that such literary forays were not considered part of the *Sapientia* project. Nor did Deschamps give any indication in this occasional poetry that he participated in this project. In fact, one is hard pressed to find any reference in Deschamps's poetry dating from the Wise King's reign that refers to the sovereign's learned pursuits; instead, on the rare occasion when the poet speaks openly of Charles V's reign, he promotes a more traditional image of the warrior-king. However, it does appear that other works by Deschamps would have easily fit into the *Sapientia* project. We have already heard about the "book of memory" intended to memorialize the Valois dynasty by focusing on Charles V. That work has not survived, but another that suggests a strong affiliation with the king's *Sapientia* project is the *Double lai de la fragilité*, to which we now turn.

The *Fragilité* remains an enigmatic work in Deschamps's corpus, and questions concerning its intended recipient remain unresolved. These questions are driven by BnF, MS fr. 20029, a luxury copy of the work that openly expresses its own hesitation about the intended recipient. The codex opens with a frontispiece depicting the poet kneeling before an unidentified and unrecognizable king. In spite of a colophon that links the work's completion to the reign of Charles VI, Michael Camille persuasively argued that Charles V rather than Charles VI was the more likely intended recipient of this work. For Camille, the extended meditation on the decaying body and death central to this work best reflects the personal inclinations of Charles V in his final years, when he behaved "as a morbid hypochondriac."[11] There are, however, even more compelling reasons to associate this work with the Wise King. First, the *Fragilité* reflects the same intellectual and devotional interests that led Charles V to commission the *Voies de Dieu* from Deschamps's fellow sergeant-at-arms Jacques Bauchant.

Like Bauchant's work, the *Fragilité* is a vernacular translation of a devotional work, in this case, the popular Latin text by Lotari dei Conti di Segni, later Pope Innocent III, entitled *De Miseria humanae conditionis*, which had already been presented in prose translation to Charles V in 1372.[12] What sets Deschamps's translation apart from this other version is that his version represents a selective translation in verse form, a curious choice given Charles V's apparent disinterest in contemporary poetry. Adding to the uniqueness of the poeticized text is the highly original manuscript copy of the work unquestionably produced for a Valois king.

Measuring 270 × 185 millimetres and containing only twenty-four folios, BnF, MS fr. 20029 may initially strike the viewer as a modest object, but Geneviève Hasenohr has spotlighted the uniqueness of the manuscript layout, while Michael Camille qualified the codex as deserving "to be ranked alongside more famous contemporary productions like the *Grandes Heures* made for the duke of Berry and the *Grandes Chroniques* made for Charles V."[13] Moreover, the message communicated by the codex's layout deserves to be recognized as one of the most powerful visual expressions of Charles V's promotion of vernacular translations. Unlike any of the king's identified commissioned translations, MS fr. 20029 is a bilingual text whose layout relegates the original Latin to the margins and reserves centre stage for the verse translation. That is, in spite of ample space available on each folio, the Latin text is unnecessarily condensed into compact and heavily abbreviated passages that create an interpretative barrier between text and reader. In contrast to this unwelcoming layout of the Latin passages, the verse translation is given free rein to extend across an expansive first column. Line fillers and marginal pen flourishes spotlight the free-flowing vernacular text, in which the speaker's lament takes on far greater emotive qualities than afforded in the Latin original.[14] The innovativeness of the textual layout was further enhanced by a highly original and extensive miniature cycle decorating the *Fragilité*. MS fr. 20029 allots space for thirty miniatures, of which the completed twenty-eight pen-and-ink drawings (occasionally enhanced with colour washes) frequently contain two to six frames and sometimes span the full width of the page. The artist responsible for this cycle was none other than the *Master of Death*.[15] This artist became increasingly active at Charles V's court in the last years of his reign. According to Camille, the *Master of Death* participated in the decoration of thirty-seven codices, several of which were produced for Charles V's Louvre collection, including the above-mentioned earlier prose vernacular translation of *De Miseria humanae conditionis*, a copy of the *Grandes chroniques* (BnF, MS fr. 2813), and a copy of Oresme's translation of Aristotle's *Politiques* and *Ethiques* (private collection). For Deschamps's *Fragilité*, a highly original visual cycle was conceived, one that demands careful meditation from viewers, given its originality and its complex relationship to the verse it illustrates.[16] Yet another layer of luxury is provided by the elegant calligraphy, which is enhanced by red-and-blue ink flourishes that fill in opening initials. Such attention to the artistry of the work aligns this codex with the *de luxe* manuscripts collected during Charles V's reign.

The frontispiece to MS fr. 20029 adds substantially to the importance of this codex, although Camille described the frontispiece as "measly" in comparison to the dedication scenes typically found in Charles V's commissioned manuscripts.[17] Where Camille found only disappointment when gazing on the frontispiece, I am struck by the disquieting entry into the work that it affords readers due to both the content of the miniature and its *mise en page*. The frontispiece portrays a kneeling author with an oversize book before a seated crowned figure (Figure 4.1: BnF, MS fr. 20029, fol. 4v). Deschamps's first modern editor, the Marquis de Queux de Saint-Hilaire, speculated that the royal figure was Charles VI who was "en proie à quelqu'un de ces accès de mélancolie" (suffering from one of his melancholic fits).[18] Challenging this reading is Camille's later observation that given the closing rubric's dating of the codex to 1383, to view this illustration as referencing the king's madness requires us to believe that nine years in advance of his first attack, the king's illness was diagnosed – never mind the fact that madness was rarely portrayed in medieval art, and when done, was presented through an established iconography not exhibited in this image.[19] In contrast, we know that Charles V was sickly. Might the caved-in cheekbones and the emaciated and bowed body reflect the Wise King's ill health? While still harbouring some doubt, Camille would ultimately concur with the marquis's identification of the royal figure as Charles VI and conclude that the image appeared to have been "added as an afterthought in order to make [the codex] 'fit' its new patron,"[20] Charles VI. The identity of the enthroned king is still open to debate, and the recent work of Stephen Perkinson adds to the confusion surrounding this king's identity. In *Likeness of the King*, Perkinson makes apparent the greater importance given to sartorial distinctions and accoutrements rather than to physiological traits in visualizing an individual. In this regard, we need to take into serious account the king's clothing in this miniature. In the MS fr. 20029 frontispiece, the king dons scholastic robes, which echoes the frequent portrayal of Charles V in a similar costume in his commissioned manuscripts. Even if one persists in identifying the represented king as

Figure 4.1: Frontispiece to Eustache Deschamps, *Double lai de la fragilité*, Paris, Bibliothèque nationale de France, MS fr. 20029, fol. 4v.

Charles VI, it ought to be taken into account that the *Master of Death* might have deliberately imposed the former king's learned costume on his youthful replacement in an effort to cast his new sovereign as a worthy continuator of the Wise King's legacy.

To return to Camille's qualification of the frontispiece as "measly," we also need to factor in that it is not the miniature itself that disappoints; rather, it is its placement at the top of an otherwise empty page that disturbs the viewer. After all, miniatures of similar dimensions appear throughout this codex and other works by this master,[21] and it is not uncommon to find similar dimensions reserved for contemporary frontispieces.[22] We generally assume that a frontispiece would have been the last stage in manuscript production after the text had been transcribed. Nonetheless, this assumption does not preclude the possibility that this opening image was produced with the expectation of an introductory address to follow. This frontispiece strikes us as odd precisely because we seem to have fallen upon an incomplete paratextual framework. It is as if the folio still awaits a dedicatory address. Reinforcing this idea that MS fr. 20029 is missing this key paratextual element is that the crucial information one would expect to have found in this address – namely, the intended recipient's name – is lacking. As MS fr. 20029 opens with an image of a king that lacks an address identifying the sovereign, so too the codex closes with an explicit that, at least at an early stage, also faltered on the issue of the intended recipient's identity. When originally composed, the explicit in MS fr. 20029 communicated its own degree of uncertainty regarding the intended recipient's identity with another visual expression of gaping silence. Here follows the original text with abbreviations expanded and, most significantly, with blank spaces that would be filled in by a later hand indicated:

> Ci fine le livret de la fragile/ te de dumaine nature fait [et] com/ pile p[ar] maniere de double lay// p[ar] Eustace morel de v[er]tus es/ cuier [et] huissier darmes du/ roy charle le ___chastelain/ de fymes et a li presente le ___ jour davrilg après/ saintes pasques lan de/ grace n[ot]re s[eigneur] mil .ccc. qua/ tre vins [et]troys (fol. 21v)

> (Here finishes the *Book of the Fragility of Human Nature*, composed and compiled in the form of a double lay by Eustache Morel of Vertus, sergeant-at-arms of King Charles the ___, squire of Fimes and on this present ___ day of April after Easter in the year of our lord, 1383)

At an undisclosed later date, another scribe inserted the missing regnal roman numeral for the king as "le quint" (the fifth) and the day of presentation as 28 April. One can only speculate as to the cause of the original silence and the significance of the information later inserted. Does the initial silence reflect the poet's precarious state at the outset of Charles VI's reign, when his position as a sergeant-at-arms was in jeopardy?[23] If so, was the final decision to link Deschamps to the deceased king an indicator that he was no longer viewed as a royal servant? Or was the information meant to inspire a sense of obligation in the new king that he must honour his father's servant? Or did the reference have nothing to do with the poet and serve instead as a way of honouring the deceased king's inspirational role in this work? Finally, might we interpret the later addition of Charles V as an indirect acknowledgment that the current young king would take little personal interest in this work? As with the frontispiece to this codex, the explicit leaves the audience uncertain as to Deschamps's intended royal recipient. In the expected spaces where poet and scribe might have detailed a patronage history for this work, we gaze uncomfortably on palpable confusion and uncertainty.

Whereas the paratext to MS fr. 20029 fails to provide a stable narrative concerning the intended royal recipient of this codex, it leaves little room for confusion when it comes to identifying the author. In fact, the framing texts and illustrations in MS fr. 20029 stand out for their uncommon celebration of the vernacular author. Concerning the frontispiece, the sparse decoration of the room, the vastness of the architecture, and the measured application of colour washes, combined with the compact arrangement of the human participants, pull the reader's gaze towards the presentation scene. The column impedes our view of the king draws us more deeply into the image through the spatial depth it introduces. Therein, our gaze is directed to the kneeling poet and the disproportionately large book he holds. Contained in separate arched alcoves, poet and king are nonetheless linked via the book that is placed on the central axis. With the king and the attendants turned to the poet, so too our gaze moves quickly past the book to the poet's body, which is further enhanced by the artistic attention afforded it. Elegant lines fill out the poet's form and distinguish him from the crouched bodies of the king and his men. The *Master of Death* also includes several symbolic objects and distinctive artistic techniques to distinguish Deschamps. A baton held against his left shoulder identifies him as a sergeant-at-arms, while a crown of roses confirms his status as an accomplished poet. The poet's crown received uncommonly detailed attention to assure that it would stand out against the negative space framing the presentation scene. In contrast to the flat yellow colour wash used to enhance the king's diadem, the poet's crown is accentuated with heavy beads of red, white, and green paint to provide colour, weight, and texture. The *Master of Death* further assured that our gaze would be drawn to the poet by extending his foot outside the frame, a visual tactic that impresses on the reader the link between the book the poet holds and the parchment upon which he now appears. Finally, the oversized book that the *Master of Death* places in the poet's hands communicates the seriousness of the work, a point reinforced by the Latin rubric on the facing page, where Deschamps is identified by his learned role rather than by his court function: "m[a]g[is]t[ru]m Eustachi[um] Morelli de Virtute" (Master Eustache Morel of Virtus) (fol. 5r).

Even more striking is the closing illustration in MS fr. 20029, which precedes the final rubric that testifies to scribal hesitation concerning the identity of the royal subject. In contrast to this confused written account of royal involvement, the final image of the cycle foregoes depiction of earthly royalty to provide a new vision of exchange. This miniature precedes a closing prayer addressed to the Virgin. Here, Deschamps appears, once again, with the baton, and in place of his coloured crown of flowers he donned in the frontispiece, he now wears a belt highlighted with red

Figure 4.2: Poet kneeling before the Virgin Mary, Eustache Deschamps, *Double lai de la fragilité*, Paris, Bibliothèque nationale de France, MS fr. 20029, fol. 21v.

ink (Figure 4.2: BnF, MS fr. 20029, fol. 21v). In place of earthly royalty, the Virgin Mary appears before the kneeling poet. A rose placed in the Virgin's hand echoes the flowers of the poet's headdress and, now, the colouring of his belt. This visual resonance may have been intended to express ideas similar to Machaut's recent claims in his Prologue that his poetic talents were divinely bestowed (see previous chapter). What is certain is that the final miniature leaves open to interpretation whether the poet kneels in gratitude for gifts received by the Virgin or to beseech that she accept his versified prayer.

The exchange history of the *Fragilité* is further complicated by the absence of details concerning its actual circulation. The work never figured in the Louvre library inventory, and the original owner of MS fr. 20029 remains a mystery. Deschamps provided no clues for us to understand this case, either here or in other works. He never referenced this *lai* in later writings, nor did he discuss more generally any possible translation dealings with Charles V. His contemporaries, however, encourage us to imagine such a transaction. Beyond the involvement of a court-affiliated miniaturist and the scribe who eventually linked Deschamps to Charles V in the closing rubric, Philippe de Mézières deliberately associated Deschamps with Charles V's commissioned writers in his *Songe du Vieil Pelerin*, which he presented to Charles VI in 1389. When encouraging the young monarch to read the great works commissioned by his father, he listed the commissioned translations of Raoul de Presles and Denis Foulechat and then added: "tu puez bien lire aussi et ouyr les dictez vertueulx de ton serviteur et officier Eustache Morel" (you can also read and listen to the virtuous poetry of your servant and officer Eustache Morel).[24] For Philippe de Mézières, Deschamps, whose family name was Morel, belonged alongside the members of the Wise King's learned coterie and now merited recognition as a bridging figure between the reigns of father and son. In the end, little can be said with certainty regarding Deschamps's role as a writer and poet at the court of Charles V, although there is tantalizing evidence to suggest that he held a more elevated status than that of a mere poet of occasional verse. It may be that Deschamps participated in a movement at the king's court that continues to elude us, a movement that potentially sought to carve out space for original vernacular writings and, perhaps, even poetry, in the king's *Sapientia* project. Had Charles V lived even a few years longer and been able to examine MS fr. 20029, he would have discovered a radical example of the capacity of vernacular poetry to express spiritual, scientific, and political opinions. Such was not to be the case.

On 16 September 1380, the Wise King died, and the Valois dynasty worked quickly to assure the line by crowning a twelve-year-old king. For the next forty-two years, Charles VI would sit on the throne, but rarely would he rule. The ambitious textual-commissioning campaign of his father was one of many promising undertakings that evaporated seemingly overnight. The intellectual community that Charles V had fostered quickly dispersed in the days and months following his death. In contrast, Deschamps remained at the royal court. Much of his poetry registers his efforts to maintain a role for himself at court both as a sergeant-at-arms and as a moral voice. This same poetry, however, tracks his profound disappointment regarding the dramatic cultural shifts that transpired at court and of his failed attempts to convince the new king of the value of vernacular verse. Faced with what he perceived as a devaluation of knowledge and wisdom, Deschamps radically reconceptualized literary exchange dynamics over the course of his troubled dealings with Charles VI. No longer were writers dealing with a learned king who invested in knowledge; rather, they were confronted with a child who, at least as far as Deschamps was concerned, first needed to be schooled in the power of poetry.

Royal Patronage in Charles V's Wake

In August 1380, Charles V left Paris for Beauté-sur-Marne to convalesce, when his health took an unexpected turn for the worse, and on 16 September 1380, France lost its king. In the aftermath of Charles V's death, Deschamps hastily composed the previously mentioned Ballade 250, addressed to the new king, which begins, "Au Roy supplie Eustaces humblement" (Eustache humbly begs the king) (B250, line 1). As he would later do in Ballade 1125, the poet called attention to his extensive service to the dynasty. Once again, Ballade 250 dates Deschamps's service back to 1360 when he escorted Isabelle de France, Charles VI's aunt and daughter of Philip the Bold, to her marriage with Jean Galéas Visconti. He further affirms his sustained presence at court thereafter when declaring that he has served as "huissier d'armes jadis treslonguement" (sergeant-at-arms since long ago) (B250, line 3) and, then, more deliberately, when associating himself with the Valois dynasty, "vos ancesseurs a servi longuement" (your ancestors he has long served) (B250, line 11). This versified *curriculum vitae* was surely composed with the intent of persuading the young king to renew Deschamps's court position, a point explicitly articulated in the refrain that requests on behalf of "Eustace" that he "retenue ait et confirmacion"(be retained and confirmed) (B250, refrain). Positioning himself at the nexus of the royal line joining Charles VI to past Valois kings, Deschamps clearly hoped to be regarded as a pivotal member of the newly formed court. Beyond seeking to retain his position as sergeant-at-arms, Deschamps used Ballade 250 to assert his status as a learned poet who could inform, comfort, and support a child-king found too early in the seat of authority and unprepared for the ensuing political machinations. In fact, this poem can be aligned with a constellation of poems rapidly penned in the immediate aftermath of Charles V's passing. These compositions include two works lamenting the passing of Charles V (to be associated with what Clotilde Dauphant refers to as a "cycle" related to Charles VI's coronation),[25] a lyric prayer addressed to the Virgin Mary in the young monarch's voice, and several lengthier poems that read like a crash course in leadership for a child-king. Deschamps, however, was writing in a vacuum. For with Charles V's passing, so too evaporated interest in intellectual pursuits.[26]

Court records post-dating Charles V's death testify to an abrupt ending of royally sanctioned intellectual life. It is impossible to know how many writers and artisans were carrying out book commissions at the time of the king's death, but what is clear is that learned activity came to a sudden halt even though we know that Charles V's predilection for texts had far from waned in his final years. For instance, upon completing his *Cité*, Raoul de Presles received a second commission for a new translation of the Bible. Presles was surely hard at work on this project when the king passed, and yet he abandoned the project soon thereafter. There is also reason to believe that Simon de Hesdin was in the midst of his translation of Valerius Maximus's *Facta et dicta memorabilia* at the time of the king's death because even though the opening rubrics to the royal copy date it to 1375, Hesdin begins the prologue on a mournful tone, in which he bemoans the pointlessness of writing a typical dedication given the "brieveté et fragilité de ceste douleureuse vie temporele, la constance de l'inconstance et variabilité de fortune" (brevity and fragility of this painful terrestrial life, the certainty of uncertainty and the variability of fortune).[27] Such a declaration to forego praise of his king seems odd unless motivated by the king's recent death. The accompanying frontispiece to this codex encourages us to believe that at least the prologue postdated Charles V's death since the translator is depicted attempting to pass his book to the king across a pronounced territorial divide. That neither Presles nor Hesdin completed their translations substantiates suspicions that the court witnessed a swift collapse of the *Sapientia* project.[28] While true that these two men, as well as Nicole Oresme and Jean Daudin, died three years after Charles V's passing, other commissioned writers simply disappear from history. Where information on Charles V's commissioned writers is available, it usually points to writers having abandoned literary activity after 1380. Jean Golein, the most prolific of Charles V's writers, for instance, completed his last known commissioned translation, the *Information des princes*, in 1379 and then appears in records only because of his diplomatic service to Clément VII.[29] Similarly, Mézières immediately retired to the Convent of the Celestines in 1380, while Pierre d'Orgemont, responsible for the *Grandes chroniques*, abandoned this project and headed to Méry.[30] These last two men did eventually re-enter royal service, and, exceptionally, Mézières returned to writing to compose for Charles VI the *Songe du Vieil Pelerin* between 1386 and 1389.

This halt in royal commissioning of writings following Charles V's death was surely motivated by Charles VI's preference for the battlefield over book learning. In fact, the young king spent much of his first years quelling uprisings provoked both by the new tax policies implemented just prior to his father's death and by his uncles' political machinations.[31] This is not to say that the young Charles ignored entirely the royal collection. Records show that he removed several works from the Louvre library, of which a good portion dealt with chivalric romance and adventure.[32] These last works appear to have deeply informed Charles VI's court, where events were often cast in an aura of romance inspired by the Arthurian literature he preferred. For example, the young king's adoption of the flying stag as his emblem linked him to this mythical world of romance and he also drew freely from these fictions when organizing tournaments and celebrations linked to May Day, birthdays, as well as the new queen's entry into Paris.[33] In this sense, the royal library functioned more as a resource and inspiration for entertainment at the court of Charles VI than as a dynastic treasure. This downgrading of the royal library's importance helps explain the new king's failure to protect the collection. Approximately 150 works listed in the 1380 inventory of the collection disappeared over the early years of Charles VI's reign. Many of these losses were due to the royal uncles, who pilfered the collection to fill their own libraries.[34] The duke of Anjou alone took ownership of approximately forty books after his father's death.[35] Charles VI proved no better than his uncles in this regard since he regularly turned to the royal library for gifts: for example, in 1381, he presented the duchess of Burgundy with gifts of his father's books, including a *Légende dorée*, a French Bible, a volume of Arthurian works, and a book of hours.[36] Much is made of the fact that the 1411 library inventory documents the addition of 210 books to Charles V's collection; yet more than half of these acquisitions were copies of Latin writings, a fact that counters the keystone of the *Sapientia* project to promote the vernacularisation of knowledge.[37] This later inventory does, however, show that Charles VI paid at least for the production of two books of hours,[38] and that his reign also saw the return of several works once owned by Valois rulers, some even garnering royal signatures of past kings.[39] Otherwise, only two translations of Latin writings into the vernacular entered the royal library during Charles VI's reign,[40] and only four entries document new or recent compositions.[41] Curiously, major works addressed to Charles VI, including writings by Deschamps, Mézières, Christine de Pizan, and Pierre Salmon, do not figure in either the 1411 or 1423 library inventories.

In spite of abandoning the active role his father had assumed within the book community, Charles VI clearly inspired vernacular writers. Jacques Krynen speaks of an "intensification" of political writings during this period,[42] and Jean Devaux goes so far as to refer to this period as having witnessed "un essor artistique sans précédent" (an artistic development without precedent).[43] Regardless of his intellectual disengagement, Charles VI frequently received unsolicited writings presented as advice literature for assuring good government. One of the earliest such works suggests a deliberate effort to revive earlier models of learning; in 1385, Robert Gervais, Bishop of Senez, presented Charles VI with a new Latin Mirror of Princes, the *Speculum morale regium*, that made no pretence of figuring as a continuation of the previous king's vernacular campaign. Apart from Gervais, however, most authors presented unsolicited vernacular writings to Charles VI only after his 1388 declaration of personal rule. We date to this period two important compositions: Bovet's second redaction of the *Arbre de batailles* and Mézières's *Songe du Vieil Pelerin*, both of which explicitly sought to council the young king at this crucial transitional moment.[44] Mézières declares in his lengthy prologue that he, the "Vieil Pelerin," desires to present this work to Charles VI, identified by his chosen emblem, the "Cerf Volant," precisely because he has finally declared independent rule:

> Le Vieil Pelerin doncques au derrain quartier de sa vie, foible arquemiste bien garny de ignorance et de toute fragilite, en l'esperance de l'aide de la tresdoulce Vierge Marie, a revele son songe et par escript presente au jeune Cerf Volant, dignement sacre et couronne des blanches fleurs dorees, et roy tout seul du royaume de France, son souverain seigneur temporal et naturel.[45]
>
> (The Old Pilgrim in the last quarter of his life, a weak swordsman defined by ignorance and all forms of fragility, with the hope of aid from the very gentle Virgin Mary, revealed his dream and, through writing, presents it to the young Flying Stag, rightly invested and crowned with golden white flowers, and king all alone of the kingdom of France, her sovereign temporal and natural lord.)

Similarly, Bovet informs Charles VI that he has undertaken "to compose some new things" (faire aucunes nouvelles choses) so that

> vostre jeunesse soit informée de plusieurs entendemens de la sainte Escripture et d'aultre part afin que vostre volonté soit de plus en plus en pensée de faire et donner secours à la sainte foy de Jhesucrist ...[46]
>
> (your youth might be informed by much wisdom contained in Scripture and, also, so that your desire be increasingly oriented toward helping the sacred faith of Jesus Christ ...)

Both men entered the king's service thereafter, and Bovet's works were among the rare new vernacular compositions added to the Louvre library during Charles VI's reign.[47]

While Charles VI's declaration of personal rule stimulated new writings, his first mental crisis in 1392 put an end to this literary activity. Thereafter, the rare author who addressed the king folded the sovereign into a collective of noble readers identified as privileged addressees. As for royal commissions of new vernacular works, one must wait two decades before the king's secretary, Pierre Salmon, would claim in 1409 to have composed his *Dialogues* at the king's request.[48] As Anne D. Hedemen has observed, however, Salmon "diminishes the king's role" because "unlike his father, Charles VI was not an active participant in the project."[49] In spite of identifying his work as a commission, Salmon presents his book as an unsolicited gift in the prologue, adding that although his "don" [gift] is not typical of the material treasures offered a king,[50] he hopes, nonetheless, that the king will agree to "le visiter et estudier de fois à autre" (to frequent it and study it from time to time).[51] Striking is the difference between Salmon's defence of his book offering and the efforts of Charles V's commissioned writers to identify their gifts as worthy – and clearly appreciated – gifts.

Against this backdrop Deschamps cuts a curious profile. At least over the first sixteen years of Charles VI's reign, Deschamps persisted as no other writer would in his efforts to engage the young king in a literary exchange that he believed would benefit his sovereign by guiding him in moral, political, spiritual, and historical issues. As noted, Deschamps lost no time in addressing the king in lyric form. Following that initial address to the newly crowned young king, Deschamps produced numerous works directed to Charles VI through the early bouts of madness and even when the poet later transferred to Louis of Orléans's household. Let us turn to Deschamps's early poetry addressed to Charles VI to examine his initial efforts to maintain a sustained poetic presence at the royal court, before taking into account the ensuing altered exchange paradigm he presented years later.

"Or pran garde a la dureté ... que je diray": Deschamps and the Young King Charles VI

To appreciate the importance of Deschamps's threat in 1396 to abandon his "book of memory," one needs to examine his early writings directed to Charles VI. Three prominent lyric categories emerge in the poetry that

Deschamps wrote for Charles VI during the first two decades of his reign. They are 1) *poésie de circonstance*, modelled on poetry composed for the previous monarch; 2) advice poetry that sought to inform and educate the young king; and 3) supplication poetry that argued for positions, funds, and rights deemed by Deschamps to be his rightful due because of his official service to the crown. This poetry sketches out dramatically different dynamics from the discourse of literary engagement authored by Charles V's commissioned writers. Over the course of these works addressed to the young king, Deschamps would radically rethink his relationship to the sovereign and the purpose of his poetic gift. He would imagine a new literary economy in which he occupied the role of a donor in possession of a dangerous and unwanted gift, whereas the king, much in the spirt of Machaut's disgruntled *Confort* reader, assumed the role of an unwilling and ungrateful recipient.

Deschamps's early addresses to Charles VI reveal him occupying the same role he had with Wise King: that is, as a porte-parole who produced *poésie de circonstance* advertising and celebrating important events at the royal court. Poems in this category celebrate the birth of Charles VI's sons (B81, B273, V759, and B1142), the king's birthday (B77), as well as royal festivities and jousting tournaments (B362, B444, B501, and B521). A slight difference between occasional poems and those addressed to the former king is the increased presence of the poet's personal views. In a constellation of *poèmes de circonstance* that Clotilde Dauphant calls the "cycle de l'avènement de Charles VI," for instance, the poet inserts himself into the royal narrative. Dauphant's cycle includes nine ballades that she dates to around 1380.[52] Three of these poems deal directly with Charles V's death, while one looks forward to the new era marked by Charles VI's coronation. As is to be expected, the three ballades on the king's passing, Ballade 164 to Ballade 166, speak of the kingdom's great loss and commemorate the deceased king's accomplishments. Thus, France first appears as a "vefve" (widow) (B164, line 9) and "orpheline" (orphan) (B164, line 17), while the next poem evokes the sorrow experienced by the "François jeunes et anciens/ Par le trespas du roy Charles le Saige" (both young and old Frenchmen due to the passing of King Charles the Wise) (B165, lines 9–10). The Wise King is remembered for his wisdom, for his success in reconquering territories, and for amassing wealth as well as building castles (B165, lines 13–15). Ballade 166 details the specific regrets of royal servants. As with the previous ballade, Deschamps reserves particular praise for deceased king's royal investment in institutions (B166, lines 21–6), and he further celebrates Charles V's largesse and benevolence towards servants (B166, lines 8–9). In closing, the Celestin monks are reminded to pray for the soul of their protector (B166, lines 28–30).

In other poems linked with the Wise King's passing, Deschamps shifted the gaze to consider the new king and, in so doing, took advantage of the opportunity to cultivate a new poetic identity. In Ballade 168 of the cycle, the poet reorients his audience to introduce Charles VI to his people. Here, the king's name etymologically assures that "li jeunes roys" (the young king) (B168, line 4) already possesses the expected qualities of a leader. The poet reserves special praise for the young king's success in retaining the throne in the face of an English threat. This inaugural sovereign act bodes well for ultimate victory over the king of England, identified here as a leopard:

En .xiii.e an vient a seignourier,
Et a garder son regne des Anglois,
Et si ami le veulent bien aidier,
Vuidier fera le lieppart de son bois. (B 168, lines 17–20)

(In his thirteenth year, he became lord and protected his kingdom from the English and if his friends want to help him, he will rid his woods of the leopard.)

In this brief passage, Deschamps shifts from providing an ideal moral portrait of the new leader to recording the hope that this new reign will augur the end of war. Peace throughout the land looms large among expectations and is articulated as both a prayer and a prophecy: "Or lui doint Dieux bien achever sa guerre!" (May God allow him to bring a successful end to his war!) (B168, refrain). This shift from promoting events, as was common in Deschamps's *poésie de circonstance*, to interjecting prophecies and prayer announces the poet's ambitions to contribute to shaping the king's royal identity. For instance, the final stanza of Ballade 168 extends the command in Ballade 166 that the monks pray for their deceased king to call on everyone to pray for the new sovereign according to the poet's instruction. Deschamps calls for prayers to end of the war with England:

Prions en tuit, crions a haulte voix:
Or lui doint Dieux bien achever sa guerre! (B168, lines 23–4)

(Let us all pray, let us cry out with loud voices: may God allow him to bring a successful end to his war!)

Ballade 168 makes clear what the poet has to offer the new king. First, as a mediator, Deschamps can communicate to the people an ideal portrait of the young king. Second, breaking with his previous practice of self-effacement, Deschamps positions himself as a moral voice prepared to assist his king.

Although not identified as part of Dauphant's "cycle du couronnement," Chanson Royale 338 merits being read alongside these writings because it documents similar efforts to position the poet as a moral and spiritual guide to the newly crowned sovereign. The poet begins by describing a worthy king as one who "doit estre benigne,/ Misericors, doulz et plain de pité" (must be benevolent, merciful, sweet and full of pity) (CR338, lines 3–4). This list of appropriate characteristics and practices of the ideal king culminates with the naming of great men who "tint ceste discipline" (held this practice) (CR338, line 41), including illustrious leaders ranging from Hector and David to Arthur and Charlemagne. Turning directly to the intended noble audience, the poet counsels:

> Princes et roys de bon entendement,
> Qui avez prins vostre couronnement
> Faictes lire ma chançon pluseurs foys
> Se bien y a, faites le doucement,
> Et lors serez en vo gouvernement
> Preux et vaillant, doulz, larges et courtois (CR338, lines 51–6)
>
> (Worthy prince and king who has taken the crown, have read aloud my song multiple times and if done, do so thoughtfully and, as a result, you will rule with courage and valiance, gentleness, largesse, and courtesy)

In this manner, Chanson Royale 338 explicitly points to Deschamps's poetry as assuring the king's greatness, not simply by advertising his successes but also by communicating lessons that, through study and repetition, can shape the royal consciousness.

Deschamps was even more deliberate in articulating a new role for himself eight years later when Charles VI declared independent rule. Chanson Royale 1353 provides a scripted prayer in the young king's voice. Rather than celebrate the king's newfound power, the prayer emphasizes Charles VI's vulnerability and need for both spiritual and moral guidance. The prayer opens with the king voicing intellectual and physical shortcomings – "Juenes de sens et po puissans de corps" (young in wisdom and of little physical strength) (CR1353, line 1) – followed by an acknowledgment of his complete isolation and lack of guidance – "sanz pere … sanz mere … sanz amis" (without father … without mother … without friends) (CR1353, lines 6–7). Like the "widowed" and "orphaned" France of the earlier Ballade 164, the child-king is now portrayed as an orphan who neither has "parent ne parente,/ N'amour n'a lieu" (father nor mother, love nowhere to be found) (CR1353, lines 13–14). Development of his social isolation dominates the third stanza, in which both his people and his enemies are described as opposing him: "Mon peuple est dur et mes ennemis fors" (my people are harsh and my enemies strong) (CR1353, line 17). The next two stanzas generate an allegory of the struggles that led him to declare personal rule in 1388. In the final stanza, Charles VI voices a promise to protect his people: "un seul pastour sera, tel est m'entente" (a single pastor there will be, such is my intent) (CR1353, line 39). In the envoy, however, the poetic voice emerges to call attention to the king's precarious state; Charles VI is depicted as "a la moitié mors" (half dead) (CR1353, line 41) due to the overwhelming discord of his regime. The poet blames the situation on the king's uncles, who oversaw the kingdom: "ly regent mainent vie envieuse" (the regents lead a selfish life) (CR1353, line 43). In the final lines of the envoy, Deschamps joins Charles VI by adopting the king's plea of the refrain as his own to plead directly to the Virgin Mary to protect him: "Secourez moy, Vierge tresprecieuse!" (Help me, most precious Virgin!) (CR1353, refrain). This scripted prayer gives expression to a new intimacy between poet and king. It recognizes the king's vulnerability and inexperience and proposes the poet as one who joins him in his hopes and who can provide the guidance he needs. Whereas Charles V's writers had offered their king intellectual friendship, Deschamps modelled in this poem a new arrangement between a young king and a wizened poet whose voices and desires united in prayer on behalf of the kingdom.

The "Lay du roy," also likely composed around 1388, provides an even more explicit poetic declaration of Deschamps's interest in counselling the king. This poem plays off of the conventional language that had become common fare in works dedicated to the previous monarch to sketch out the new relationship binding poet and king. Deschamps begins by identifying his status in the third person as a "subgiez a son Roy/ Et son seignour" (subject of his king and his lord) (L311, lines 5–6) to whom he offers the present work – "Prandre en gré et ma clamour/ Retenir" (accept and keep in mind my cry) (L311, lines 13–14). The poem references the king's "grand benignité" (great kindness) (L311, line 23), which the poet then links to his own history at court of being "nourris" (taken care of/nourished) (L311, line 26). The fourth stanza, however, adopts an unexpected tone to issue a warning for what follows: "Or pran garde a la durté/ ... / Que je diray" (But beware of the severities [...] that I will pronounce) (L311, lines 33–5). The poet thereafter abandons the ritualistic rhetoric of praise to speak bluntly of the challenges the young king has already faced and the poet's responsibility to teach the king about "the ways of honour, courage and valour":

> Prince, pour la grant honnour,
> La reverence et amour,
> L'obeissance et cremour
> Que je te doy,
> Comme subgiez a son roy
> Et son seignour
> Naturelment, mon labour
> Met et employ
> A t'y descripre le ploy
> D'onneur, de prouesce et foy
> Et de valour (L311, lines 1–11)

> (Prince, because of the great honour, reverence, love, obedience, and fear that I owe you as a subject of his king and natural lord, I put my labour and my efforts to describing for you the ways of honour, courage, faith and valour)

By identifying this poem and its message as a duty owed his king, Deschamps made apparent his dependence on the well-established line of thought promoted by Charles V's commissioned writers. As noted in chapter 2, commissioned writers during the previous reign frequently sought to convert the king's order into an offering that emphasized the labour they willingly undertook on his behalf. Deschamps appropriates a similar rhetoric to dramatically different ends. He acknowledges in this poem that he was neither asked to compose this work, nor did he expect its grateful acceptance. Deschamps anticipates that the king might, in fact, take offence at his unsolicited advice. He offers it to him ("prandre en gré"), all the while advising the king to brace himself ("pran garde") for what follows. Similarly, while Deschamps may adopt the language of subordination and fear – "reverence," "obeisance et cremour" – to position his poetry as an unsolicited offering, he also qualifies his poetry as a duty.

He "labours" poetically on behalf of his king so that Charles might learn of his own responsibility to reign with "honour, courage, faith and valour." The poem thereafter lists the king's duties, which range from being truthful, loyal, and just to practising moderation in dress, wine, and entertainment. These royal obligations figure as orders rather than as suggestions: "Soit Vérité en ta bouche" (let there be truth in your mouth) (L311, line 85), "Soies au mauvais crueux,/ Aux debonnaires piteux;/ Fay tes chasteaux retenir" (be ruthless with the bad; understanding with those who are good; hold on to your castles) (L311, lines 115–17), "Vis selon ta revenue" (live according to your means) (L311, line 125). Perhaps most striking, given Charles VI's penchant for frequent festivities, the poet counsels him to refrain from celebration until peace is achieved:

Et comme tu paix aras,
Jouster, tournoier pourras
Et mener vie joieuse,
Dancier et chanter feras,
Et autre heure chaceras
Et menrras vie amoureuse. (L311, lines 200–5)[53]

(And when you have peace, you will be able to joust, participate in tournaments, and live a joyous life, dance and sing you shall, and, at another time, you shall hunt and lead an amorous life.)

The poet makes clear in this passage that the king's duties ought to precede his pursuit of pleasure. At the outset of the "Lay du roy," Deschamps relied heavily on conventional gifting language that, effectively, drew the king into a binding arrangement in which he had little choice other than to accept the text. Once accepted, the text obliges the king to abide by the poet's counsel or risk being exposed as an unworthy leader. Deschamps's poem then communicates a series of ultimatums that are loosely disguised warnings and firm counsel on appropriate royal conduct. Through this lay, Deschamps makes explicit the extent to which literary dynamics shifted with the rise of Charles VI. No longer did royal desire drive writing; instead, the poet's duty obliged him to speak out.

Deschamps's approach to poetry as a moral duty to expose the political and intellectual setbacks linked to Charles VI marks two additional works composed in the years leading up to the young king's declaration of independent rule in 1388.[54] These two lengthy texts, the "Lay de Franchise" (L307) and the "Fiction de l'aigle" (L1189), present a strong critique of royal affairs that addresses concerns ranging from the king's youth and need for instruction (and reprimand) to the problematic Flanders campaigns, to the financial disarray, bureaucratic collapse, and political struggles of the early years of the reign. These poems also allude to the loss of authority and respect owed to the wise men who have been cast off by the new court. On this last issue, the poet expresses his disillusionment with the court of Charles VI most powerfully by contrasting contemporary realities with the previous reign. In the case of the "Lay de Franchise," the poet sets out on a beautiful spring day for a walk in the countryside that leads him to physical remnants of Charles V's reign. As Miren Lacassagne has observed, the setting likely references the royal domains of Vincennes and Beauté-sur-Marne, both of which were projects funded by Charles V.[55] The poet eventually takes refuge behind a bush to enjoy the songbirds, only to have his reveries interrupted by a "grant bruit" (great noise) (L307, line 145) that troubles his thinking – "ma memoire troublée" (my thinking is troubled) (L307, line 147). The noise turns out to be the sounds of jousting from the valley below, and when a raucous group of men and ladies pass, the poet identifies the source to be the king's May Day festivities (L307, lines 149–56). The retinue stops in front of the poet's hideout, thereby allowing the poet to view the king, whom he describes as "plus bel, plus doulz de maniere acesmée,/ .xvi. ans lui pot bien Nature donner" (very handsome, very well mannered, and well dressed, 16 years old would Nature give him) (L307, lines 151–2). He further observes the exchange of gifts, May Day promises, the performance of minstrels, and the laying out of fine fabrics in anticipation of a copious banquet. Contrary to expectations, however, the poet takes the first opportunity to scamper away like an animal from his hiding place ("De mon buisson sailli comme une beste," "from my bush, I ran like an animal," L307, line 261). His evasion leads him to an alternative scene of May Day celebrations conducted by Robin and Marion, who commemorate the day with gentle song, water, and simple bread. The poet approves of this scene, whereas he harshly judges the lifestyle of courtiers. Even more striking than this final contrast between court life and that of Robin and Marion are the differences between the two reigns detailed at the poem's outset.

That the setting of the "Lay de Franchise" concerns the two renovated chateaux that served as retreats from the Louvre palace during Charles V's reign is all the more important given the language Deschamps adopts to describe these spaces and their history. The poet refers to Charles V as the creator of the buildings only through reference to his qualities of power and wisdom (L307, line 80). When describing the first chateau, likely

Vincennes, Deschamps qualifies it as "grant" (big), "fort" (strong), and "riche" (rich) (L307, lines 69–71) and, most notably, he marvels over its structure, which encourages study and a sense of safety: "Chascune tour sembloit une abbaie,/ Assault ne craint ne siege ne saillie" (Each tower was like an abbey, no assault, no siege, no attack was feared) (L307, lines 84–5). These safe spaces are then "fermé de merveilleus pouoir" (enclosed in marvellous power) (L307, lines 67–8) by the large park joining Vincennes and Beauté-sur-Marne. It is against this formidable backdrop displaying the power and vision of the past king that the young king prances into view. As Susanna Bliggenstorfer aptly describes his appearance in the poem, Charles VI represents a "destinataire très peu visible" (recipient only slightly visible).[56] To be more precise, Charles VI enters the lay as a glimmering mirage emerging from the noises and the riches that surround him (L307, ll. 146–82). More importantly, by the end of the poem, the young king functions as a mere phantom who scarcely merits a dedication. The two-line dedication addressed to Charles VI constitutes an abrupt end to the lay. Moreover, given that Deschamps adopts the third person to reference the king, even the conventional language of gifting cannot mask the obvious distance now established between poet and king:

Or lui suppli que sa douce semblance
Reçoive en gré ce lay au departir (L307, lines 311–12)

(So I request of him that his sweet semblance willingly receive this lay in parting)

As with the "Lay du roy," the "Lay de Franchise" uses gifting discourse not to reflect a partnership but to highlight a deliberate resistance to exchange. Rather than use his poetry to forge an intellectual partnership, Deschamps expresses his sense of exclusion and isolation as well as his desire to break ties with the king.

The "Fiction de l'aigle" pushes further the negative comparison of the reigns of Charles V and Charles VI. It communicates this message through a less-than-subtle allegorical tale about the transfer of power from an eagle, a clear reference to Charles V,[57] to his young heir, who is ill equipped for the job. Deschamps's tale begins by detailing the organization and practices at the Eagle's court before announcing that while having achieved "celle grant prosperité,/ ... ce bien, ... celle unité" (this great prosperity, ... this good, ... this unity) (L1189, lines 195–6), the Eagle's sudden death leaves "un jeusne hoir en son herité" (a young heir as his inheritor) (L1189, line 199). The young Eagle proves poorly positioned to perpetuate his father's successes, a failure that the poet blames primarily on the poor counsel the son receives from greedy court members. Nonetheless, the poet holds the young king responsible for the "destruction de pays" (destruction of the land) (L1189, line 283). When all is lost, the young Eagle finally turns to the "vielz oyseaulx" (old birds) (L1189, line 323) for help. Their counsel allows Deschamps to address the many failures he has witnessed at the royal court while also providing him the opportunity to advise the young ruler to study the worthy model provided by his father's legacy:

> Tu vois les traces de ton pere,
> Dont la vie fut belle et clere,
> Et comment il fu veritable:
> Or fay que sa vertu appere
> En toy, car filz ne degenere,
> Par nature, de son semblable (L1189, lines 511–16)
>
> (You see the traces of your father whose life was beautiful and transparent and how he was truthful: make it that his virtue appears in you, because a son does not normally lose the qualities of his ancestors)

Because this poem provides a clear record of the father's legacy, his "traces," the poet concludes with the advice that the son use this very work to recall his father's reign:

> Je croy que je tairoy a tant
> Mon chastoy, car en recitant
> De ton bon pere le sçavoir,
> Est assez cler en apparant
> En quel guise il fut gouvernant,
> Tant qu'il estoit riches d'avoir,
> Or fay donc ton sens apparoir,
> Selon son fait, d'or en avant,
> Et se tu lis ce dit souvent
> Tu en deveras mieulx valoir (L1189, lines 541–50)
>
> (I think I will silence my critiques for now because in reciting the wisdom of your good father, it is obvious his method of governing, so wealthy

was he in qualities. So make it that your understanding reflects his actions from here on out and if you read this *dit* often, you should be more worthy of it)

For the second time in forty lines, the poet has counselled the king to behave more like his father – to be his father's "semblable" and to "reflect" (apparoir) on his father's actions. As already witnessed in the Chanson Royale 338, Deschamps, here again, directs the king to find wisdom in his poetry. The pronoun "en" in line 550 used to identify what Charles VI will gain in studying this poem is sufficiently ambiguous as to suggest that he might earn access to his father's wisdom or, more provocatively, that he might merit similar poetry written for him.

Deschamps was not shy in pairing the capacity for poetry to provide needed advice with its role in securing a man's fame. In an undated ballade on the importance of memory, the poet stresses that writing, sculpture, and painting all serve to assure that the dead are remembered:

Mais Memoire, qui tant a proufité
Par le moien de lettre et d'escripture,
Et figurer de taille ou en painture
...
Font après mort congnoistre creature (Ballade 967, lines 5–9)

(Memory, which has so greatly benefited from letters and writing and sculpture and painting, assures that after death, men are known)

In the *Miroir de mariage*, Deschamps elaborates on this point when blaming ungifted writers for forgotten great men:

Et certes maint vaillant baron,
Maint chevalier et maint servent,
Qui furent ou temps cy devant
Preux, hardiz et batillereux,
Conquerans et chevalereux,
Sont mis en oubli tout a plain
Par la faulte d'un escripvain;
Pour ce que ceuls qui depuis furent
N'en escriprent pas ce qu'ils durent (lines 8074–82)

(It is true that many worthy barons, many knights and many servants, who in the past were courageous, strong, pugnacious, victorious, and knightly, have been completely forgotten because of a writer, because men of the past failed to write works that would endure)

As we shall see, besides the risk of writers failing to compose worthy works that would commemorate the achievements of great men, Deschamps revealed an even greater threat for leaders – that the poet might memorialize unacceptable behaviour and practices. This theme takes shape in several of Deschamps's commonly labelled supplication poems. In these works in which the king's sergeant-at-arms requested funds owed for his past services, Deschamps wielded poetry as a powerful weapon that could cause great harm to the king's reputation. In these writings, a new model of literary exchange is developed, one in which poetry functions as a dangerous gift.

Poisoned Poetry

Over the course of Charles VI's reign, Deschamps's poetics shifted in important ways that recall the fundamentally ambivalent nature of the gift, which Mauss points out communicates at its etymological core the notion of "poison."[58] This double function of poetry as both a gift and a curse is most apparent in Deschamps's so-called supplication poems addressed to Charles VI, in which the poet registers the failures of his superiors to honour financial and material promises and obligations. In these poems, shaming emerges as a powerful counter-threat to Charles VI's failures to satisfy his debts to Deschamps for his services as a sergeant-at-arms and bailiff. In separate studies, Susanna Bliggenstorfer and James Laidlaw have offered compelling evidence that these poetic demands played an important role in Deschamps's real-life pursuit of reimbursement, recompense, and renewal of positions over the years.[59] Laidlaw, in particular, has brought attention to the inclusion of some of Deschamps's supplication ballades in court records as supporting matter for the poet's officially registered complaints.[60] In addition to effecting change in the poet's daily life, this poetry also orchestrated a startling reversal of expected literary exchange dynamics. In these poems, Deschamps explicitly stated that the pursued recompense was no more related to his poetic service than these poems represented gift offerings. Instead, poetry serves in these cases as a vehicle to communicate the author's needs and desires as much as his right to speak out against the moral shortcomings of his addressees. In these instances, Deschamps's poems issued both orders and potential curses directed to superiors. The "supplication" poems reveal time and again that should leaders fail to abide the poet's advice, the poet could just as easily use his words to unmake as to make their reputations.

To return to Ballade 250, in which Deschamps advertised his long service to the royal family on the eve of Charles V's death, poetry serves to communicate the writer's needs rather than satisfy royal desire. In the final lines of the envoy, the poet announces this radical reversal of literary dynamics. Here, the poet reverses the language of the commission to call for a royal order that would secure his court position. Again, speaking of himself in the third person, Deschamps requests that the king decree the renewal of his court position:

Or soit par vous commandé
Sa lettre aussi com nouveau don donné,
Et qu'om le paye sanz contradicion,
Et de grace que le povre brullé [i.e., Eustace]
Retenue ait et confirmacion (B250, lines 26–30)

(Let his letter be ordered by you as a new gift given and let it be paid without hesitation and let it be, by grace, that the poor burnt man be retained and confirmed)

Deschamps couches his request to retain his position in an overtaxed language of gifting, one that identifies the king's potential generosity as a "nouveau don donné." Far from crediting Charles VI as a generous giver of gifts, however, the requested "gift" is configured as reparations for previous injustices ("le paye sanz contradicion"). By identifying himself here as "le povre brullé" – a disturbing allusion to the loss of his lands in Vertus due to fire during a chevauchée in August of 1380, a month before Charles V's death – Deschamps thus labels himself as someone scarred by previous royal gifts of land and service.[61] In this respect, this request for the new king's aid serves to correct a past exchange gone awry rather than represent a new cycle of giving with the young sovereign. Stated otherwise, the gift requested of Charles VI early in his reign already figures as a due. Deschamps's highly original gift account(ing), in this instance, reverses convention in other ways as well. First, he positions the king as answerable to the poet's commission/command ("Or soit par vous commandé"). Then, he announces that what he desires from the king is nothing less than a royal text authored by him; that is, a "letter" of confirmation that would secure Deschamps's reinstatement as a sergeant-at-arms.

In yet another poem addressed to Charles VI that registers the king's debt to Deschamps, the poet recalls his incessant travel as a royal messenger over the previous five years. The poem details Deschamps's tireless efforts to receive his due for service as a sergeant-at-arms:

Il a cinq ans que mes corps ne cessa
De poursuir, d'impetrer mandemens
Boiste porter puis de la, puis de ça
Et s'avez fait pluseurs commandemens
Aux generaulx, de bouche et par voz gens,
Que de voz dons fusse sactifiez,
Dont riens n'ont fait, dont pas je ne suy liez (B1168, lines 1–3)

(It has been five years that my body has not stopped searching and soliciting orders transported in boxes first here, then there, and regardless of whether you ordered several times the generals, whether in person or by your people, that I receive your gifts, nothing has been done. About this, I am far from pleased)

In this ballade, the poet complains of having not yet received reward for his service. No one has done anything about his situation, the poet explains later, because he has been forgotten: "je suy touz oubliez" (I am completely forgotten) (B1168, line 9). The refrain, however, blames the poet himself because he naively believed promises made: "En si faiz dons mauvais fier se fet" (According to the facts, it is foolish to place one's trust in gifts) (B1168, refrain). Beyond registering such a biting complaint that insinuates the untrustworthiness of the king's promise, the structure and homophonic play of the refrain severely undermine the fundamentals of a gifting economy. The alliterative framing – "si faiz" and "fier se fet" – contrasts the facts (faiz) with the poet's foolish belief in the king's word (fier se fet). At the centre of the alliterated line stand the disputed gifts, now portrayed as "bad gifts" or "dons mauvais."

The notion of superiors offering only "bad gifts" takes on increasing significance in the envoy, where the poet requests that the king fulfil his promises and give him his rightful "due" (deuz):

Princes, soiez de voz dons recordans
Et de voz diz, l'un a l'autre acordans:

En vo grace de tous poins me soubmet;
Deuz me sont voz dons depuis cinq ans,
Mais, se sur eulx n'ay mes .iiii.c frans,
En si faiz dons mauvais fier se fet (B1168, lines 31–6)

(Prince, take responsibility for your promised gifts and for your word. May the two be in harmony. To your grace, I submit myself on all points: due to me are your gifts, now going on five years, and yet, of them, I still don't have my 400 francs. According to the facts, it is foolish to place one's trust in gifts [*or*] According to the facts, he [the poet] has put his trust in bad gifts)

Deschamps exposes here the realities of the economic system in which gifting language in late-medieval French served to disguise a bastardized feudal economy.[62] He also draws attention to the hidden economics of poetry when alluding to the recording of princely gifts in the opening line to the envoy. The poet requests that the prince assure that his promises ("voz diz") be documented, presumably by the treasurer, so that Deschamps might receive the 400 francs owed him. This surprisingly blunt request for money also registers a poetic threat since the term "recordans" used to request the recording of the king's promise also alludes to the notion of remembrance. At the same time that Deschamps calls for his dues to be documented, he gives the king his due. That is, he produces a poem that records and publicizes the sovereign's "dons mauvais," which translates as "bad gifts," but constitutes a loosely veiled allusion to "empty promises."

In another supplication poem, Deschamps states explicitly the threat of poetry for leaders who fail to give rightful due to their men. In the envoy to Ballade 1301, Deschamps claims that he will be "ruined" if his lords do not come to his aid: "Mes seigneurs, je suis desconfis/ Se vo pité n'y remedie" (My lords, I am ruined if you do not take pity on me) (B1301, lines 25–6). Once again, the problem stems from the king's failure to give the servant his due for past work. Here, Deschamps refers to promissory notes – "mes dons du roy sont escrips" (my gifts from the king are documented) (B1301, line 12) – that have yet to be satisfied. The poet first likens his current situation to that of the street vendors whose cries open the poem, only to then distinguish himself from the vendors who hawk clothing, mousetraps, and food because his wares prove worthless. All he has to sell are the empty promises of his masters:

Coffin porter, et le cabas
Des supplicacions toudis,

Et une boiste pour les ras
Ou mes dons du roy sont escrips (B1301, lines 9–12)

(A portable coffin and a basket of repeated supplications and a rat's box where my gifts from the king are written)

In place of clothing, he has a coffin; instead of food goods, he carries a basket of supplications (presumably the ones he submitted in poetic form); and rather than a mousetrap, he possesses a rat's nest stuffed with useless written royal promises. The worthlessness of his possessions leaves him no choice but to threaten his superiors:

S'en mon fait n'est remede mis,
Crier me fault: "Oublie, oublie!" (B1301, lines 23–4)

(If there is no remedy made on my behalf, I must cry out: "Forgotten! Forgotten!")

Pay up or suffer public shame, he menaces. If no recompense ensues, the poet promises to join the city chorus with his own unique cry for justice, a cry that will expose his lords' failure to keep promises. In contrast to the complaint of Ballade 1168 regarding "bad gifts," this ballade aggressively seeks to shame the monarchy into action and to warn princes that they too run the risk of being forgotten or, worse, remembered only by the poet's accusatory cry.

The risk of poetic shaming because of unpaid debts receives its most menacing treatment in Ballade 788, in which Deschamps directly addresses the king: "Au roy supplie Eustace, vostre huissier" (To the king begs Eustache, your sergeant-at-arms) (B788, line 1). The opening line adopts the formality of an officially registered demand that is then followed by the poet's threat to abandon both his court position and all lyric activity if his request remains unanswered. He recalls for the king the history behind his supplication. Four years earlier, the king visited Deschamps (referred to in the third person): "Quant vous fustes son hostel visitans" (when you visited his home) (B788, line 4). At that time, the king promised to release 200 francs to cover the visit. With this promise still to be satisfied, Deschamps urges the king to fulfil his debt – "Et le faictes ordonner le premier" (Make it of the first order) (B788, line 17); otherwise, the poet will be reduced to becoming a sheepherder to assure his survival. Should this transpire, Deschamps warns his king, he will cease to write but will never remain silent. Instead, he promises to call out the king's treasurer, Jean de Montaigu, for his crimes:

> Plus ne fera chançons, livre ne chans,
> Ainsois joura de la turelurette
> Et s'en yra dire, come uns truans,
> A Montagu qu'il ly paye sa debte (B788, lines 21–4)
>
> (I will no longer make music, books or song, instead I will play the flute and will go about saying, like a vagabond, "that Monta[i]gu pay his debt to him!")

In place of works that might celebrate the king, Deschamps threatens to pick up the musical instrument most often associated with the rumours and deceptions of minstrels, and to go about singing, to the king's shame, of unpaid royal debts. This threat to replace works written for the king with songs exposing royal failings attributes uncommon worth to poetry. Deschamps threatens that his poetic gift will no longer support but, instead, will serve to harm his sovereign's legacy. We could not be further from the literary exchange dynamics celebrated by Charles V's commissioned writers. Deschamps leaves no room in literary exchange for the king to benefit. Rather than position his writing as answering the patron's pleasure or as offering the writer's gift to a worthy recipient, Deschamps presents poetry as outside of the realm of negotiations. Rather than a means of forging an intimate relationship, in Deschamps's hands, poetry divides maker and ruler.

Deschamps's many threats of how he might harm the king's reputation with his verse eventually culminated in his declared intention to cease writing on his king's behalf and to exit the court, as did many of his fellow writers following the king's first mental attack in 1392. These writers began migrating to Valois satellite courts, especially to the courts of the frequently feuding princes, the dukes of Orleans and Burgundy. A case in point is Bovet, who, as previously noted, presented the young king with his *Arbre de batailles* in 1389, but when he completed the *Apparicion maistre Jehan de Meun* in 1398 and in spite of still being officially in the king's service, Bovet composed three different dedications addressing the duke of Orléans, the duchess of Orléans, and the treasurer Jean de Montaigu.[63] Even Christine de Pizan, who addressed the *Chemin* to the king in 1403, provided several members of the Valois dynasty with copies of the same work. Similarly, one year after the king's first mental attack, Deschamps completed two works: the *Art de dictier* for an unidentified prince – perhaps Louis of Orléans, who showed a pronounced interest in poetry – and the *Dolente et piteuse complainte de l'Eglise moult desolée au jour d'ui*, a translation from Latin into the vernacular that, according to Tainguy, was undertaken for Philip of Burgundy.[64] That same year, Deschamps would take up position at the court of the king's brother Louis of Orléans as "conseiller" (advisor) and "maître d'hôtel" (steward), although he retained his title as the king's sergeant-at-arms until his own death.[65]

Breaking the Cycle: The "Livre de memoire" and Deschamps's Relinquishing of His Lyric Duties

Deschamps's reversal of conventional literary dynamics that redefined poetry as capable of either contributing to one's legacy or meting out justice owed a great deal to both Charles V's former commissioned writers and Machaut. The commissioned writers, as discussed in chapter 2, played a crucial role in presenting literary exchange as an expression of archaic gifting in which their learning represented an inestimable treasure offered their king because he recognized the value of knowledge. Drawing on this philosophy of intellectual exchange promoted by the commissioned writers, Deschamps repeatedly proclaimed the value and power of his poetry as a source of moral, spiritual, and political wisdom that could either benefit leaders or damage their legacy. His insistence that poetry served to enlighten those in need of guidance resonates with Machaut's declaration in his Prologue that poetry was a divine gift that the author, in turn, was expected to share with a worthy audience. Combining these earlier philosophies regarding literary value, Deschamps established poetry as the writer's treasure, and in his literary world, the poet could choose to share his riches with privileged and knowledgeable members of this learned sodality or use his gift to exclude individuals from the community. In his treatise on poetic composition, the *Art de dictier*, Deschamps makes this second point clear when identifying verse as an "art" that although equal to the seven liberal arts, differed because only a select few naturally possessed the talent. That is, in contrast to the liberal arts tradition that seeks "aprandre … d'icuels ars" (to teach these arts) to the sons of nobility,[66] poetry "ne puet estre aprinse a nul" (cannot be taught to anyone) (7: 270). Deschamps further distinguishes the art of composing poetry by claiming its status as a natural talent worthy of the title of "musique naturele" (natural music) (7:270). Deschamps emphasizes this point when laying out the rules of poetry:

Et de ceste musique naturele et comment homme, depuis qu'il se met naturelement a ce faire, ce que nul, tant fust saiges le maistre ne le disciple, ne lui sçavroit aprandre, se de son propre et naturel mouvement ne se faisoit, vueil je traictier principaument, en baillant et enseignant un petit de regle ci après declarée a ceuls que nature avra encliné ou enclinera a ceste naturele musique. (7:272)

(And regarding this natural music and how man, ever since he set himself to do it naturally, that which no one, no matter how wise the master or the disciple, could know how to teach he who was not inclined to do it, I want to address this first by offering and teaching the rules hereafter detailed to those who by nature will have been inclined or will be inclined to practice this natural music.)

The repetition of variations of "natural" in this pronouncement echoes Machaut's Prologue in which he declared to have received his poetic abilities as a gift from Lady Nature. In Deschamps's case, he asserts that he cannot teach to the "un-inclined" what comes "naturally" to him. To the unidentified prince who commissioned the work, therefore, all Deschamps can "give" are rules to describe poetry; he cannot teach the addressee the art of poetry. This insistence on the poetic gift registers one more example of Deschamps's disruption of conventional dynamics. The poet may have agreed to answer the patron's request for this treatise, but he placed limits on the prince's ability to profit from this work or to appropriate the knowledge contained therein.

For all of his threats to use poetry against his superiors and to deny them access to the lyric world, Deschamps admitted in four poems dating from around 1396 that he had long placed his writing talents in the service of his masters rather than horde this wealth. These poems (Ballades 1124, 1125, 1130, and 1148) allude to a work undertaken in the name of the Valois dynasty.[67] As discussed at the outset of this chapter, Ballade 1125 speaks of a "livre de memoire," which the poet claims was intended to commemorate both Charles V and his sons and which he claims to have been writing for thirty-two years. Since the stated intention is to begin by celebrating Charles V, it is reasonable to date the beginning of this project to the start of Charles V's reign in 1364. As such, the end date for the composition of this work would be 1396, which brings us to the year of the royal wedding between Richard II of England and the Valois Princess Isabelle of France. Two additional ballades reinforce this identification of the 1396 wedding as the end date for the "livre de memoire." Long regarded as a companion poem to Ballade 1125, Ballade 1124 lists the official wedding ceremony that took place on 31 October 1396 among events the poet witnessed during his lifetime. In addition, Ballades 1130 and 1148, in which there is also mention of a book project, reference the peace negotiations linked to this marriage that took place in the St Omer region three days prior to the marriage festivities and that led to the announcement of a twenty-eight-year truce. Ballade 1148 further links itself to the wedding through internal dating because it mentions that the anticipated "final peace" would conclude the present "debat d'Angleterre et de France" (conflict between England and France). The poet dates this conflict back sixty years, which would return us to the 1330s if we date the poet's composition to 1396. As is well known, it was, in fact, in 1337 that Edward III reasserted his claim to the French throne.

These four poems are also linked by their treatment of the poet's history of recording key moments of the Valois dynasty and his current decision to abandon this work. Ballade 1124 reads like a table of contents for the "livre de memoire" named in the subsequent Ballade 1125. Among the key events of the Valois dynasty listed in Ballade 1124, we find mention of the reign of four kings (presumably, a reference to the French Valois kings from Philip VI through Charles VI), the heroic feats of Bertrand of Guesclin (d. 1380), the incessant fighting over the last fifty years (a reference that takes us back to the first major English victory at Crécy in 1446), as well as the coronation of Charles VI and his victories in Flanders (after declaring majority in 1388), and, finally, the marriages of both Charles VI in 1385 and of Richard II in 1396. The refrain concludes, however, that these events represent worthless knowledge: "C'est tout neant des choses de ce monde" (All things of this world are nothing) (B1124, refrain). The three remaining works explicitly reference a book project that is also understood as suddenly irrelevant. Beyond the reference to a "livre de memoire" (B1125, line 1), the poet mentions an "euvre" (work) that he intends to cease writing (B1130, line 28) and a "livre ... enclos soubz serre" (book held under lock and key) (B1148, line 29) that the poet declares will remain sealed unless peace is achieved. In Ballade 1130, an anonymous interlocutor further identifies the poet as a royal chronicler who is assumed to have attended the royal wedding in 1396 (line 6). In all four of these poems, mention of Deschamps's literary activity on behalf of the dynasty is linked to his determination to abandon the assignment. This book, held "under lock and key," shall remain hidden, the poet threatens; therefore, the dynasty's accomplishments will fall from memory. The poet is not shy in blaming the king's broken promises for having provoked his decision to abandon the book.

The 1396 royal wedding that united the English king and the Valois princess held the promise of a final peace that would end the long drawn-out conflict. It is easy to imagine that the author of the "livre de memoire" anticipated that the discussions and celebrations would represent the final chapter of a work long in the making. Such was a sentiment clearly shared among the *literati*; after all, Deschamps was not the only writer on hand for these ceremonies, so great was the promise that this union announced a final peace between the warring parties. Both Pierre Salmon and Jean Froissart spoke of their attendance at the wedding.[68] However, both Deschamps and Froissart acknowledged that they were denied direct participation in negotiations; both were, in fact, corralled in the town of Liques, which was equidistance from the two royal camps, an apparent holding camp for the public. Froissart did not complain about his exclusion from the high-level talks that took place during the four days leading up to the first meeting of the newlyweds on 31 October. Deschamps, however, authored a different story. He openly complained about his exclusion from events. Deschamps directed his grievances to his lords, both the king and the king's brother Louis, whom he accused of having failed to recognize his writer status and thus failed to secure him the right to attend events.

In Ballade 1130, Deschamps ingeniously couched his indignation concerning the royal wedding in a verse dialogue set in the early days after the event. The exchange begins with a question from an unidentified interlocutor about the poet's recent travels: "Dont venez vous? – Je viens de Saint Omer" (Where are you coming from? – I come from Saint Omer) (B1130, line 1). The poet's interlocutor then inquires:

> – Or me dittes des nouvelles des roys.
> Les avez veuz aux tentes assembler?
> Arons nous paix de tous poins ceste foys?
> Dittes nous ent, car vous avez la vois
> D'avoir escript de leurs faiz queroniques (B1130, lines 2–6)
>
> (Do tell me news of the kings. Did you see them come together in the tents? Will we have peace on all fronts this time? Tell us about it since you have the reputation to have written chronicles about their deeds.)

Through his anonymous interlocutor, Deschamps indirectly proclaims for himself an official role as a writer at the king's court and, furthermore, he affords substantial power and authority to the position. More than simply assuming that Deschamps has access to the private spaces of the royal tents and is privy to the secret negotiations between the two kingdoms, the interlocutor assigns the poet the role of porte-parole or the "voice" of royalty and thus responsible for recording their accomplishments. According to Deschamps, the interlocutor's favourable account of the poet's court status could not be further from reality. Contrary to the interlocutor's assumption that the poet enjoyed special privileges, the poet speaks of his confinement in Liques, where he did little more than stare at the church steeple: " – Je vous jure, sur Dieu et sur la crois,/ Je n'ay riens veu fors le moustier de Liques" (I swear to you, by God and the cross, I saw nothing apart from the church of Liques) (B1130, lines 7–8). The second stanza develops this idea when admitting that "Quant a chose dont je doye parler" (Regarding those things about which I'm expected to speak) (B1130, line 9), the poet can respond to his interlocutor's questions with nothing more than mention of random sightings and hearsay. The poet acknowledges having seen the English "venir et aler/ Vers la roine d'Angleterre" (come and go towards the queen of England) (B1130, lines 11–12) and he has heard say ("si dit on," B1130, line 13) that at the end of the month, they would take their new queen to Calais. Apart from this secondhand information, the poet can only bear witness to the little esteem he enjoys at court. Having passed his time far from the royal tents, the poet can speak of nothing but royal equestrian finery and the stables where the royal horses were housed. In place of salient details about the kings' conversations, all he can tell of is a wily Breton valet who stole both his money and horse (B1130, lines 20–3).

Turning to the princes in the envoy, most likely the king and his brother Louis, the poet lays out the repercussions of his exclusion from events:

Princes, j'aray bien pou a sermonner,
A escripre, n'a voz faiz ordonner
De ce traicté des noces autentiques,
Et pour ce vueil cy mon euvre finer,
Et en finant puis bien a tous jurer:
Je n'ay riens veu fors le moustier de Liques (B1130, Envoy, lines 25–30)

(Princes, I shall have very little to speak of in writing, nor can I speak of your role in the treaty linked to this marriage. For this reason, I wish to finish here my work and, as a conclusion, I can swear to all that I saw nothing apart from the church of Liques.)

Whereas the interlocutor began by identifying the poet as a royal chronicler responsible for knowing, promoting, and recording royal events, Deschamps exposes the extent to which he cannot fulfil this role, and through no fault of his own. Given his exclusion from royal events, he announces "the end of his work." This "euvre" speaks directly to the present poem, which he addresses to the princes as a poor replacement for a work that might have commemorated this major event and publicized the details of the peace treaty. The expression, "cy mon euvre finer," further calls to mind the declaration with which Ballade 1125 opens: "Je vueil cesser mon livre de memoire" (I want to end my book of memory) (B1125, line 1). As such, it invites us to interpret the statement as an epitaph marking the end of a larger work that would never see the light of day.

Where a stranger identifies Deschamps in Ballade 1130 as an official court writer known to chronicle and publicize royal events, Ballade 1125 claims that for thirty-two years, Deschamps has dedicated his time to a work about the Valois dynasty, beginning with "Du saige roy Charle le quint l'istoire" (the history of the Wise King Charles V) (line 3). Over its three stanzas, Ballade 1125 develops some of the ideas that are ostensibly treated in the book. Although it identifies the history of Charles V as the heart of the text, the poem affords the majority of the first twelve-line stanza and the complete second stanza to the renowned Constable Bertrand of Guesclin. Rather than focus on the constable's accomplishments, however, the poet details the public mourning and unprecedented funeral ceremony in honour of a man whose greatest desire was "garder l'utilité publique" (to protect the public good) (B1125, line 6). Both the constable's honourable intentions and the respect afforded him justify the refrain: "Noble chose est de bon renom acquerre!" (It is a noble thing to acquire good fame!) (B1125, refrain). Deschamps developed this same idea in the companion poem Ballade 1148 in which he promised that his "livre ... soubz serre" (book under lock) (B1148, line 29) would function as a terrestrial counterpart to the "livre de vie" (book of life) (B1148, line 21). This book was to circulate throughout the world and publicize the names of those who achieve peace ("En trestous biens leurs noms perpetuer/ En bon renom, qui par tout le monde erre," "In all good ways perpetuate their name and good fame, which will pass around the world," B1148, lines 25–6). If the book in Ballade 1148 holds the promise of someday being made available, the book mentioned in Ballade 1125 traces a much more sombre trajectory. Leaving behind "ceste vie en gloire" (this life of glory) (B1125, line 25) associated with Charles V, the poet turns to the king's sons to first present a tally of the "grans meschiez" (great failures)

(B1125, line 28) they have experienced. The poet further declares, "le temps fut lors inique" (times have since been cruel) (B1125, line 30). While the poet acknowledges that since Charles VI assumed independent rule in November 1388, the political circumstances have slightly improved ("La chose fut assez bien gouvernée," "things have been pretty well governed," B1125, line 32), the poet's lot has worsened:

Puis son sacre me fut paine donnée
Estans o eulx, d'encerchier et enquerre
Et d'escripre leurs faiz par la contrée;
Noble chose est de bon renom acquerre! (B1125, lines 33–6)

(Since his coronation, I have only endured trouble being with them, seeking out and inquiring and writing about their deed throughout the lands; it is a noble thing to acquire good fame!)

Deschamps provides no envoy to this work and instead abruptly concludes with reference to his difficulty (paine) in writing about the brothers' rule. In contrast to his inability to record their successes, the repeated refrain evokes their obvious desire for fame, which now seems to be put at risk by the promise of sudden poetic silence. Countering Machaut's anxieties that a patron would assure the poet's effacement, Deschamps reverses this fear when suggesting that the poet possesses the ability to efface all textual trace of an unworthy prince. Denied access to the princes, the poet sums up the lives of Charles VI and Louis of Orléans in the last stanza as a series of unfortunate or unremarkable events that merit only the most mediocre of praise: "La chose fut assez bien gouvernée" (B1125, line 32). With nothing more to say, the poet leaves his readers, both the princes and later audiences, to contemplate the risk of a poet turning the conventional literary exchange dynamic on its head to present his superiors with their rightful due.

In the end, it matters little whether the "livre de memoire" was an actual book. Nor does it matter that archival evidence of Deschamps receiving a royal commission is lacking. Deschamps's claims may be as much of a fiction as those of Machaut's anxious doppelgängers. What does matter is that Deschamps conceived of his lyric endeavours as pointing to something needed and desired by his Valois lords. When comparing Deschamps's poems addressed to Charles V with those addressed to Charles VI, we detect an important transition in his treatment of the poet's role. In his earlier works for Charles V, he submitted fully his talents to the king's purpose, much in the manner of the commissioned writers, possibly going so far as to pursue a verse translation project to honour the king's interests (if not in direct response to a royal commission). When Charles VI assumed the throne, Deschamps first justified composing poetry for the child-king based on a sense of intellectual and moral duty owed his sovereign, a perspective in harmony both with Machaut's presentation of the poet and his art as providing moral guidance and comfort as well as with the commissioned writers' belief that they were supporting the Wise King's pursuit of knowledge through their learned labour. Deschamps has us believe that without having been solicited and with the awareness that his works might not be desirable, he nonetheless produced a series of works directed to the young king. Nevertheless, Deschamps made clear that he expected a return on his efforts and thus he openly discussed the dues the Valois dynasty owed him. Far from contaminating his poetry by demanding financial recompense for his writings, he instead spoke of literary exchange as entailing the recipient's obligatory acceptance and appreciation of the writer's gift. When he demanded financial recompense, it was systematically linked to his official court positions, but he also threatened that his poetry could serve to mete out "poetic justice." His solicitation poems communicate an unprecedented statement regarding the power of poetry to go beyond making public the dues owed a servant of the crown so as to deliver to the royal family what was its rightful due – in this instance, not praise but exposure of royal failures. In the constellation of poems composed around the 1396 royal wedding, we witness another stage in Deschamps's understanding and articulation of his role as a poet. Claiming a long history of serving the Valois dynasty as a chronicler who was to commemorate and assure the dissemination of the history of his noble subjects, Deschamps spoke not of what was his rightful due, nor of his duty to his masters. Instead, he drew attention to the poetic silence they merited in exchange for their failure to recognize the importance of poetry and learning. In 1396, Deschamps declared that it was no longer his duty to compose works that might secure his leaders' legacy, because, in fact, they could no longer claim such works as their rightful due. To emphasize the profound breakdown that resulted from this event, Deschamps performed in a number of poems addressed to Charles VI the antithesis of the presentation scene. Rather than portraying himself as kneeling before his king, and rather than soliciting his king's benevolence and goodwill, Deschamps arrived empty handed. Or worse, he held out the promise of a gift that contained a powerful curse.

The radical shift in court culture following Charles V's death led Deschamps to re-conceptualize the function of poetry and re-theorize its circulation dynamics. So distinctive are the literary dynamics detailed by Deschamps in his corpus that related terminology must be used with great caution. To identify Charles VI as fulfilling a patron-function in Deschamps's poetic world would be to ignore the profound discrepancies between the idealized accounts of literary engagement linked with Charles V's commissioned writers and Deschamps's account of his literary dealings with Charles VI. Charles VI appears to have neither exerted direct power over the book community nor cultivated goodwill and fidelity among contemporary writers. Little evidence from his reign points to writers either receiving royal commissions or royal reward for text-offerings presented to the king. Literary activity at the court of Charles VI appears to have been limited to writers addressing the monarch in their writing and, on occasion, presenting him with manuscript copies of these works. Charles VI functioned, at best, as a passive placeholder in the literary circuit. This lack of both intellectual and financial investment in texts might be said to have indebted him to the learned community. Deschamps's poetry suggests as much in his account of his own literary dealings with the king.

Deschamps's younger contemporary, Christine de Pizan, provides further insight into the challenges facing writers during the reign of Charles VI. By the time she entered the literary scene, there was little reason to turn to the sitting king as a potential patron, so incapacitated was he from his struggles with mental illness. Instead, Christine followed the intellectual migration to the Orléans household. In contrast to Deschamps who, at least in 1396, grouped the duke with his brother as so indifferent to his writings that he deemed both of them unworthy of his riches, Christine recognized Louis of Orléans as the most viable Valois prince to revive the Wise King's literary legacy. She was both earnest in her support of Duke Louis's claim to his father's learned legacy and relentless in her determined pursuit of a commission from Louis between 1402 and 1404 that would confirm her hopes for him. That Christine's venture failed is an essential chapter in the history of literary exchange dynamics during the early reign of the Valois dynasty.

Chapter Five

The Pursuit of Patronage: From Christine de Pizan's Troubled Dealings with Louis of Orléans to Marketing Nostalgia

With the first signs of Charles VI's mental illness emerging in 1392, any hopes that the fourth Valois king might reignite his father's *Sapientia* project were dashed. The learned community that had briefly re-emerged after the king's declaration of independent rule in 1389 shifted its energies to the alternative face of royal power, the king's brother Louis. Prince Louis encouraged this exodus, especially after his naming as duke of Orléans in 1392, at which point he made a concerted effort to model himself after his father. As duke, Louis aggressively sought to revive Charles V's practice of supporting book culture. He invested heavily in manuscripts, both old and new; saw to the construction at his Paris residence of a private library modelled on the Louvre library; and pursued the translation campaign of his ancestors. To achieve these projects, Duke Louis absorbed into his household many of the key learned men who had contributed to Charles V's creation of the royal library, including translators and librarians as well as scribes, illuminators, and his father's architect. Contemporary writers followed this migration. Among these writers, Christine de Pizan (c. 1364–c. 1430) stands out for her concerted efforts to curry the duke's favour. From 1400 to 1404, she composed four works in his honour, in which she expressly set out to position the duke in the intellectual seat once occupied by his father. Contrary to Deschamps, who openly declared his disappointment with both royal princes and, ultimately, his refusal to use his literary gift to secure their legacy, Christine identified Duke Louis as the worthy inheritor of the Wise King's learned legacy and anticipated that he would revive his father's commissioning practices.

Christine's fame as a writer developed over the last decade of the fourteenth century, and by 1399, she had composed hundreds of discrete poems. At that stage, she shifted to thinking of her literary forays as a corpus and, in 1399, gathered together these works to produce an early lyric anthology of her writings that she entitled the *Cent ballades*. This early poetry focused primarily on issues of the heart, and as she ventured into lengthier verse writings, she respected the same themes while also taking into account the impact of political reality on sentimental life. In the *Dit de Poissy*, which Christine dated to April 1400, for example, the recorded debate pits the suffering of a knight snubbed by his lady against a lady whose knight was taken prisoner at Nicopolis. Christine offered this work to a celebrated knight at the royal court, the seneschal of Hainaut, Jean de Werchin, who was also a minor poet. As Françoise Autrand observes, this address to the seneschal reflects Christine's concerted effort in her early years of writing to attract the attention of the literary community, which Autrand considers to have included the learned linked to the university, the "first humanists" who held chancellery positions, and respected knights with a passion for composing poetry.[1] By all accounts, Christine's efforts paid off, and her works were quickly in demand. In fact, the liminary ballade to the *Cent ballades* explains that it was by demand of her public that she had decided to organize this anthology.[2] Christine, however, appears to have quickly tired of the public's demand for love poetry and she even came to regard their requests for this verse as an imposition. In two undated writings, the *Livre du duc des vrais amants* and the *Cent ballades d'amant et de dame*, the poet identifies these works as unwanted commissions that required her to write about subjects of no interest to her.[3] Christine's distaste for these commissions could lead us to conclude that, like Machaut, she viewed patronage as an arrangement that did more harm than good but for the fact that her writings also bear witness to her abiding desire to revive the ideal of literary patronage promoted by Charles V's commissioned writers. Dissatisfied with her fame as a writer of love poetry, Christine turned her attention to participating in a more illustrious and restricted circle of writers who sought to use their writerly gifts to affect political change. Christine set her sights on acquiring patrons who would recognize her as capable of partnering with them to assure a victorious future for France.

This chapter revisits and redirects a question I previously pursued in relation to Christine's work: "What is a patron?" Here the focus shifts from how these accounts bolstered Christine's authority to her efforts to negotiate the divide between a past patronage ideal, founded on the concept of intellectual partnership, and a contemporary failure of the nobility to assume an engaged role in the literary economy. Christine was wedded to the patronage associated with Charles V in which an intellectual partnership was forged, and she sought to revive this ideal as once expressed by the Wise King's commissioned writers. For, as Liliane Dulac has observed, Christine relentlessly referenced the "mythe bénéfique du 'sage roi'" (beneficial myth of the Wise King) not only because it had become a "symbole d'un idéal monarchique" (symbol of a monarchical ideal), but also very simply because it had become the "figure tutélaire qu'évoque l'écrivain politique effrayé de son impuissance présente" (the dominant figure that the political writer, terrified by her present powerlessness, evoked).[4] Dulac's focus on Charles V's political importance, nonetheless, overlooks Christine's emphasis on the Wise King's mythic status as a revered member of the intellectual community. In this regard, Christine's belief that her "present powerlessness" might be altered by a patron in the mould of the idealized Charles V led her to pursue the patronage of a powerful literary partner. Christine's pursuit of patronage was infused with a nostalgic desire to revive the intellectual community she associated with Charles V. Thus, in contrast to Machaut and Deschamps, Christine viewed clientelism as a boon not just for the writer but also for society at large: she did not see it as exclusively serving the patron's pleasure but, rather, as also assuring the common good. Christine called on Louis of Orléans to fulfil this role. Unfortunately for Christine and her contemporaries, the duke appears to have had little interest in reviving his father's literary clientelism, whether to become the patron who supported intellectual labour to strengthen his reputation as his father did or, more idealistically, to embody the idealized vision of his father as joining with the learned to promote and protect knowledge. Instead, Duke Louis's involvement with the writing community echoed his reigning brother's practices; while writers addressed works to the duke and sought to initiate close intellectual relations with him, there is no evidence to suggest that he accepted their invitations. Perhaps in response to the duke's noncommittal stance, Christine changed literary tactics around 1402, when she expanded her call for a revival of intellectual partnerships between nobility and the learned beyond Louis. To develop this point, this chapter first examines Louis of Orléans's use of book culture to position himself as his father's worthy heir, then turns to Christine's support of these efforts in four *dits*. These works are the *Débat de deux amans* (c. 1400–2), the *Epistre Othéa* (c. 1401–2), the *Dit de la rose* (1402), and the *Livre de la Prod'hommie*, (c. 1402–4). Each work offers rich textual and visual examples of Christine manipulating archaic gifting and contemporary public gifting rituals to guide Louis towards the understanding that by commissioning a work from her, he would achieve the full expression of his claim to Charles V's legacy. Without the ducal commission ever taking shape, Christine eventually shifted attention away from Duke Louis to pursue a practice that critics date to this period: the distribution of multiple copies of a single composition to a wide audience.[5] The earliest examples of Christine adopting this practice concern works originally dedicated to Duke Louis that she later redistributed to potential patrons, but over time, we witness an important shift in which Christine began naming several princes in a single dedication. These new strategies, however, never strayed from Christine's stated ambition of acquiring a dedicated patron. In 1404, Charles V's brother, Duke Philip of Burgundy, who had been the beneficiary of several book-gifts from Christine, answered her call and commissioned a biography of Charles V. This commission and its ensuing complications will be the subject of the next chapter.

Louis of Orléans's Self-Fashioning as His Father's Intellectual Heir

When turning to Louis of Orléans as a worthy continuator of Charles V's learned legacy, Christine was responding to the duke's own political self-fashioning as his father's intellectual heir and as a viable replacement for his ailing royal brother. Louis's claims took on particular urgency in light of the political vacuum that surrounded the king's descent into madness. From 1392 until 1396, Charles VI suffered recurring bouts of madness that led the Religieux de Saint-Denis to refer to a "chronic illness."[6] It was clear that this sickness would not pass, and political action was taken during the king's lucid periods to protect the throne. A royal ordinance in January 1393 declared that Louis of Orléans would serve as regent in his brother's "absence" (a euphemism soon adopted to reference the king's periods of madness). The Religieux de Saint-Denis reiterated this point, declaring that due to Louis's proximity to the crown (*tanquam propinquiorem corone*), he should reign in the king's place.[7] Louis of Orléans's capacity to rule and to inspire those around him, however, was regularly challenged by the Burgundian faction. Duke Philip of Burgundy disputed at every turn Louis's position as second in command. Countering his uncle with efforts to bolster his own authority, Duke Louis adopted the role of the wise and prudent leader, modelled on his celebrated father. Nowhere is Louis's imitation of the Wise King more apparent than in his investment in book culture.

That Louis of Orléans considered support of vernacular writing as a responsibility of the royal line is apparent in the growth of his personal library over the years. Although we lack an inventory of his book collection, treasury records give us some idea of its contents as it developed from 1389 until his assassination in 1407. Scholars estimate that at the time of Duke Louis's death, his library contained between 100 and 200 books, a collection that was comparable, if not superior, to the contemporary collections of his uncles, the dukes of Berry and Burgundy.[8] Two important events occurred in 1389 that triggered Prince Louis's book-collecting practices: he began receiving a fixed allowance from the royal coffers and he married Valentina Visconti, who brought both wealth and books to the marriage.[9] It was, however, when he acquired the titles of duke of Orléans and then regent during the king's absences that Louis began in earnest to build up his still-modest book collection. During this period, he purchased several books that had been part of his great-aunt Blanche of Orléans's impressive collection, as well as titles from booksellers.[10] So significant was the duke's investment in books that Christopher R. Shultz refers to 1394–8 as the period of "Louis' campaign of manuscript production,"[11] an obvious nod to Charles V's so-called translation campaign. During this four-year period, the duke appointed the bookseller Thevenin Angevin to oversee the continued growth of his collection. On Louis's behalf, Angevin purchased parchment and secured the services of scribes and illuminators to produce new copies of vernacular translations long associated with the Valois dynasty.[12] These commissions ranged from new copies of Jean de Vignay's *Miroir historiale*, first dedicated to Queen Jeanne of Burgundy to new editions of several works commissioned by Louis's father, including Raoul de Presles's *Cité* and the complete set of Nicole Oresme's translations of Aristotle.[13] Other key purchases during this period comprised copies acquired directly from Charles V's favoured scribe, Henri du Trevou. These titles include Pierre Bersuire's *Tite-Live*, first translated for Louis's grandfather, as well as copies of the *Chroniques historiées*; and the *Racional*.[14] The duke's entourage also contributed to his library. Nobles ranging from Amaury d'Orgement, Lord of Chantilly, to Duke Philip of Burgundy presented him with book-gifts over the years.[15] Contemporary writers also encouraged the duke's interests. For example, Jean Froissart presented him with a copy of the now-lost *Dits royaulx* and as noted in the previous chapter, Deschamps possibly composed the *Art de dictier* for the duke around the same time.[16] In spite of Deschamps's claims in 1396 that he would no longer write for the royal brothers, he clearly remained committed to promoting verse as an important resource for intellectual, spiritual, and moral wisdom since, in 1398, he procured for the duke the complete *Pelerinage* series authored by Guillaume de Diguileville.[17] In addition to these acquisitions, Duke Louis invested in projects directly associated with his father; for example, he sponsored the continuation of the Jean de Sy French Bible translation that had previously been financed by his grandfather and father. Household inventories detail support for this project, which involved numerous rewards between 1397 and 1398 to named translators throughout the kingdom for their contribution to the "Bible en françois, laquelle fist commencier le roy Jehan" (the French Bible that was begun by King John).[18] Such attentiveness to the legacy of this learned Valois tradition makes legible the symbolic function Duke Louis attributed to investment in books. Yet another powerful indicator of the duke's commitment to assuming the role of sponsor of intellectual endeavours during these years concerns the presence of Gilles Malet, Charles V's former librarian, in ducal treasury records, a likely indication that Malet was involved with Louis's library.[19] Likewise, in 1397, Louis would enlist the services of another key contributor to his father's *Sapientia* project, Raymond du Temple, the architect responsible for the Louvre library, who would oversee the installation of a formal library at Duke Louis's new hotel in Paris.[20] After the many years during which Charles V's project had lain fallow, Duke Louis's interest in bringing to his court the skilled men who made up his father's elite coterie was surely viewed as evidence of an intellectual revival.

Contemporary writers provide important insight into the book community's perception of this activity and of the duke's promise as a literary patron. We saw in the last chapter the harshness with which Deschamps dealt collectively with the royal brothers in 1396, but hints of a more complicated relationship between the poet and Duke Louis emerge in court records and even in Deschamps's writings addressed exclusively to the duke. Beyond joining the duke's household as his *maître d'hôtel* in 1393, there is evidence that Deschamps shared with the prince a mutual appreciation for poetry. Duke Louis tried his hand at poetry, of which we find examples that include a response to Jean le Seneschal's *Cent ballades* and a poetic response to one of Deschamps's supplication poems.[21] These poetic forays strengthen the hypothesis that Louis of Orléans was the unidentified patron who requested Deschamps's *Art de dictier* in 1393. Deschamps also offered Louis New Year's wishes in poetic form that reinforced Louis's self-fashioning as his father's worthy heir. In the undated Ballade 293 presented to the duke as a New Year's gift, Deschamps wishes for the duke that God bestow on him many of the great qualities so often attributed to Charles V, including the wisdom of Solomon and the power of Alexander, while also wishing victories in far-off lands comparable to those enjoyed by Charlemagne and Louis the Conqueror, significantly, worthy namesakes of father and son. As flattering as these comparisons may be, it is key to recognize that Deschamps links them to a hoped-for future rather than claiming that Louis already possesses such qualities. Moreover, the poet warns the duke that his wishes hold only "tant que France soit par vous honourée" (as long as France is honoured by you) (refrain).

Two other contemporary writers who cautiously identified Duke Louis as the worthy heir of the Wise King's learned legacy were Honorat Bovet (born c. 1340–50; died 1410) and Jacques Legrand (born c. 1360; died c. 1415–18). Bovet was associated with the court of Louis's uncle and most immediate namesake, Louis II of Anjou. Nine years after presenting Charles VI with the *Arbre de bataille*, Bovet directed his *Apparicion* to the court of Orléans and composed two independent dedications for the duke and the duchess. The *Apparicion* casts a critical gaze on contemporary political affairs at the same time that it expresses support for the king and his brother. In his address to Louis of Orléans, Bovet confirms Louis's important role in counselling his brother the king and in governing the kingdom when reminding him that he would be divinely judged by these services:

> Et sy fauldra que par devant Dieu une foys rendés compte de l'administracion que [Dieu] vous a donnee ou commise en cestuy mortel monde et des consaulx que vous aurez donnés a vostre seigneur vostre frere pour lui aidier a gouverner son royaume.

> (And thus will you one day be obliged to give an accounting before God of the administration He gave you or to which He assigned you in this mortal realm, and of the counsel you will have given to your Lord, your brother, in helping him to govern his kingdom.)[22]

In a similar fashion, the *Archiloge Sophie* by Jacques Legrand (1400) acknowledges the duke's dominant role in the kingdom: "en estat vous estes tres souverain" (in the kingdom you are very sovereign).[23]

Both writers advise that Louis imitate his father to assure good leadership. Bovet counsels Louis to recognize learning as a prerequisite for good leadership, all the while acknowledging that it is the rare leader who values such things. The duke's father, of course, stands as one exception to the rule:

> Avec tout ce est il bonne chose de veoir aucuns fruiz de l'escripture; car disoit li bons philosophes Socrotes que lors seroit ly siecles beneurés quant les roys et les princes sauroient ou quant se mettroyent en estude de scavoir. Et sy

a bien grant temps que ly mondes n'ot princes qui guerez s'adonnassent a estude de scavoir. Car puys que mourut ly bons roys Robers de Cedille qui fut de vostre sang et fut moult grant clerc, nous avons eu pou princes qui bienne amassent science, fors vostre pere qui Dieu face mercy; car il l'ama et sy fist il les bons clers.

(In all of this, it is a good thing to see some of the fruits of learning, for this is what the good philosopher Socrates said, that the world would be blessed when kings and princes were learned, or when they applied themselves to the acquisition of learning. And so it has been a long time that the world has lacked princes who cared to devote themselves to the acquisition of knowledge. Because since the death of Robert of Sicily, who was of royal blood and was a great scholar, we have had few princes who really loved learning, one exception being your father, God rest his soul, because he loved it and loved good scholars as well.) (*Apparicion*, 60–1)

This nod to Louis's father's learned reputation stops short of placing the son in the father's seat. In fact, much like Deschamps who practised caution in assigning praise to Louis, Bovet limits his praise to rumours of the duke's book-collecting interests:

Et combien que je n'ay eu ou temps passé vostre congnoissance ny accointement de vostre noble estat, pour ce que j'ay entendu que vous amés les livres, j'ay escript une petite chosette que se tout vault petit, mais que soit au plaisir de Dieu et de vostre seignourie, mes cuers en sera plus appaisiez.

(And even though in the past I was not known to you nor part of your court, having heard that you love books, I wrote a little thing of little worth; but should it please God and your Lordship, my heart will be more at ease because of it.) (*Apparicion*, 62–3, translation altered)

In contrast to Bovet's cautious allusion to the duke's potential attraction to learned matter, Legrand reserves fulsome praise for the young duke, whom he claims openly displays an interest "en sapience et en vraie science" (in wisdom and in true learning) (*Archiloge Sophie*, 25).

That we have no evidence that the works of Deschamps, Bovet, and Legrand figured in the duke's personal library suggests that the duke did not commit to these writers in any sustained manner. In the cases of Deschamps and Bovet, there is reason to believe that they eventually shifted their attentions to Duke Philip of Burgundy, who proved to be more interested in their learned labours. As already discussed, as early as 1393, Tainguy claimed that Deschamps's *Dolente et piteuse complainte de l'Eglise moult desolée au jour d'ui* was produced "au commandement de monseigneur de Bourgongne" (by the order of the lord of Burgundy).[24] As concerns Bovet, when he offered Duke Louis the *Apparicion*, he also presented Duke Philip with his own personalized copy of the work.[25] As for Legrand's *Archiloge Sophie* addressed to Duke Louis, it appears to have never been completed (a possible indicator of the duke's lack of support for the project).[26] The examples of these writers' brief dealings with Duke Louis suggest a troubling pattern of literary engagement. Their cases provide little evidence that the prince followed in his father's footsteps as a benefactor who, in Bovet's words, "loved knowledge and scholars as well." Instead, Duke Louis appears to have shared more in common with his reigning brother, who practised at best benevolent indifference. It is true that like his father, Louis supported the continuation and recopying of vernacular translations, particularly those linked to previous rulers; nonetheless, most of the literary activity linked to him constitutes unsolicited writings, for which their authors appear to have had little success in securing support.

Lending Support to Louis of Orléans: Christine's Efforts to Position the Duke as the Wise King's Intellectual Heir

Christine joined fellow writers at the outset in recognizing Louis of Orléans's interest in reviving his father's learned legacy, but she proved far more persistent in her efforts to secure a commitment from the duke. As Tracy Adams demonstrates in *Christine de Pizan and the Fight for France*, the author harboured a lifelong commitment to the Orléanist cause. From the outset of the king's mental crisis, Adams maintains, Christine recognized Louis as the only true heir to the throne after Charles VI. Further bolstering Adams's contention is evidence that Christine championed the duke's self-positioning as Charles V's worthy heir as part of his quest to appear as the logical substitute for his brother. Between 1399 and Louis's assassination in 1407, Christine authored four new compositions that openly supported the duke of Orléans; prepared for him supervised copies of her writings;[27] and regularly reserved the highest praise for him in her texts (even those not directly addressed to him).

Before analysing Christine's account of literary exchange with Louis of Orléans, it is important to address the chronology of her four works that single him out as the privileged recipient. Only one of these texts is internally dated. The *Rose* dates its completion to Valentine's Day 1401

(1402 n.s.) and claims to detail events that transpired at recent New Year's festivities hosted by the duke of Orléans. Both the *Deux amans* and the *Othéa* are presumed to predate the *Rose* by no more than two years. The dating of the *Prod'hommie* proves more difficult to establish. The *Prod'hommie* internally references a previous presentation to the duke of a "petit epistre adrecent a vostre dignité"[28] (little letter addressed to your Highness) that led to a ducal invitation for the author to visit his court. Jean-Louis Picherit argues that this "petit epistre" references the *Othéa*, which suggests that the work could not have been produced before 1402.[29] This study, however, maintains that the *Prod'hommie* could just as easily postdate the *Rose* since in this last work, Lady Loyalty leaves the poet with a letter detailing the rules of the "Order of the Rose" created at Duke Louis's court (lines 558–93). As regards the *terminus ad quem* of this work, Angus Kennedy convincingly argues for its completion no later than 1404.[30] With these points in mind, this study positions the composition of the *Prod'hommie* as the likely final work that Christine addressed to Louis exclusively before accepting his uncle's 1404 commission for a biography of Charles V, which is the subject of the next chapter.

In works addressed to Louis, Christine enthusiastically endorsed the duke's self-fashioning as his father's learned heir. Whereas Deschamps and Bovet proved reluctant to recognize Louis as having completely assumed his father's position, and whereas they and Legrand made clear their belief that Louis needed their guidance, Christine openly recognized the duke as a model in the tradition of his father – one who deserved praise and admiration. The pedantic approach adopted by Christine's male counterparts may be credited to their age and status. These men were all twenty to thirty years senior to the duke at the time of writing. Thus, in the case of Deschamps's declarations of ending his service as the "chronicler" of the Valois dynasty in 1396, which was addressed in the previous chapter, the duke was only twenty-four while Deschamps was in his mid-fifties. In addition to seniority, Bovet and Legrand also enjoyed strong reputations as leading moral voices in both ecclesiastic and court circles.[31] In contrast, not only was Christine a woman in a man's world and of humble standing, but she was also only eight years the duke's senior. Christine's gender, status, and age may explain in part the laudatory portrait of Louis she would provide. It must, however, be recognized that Christine's praise for the duke resulted in the most extensive argument in contemporary literature for Louis as the true inheritor of his father's legacy.

In her first lengthy work dedicated to Louis of Orléans, the *Deux amans*, Christine drew abundantly on the Valois legacy to position the duke as more than a worthy judge of the enclosed amorous debate; according to the poet, he was the only logical choice. Similar to Bovet and Legrand, Christine insisted on the duke's royal lineage, and similar to Legrand, she unhesitatingly linked Louis to his father's learned legacy. With her first utterance, she confers on Louis his father's distinguishing quality of wisdom: "prince royal renommé de sagece" (royal prince renowned for wisdom).[32] For the obtuse reader who might not appreciate the association, Christine thereafter bluntly states the filial bond: "Filz de Charles, le bon roy charitable" (son of Charles, the good and charitable king) (*Deux amans*, line 6). In comparison to Bovet, who afforded the duke a reputation based solely on his bibliophilia, Christine identifies Louis as an avid reader who favours texts that are "vertüeux et sage" (virtuous and wise) (*Deux amans*, line 18), "soient rimes ou proses" (whether in verse or prose) (*Deux amans*, line 23). This last observation personalized Louis's literary interests, since new poetry, as we have seen, was virtually absent from Charles V's library. In Christine's text, Louis also figures as a discriminating reader who possesses both virtue and wisdom. For this reason, it is only fitting that Louis should be chosen by the debating lovers to judge their conflict. This last fictional conceit allows Christine to insinuate that the public shares her views concerning the duke, while it also harks back to Charles V's similar placement as judge of debaters in Trémaugon's *Vergier*.[33]

Christine endorses Louis's claim to his father's legacy again at the outset of the *Othéa*:

> Et a vous, tres noble prince excellent,
> D'Orlïens duc Loÿs de grant renom,
> Filz de Charles roy quint de cellui nom,
> Qui, fors le roy, ne congnoiscez greigneur.[34]

> (And to you, very noble and excellent prince, Duke Louis of Orleans of great renown, son of Charles, fifth of the name, who, apart from the king, I know no greater.)

While the reference to the unnamed king in this address may allude to Charles VI, the naming of Charles V in the preceding line invites us to understand that only Louis's father stood as his superior.[35] In the *Othéa*, Christine also positions Louis as a leader attentive to promoting ethical behaviour. Critics have acknowledged that given Duke Louis's age and his status as second in command of the kingdom for nearly a decade when Christine composed the *Othéa*, he was surely not the intended reader of this courtesy book that provided moral instruction for a young prince. Sandra Hindman suggests that the work was most likely directed to young men at court, while Adams proposes the dauphin as the intended reader.[36] For both critics, Duke Louis functioned as a mentor for the younger intended readership of this work. In this regard, Christine provided the duke with a new identity distinctive from the role Bovet and Legrand proposed for him. In Christine's literary world, the duke was not in need of guidance; rather, he was poised to serve as a promoter and a paradigm of the ethical behaviour detailed in her work.

Early copies of the *Othéa*, including BnF, MS fr. 848, the likely copy that Christine presented to the duke, reinforce Louis's role as a mentor and model.[37] The manuscript opens with facing-page miniatures that combine a standard presentation scene on the first folio, which shows Christine offering her book on bended knee to the duke, with a facing folio depiction of the goddess Othéa reaching out from the clouds to offer Hector her letter.[38] Hindman considers that the pairing of these images "prompts the viewer to identify Christine as Othéa and Louis as Hector."[39] At the same time, she admits that the careful detail afforded the duke in this presentation scene makes it impossible to see the two men as interchangeable.[40] In contrast to the young Hector, who obediently reaches up to receive a message from Othéa in the second miniature, the duke appears in the facing-page presentation scene in MS fr. 848 as a dominant figure. Louis's position as second in command to the king is expressed through the stature afforded him and the prominent presence of the ducal baton held by a member of his entourage. Where a deliberate overlap does seem to emerge between the two images is in the positioning of Louis and the goddess Othéa. By placing the two in the same hieratic position, the miniaturist encourages us to consider that the sagacity for which Othéa is celebrated redounds on Louis, who assumes alongside her the position of a wise and learned leader.[41]

Christine would place the duke in the company of another powerful allegorical figure in the *Rose* (1402). Again, although parallels along gender lines might encourage an initial reading of Lady Loyalty as a lofty double of the female poet, the text makes clear that Lady Loyalty favours the gathering hosted by the duke because he and his entourage embody the ideals she has come to promote.[42] Christine's role in this process is laid out by Lady Loyalty, who visits the poet in the night to request that she commemorate in verse the establishment of the Order of the Rose at the duke's court (*Rose*, lines 519–27). In this regard, Christine's role is restricted to that of a porte-parole. Once again, the focus remains on Louis, who is singled out as a model of desirable behaviour.

The *Prod'hommie* goes even further than either the *Othéa* or the *Rose* in depicting Louis as model and mentor. In this final work that Christine addressed exclusively to the duke, he functions as the direct source of wisdom. Gone are fictional characters requesting the duke's judgment or lessons on ethical behaviour that have received the duke's stamp of approval. In place of these fictional voices, Christine identifies the duke as the source of the wisdom to be detailed in this work. The writer explains that having received a ducal invitation to visit Louis's court, she hears him speak firsthand on ethical matters, and this experience serves to confirm the author's previous praise of the duke:

> J'ay cause maintenant et de nouvel plus que oncques mais d'encore recorder et derechief certifiant et notifiant tant la vraie opinion que j'en avoie comme l'experience que je sentoie de ce que autrefois ay dit de vostre grant savoir et autres vertus tres dignes de recommendacion et loeunge. (MS Reg. Lat. 1238, fol. 1)

> (I now have more than ever reason to testify anew and certify and ratify once more the correct belief that I had previously stated based on my experience and my belief that your great knowledge and other virtues deserve recognition and praise.)

In this case, Louis is likened to Julius Caesar, for as the emperor's "dignes et loables" (worthy and praiseworthy) words merited being recorded, so too do the "mos beaulz et paroles dignes issans de vostre bouche, tres noble duc" (beautiful words and worthy language issued from your mouth, very noble duke) (MS Reg. Lat. 1238, folio 1v) deserve to be transcribed by Christine. The duke could not have asked for a better-written recognition of his efforts to assume his father's mantle. Nonetheless, in spite of this glowing comparison of son to father based on their shared wisdom, commitment to ethical conduct, and rhetorical eloquence, Christine signals one final but crucial practice that Duke Louis must display if he is to stand in for his father: he must provide evidence of support for intellectual activity. For Louis of Orléans to assume the intellectual banner of his father, he was expected to revive the former king's literary commissioning practices and to recognize writers as crucial contributors to the kingdom.

Scripting Charles V's Literary Engagement as a Shared Legacy

When promoting Louis's status as a learned prince, Christine introduced a number of rhetorical strategies that modelled what was required to perform as a viable patron. Christine clearly drew inspiration from the accounts she read in Charles V's commissioned books to communicate this message.[43] For instance, in the *Deux amans*, Christine adapted a popular model of this exchange inspired by Trémaugon's *Vergier* when inviting Louis to sit in judgment of the recorded debate. Reminiscent of Trémaugon's crediting of the king with having inspired the debate detailed in his text, Christine presents the duke's anticipated response to the debate as less of a ruling on the exchange itself and more as evidence of a collaborative enterprise between poet and prince. She ingeniously communicates a sense of collaborative exchange by explicitly pairing her "petit dit" (little text) (*Deux amans*, line 46) with her request to the duke that he supply a judgment, here identified as "vostre dit" (your response) (*Deux amans*, line 65). This poet-prince exchange serves as the subject of an opening miniature in all seven author-supervised extant copies of the *Deux amans*.[44] Among these copies, Reno and Ouy identify Bnf, MS fr. 1740 as "le plus ancien témoin de l'oeuvre" (the oldest witness of the work), which their team also presumes to have been transcribed and decorated under Christine's supervision for the duke's pleasure.[45] The frontispiece to MS fr. 1740 sets the tone for the duke's anticipated engagement with the work (Figure 5.1: BnF, MS fr. 1740, fol. 1r). To this end, it manipulates the conventional iconography of a presentation scene to emphasize the collaboration and reciprocation treated in the accompanying prologue. The artist, identified as a member of the *Master of the Couronnement de la Vierge* workshop and who worked on several of Christine's early books,[46] portrays the poet kneeling before the seated duke with an unfurled scroll in hand. The visual presentation of the duke corresponds perfectly to the opening line of the prologue, "Prince royal, renommé de sagece" (Royal prince, renowned for wisdom) (*Deux amans*, line 1). The fleur-de-lis backdrop confirms his royal standing, while he assumes the posture of the wise leader, enthroned with hand raised. Behind the poet, the two debaters are depicted engaged in conversation. Christine points with one hand to the debaters behind her while her body turns towards the duke, to whom she hands over the scroll. This gesture communicates a double message: the scroll functions as a written record of the debate between the two lovers behind her, while its blank state symbolically reserves space for the duke's requested response, his "dit." That the

Figure 5.1: Frontispiece, Christine de Pizan, *Débat de deux amans*, Paris, Bibliothèque nationale de France, MS fr. 1740, fol. 1r.

duke takes hold of the scroll with one hand while raising the other as if in preparation to speak reinforces the double role assigned the scroll. His posture simultaneously indicates his acceptance of the text and his willingness to share his views on the debate.

The *Othéa* prologue, produced a year after the *Deux amans*, adopts a new strategy for urging the duke to view Christine as an intellectual partner. Instead of scripting a future exchange with the duke, Christine daringly intertwines their destinies by revealing an important overlap in their genealogies that points to a shared legacy. As already discussed, the prologue bolsters Louis's own self-fashioning by emphasizing the intellectual lineage binding him to the Wise King. This learned genealogy that seems to bypass the firstborn sitting king resonates with Christine's own self-proclaimed genealogy thereafter. In lieu of self-naming, the poet identifies herself via the father: "fille jadis philosophe et docteur" (daughter of the deceased philosopher and doctor), who is then identified as "Maistre Thomas de Pizan" (*Othéa*, lines 19 and 24, respectively). She credits her father for any knowledge she possesses, although she claims to be an unworthy match to his wisdom: "je n'ay sentement/ En sens fondé, n'en ce cas ressemble/ Mon bon père" (I do not have knowledge in the profound sense and in this case, do not resemble my good father) (*Othéa*, lines 36–8). This modesty only loosely disguises the daring new familial genealogies that Christine establishes, ones in which the second living son of a king and the daughter of a doctor become the inheritors of paternal intellectual wealth. Christine calls attention to this suggested overlap in their family narratives when reminding Louis of her father's service to his father: "philosophe et docteur/ Qui conseiller et humble serviteur/ Vostre pere fu" (the philosopher and doctor who was an advisor and humble servant to your father) (*Othéa*, lines 19–21). Having effectively written herself into the Valois family legacy through this reminder of past interfamilial bonds, Christine thus justifies her desire (and right) to serve the duke. This new family narrative powerfully implies that, together, Louis and Christine represent the only chance for their fathers' legacy to survive. Christine maximized exposure of this daring proposal by inserting the work into the New Year's gifting economy, a ritualized exchange ceremony that made public the relationship she sought to secure. Such had been her intention from the outset, as she claims to have always conceived of the *Othéa* as a New Year's gift for the duke:

> … entrepris ay, …
> Presentement ceste oeuvre a rimoyer,

Mon redoubté, pour la vous envoyer
Le premier jour que l'an se renouvelle (*Othéa*, lines 30–3)

(I have now undertaken to rhyme this work, my esteemed prince, so as to send it to you on the first day of the year)

In the accompanying frontispiece to the duke's copy, MS fr. 848, this hoped-for exchange is carefully rendered. Upon gazing on this image, the duke would have discovered that both the illustration and the dedication firmly located him in the patron's seat once assigned his father. The addition of the men who witness the transaction brings added weight to the duke's positioning as the desired patron, since their very presence transforms the intimate exchange into a public performance. In so doing, they also signal the duke's official obligation to reciprocate if he is to maintain this elevated status as a generous and benevolent prince.

Work on New Year's gifting has tended to overlook the logic behind subordinate giving such as we see Christine re-enact in the frontispiece and prologue to the *Othéa*. In her thought-provoking work on the revival of this ceremony in the late Middle Ages, Brigitte Buettner speculates that the Valois dynasty restored the New Year's ritual to counter a growing market-driven society that threatened to undermine the archaic affiliations key to the continued dominance of nobility.[47] Both giving and receiving strengthened this reassertion of dominance since these gifts served to solidify alliances, strengthen fidelity among servants, and advertise wealth and taste. Inventory records reveal that the Duke of Orléans avidly participated in these ceremonies, with about 15 per cent of his annual income in the 1390s reserved for purchasing gifts in advance for his household and peers.[48] In this regard, the participation of Christine and other writers in this annual ritual can be interpreted as their willingness to encourage the archaic ideals of their superiors. It is equally likely that their efforts were self-serving. By inserting one's writings into the official gifting economy of checks and balances, authors surely increased their chances of reward and recognition. In addition, the ceremony provided a public opportunity to position their compositions as desired treasures with both material and intellectual value. When a writer used the paratext to document the insertion of the literary text into this exchange economy, as Christine did, there was also the opportunity to hold the recipient accountable for the offering. For as Buettner also notes, this ritual served as an important site for articulating relationships:

> Semi-public rituals like the annual offering of New Year's gifts provided a festive forum in which the appropriateness of things and actions could be evaluated. Its participants were called on to play the role of eyewitnesses who could see, discuss, broadcast, and remember what was given by whom to whom, and of translators of the language of objects who could discriminate between things that signified and those that remained silent, who could read between the lines and folds of what changed hands.[49]

That Christine regularly retained these original accounts of her text's biography in later copies intended for new readers suggests that in addition to bolstering her authority in the eyes of new recipients,[50] these ritual reproductions assured a focused gaze on the original recipient's role in the exchange. The recipient would thereby be recognized as holding a privileged status while at the same time being held publicly accountable for reciprocation.

Christine is careful to communicate in the prologue to the *Othéa* that, as a New Year's gift, her text enters into a circuit that anticipates, even requires, reciprocation. She first emphasizes the value of her work through her own investment in the work, which required intellectual labour ("labour d'estude," *Othéa*, line 50). She implicates the duke in the circle of exchange in a line that stands out in the dedication for its break with the otherwise consistent decasyllabic metre. Christine's single-line scripted performance of the book offering extends the number of syllables to introduce the loftier alexandrine metre: "A vous, mon redoubté seigneur, pour qui l'emprens" (to you, my esteemed Lord, for whom I undertook this) (*Othéa*, line 63). In a seemingly deliberate attempt to have the eye and ear linger on this declaration, the poetic voice extends the metre, bringing particular attention to the final two syllables of the line, whereupon the semiotic complexity of "l'emprens" becomes apparent. When divorced from its context, as the expanded metre invites us to do, "l'emprens" wavers between an acknowledgment of the poet's service to the duke ("I undertook this work") and a command that the prince take hold of/accept the book ("you take it"). The reciprocation set in motion by this line plays out in the initial presentation miniature.

In these early *dits* addressed to the duke, we observe Christine manipulating rhetoric and gifting rituals to implicate the duke in the exchange process. In the *Deux amans*, she invited the duke to respond to her work with his judgment, whereas in the *Othéa*, she publicized the duke's receipt of a New Year's gift that required reciprocation if an archaic tradition was to win out over the increasingly market-driven economy of late-medieval

France. In spite of her savvy manipulation of contemporary rituals and social anxieties, Christine does not appear to have been successful in persuading Duke Louis to serve as her literary patron in any sustained or active manner. There is no record in the ducal accounts of Christine receiving a reward for her literary gifts and no indication in Christine's writings that she received from Duke Louis either a reward or a commission. It may very well be that Christine sought to recall this unfulfilled obligation to reciprocate when staging the presentations of the *Rose* and the *Prod'hommie* in the ensuing years.

Although the *Rose* lacks a dedication, it is also inserted into ritualized gifting traditions within the fictional narrative. The poet links the poem to two ritualized gifting events. She first identifies a past New Year's banquet at the Orléans court as the site of the events to be detailed in the text. Second, the poet reveals her plan to present the completed work on Valentine's Day, yet another potential gifting moment on the late-medieval calendar.[51] Christine's decision to position this fictional narrative between these two public gift holidays may have served as a subtle reminder to the duke of her previous New Year's offering of the *Othéa*. As we shall see in the next chapter, she used a similar technique later in the commissioned biography of Charles V to recall an earlier New Year's book offering presented to the duke of Burgundy. Here, Christine makes use of the fictional veil to model more explicitly the literary relationship she desires. Christine provides a scripted performance of a literary commission in which Lady Loyalty visits Christine after the duke's banquet to communicate an order from the God of Love that the previous New Year's event "soit/ publiée ... / Et qu'on le sache en maint paÿs" (be announced ... And that one know of it throughout the country) (*Rose*, lines 498–500). The poet responds to the commission with delight:

Lye fuz de la vision
Et d'avoir tel commission;
Car combien que je ne le vaille
Ay je desir que nul ne faille,
Et pour ce moy, qui suis commise
A ce, ne doy estre remise
De faire si bien mon devoir. (*Rose*, lines 594–600)

(I was delighted by the vision and to have received such a commission because as much as I am unworthy, I desired more than anyone to do it and for this reason, I committed myself to it and do not have to be reminded to do my best.)

To my knowledge, this passage records the earliest use of the term "commission" in French linked to a request for a literary text. Christine emphasizes the importance of this term when using the adjectival form of the order to express her personal dedication to this enterprise ("suis commise"). In so doing, she signals the binding contract dictating all forms of exchange that oblige both parties to commit to the enterprise, while also clearly positioning herself as a willing client prepared to satisfy the patron's pleasure.

The fictional conceit on display here is intriguing. Similar to the *Deux amans*, in which Christine justified presenting the work to the duke based on the desires of the debaters, the present justification for composing this work stems from a "divine" commission that she commemorate and publicize an event previously headed by Louis of Orléans. For Adams, Christine composed the poem to counter Louis's marginalization in the *cour amoureuse* that had been recently formed by Philip of Burgundy and Louis of Bourbon.[52] While potentially true that Christine had the duke's interests at heart in composing this work, she also shows concern for her own positioning and she made sure to reserve for herself a vital role as one who could promote his interests. Herein, Louis emerges as a model prince who cultivates ideal behaviour in those around him, a prince who has earned the admiration of no less than the God of Love. It is also noteworthy that this *dit* presents Louis's court as a site of poetic collaboration since we are told that this New Year's dinner involved both good food, "beaulx livres et de dis" (good books and *dits*) (*Rose*, lines 71–2), and even poetry composed by the participants (" … de balades … qui … chascun devisoit," *Rose*, line 72–3). In spite of the high praise afforded Louis in this text, it appears that this work had no more success in eliciting a literary commission from the duke than Christine's *Othéa*. There is no trace of a copy of the work presented to Louis and, moreover, its circulation was highly limited. In addition, even though included in the first two iterations of her collected works manuscripts (Chantilly, Bibliothèque du château, MSS 492 and 493, and BnF, MS fr. 12779), neither rendition includes an opening miniature that might have confirmed Louis's status as the intended recipient. In subsequent years, the *Rose* disappeared entirely from Christine's repertoire, figuring in neither of the two extant luxury copies of her collected works that were owned by the duke of Berry and the queen of France.[53]

In the *Prod'hommie*, Christine adopts a very different tone from that of her previous works addressed to Duke Louis. Jean-Louis Picherit has already observed that the *Prod'hommie* seems to harbour some tension between the poet and the duke, and he reads this composition as a conciliatory work in which Christine attempted to remedy the situation.[54] The source of these tensions, according to Picherit, stemmed from the duke, but Christine's own opening account of the genesis of this work suggests that she harboured her own frustrations towards Louis. The poet implies herein that past efforts to curry the duke's favour went unnoticed. The prologue to the *Prod'hommie* recounts that Christine was invited to attend a closed court session during which Louis of Orléans publicly shared his views on moral conduct. For the first time in her writings, Christine openly refers to having presented the duke with previous works by speaking of an earlier gift of a "petit epistre" (little letter) (MS Reg. Lat. 1238, fol. 1v), but she hastens to disassociate that present from the duke's current invitation. Addressing the duke directly, she observes that "cy ne laissastez pas pour la petite faculté de moy femme transportee devant vous" (this [i.e., the "little letter"] does not justify that given my meager intellectual capacities, a woman was brought before you") (MS Reg. Lat. 1238, fol. 1v). Instead, Christine seems to imply that the duke never took serious notice of her until hearing of her growing reputation as someone interested in learning: "je suppose que la reputacion que avez que j'aime science et estude ... en est cause" (I suppose that the reputation concerning my love for knowledge and study ... is the reason) (MS Reg. Lat. 1238, fol. 1v). If Christine seems somewhat hopeful here – after all, she surmises that the duke appreciates her learned reputation – she also invites us to view her past textual offerings to the duke as scarcely acknowledged and she sets up the potential for ducal reciprocation only to deny the link. At best, Christine encourages us to believe that the duke invited her to court because she was a curiosity.[55] What does become increasingly evident is that Christine does not view his invitation as a solicitation of her learned talents, but rather as an opportunity for him to display his intellectual abilities. Nevertheless, Christine makes one last attempt to communicate to the duke her value as an intellectual partner.

In spite of this less-than-subtle nod to her growing reputation, Christine went to great lengths in the *Prod'hommie* to subordinate her abilities to the duke's wisdom as much as to his rhetorical talents. To this end, she recounts that during her court visit she remained "en silence" (in silence) so as to better hear Duke Louis's "paroles non pas frivoles ne de choses vaines mais de tres beaulx mos substanciux et pleine de profitable liqueur" (words that were neither frivolous nor about vain topics but beautiful words of substance and filled with profound liqueur) (MS Reg. Lat. 1238, fol. 1v). Clearly, Christine's earlier efforts to position Louis as the source of great wisdom are, once again, on display. Far from identifying him as a student she might school in appropriate ethical practices, as did her contemporaries Deschamps, Bovet, and Legrand, Christine presents the duke as a model for all, including herself. Even more explicitly, she refers to Duke Louis as a wise leader who, like a Julius Caesar, enlightened his people. As she "tenoit esmerveillee devant [sa] face" (stood in amazement in his presence) (MS Reg. Lat. 1238, fol. 2r) when he spoke, so too would the people of France find in him an extraordinary leader. When concluding the work, she is again careful to articulate her subordination to the prince. She qualifies the work as a product by and for him: "cy feray orez fin a l'euvre qui par vous et pour vous moy vostre servente et obeisant Cristine femme [...] ay accomplie" (here I will complete a work that I, your servant and the obedient woman Christine, have accomplished through you and for you) (MS Reg. Lat. 1238, fol. 46). She adds thereafter that the work "recounted here" ("icy narrées") reproduces "des premises qui de vous ont eu leur commencement" (the ideas that originated with you) (MS Reg. Lat. 1238, fol. 46). Furthermore, Christine refers to herself in the closing rubric to this work as a simple "antygraphe," a term unique to her that limited her involvement to that of a recorder of the words of others.[56] Finally, in the only contemporary extant version of the work, the duke is exclusively credited as the text's source: *la descripcion et diffinicion de la prodommie de l'omme selon l'opinion de monseigneur le duc d'Orlians* (the description and definition of the prudence of man according to the opinion of my Lord, the duke of Orléans) (MS Reg. Lat. 1238, fol. 1). It would be to a later hand to add Christine's name in the margins of this opening rubric.[57] Otherwise, Christine identifies herself only in the final lines of the text as "vostre servente et obeisant Cristine femme" (your obedient servant, the woman Christine) (MS Reg. Lat. 1238, fol. 46). It may appear that we encounter here an example of what Douglas Kelly identifies as a common poet-prince dynamic in which the prince assumes the role of "source, planner, and architect of artistic productions" while the poet serves as a mere mouthpiece[58] were it not for the fact that Christine gives no indication that the duke commissioned this work, and thus his actual involvement in the production of the text remains in question.

It is no small irony that the *Prod'hommie* holds the rare distinction of figuring in the duke's inventory[59] because Christine decisively changed literary strategies following this work and substantially tempered her enthusiastic support of the duke's patronage thereafter. Although Christine placed Louis in the seat of learned authority in this final work focused on him, she was careful to not confuse this seat with the mythical patronal seat once occupied by his father Charles V. Christine fully attributes the wisdom contained within this book to Duke Louis. She further recognizes that his invitation gave her the opportunity to hear and record his words. She even credits him with recognizing her learned reputation. Nonetheless, unlike her earlier works, she withholds from him any semblance of possessing his father's interest in engaging with the intellectual community. Duke Louis so fully occupies the seat of learning that he leaves no room for intellectual partners. All he requires is a scribe to record his words. The *Prod'hommie* would be the final composition that Christine addressed so prominently and exclusively to the duke of Orléans, although she would continue to praise him in subsequent works.[60] Beginning as early as 1402, Christine started to recast her writings as gifts intended for a diverse community and she even reworked texts first composed for the duke to redistribute to a larger audience. The strategies she adopted to normalize the decision to offer works initially dedicated to a single potential sponsor to new readers reveal an important shift in her understanding of the function of the gift-text and, more importantly, of the role that accounts of past literary exchange, real or imagined, might play in reviving Charles V's legacy. Going forward, the literary gift would serve to cultivate desire and to trigger need in the reader; in short, the gift-text now figured as a call for potential patrons to consider the relationship they might have with the poet should they solicit her talents.

Competitive Sponsorship and Fostering Conspicuous Consumption: Christine's Pursuit of Alternate Partners

Beginning as early as 1402, Christine redistributed at least two of the four works originally dedicated to Louis as gifts to others. Christine's decision to distribute among multiple worthy parties works initially dedicated to Duke Louis and, then, identical copies of her subsequent writings reflects her savvy appropriation of the practices and customs of ritual gifting among nobility. As late-medieval nobility turned to the contemporary market to acquire mass-produced tokens – such as broaches, necklaces, clothing items or fabric, goblets, and carafes – to re-enact archaic forms of gifting, so too did Christine see to the production of multiple copies of her works, which she then circulated in an effort to advertise her literary gift. Extant manuscripts of the *Deux amans* and the *Othéa* suggest that Christine composed new dedications for these works, which presented a second wave of privileged recipients with an account of literary exchange that differed from the arrangement she had imagined with Duke Louis.

These new dedications did not place the latest addressee in the patronal seat left vacant by the duke. Instead, they presented literary exchange as a nostalgic performance intended to trigger desire for Christine's literary gift. Through the re-enactment of the presentation performance that had defined the Wise King's public persona and that was now associated with his second surviving son, the author offered newly chosen recipients the chance to insert themselves into this lofty narrative.

We know little surrounding Christine's presentation of the *Deux amans* to Duke Louis, but we learn in a second single-work copy of the text that, in 1403, she repackaged the gift as a New Year's offering for the newly appointed constable of Paris, Charles d'Albret.[61] The constable's presentation copy (Brussels, Bibliothèque royale de Belgique, MS 11034) does not rewrite the original dedication to Duke Louis; instead the duke's dedication is prefaced with a new address to the constable.[62] Barbara K. Altmann understands the new prologue as an attempt "to reconcile sending a presentation copy of the poem to Charles d'Albret despite the fact that the text itself contains a dedication to Louis, duke of Orléans."[63] To be certain, negotiating this delicate transaction demanded careful attention, especially given that the new dedication drew on the same fictional conceit used in the original address to Louis to justify this second book presentation. As the original dedication claimed that the debaters had sought out Louis as their judge, so too the new dedication in MS 11034 claims that these same debaters also recognized the constable's opinion as equally desirable.[64] The final stanza of this new dedication, however, hints at the poet's actual intentions:

> Mon redoubté seigneur des milliers trente,
> Me recommend a vo bonté hautaine
> Cui mon service ottroy sanz estre lente;
> Si le vueilliez recevoir pour estraine. ("Albret Dedication," lines 31–4)

> (My revered Lord of thousands of men, I submit myself to your noble goodness, to whom my services are given without hesitation; if you are willing to accept [this work] as a New Year's gift.)

When addressing Charles d'Albret, Christine makes an important distinction between this copy that serves to advertise her services rather than to celebrate the constable's authority, whereas her original intention when she first presented the work to Duke Louis was to advertise his power and her submission to his authority.

The artist of the opening miniature to MS 11034 played an instrumental role in articulating the difference between the two narratives of literary exchange documented by the double dedication heading MS 11304 (Figure 5.2: Brussels, KBR, MS 11034, fol. 2r). At first glance, the MS 11034 frontispiece appears to reproduce the presentation scene already heading MS fr. 1740, which scholars consider to have been Duke Louis's personal copy. The central scene in both codices portrays the poet presenting the poem to Duke Louis with the debaters behind her. The artist responsible for the constable's copy of the *Deux amans*, however, modified the donation scene by inserting in the background a second ceremonial event. The two men behind Duke Louis's throne do not engage with the book presentation transpiring before them and appear, instead, to re-enact a separate ceremony.[65] In fact, this scene of one man extending a baton to the shoulder of a figure donning a sack cap may very well reference the ceremonial naming of Charles d'Albret as the new constable.[66] If indeed the case, MS 11034 provides a visual trace of efforts to negotiate the passing of the *Deux amans* from Louis to a new privileged reader. The image achieves this negotiation not only through reference to the constable's recent court promotion, which occurs in the background, but also by anticipating the relationship the constable might have with the text. All the while acknowledging Louis as the first recipient, the foregrounded presentation scene invites the constable to imagine himself as stepping out of the shadows to assume the lofty position of someone worthy of receiving a poet's text, which is proferred on bended knee. These textual and visual adjustments to the original dedication shrewdly withhold from the constable immediate access to the patron's seat, although the poet extends an invitation to him to consider accepting her offered services and, by extension, the status such an act would confer on him ("Albret Dedication," line 34).

Extant manuscripts of the *Othéa* point to a similar circulation strategy to the one on display in Charles d'Albret's personalized copy of the *Deux amans*. Extant copies of the *Othéa*, although not directly linked to the poet, offer provocative evidence that between 1402 and 1406, Christine composed new dedications intended to redirect this work to other noble readers.[67] These later manuscripts suggestively point to three noblemen as later recipients of personalized copies of the *Othéa*: Henry IV of England, Duke John of Berry, and Duke Philip of Burgundy. The addresses to the two dukes differ from one another only in the insertion of each duke's name, while the address to Henry IV identifies him by his sovereign title and alters key passages that delineate the exchange.[68] Two of the

Figure 5.2: Presentation scene, Christine de Pizan, *Débat de deux amans*, Brussels, Bibliothèque royale de Belgique, MS 11034, fol. 2r.

extant copies containing these alternative dedications also include tailored frontispieces that suggest either that Christine ordered new presentation scenes to portray each duke in the seat once reserved for Duke Louis or that later bookmakers found it inappropriate to dedicate the work to one prince while referring to another as occupying the seat of authority.[69]

In a strategy reminiscent of tactics used in the dedicatory matter added to Charles d'Albret's copy of the *Deux amans*, these later rededications of the *Othéa* refrained from fully substituting Louis with the new dedicatees and opted instead to articulate a different relationship with each addressee. The address to the king of England is most striking in this arena. The impetus behind Christine's decision to send a copy of her *Othéa* to Henry IV may explain some of its distinctive components. It is possible that she sent the work as a form of ransom to secure the return of her son after political events jeopardized his safety in England.[70] These circumstances may explain why Christine appears to have avoided any suggestion that the work issued an invitation for the English king to commission future works. She was careful in her address to the unnamed king to maintain a certain distance from him. Thus, whereas she conceived of Duke Louis's appreciation of her work as conferring back to her "grant gloire" ("much glory," *Othéa*, line 29), the poet simply claims the English king's pleasure to be motivation enough to send a copy to him (*Othéa*, p. 502, lines 21–4). Nor does she identify the king as the motivating source for composing the work, as she declared in her address to Duke Louis. Instead, Christine informs the king that she wrote the work to celebrate chivalry in general:

> Pur le desir qu'ay que chivalrie
> Soit en tout temps augmentee et flourie,
> Ay je volu cest oeuvre cy emprendre. (*Othéa*, p. 502, lines 41–3)
>
> (Because of my wish that chivalry at all times grows and flourishes, I wanted to undertake this present work.)

This new explanation for the work strips "emprendre" of the semiotic complexity and metrical distinction examined in Christine's alternative address to Louis. Here, she appears keen to position her offering as one not expecting a return, a point reinforced by the closing to King Henry's dedication. in which she declares, "A vous, tresredoubté que je desir/ Servir, doubter, amer, faire plaisir" (To you, most revered whom I desire to serve, love, and please) (*Othéa*, p. 503, lines 53–4). For Christine, this tendered copy of her book represents not a gift-offering but a transaction intended to secure her son's return.

The finality of her dealings with the king is most clearly appreciated when compared with the new addresses likely composed by Christine to head copies of the *Othéa* presented to the dukes of Berry and Burgundy. When addressing the Valois uncles, the poet echoes the hope expressed in her address to Charles d'Albret in the *Deux amans* that her offering might lead to a future commission. The new dedications elaborate further on the "labour d'estude" (labour of study) (*Othéa*, line 50), which Christine previously spotlighted in her address to Duke Louis. In these later dedications, the term "labour" appears twice in each to signal two stages of production:

> Prince digne, et comme desireuse
> De vous servir, se feusse si eureuse,
> Je vous fais don de mon petit labour,
> Afin que vous voyez com je labour
> A mon pouoir a l'augmentacïon
> De vaillantise. (*Othéa*, p. 505, lines 21–6; p. 508, lines 21–6)
>
> (Worthy prince, wishing to serve you, so happy would I be, I thus offer you my little work so that you can see how I labor as I am able to celebrate valor.)

In the first instance, "petit labour" identifies the book-gift, which then leads to the advertisement of the learned labour required to compose this poem. As already witnessed in her address to Charles d'Albret, each of these book presentations communicates the poet's desire to serve both dukes in the future. Specifically, she aspires that her offering will trigger in each of them a hunger, an "appetite," for more of her writings:

> Combien qu'en moy ait savoir trop petit
> Parquoy aucun peust prendre appetit
> En mes dittiez pour doctrine y aprendre. (*Othéa*, p. 505, lines 27–9; p. 508, lines 27–9)
>
> (Even though my knowledge is modest, perhaps some might acquire an appetite for my writings, for the doctrine they can teach.)

As was the case with the constable, these new dedications do not cast the dukes as patrons of this work. Instead, these new copies publicize a willingness to collaborate in the future with each duke on other enterprises. While these gift-copies of works previously composed for Duke Louis may still represent unsolicited gifts, they are presented to new recipients as material products that serve the author's intentions, whether that is to secure the return of her son, as was the likely case with the king of England, or to advertise her talents to other potential Valois sponsors.

The two remaining works associated with Louis experienced very different afterlives that stand in stark contrast to those of the *Deux amans* and the *Othéa*. As already mentioned regarding the *Rose*, there are no extant single copies of it, and its presence in the collected-works manuscripts supervised by Christine in subsequent years was irregular. To reiterate, the poem appeared in the earliest collections supervised by the author, only to disappear from the lineup in the collections acquired by the duke of Berry in 1408 and the queen of France around 1414.[71] Likewise, the *Prod'hommie* is extant in only one author-supervised manuscript now housed at the Vatican. This last work would reappear with a new title and stripped of its framing address to Duke Louis in later author-supervised complete-works collections.[72] In this later rendition of the *Prod'hommie* text, it is Christine, not Duke Louis, who is identified as the source of the contained wisdom. This reattribution of the wisdom contained within is made even more explicit by the new closing rubric attached to the retitled work, the *Livre de Prudence*. Whereas the closing rubric in the *Prod'hommie* reduced Christine's role to that of "antygraphe," the closing rubric to the *Livre de Prudence* declares the work to have been "fait et compilé par Christine de Pizan" (made and compiled by Christine de Pizan).[73] The surprising appropriation by Christine of words and ideas formerly attributed to the duke led Christine Reno to conclude that the author must have received at least "tacit" approval from Louis before repackaging the *Prod'hommie* as a new work.[74] It is equally possible that Christine was no longer willing to be satisfied with the role of passive scribe and sought to reclaim her learned labour.

The afterlives of the works that Christine originally dedicated to Louis of Orléans detail different models of literary exchange used by the author when circulating her writings. In all cases, when first presenting these works to Duke Louis, there was an insistence on their status as what Mauss refers to as "free and disinterested" gifts that, nonetheless, expressed a desire for a very particular version of literary reciprocation. Addresses to the duke of Orléans make clear that Christine hoped that her unsolicited gifts would lead to an intimate intellectual partnership with the duke in which, together, they would assure their fathers' legacies.

It appears that Duke Louis never sufficiently assumed the role of patron that Christine sketched out for him, and this failure to respond to her offerings led Christine to recirculate the works to other potential sponsors. In these subsequent quests for sponsorship, she retained the language and patterns of gifting initially used to address Duke Louis and, at least in some cases, even retained the narrative of past intimacy, real or imagined, with the duke. In either scenario, the intent appears to have been to incite in her new audience a nostalgic desire – an "appetite" – for the type of literary relations so vividly celebrated in Charles V's books and reproduced in her own, even if an uncooperative prince occupied the patron's seat. That said, Christine's works make clear that for this past model to be revived, new recipients were required to respond to the writer's gift by requesting new works from her, thereby truly assuming the role of a literary patron.

By 1403 Christine seems to have fully embraced the value of distributing her texts to multiple potential patrons as symbolic gifts intended to trigger a desire for intellectual intimacy reminiscent of the Wise King's literary dealings with the commissioned writers. Two new compositions produced that year, the *Chemin* and the *Mutacion*, detail different but complementary strategies. In these works, Christine stepped away from the conventional single-patron model to cultivate instead competition for the role of sponsor from the outset. The dedication to the *Chemin* explicitly details this strategy. This work begins by assigning the patron-function to Charles VI:

> A vous, bon roy de France redoubtable,
> Le VIe Charles du nom nottable,
> Que Dieu maintiengne en joye et en santé
> Mon petit dit soit premier presenté. [75]

> (To you, good and esteemed King of France, Charles, the sixth of this worthy name – that God keep you in joy and health – my little work shall be presented first.)

Clearly, the mad king could not live up to the obligations of a real patron.[76] Significantly, Christine identifies Charles VI as only the first recipient of the text at the outset of this work. The next line expands Christine's audience to include the Valois dukes: "Et puis a vous, haulx ducs magniffiez,/ D'ycelle flour fais" (and then to you, great and magnificent dukes born of the flower [i.e., fleur de lis]) (*Chemin*, lines 15–16). Christine encourages these men, as she had with the repackaged *Othéa*, to see their gift-copy as evidence of her desire to serve them, which she states directly as the "desir/ Qu'ay de servir ou faire aucun plaisir/ A vostre tres digne et haulte noblece" (desire that I have to serve or accomplish any pleasure for you, most worthy and of high nobility) (*Chemin*, lines 29–31). The material history of the *Chemin* confirms that the dukes of Berry, Burgundy, and Orléans all possessed personal but not personalized copies of this work by 1404.[77] Each of their copies retained the original dedication in which Charles VI enjoyed the privileged role as first recipient, and their accompanying presentation miniatures reinforced the king's singular honour by portraying the poet with book in hand and on bended knee before him rather than before one of the dukes. This nostalgic scene surely served as a haunting reminder of the patron scenes decorating Charles V's previously commissioned texts, especially given the disturbing present reality of an incapacitated king.

Scholarship on nostalgia and its relationship to memory can be helpful in understanding Christine's unique usage of an account of past literary exchange to inspire future activity. Eric Hobsbawm observes that "the ongoing reconstruction of the past is an act not only of recontextualization but of invention"; Svetlana Boym identifies nostalgia as a "romance with one's own fantasy"; and Bakhtin positions nostalgia as a "historical inversion" in which "the ideal that is not being lived now … is projected into the past."[78] In essence, nostalgia studies encourage us to see in Christine's efforts to register a past model of ideal/idealized proportions an attempt to shape her future dealings. Whereas the nostalgic is often accused of wallowing in the past, Christine proves different. In place of an uncritical revival, her textual and visual testimonies of dealing with multiple patrons function as sites of complex negotiations between past ideals and present realities. In Christine's writings, we witness her unique effort to force an economic conversion by imposing on the competitive consumption practices of her privileged audience a nostalgic memory of a time when the writer's gift represented the most coveted of possessions.

Christine's treatment of audience relations reveals a shrewd manipulation both of Charles V's legacy and of market demand for her works to create an unprecedented hybrid economy for her books. Christine benefited from the unique take on gift distribution central to the Valois revival of holiday gifting ceremonies to assure larger circulation of her works that she had begun to produce in multiple copies. These copies served as tokens *representing* exchange and intimacy, but they explicitly kept the privileged readers at a remove from the depicted event. Recipients of these copies could gaze on the inaugural gifting scene, but they were not allowed to see themselves as direct participants in the transaction. Instead, Christine advertised her literary gift, her willingness to foster a nostalgic longing for this lost past, and her capacity to revive past practices. That she declared such an arrangement was theirs for the taking justified her multi-pronged distribution and, moreover, it achieved the desired effect. In 1404, Duke Philip of Burgundy commissioned a new work from Christine – fittingly, a biography of his brother Charles V. Christine was quick to sketch out the events that surrounded this most desirable commission, which she dated back to her previous presentation to the duke in 1403 of one of several copies of the *Mutacion*, a work that proclaimed no one as patron and yet succeeded in securing a subsequent commission. It is this form of literary circulation, developed in Christine's biography of Charles V, to which we turn in the final chapter.

Chapter Six

The Curse of the Commission: Christine de Pizan on Sacrificing Charles V's Biography

The previous chapter focused on Christine de Pizan's failed pursuit of a commission from Louis of Orléans and her eventual decision to redistribute texts originally dedicated to the duke to others who might be willing to revive the literary practice so closely associated with Charles V. This strategy allowed Christine to advertise her literary gift to these potential sponsors and to invite them to imagine themselves in the seat previously reserved for Duke Louis. Christine's tactics signalled an important shift in views on literary engagement in the wake of Charles V's commissioning activity, a shift that cast literary clientelism in a nostalgic light, a perspective that was due in large part to the early efforts of the king's commissioned writers and illustrators to present his literary dealings as motivated by the king's intellectual commitment rather than by personal interest in acquiring symbols of power and prestige. Given that Christine's initial efforts appear to have never achieved the desired outcome with Duke Louis, we need to be attentive to what these accounts might have represented for both author and audience thereafter. For when redistributing narratives that had initially served as invitations to Duke Louis to participate in the type of intimate intellectual exchange famously associated with his father, Christine was peddling an illusion that had long fallen out of favour. It has been remarked at several points in this study, but it bears repeating that one is hard pressed to find archival evidence of the Valois princes commissioning works from contemporary writers in the immediate decades following Charles V's death. Instead, the dominant form of literary exchange involved unsolicited giving initiated by writers. Christine followed this more common pattern while never failing to cast her gift as an invitation to recipients to consider reviving the literary practices that had assured the Wise King's revered status. Note the extent to which Christine walked a fine line between the idealized model detailed in Charles V's commissioned works and the sceptical take on the literary commission that was developed in Machaut's writings and eventually embraced by Deschamps as a true reflection of court life during Charles VI's reign. Worthy of our consideration is also the likely ambivalence of the ruling class regarding the literary economy. Even if disinterested in reviving the commission, the nobility surely appreciated invitations by writers like Christine to assume the patronal seat left empty following Charles V's sudden death. The competitive consumption practices that stimulated gifting in late-medieval aristocratic circles surely kicked in when a writer openly announced that new owners might acquire another's riches. How else are we to understand the fact that Christine's tactic of redistributing her works that still bore the mark of the initial recipient led to subsequent commissions for copies of her works? As discussed, we find this pattern evoked in the *Cent ballades,* where Christine justifies repackaging her past poetry based on audience demand. Yet another example of this tactic used as an advertising strategy to be discussed appears at the head of the anthology of her works produced on demand for the queen of France, where she advertised her diverse readership in opening miniatures and prologues to individual works.[1] This pattern of commemorating past literary exchange is, however, most powerfully detailed in Christine's account of receiving her first desired commission from Duke Philip of Burgundy. The *Fais et bonnes meurs du sage roy Charles V* commissioned by Duke Philip stands out as one of the most spectacular and loaded literary commissions ordered by a Valois prince since the abrupt collapse of the Wise King's *Sapientia* project.[2]

In 1404, Duke Louis's uncle, Duke Philip the Bold of Burgundy, commissioned from Christine the biography of none other than his deceased brother, Charles V. This extraordinary request to commemorate through writing the Wise King's legacy was made even grander by the duke's spectacular re-enactment of the deceased king's revered clientelistic literary practices. This re-enactment was far from coincidental, and it surely reflected the "growing nostalgia for the reign of Charles V" that pervaded the period.[3] In addition, as Suzanne Solente has observed in her edition of the work, this commission held particular significance for the duke, who could count it as "une victoire de plus dans sa lutte contre le frère de Charles VI" (one more victory in his fight with the brother of Charles VI).[4] Indeed, with this single gesture, Duke Philip publicly deposed his nephew, who had pretensions of assuming the patronal seat once occupied by Charles V. Duke Philip had long fashioned himself as a powerful alternative to the failing leadership of his nephews, and by personally assuring his illustrious brother's legacy, he made a decisive grab for this learned heritage. That Duke Philip chose the royal brothers' most devout and prolific supporter among the Parisian *literati* to produce this work undoubtedly enhanced this political upstaging. Christine aided in the uncle's efforts by giving his request the recognition it deserved in the opening chapter of *Charles V*, where the commissioning scene is meticulously documented to assure that all witness the ritualized transfer of intellectual authority to Duke Philip. Although Christine's shift in allegiance to the very prince who had long challenged Louis's right and ability to rule could not have been taken casually, she would from that day forward recognize the Burgundian commission as a pivotal moment in her own narrative and credit Duke Philip alone with having revived the learned and literary practices of his illustrious royal brother. What resulted from political manoeuvring for the duke was decidedly repackaged by Christine as a nostalgic nod to what she perceived as the golden age of literary patronage.

The promise represented by Duke Philip's commission was, however, short lived. Approximately four months after having solicited the biography, Duke Philip unexpectedly died on 27 April 1404, and with his death, the commission collapsed. The duke's death shattered Christine's hopes of a new era of Valois literary clientelism. She bears witness to her enduring disappointment one year later in the *Livre de l'advision Cristine*, in which she refers to the duke's passing as "[s]a plus grant perte" (her greatest loss)[5] – a loss so great that it trumped the earlier deaths of her beloved husband and her father. She further claims in this pseudo-autobiography that his death represented a personal attack by Lady Fortune who felt "haineuse envie" (hateful jealousy) towards the writer (*Advision*, 114). Christine's continued bewilderment in face of this mortal blow is fully captured in her highly stylized remembrance of their brief collaboration:

> de sa bouche me charga, [...], comme il desirast que la belle vie et notables fais du saige roy sus dist fust en propre volume mise en registre affin que perpetuelle mémoire demourast au monde par bon example de son noble nom, que je compillasse desdictes choses certain volume – helas! et tost après, lors que sa grace vers moy de plus en plus croissoit, le me tolli par Mort la desloyale! (*Advision*, 114)

> (From his mouth he notified me, [...], that he desired that the good life and noble deeds of the Wise King be appropriately recorded in writing so that in this world, perpetual memory would endure of the good example of his noble name; and that on this subject, I was to compose a work – but, alas, soon

> thereafter, just as his favour towards me grew more and more, he was torn from me by disloyal Death!)

That the commission had not yet been completed when Philip died – the "livre qu'il me commanda, non encore lors achevé" (the book he ordered from me that was not yet completed) (*Advision*, 115) – made the duke's death all the more bitter.

The frustration that Christine expressed in this later text revealed itself quite differently in the actual biography, which she did manage to complete in the subsequent months. As fate would have it, Christine dated the completion of Part 1 of *Charles V* to one day after the duke's death. She gave no indication when signing off on this first section that she was aware of the tragic events that had transpired. By the time she began Part 2, however, she had learned of the duke's passing and she responded with a public promise to complete the assignment in spite of this major setback. Christine's loyalty to the duke's wishes set her apart from her contemporaries, the Limbourg brothers. In April 1404, the brothers were midway through a 1402 contractual agreement to decorate Duke Philip's *Bible moralisée*, which only three months prior, the duke had extended with another four-year contract.[6] In spite of these binding agreements, the brothers abandoned the assignment following the duke's death.[7] Christine, in contrast, completed the commissioned biography, but not without much struggle. The biography of Charles V authored by Christine bears witness to these struggles in asides that find the author grappling with the ethical responsibility, the contractual constraints, and the personal disappointment that shrouded the now-orphaned commission. For Christine, what had once been a boon became a curse. In the aftermath of Duke Philip's death, Christine found herself yoked to a text and a nostalgic memory that she alone seemed to value. What might have been the greatest literary expression of Charles V's legacy ended up exposing the problems inherent in the clientelistic model the Wise King had come to embody and that Christine had aggressively pursued.

This chapter begins with a brief overview of the duke of Burgundy's investment in letters before examining Christine's account of their dealings at the outset of *Charles V*. Attention is then given to authorial asides in the commissioned biography that redirect the work to a new audience. This audience encompassed both assenting interlocutors, who participated in the building of the king's *memoria*,[8] and hostile opponents, who threatened the textual monument intended to honour both the Wise King and his brother. Of particular importance are asides in Part 2 of the biography, in which Christine openly struggles with an imaginary antagonistic audience whom she describes as "envieux ou mesdisens" (envious people or slanderers) who are eager "to accuse [her] of lying or breaking her promise" (chargier de mençonge ou faulte de promesse).[9] Their criticisms, which are registered in Part 2, lead to the adoption of extreme measures in Part 3, in which the duke's orphaned commission is re-conceptualized as a sacrificial offering presented to the deceased king. Georges Bataille teaches us that sacrifice, as the purest form of gifting, allows one to "restor[e] a lost value through a relinquishment of that value" by practising uncalculated generosity.[10] This radical re-imagining of exchange is played out in Christine's treatment of the biography. Christine ultimately freed the text from the contractual bind of the commission, although this act left her in possession of an unwanted object whose very existence simultaneously commemorated two celebrated deceased patrons and the literary economy that they alone had sustained. In the biography, she mourned the collapse of this nostalgic ideal of literary dynamics built on intellectual friendship. The final section of this chapter turns to the material traces of *Charles V*, which allow us to track the effect of this sacrificial act on the text's survival, a process that casts a wider gaze on the fate of the commission during the final and most difficult years of Charles VI's reign.

Duke Philip of Burgundy's Library and Christine's Early Contributions to his Collection

It is no surprise that Christine turned to Duke Philip the Bold as a potential sponsor of her work. For Patrick de Winter, the duke of Burgundy emerged as the true perpetuator of Charles V's legacy because he alone exhibited strong interests in "les courants littéraires nouveaux" (new literary currents) and because of his leading role as a "promoteur d'importants projets artistiques" (promoter of important artistic project).[11] There are many indications that Charles V's youngest brother took an early active interest in book culture, and as his fortunes increased, so too did his investment in luxury books. As early as 1375, Duke Philip had culled together a personal library modelled on his brother's Louvre collection (hence, nearly a decade before his nephew Louis would invest seriously in his own replica of the Louvre library). Several of the duke's prized holdings actually came from the royal collection in the form of "certains livres" (some books) that the librarian Gilles Malet presented to Philip.[12] The duke also received directly from Charles VI and Queen Isabeau gifts of at least eight more books pulled from the royal shelves.[13]

Add to this booty that when the duke of Anjou died in 1385, not all of the forty-some works that he had originally taken from the royal library were returned to the Louvre; some made their way to Duke Philip's residence, including Charles V's personal copies of Oresme's translations of Aristotle.[14] In 1398 the duke would pilfer yet another treasure from the royal library, the copy of the *Bible moralisée* owned by his father King John the Good, a work that he was said to have "borrowed," but that was never returned.[15] As they did with other princes who showed an interest in book culture, contemporary writers curried Duke Philip's favour. Several of the writers mentioned in previous chapters who had written for Valois royalty turned their sights on the duke after first trying their chances with his royal nephews. In the final decade of the fourteenth century, as already stated, Honorat Bovet provided Duke Philip with copies of his *Arbre des batailles* and *Apparicion maistre Jehan de Meun*, which had been presented to the royal brothers, and Eustache Deschamps may have produced at the duke's request his translation, the *Dolente et piteuse complainte de l'Eglise moult desolée au jour d'ui*.[16] Other writers of varied backgrounds also presented Duke Philip with new compositions over the years, including Gace de la Buigne, Philippe de Mézières, Jean Créton, Gaston Fébus, Jean Gerson, and Nicolas de Clamanges.[17] Perhaps not coincidentally, just as Louis of Orléans's "campaign of manuscript production" of 1394–8 was assuring a replica of the Louvre library at his own Paris hotel,[18] Duke Philip appears to have turned increased attention to his own book collection. Like his nephew, Duke Philip acquired new copies of works already contained in the royal library. The Rapondi brothers were the duke's preferred book merchants and they secured for him copies of the *Propriété des choses, Decades*, and the *Fleurs des histoires de la terre d'Orient* to the *Legende dorée* and a new Bible.[19] It is also during this period that Duke Philip agreed to pay a monthly salary and provide food and lodging to the already mentioned Limbourg brothers to assure decoration of a new *Bible moralisée*. In 1403, in addition to receiving luxury copies of Christine's *Chemin* and the *Mutacion*, the duke obtained, with the help of the Rapondi brothers, the first French translations of Boccaccio's *De mulieribus claris* (BnF, MS fr. 12420) and the *Decameron*; these dealings with the Rapondi brothers speak to the duke's willingness to pay handsomely – anywhere from 300 to 700 gold francs – for worthy books to enhance his collection.[20] In this regard, Philip far surpassed his nephew Louis in his financial investment in new literary works, even though he possessed fewer books than Louis during this period.

As discussed in the previous chapter, Christine likely began her campaign to attract Duke Philip's patronage in 1402, when she presented him with a tailored copy of the *Othéa*. The following year, she offered him copies of her new writings, the *Chemin* and the *Mutacion*. One or both of the gift-texts submitted to the duke prior to the *Mutacion* surely inspired Duke Philip's gift in September 1403 to Christine of "un hanap et une aiguiere d'argent" (a goblet and a carafe in silver) valued at 50 francs.[21] Let us note, however, that this sum constitutes a fairly modest reward, given the quality of books we believe Christine offered him. Although the actual *Othéa* copy presented to the duke remains unknown, several extant copies of the last two works have been proposed as the likely originals obtained by Duke Philip. Regarding the *Chemin*, scholars debate which of the two nearly identical extant copies of this work now housed in Belgium represents the duke's presentation copy, although most lean towards Brussels, Bibliothèque royale de Belgique, MS 10983.[22] Scholars concur that Brussels, Bibliothèque royale de Belgique, MS 9508 is the copy of the *Mutacion* that Christine offered the duke as a New Year's gift in 1403. All three of these codices clearly testify to Christine's efforts to cultivate desire for her work through an astute management of their messaging capacity. First, in all three cases, it has been hypothesized that Christine personally transcribed these copies.[23] Second, with their high-quality parchment, ample page layout, and refined miniature cycles and decoration, these codices clearly catered to the duke's luxury book tastes. They are imposing book-objects, with the two nearly identical copies of the *Chemin* measuring 280 × 190 millimetres and 289 × 209 millimetres, and the *Mutacion* exhibiting even more imposing measurements at 349 × 254 millimetres and its 190 folios double the volume of the *Chemin* copies.[24] For these reasons, it can be said that these three copies are marked by a "semiotic complexity" that Arjun Appadurai finds to be typical of luxury objects.[25] Thus, at the same time that we witness Christine using the paratextual and material space of the *Chemin* copies to encourage a nostalgic consideration of past literary dynamics, as discussed in the previous chapter, we also see her producing luxury copies of her works that would speak to the competitive consumption practices that fuelled the growth of late-medieval private libraries.[26] We have already considered this strategy as it is manifested in the liminary material heading all extant copies of the *Chemin*. To reiterate the point, Christine first identified Charles VI as the privileged recipient in the prologue, only to then expand her audience immediately thereafter to include as worthy recipients of her writing "haulx ducs" (great dukes) (*Chemin*, lines 15–16) or "princes poissans" (powerful princes) (*Chemin*, line 55). In spite of this verbal acknowledgment of the possibility that other princes besides the king might fulfil the patron-function, Christine secured a standard opening miniature depicting Charles VI in the patronal seat for author-supervised copies of the *Chemin*. The scene surely struck contemporary viewers as incongruous given the king's infirmity, not to mention his abiding disinterest in learned writings. This obvious contradiction between the depicted scene and contemporary realities suggests that the *Chemin* presentation scene and the initial dedication to the king were not intended to model desired royal response nor to celebrate and memorialize the reigning king's status as a promoter of literary activity. Instead, they functioned as an invitation to subsequent recipients of the work to imagine themselves in the lofty seat assigned (inappropriately) to the king in their copies of the work. This reading of the opening to the *Chemin* invites us to consider that Christine's New Year's gifting of luxury books benefited from both the nostalgic thrust and the competitive consumption practices at the heart of these ceremonies to underscore the important role her writings could play in a prince's self-identification with Charles V.

The stock miniature decorating the author-supervised copies of the *Chemin* further encourages us to interpret the textual and visual re-enactment of the presentation ritual as performed not so much for the king as for those men who received copies of this work.[27] In all concerned copies, Charles VI is depicted receiving the book from the kneeling poet while a crowd of onlookers observes the scene. Regarding these bystanders, James Laidlaw asks whether they might not, in fact, represent the "princes poissans" referenced in the prologue.[28] We already observed in the previous chapter that in the same year of completing the *Chemin*, Christine adopted a similar strategy to personalize Charles d'Albret's copy of the *Deux amans*. To recap, in the constable's codex, inserted behind the scene of the author presenting her work to Duke Louis, two men are depicted engaged in a separate ceremony that could be interpreted as a visual reference to Charles's dubbing as constable earlier that year. (See Figure 5.2: Brussels, Bibliothèque royale de Belgique, MS 11034, fol. 2r.) In the *Chemin* copies, however, the situation differs in important ways from this personalized copy of the *Deux amans*. In the stock image opening all extant author-supervised *Chemin* copies, the men depicted on the sidelines give their full attention to the scene transpiring before them (Figure 6.1: Brussels, Bibliothèque royale de Belgique, MS 10983, fol. 1r). No other ceremony distracts them from the central event, in which they are afforded only a peripheral role. The orientation of their gaze, their posture, and their unusual crowding around

Figure 6.1: Presentation scene, Christine de Pizan, The *Livre du chemin de longue étude*, Brussels, Bibliothèque royale de Belgique, MS 10983, fol. 1r.

the presentation scene underscore the importance of the book exchange. The intensity of this compressed scene offers rare insight into the pathos behind the competitiveness and conspicuous consumption practices that fuelled luxury book acquisition in the late Middle Ages. That the image's central event pretends to document the official moment when the *Chemin* would have entered the royal space to be transported, presumably, to the Louvre library may have been a deliberate effort on Christine's part to encourage the Valois princes to view her work as necessary for their own libraries, which, after all, replicated in large part the royal library.

Slightly different from the *Chemin* copies, copies of Christine's *Mutacion* copies do not so much depict the pathos of conspicuous consumption as they incite the desire for it. These *Mutacion* copies, produced under Christine's supervision, open with their own visual and textual scene of substantial semiotic complexity that cultivates desire. This time, however, the stock opening matter foregoes the expected references to literary exchange to focus exclusively on the female author. The decision to eliminate any reference to a potential patron for this work is all the more striking given that we know from Christine that she presented this work to at least Duke Philip as a New Year's gift in 1404.[29] Self-consciously removed from the patronage circuit or any form of gifting ritual, the *Mutacion* copies encourage instead a voyeuristic view into the intimate space of the author's study, where a woman is caught in the private act of writing. With the book open and tilted outward, viewers are invited to linger on this early stage in creative development, in which they played no role, neither as patron nor as inspiration. The shimmering gold paint and the elaborate spray border of denser and richer quality than found in the previously distributed gift-copies of the *Chemin* extend the desire provoked by this voyeuristic gaze on the woman writer outward to the experience of holding the coveted book-object. The tendrils ending with gilded leaves and occasional coloured buds communicate a sense of lushness, especially when overrunning the gold baguette to weave around the miniature and between columns. In a similar nod to the bountifulness of the book, the crenellated towers enclosing the writer push upwards beyond the column limits. Complementing this opening invitation to cast a lingering gaze on the author in her private chamber is the ensuing narrative in which a personalized account of Christine's dealings with Lady Fortune fosters even greater intimacy.[30]

It may very well have been the combination of Christine's daring allegorical account of her life's travails with the sweeping account of world history in the *Mutacion* that inspired Duke Philip to commission Charles

V's biography. That said, we should not turn a blind eye to the fact that the author's book-gifts over the previous two years had sought to cultivate in Duke Philip a desire for her work. The hope she first expressed in the revised dedication heading his copy of the *Othéa* – that Duke Philip might "acquire an appetite" ("prendre appetit," *Othéa*, p. 505, lines 27–9; p. 508, lines 27–9) for her works – bore fruit in the early part of 1404, when he requested that Christine write the biography of his brother.

A Curious History of the Commission

The three-part *Charles V* does not open with the expected presentation scene either in text or image common to royal commissions or even to Christine's earlier writings offered to powerful men. Rather than focus on the final moment of book presentation, the opening narrative concentrates on textual inception. The obvious explanation for this restricted account of the biography of the text was that Duke Philip's unanticipated death before completion of the text made the book presentation impossible. In spite of this fact, it is crucial to acknowledge that Christine refrained from acknowledging his death at the start of the book. Her decision to suppress initially any reference to this loss merits our attention, especially since there is evidence that she actively used the prologue heading Part 1 to prepare her readers for the eventual announcement of the duke's death in the prologue to Part 2 and the ensuing impact of his passing on the biography as developed in the prologue to Part 3. By restricting her opening account to the early days of textual inception rather than extending the trajectory to encompass its eventual completion, Christine succeeded in bringing along her readers as she retraced her own nostalgic literary journey in "real time." This narrative strategy resulted in one of the most in-depth and informative treatments of the effect of commissioning practices on the literary enterprise in the history of patronage (not to mention the insight it provides into Christine's own personal mourning over a lost chance to work with Duke Philip).

Part 1 opens with a prayer that God inspire Christine, while Duke Philip is immediately thereafter credited for both content and form of the present text:

> Emprens nouvelle compilacion menée en stille prosal et hors le commun ordre de mes autres choses passées, ad ce meue par estre infourmée que ainsi plaist estre fait à tres solemnel et redoubtable prince Monseigneur le duc de

> Bourgoigne, Phelippe, filz de Jehan par la grace de Dieu roy de France, par lequel commandement ceste ditte oeuvre ay emprise. (*Charles V*, part 1, chap. 1; 1:5)
>
> ([I] have undertaken a new compilation written in prose, which is different from my previous writings, and concerning this transformation, it is due to having been informed that so it pleased the very honourable and powerful prince, my lord, the duke of Burgundy, Philip, son of John, by God's grace, king of France, by whose order I undertook this work.)

In spite of firmly positioning the biography within a closed circuit uniting the duke and the writer in an explicit clientelistic exchange reminiscent of the accounts of Charles V's commissioned writers, Christine subsequently makes room for another potential audience. Repeating the practice introduced in the *Chemin*, Christine turns attention to a larger audience consisting of "princes de [France] ... et à tous nobles et ameurs de sagece pareillement" (the princes of [France] [...] and to all nobility and lovers of wisdom as well) (*Charles V*, part 1, chap. 1; 1:6). Apart from this similarity, the dynamics surrounding *Charles V* distinguish it in important ways from the *Chemin*. Unlike the earlier work, the biography first stands as a solicited work ordered by a patron and, only thereafter, as an unsolicited gift offered to others. As if this double function does not destabilize Duke Philip's relationship to the text enough, the author proceeds to redefine the work's purpose once more by identifying the deceased Wise King as the ultimate intended recipient of the work, a sacrifice in his honour, given that the dead cannot reward the living: "feu le sage roy Charles, Quint d'ycellui nom, en laquelle reverence ceste presente oeuvre est emprise" (the parted wise king Charles, fifth of the name, in whose reverence this present work is undertaken) (*Charles V*, part 1, chap. 1; 1:6). As we shall see, this three-stage pattern of conversion of the text first transforms a commissioned text into an unsolicited offering before ultimately staging it as a sacrificial work. Christine was keen, however, for her readers to experience firsthand this unfolding of events over the course of her narration.

The prologue to Part 1 encourages temporal suspension by focusing on the book's origins rather than its fate. Here, the author promises a full account of the work's genesis or "le principe et mouvement de ceste present petite compilacion" (the origins and purpose of this small compilation) (*Charles V*, part 1, chap. 2; 1:6). This account of textual inception, however, fails to acknowledge the events of 27 April 1404, which would fundamentally impact the future of the project. Instead, when turning in the next chapter to narration of events, the author manipulates time to transport readers to a recent past made immediately present: "voirs est que cest present an de grace mil .iiii. et .iii … " (it is the truth that in the present year of grace, 1403 … , (o.s.)) (*Charles V*, part 1, chap. 2; 1:6–7). From this temporal vantage point, Christine turns a nostalgic gaze on lived events. In accounting for the text's "origins," Christine recalibrates events so as to establish the duke's commission as a causal effect of her earlier New Year's gift offering of a copy of the *Mutacion*:

> Apres un mien volume appellé de la *Mutacion de Fortune*, au dit tres solemnel prince, Monseigneur de Bourgoigne, de par moy par bonne estreine presenté le premier jour de janvier, que nous disons le jour de l'an, lequel sa debonnaire humilité receupt tres amiablement et à grant joye, me fu dit et raporté par la bouche de Monbertaut, tresorier du dit seigneur, que il lui plairoit que je compillasse un traittié, touchant certaine matiere, laquelle entierement ne me declairoit, si que sceusse entendre la pure voulenté du prince; et pour ce, moy, meue de desir d'acomplir son bon vouloir selon l'estendue de mon petit enging, me transportay avec mes gens où il estoit lors, à Paris, ou chastel du Louvre. (*Charles V*, part 1, chap. 2; 1:7–8)

> (After one of my volumes entitled the *Mutacion de Fortune*, to the aforementioned most honoured prince, my lord of Burgundy, by me, as a worthy New Year's gift was presented the first day of January (which we call the first of the year), which given his debonair humility, he received very kindly and with great joy, it was thus told to me and reported by the mouth of Monbertaut, treasurer of the said lord, that it would please him that I compile a treatise dealing with a certain matter, which he would declare to me in full if I was able to hear the true wishes of the said prince; and, for this reason, I, filled with the desire to accomplish his wishes according to the abilities of my small mind, went with my people to where he was in Paris at the Louvre.)

Time collapses around Christine, who enjoys a central role as orchestrator of the exchange. By suggesting that her New Year's offering of the *Mutacion* inspired Duke Philip to solicit her services, Christine successfully produces a scenario in which the duke performs the role she had long reserved for the duke of Orléans. Yet in spite of this masterful uniting of two otherwise separate book events, Christine's stilted and halting narrative style in this passage betrays the extreme effort required to return to a past so shattered by future events. This narrative offers in place of facts a twisted account in which an unsolicited gift leads to a contractual and financial agreement within the symbolically charged space of the Louvre. When collapsing these two book-transactions into a single event – the unsolicited offering of the *Mutacion* and the commission for a new text – Christine self-consciously intertwined two distinct literary modes of exchange. The terminology provided by the anthropologist C.A. Gregory in *Gifts and Commodities* proves helpful in appreciating the import of this act. Christine opens *Charles V* with a tale of an "ambiguous economy" in which an archaic gift-act fostered consumer desire, which then led to a promise of reward in exchange for the client's services. It is significant that this conflation occurs in the context of New Year's gifting practices, a context Christine clearly favoured for presenting her writings. Let us recall Brigitte Buettner's explanation for the purpose of this public display of gifting revived by the Valois dynasty. Public gifting was a staging site where "participants were called on to play the role of eyewitnesses who could see, discuss, broadcast, and remember what was given by whom to whom."[31] Christine's account of the public gifting event at the head of the biography goes a step further since it serves here to distract her readers from reality and to forestall the inevitable future breakdown of this exchange.

Linking the commission back to a previous New Year's gift did more than signal the complexity of Christine's dealings with Duke Philip. Given Buettner's observation that the New Year's revival began in the 1380s, we can surmise that the tradition was well-established by the turn of the century.[32] We thus need to ask why Christine behaved as if her audience might not be familiar with the timing and practices of the ritual. We can accept that there was continued debate as to whether January 1 or Easter announced the new year, but Christine's naming of her offering as a New Year's gift – a "bonne estreine" – may indicate another topic of debate concerning whether a court subject's offering merited the status of a gift in the public performance of largesse. Might we also read into Christine's attention to the details of the ritual an intentional effort to make the duke's recognition of her gift obligatory? Contemporary treasury records make clear that reciprocation was key to maintaining one's status. In fact, New Year's gifting was so carefully regulated that secretaries kept inventories both of these presents and the "counter-gifts" that followed suit.[33] In September 1403, as already noted, Duke Philip gifted Christine a silver goblet and carafe, most likely for book offerings that predated the presentation of the *Mutacion* in January. That Christine's narration of this earlier book presentation in *Charles V* seamlessly transitions to the appearance of the duke's treasurer Monbertaut – the very person who would have been expected to issue a recompense – falsely prepares her readers for a conventional scene of official reciprocation. Contrary to expectations, Monbertaut does not offer recompense for the *Mutacion* and, instead, communicates the duke's desire for a new work. Monbertaut's news, therefore, simultaneously defers and extends the initial gift act since Christine's original gift-text, it is suggested, inspired the commissioning of the present biography. As such, the duke's commission represents both an unconventional reward for the earlier gift-text and a solicitation that the author produce another work that would speak to the duke's pleasure.

Following the account of the New Year's scene and the action it triggered, Part 1 transitions to a second encounter with the duke at the Louvre. Christine details this meeting with great precision, going so far as to name witnesses who might confirm her version of events. In addition to Monbertaut, two ducal squires, Jehan de Chalons and Toppin de Chantemerle, are said to have escorted Christine to the duke (*Charles V*, part 1, chap. 2; 1:8). Once Christine entered the room, it was the duke's youngest son, Antoine, the count of Retel, who observed her ensuing discussions with the duke (*Charles V*, part 1, chap. 2; 1:8). These four witnesses positioned at different stages of Christine's transactions with the duke lend an air of legality to the exchange. Christine then summarizes the duke's request as well as the promises made: "[the duke] me dist et declaira la maniere et sur quoy lui plaisoit que je ouvrasse, et, [...] maintes offres notables receues de sa benigneté" (he spoke to me and declared both the style and the content on which he desired that I work and, [...] several worthy promises from his greatness were received) (*Charles V*, part 1, chap. 2; 1:9). Here, we appreciate that Christine's decision to suspend time and to focus on textual inception allowed her to inscribe into the biography both the official request and the promise of ducal reciprocation. At the same time that Christine's opening account in the king's biography celebrates the commission of the work, it also upstages the gifting performance with hints of a binding contract. Read with the knowledge of the duke's death a few months thereafter, this account carries with it an unintended curse that threatens all involved parties. This curse has far less to do with Deschamps's stylized threats addressed to the royal brothers, which were discussed earlier, and far more to do with the predicament Deschamps likely faced when Charles V died and he was still in possession of the *Fragilité*. Here, Christine prepares us for the predicament she would face after the duke's sudden death by presenting us with the evidence of the duke's obligation to her as well as the need to fulfil his promise to protect his reputation.

The very term "commission," with its etymological origins that can be traced back to *committere*, captures the predicament on display at the outset of *Charles V*. The term intermingles notions of unity and collaboration with more troubling experiences of abandonment, liability, and conflict as related to breaking a promise or commitment. The Latin term signifies such divergent ideas as "to deliver, entrust, consign, place, commit, yield" as well as "to resign, expose, and abandon." With ties to the Indo-Iranian notion of *mitra* or "contract," the term foregrounds a system of interlocking obligations.[34] The common Middle French term used to designate a commission was the "commandement," which initially signified an "order or obligation," although by the end of the fifteenth century, the term was used more precisely to refer to an order of payment or a contracted agreement.[35] As already noted in the previous chapter, Christine introduced the term "commission" to speak of her imaginary contractual agreement with the God of Love to compose the *Dit de la Rose*, thereby placing even greater importance on the shared commitment at the core of the literary pact. The various etymological strands of the commission make clear the dangers that have always resided in this form of literary exchange, ranging from the risk of abandonment to its power to fix objects as commodities of exchange that might become the alienable possessions of their patrons, who initiated production (such as was Charles V's intention when commissioning works linked to his *Sapientia* project). It is this bond that comes to haunt Christine's *Charles V* in Parts 2 and 3.

When concluding Part 1, Christine dated completion to 28 April 1404, hence one day after the duke's death, and yet there is no acknowledgment of Philip's passing. Part 1 of the biography exists in stasis, somewhere between textual inception and the patron's death. Christine would have us understand that by the time she turned to composing Part 2, she had learned of the tragedy since she opens the new section with a lament. Her heartfelt sorrow for the duke's death culminates in a public promise to complete the assigned work and to fulfil her obligations to Duke Philip. The inevitable dilemma represented by the act of completing a commission for a deceased patron plays itself out in Part 2 as a psychomachia that pits the author against an imaginary antagonistic audience.

Creating an Audience for the Orphaned Commission

The prologue to Part 2 sketches out a dramatically altered landscape for the commissioned biography. Christine's visceral and poignant reaction to the news of Duke Philip's sudden death transports us to a new point in time in which Christine learns of the tragedy. Her "doloureuse introit" (sorrowful lament) (*Charles V*, part 2, chap. 1; 1:108) speaks to a loss not exclusive to her but rather felt by an entire community: "non mie singuliere à moy ou comm[un]e à aucuns, mais generale et expresse en maintes terres, et plus en cestui reaume" (not by me alone or to a select group but widespread and expressed in many lands, especially in this kingdom) (*Charles V*, part 2, chap. 1; 1:109–10). In spite of this shared sorrow, Christine considers herself isolated and without support: "comme femme vesve, orpheline d'amis, ay cause de douloir et plaindre cellui par lequel digne commandement j'empris ceste presente oeuvre" (as a widow, orphaned of friends, I have good reason to mourn and lament he by whose worthy commission I undertook this present work) (*Charles V*, part 2, chap. 1; 1:110–11). She articulates the collapse of her contractual relationship to the duke through the adoption of a familial language of loss and abandonment. She is both a widow and an orphan who is nonetheless still responsible for the text requested of her.

This moving description of her social isolation and abandonment heading Part 2 presages an important shift in her perceived audience. In Part 1, Christine was quick to present herself as surrounded by supporters and collaborators, such as royal servants, whose shared memories of the king were folded into the narrative (*Charles V*, part 1, chap. 1; 1:9). In that first section of the biography, Christine also frequently adopted the first-person plural to reflect this collaboration. For instance, when transitioning from the account of the duke's commission to take up the story of Charles V in Part 1, it is the communal voice that initiates the biography: "Or commençons" (So let us begin) (*Charles V*, part 1, chap. 4; 1:10). A quarter of the chapters in Part 1 are voiced by the communal "nous"[36] and, furthermore, on two occasions in the first section, she identifies the text as "nostre oeuvre" (our work) (*Charles V*, part 1, chap. 14; 1:36 and chap. 22; 1:59). All these strategies, intended to identify the biography as a communal project, fall to the wayside in Part 2. Apart from occasional references to this community, the collective is both grammatically and socially displaced in Part 2. The assertive first-person plural pronoun gives way to a subordinate and passive collective that is subject to extensive attacks from an antagonistic audience:

> Ensuivant la matiere au premier encommencée, c'est assavoir la narracion des faiz et bonnes meurs du sage roy Charles, *nous* convient, en ceste .IIe. partie du present volume, advisier comment envieux ou mesdisens, qui souvent seulent reprimer le loz des auteurs, ne *nous* puissent chargier de mençonge ou faulte de promesse par si que le propos presescript, qui fu de traitier secondement de chavalerie, puist estre empli et satisfait. (*Charles V*, part 2, chap. 2; 1:111, emphasis added)

(Continuing the matter begun in Part 1, that is, the narration of the deeds and good qualities of the wise king Charles, it is fitting for *us*, in this second part of the present volume, to face the issue of the envious or slanderers, who often make a habit of repressing the praise of authors, so that they might not accuse *us* of lying or failing to keep promises, and to this end, let the prescribed topic, which was to treat next chivalry, be fulfilled and satisfied.)

As Part 2 advances, the use of the singular powerfully expresses the writer's sudden responsibility to take sole charge of the work. In fact, the work's antagonistic audience identifies Christine alone as responsible for this text. Christine will address directly these perceived attacks for the first time in the midst of her initial discussion of Charles V's knightly accomplishments. She begins by acknowledging that some may challenge her depiction of the king as a great knight: "aucunes gens pourroient contredire à mes preuves de la chevalerie de cestui roy Charles" (some people might contradict my evidence concerning the chivalric ways of the said king Charles) (*Charles V*, part 2, chap. 10; 1:131). She then concedes that Charles never personally went to war due to frequent illness (*Charles V*, part 2, chap. 10; 1:131), but she contends that, nonetheless, his leadership makes him worthy of "le nom et tiltre de perfaitte chevalerie" (the name and title of perfect chivalry) (*Charles V*, part 2, chap. 10; 1:133). What first appears as an attack on Christine's version of events ends here with the author's successful redirection of accusations by suggesting that what is really in question is the king's honour.[37]

The next nine chapters of Part 2 shift focus from Charles V to his extended family and servants, who are said to provide further evidence of his chivalric leadership. Individual chapters treat King Charles V's brothers and their children; the king's living sons, the duke of Orléans and Charles VI; and his former constable, Bertrand de Guesclin. These men, most of whom Christine knew personally, are portrayed as sharing similarities with the Wise King. For instance, the new Burgundian duke, John the Fearless, possesses Charles V's signature qualities of wisdom and moral character; he is described as a "prince de toute bonté, de conscience salvable, juste, sage, benigne, doulz et de toutes bonnes meurs" (a prince of great goodness and a truly upright character, just, wise, generous, kind, and possessing all good qualities) (*Charles V*, part 2, chap. 13; 1:152). While such praise of Duke John of Burgundy makes sense given his father's commissioning of the present text, the fulsome praise ascribed to the Burgundian nemesis, Louis of Orléans, is less easily justified. In fact, the intellectual interests of Duke Louis, along with his uncles, the dukes of Berry and Bourbon, link them even more intimately to Charles V than Duke John could ever claim to be. Christine finds that the deceased king's brother-in-law, Louis II of Bourbon, reflects Charles V's commitment to learning through his sponsorship of "clers sages" (wise clerics), his appreciation for "livres de mouralités, de la Sainte Escripture et d'enseignemens" (books of morality, the Holy Bible and teachings), as well as his role in translating several works (*Charles V*, part 2, chap. 14; 1:159). Likewise, the duke of Berry earns praise for his collection of "beaulz livres des sciences morales et hystoires nottables des pollicies romaines ou d'autres louables enseignemens" (beautiful books of moral science and worthy histories about Roman policies and other worthy teachings) (*Charles V*, part 2, chap. 12; 1:142). As for Louis of Orléans, Christine celebrates, once more, his eloquence (*Charles V*, part 2, chap. 16; 1:173–4), thereby echoing her appreciation of his father's rhetorical skills elsewhere in the biography (*Charles V*, part 1, chap. 23; 1:60–1, and *Charles V*, part 3, chap. 5; 2:20). These mini-panegyrics of contemporaries serve as evidence of the Wise King's enduring legacy, although the author suspects that they might be misinterpreted as efforts to curry favour with future patrons.

In anticipation of audience wariness of her praise for the living, Christine addresses this issue directly in Part 2, chapter 18, where the opening rubric announces, "cy respont Cristine à aucuns redargus, que on lui pourroit faire" (here Christine responds to the various attacks that one could make against her) (*Charles V*, part 2, chap. 18; 1:180). To the first anticipated accusation related to her extended treatment of living princes – "que flaterie pour acquerir leur grace ou benefice m'a ingerée à ce dire" (that flattery intended to attract their goodwill or benefits has inspired me to say these things) (*Charles V*, part 2, chap. 18; 1:180) – Christine retorts that she has no interest in benefiting from this text and, instead, she simply wishes to complete the requested project: "aucune adulacion, n'espoir que pour ce eusse leur grace, mais, comme desir me menast de bien et deuement acomplir l'oeuvre emprise" (neither adulation nor hope of obtaining their good grace, but rather the desire to complete correctly and rightly the undertaken work inspired me) (*Charles V*, part 2, chap. 18; 1:181). She belies her own protestations when she thereafter embeds in an address to the princes to whom she has just offered such fulsome praise an imaginary performance of the conventional book-offering ritual:

> Supplie humblement a la haultece des tres poissans et redoubtez princes, dont memoire est cy faitte, qu'il leur plaise prendre en gré le petit stile et escripture

> du raport et declaracion par moy simplement expliquée de l'informacion de leurs nobles meurs. (*Charles V*, part 2, chap. 18; 1:184)
>
> (I humbly appeal to the nobility of the very powerful and revered princes who are memorialized here that they will willingly accept the humble style and writing of this report and claims simply explained by me concerning their noble practices.)

Located at the heart of the three-part biography, this ceremonious aside inserts a presentation scene that harks back to the unnamed "princes" in the opening prologue to Part 1 (*Charles V*, part 1, chap. 1; 1:6) and thus provides Christine with a new audience who might fill the void left by Duke Philip. The hope encapsulated in this imagined scene clearly reinvigorates Christine because she subsequently re-appropriates the first person plural of Part 1 that had otherwise been abandoned. The belief that her offering will be accepted by the princes inspires her anew to view the project as a collaborative endeavour: "Et comme il soit temps de [...] reprendre nostre premiere forme" (Now it is time de return to our first intention) (*Charles V*, part 2, chap. 18; 1:184).

Christine's imagined antagonistic audience refuses, however, to remain silent, and their expected complaints infiltrate the biography with even greater force as Part 2 progresses. This audience has already been shown to harbour beliefs that the author lies and practices sycophancy. But what especially aggravates her imagined audience, Christine maintains, is her audacity as a woman who dares to discuss the lives of such important men: "il leur sembloit non apertenir à ma petite faculté, qui femme suis, enregistrer les noms de si haultes personnes" (they thought it beyond my capacities, being as I am a woman, to record the names of such important people) (*Charles V*, part 2, chap. 18; 1:182). This final accusation will develop into verbal sparring as this anticipated audience comes to overshadow the biography. In contrast to previous metatextual digressions that summarized the audience's critiques, Part 2, chapter 21 gives full expression to the audience's perceived sentiments. In the midst of Christine's explanation of why the rules of chivalry must be addressed, a raucous audience interjects, "A quoy nous escript ceste femme les ordres de chevalerie que nous sçavons?" (Why does this woman write to us about the orders of chivalry of which we are already familiar?) (*Charles V*, part 2, chap. 21; 1:190). This public further accuses Christine of pilfering the work of others: "Ceste femme-cy ne dit mie de soy ce que elle explique en son livre, ains fait son traittié par procès de ce que autres auteurs on[t] dit à la lettre" (This woman here says nothing of her own that she explains in her book, rather she produces her treatise by reciting word for word what other authors have said) (*Charles V*, part 2, chap. 21; 1:190–1). No sooner does Christine mount a defence than a more damning grievance is feared to be expressed ("aucuns pourroient dire," "one might say") (*Charles V*, part 2, chap. 21; 1:191): "Presompcion meut ceste ignorant femme oser dilater de si haulte chose comme est chevalerie aussi comme se elle tendist à de ce donner discipline ou doctrine" (Presumption made it so that this ignorant woman dared elaborate on such an important subject as chivalry, as if she believed herself able to provide learning or doctrine) (*Charles V*, part 2, chap. 21; 1:191). With each interruption, the audience's aggression builds. From the dismissive "cette femme," the public escalates to the more injurious language of "ceste ignorant femme." Christine defends herself against this final tirade by calling on the authority of two powerful learned figures, Hugh of St Victor (*Charles V*, part 2, chap. 21; 1:191–2) and the goddess Minerva (*Charles V*, part 2, chap. 21; 1:192). With this final defence, Christine permanently silences her opponents, and never again do they voice their complaints in the text.

What we see transpire over the course of Part 2 is Christine's attempt to think through ways to honour the obligation of a collapsed commission while simultaneously recognizing that she must answer to new circumstances and find a new audience. As Froissart wrote in the *Prison amoureuse*, a work must circulate among readers to survive,[38] a concept echoed in Lewis Hyde's contention that "the spirit of a gift is kept alive by its constant donation."[39] If no new audience emerged for the king's biography, Christine risked both going unrewarded for the ordered text and facing the possibility that the work would fall into oblivion. The conundrum for Christine was that the work constituted a commission, and since a commission establishes a contractual transaction between a patron and a client, Christine technically had no right to appropriate and redistribute the biography the duke had ordered, because it was officially recognized as an expression of the patron's pleasure. What had once disturbed Charles V's commissioned writers on philosophical grounds had become an issue of survival for Christine – both her financial survival and the survival of the text itself, bereft of its patron. Christine's imaginary public evokes this issue when accusing her of inappropriately seeking "benefices" and "grace" from the living by identifying and praising princes who might read the work. Their accusations suggest a common belief that Christine had no right, given her previous arrangements with Duke Philip, to now appropriate the work as her own and, thereafter, to use it to her benefit to forge new literary relationships with others.

Christine revealed in her anxious imaginings about her audience that the commission was, perhaps, not the ideal she had nurtured in her earlier writings. We detect in these asides a concern that by using the abandoned text to seek new alliances, the author might find her integrity questioned. Christine conceded that some identified her as a mouthpiece for the powerful rather than as an intellectual sharing her wisdom at the same time that she blamed such complaints on underlying misogynistic sentiments, hence the rehearsal of sexist attacks launched against her. Christine's fears regarding audience reception should give us pause when looking back at Charles V's commissioned writers. Their careful avoidance of any reference to monetary reward that they may have received in exchange for services, their elaborate development of defences based on invoking intellectual labour, their methodical efforts to convert the king's ordered text into their willing gift, and their adroit negotiation of their subordination to suggest an intellectual friendship with their sovereign – might all of these strategies have been adopted with the hopes of avoiding the accusations Christine later endured? Might these very issues and the obvious double bind of the commission that Christine exposed also explain Machaut's reluctance to join in the contemporary enthusiasm for royal sponsorship? Do not his fictions of engagement expose the risks of offering one's gift to a superior? From the writer who is charged with reversing judgments to satisfy a powerful lady to demands from a prisoner king to abandon the belief that poetry healed, to instead use verse to fuel vengeance, Machaut offered up some of the most memorable medieval tales of the danger of the commission. Might Deschamps's efforts to recast the poet-prince relationship as one based on dues, debts, and duties determined by the poet have been precisely undertaken to maintain his standing as a truth teller, as the author of "dictez vertueulx," as Mézières would have it?[40] In short, in Christine's attempt to secure steady sponsorship, had she overlooked, miscalculated, or fallen victim to her own deep nostalgic longing built on childhood memories of Charles V's court, memories surely nurtured by her opportunities later in life to delve into the books he had commissioned and that she knew so well?[41]

Christine's ultimate response to her imagined readers reveals a careful negotiation of the dilemma brought on by the literary commission. She defends herself against accusations of profit seeking by asserting that rather than pursuing reward, she endeavours to complete what she referred to in the *Othéa* as an "oeuvre emprise" – a term used in that earlier case to urge Duke Louis to perform as patron. In using the term here to explain her responsibilities (*Charles V*, part 2, chap. 18; 1:181), Christine draws attention to the distinctive obligations of the commissioned writer. In this context, the Middle French term "emprendre" signals both Christine's rights and obligations in relation to the biography. Deriving from *imprehendere*, the French term acknowledges Christine's prominent role in the literary enterprise. In literal terms, as she had previously requested Duke Louis to do, she "took hold of" the work when accepting the assignment from Duke Philip. In this sense, the expression implies her responsibility to produce the requested object. The term simultaneously acknowledges Christine's obligations to the duke's memory, since an "emprise" also signifies an object or insignia worn to designate service to a superior.[42] Thus, the biography itself marked Christine as Duke Philip's client; it marked her as contractually bound to answer his request. Faced with the duke's death, Christine recognized the expectation placed on her to produce a once-desired commodity where desire no longer existed. To protect her reputation, she was obliged to complete the contracted work per its prescribed intentions, even if it meant "consigning" or "abandoning" the work to oblivion. Such is the curse of the commission, one very different from the dilemma both Deschamps and she faced when they failed to secure sponsorship from the royal brothers. Notwithstanding this distinction, both dilemmas leave a writer in a bind – their gift is also their curse.

Christine offered an ingenious, albeit desperate, solution to this dilemma in Part 3 of the king's biography. She removed the biography from its clientelistic economy, in which it had functioned as an object produced to satisfy the stated needs and desires of the patron, and she repositioned it as a sacrificial object to be inserted into a ritual performance of abandonment. That is, Christine announced she would sacrifice the text in honour of Charles V and in hopes that future audiences would honour her actions. By moving outside of the immediate, Christine aspired to restore the intimacy of intellectual exchange she had long sought in her dealings with the Valois dynasty. Echoing the classic definition of the nostalgic drive, Christine participated in "the ongoing reconstruction of the past [that] is an act not only of recontextualization but of invention."[43] This reconstruction of the past led Christine to project a nostalgic past, a past that "never was," into the future.

Sacrificing the Commission

Part 3 of *Charles V* transforms the duke's request into what Georges Bataille refers to as the ultimate gift, the sacrifice. Bataille stresses that sacrifice does not have as its goal "annihilation."[44] Instead, by removing useful products from worldly circulation, such as the sacrificial animal, the sacrificer practises incalculable generosity and imbues the chosen object with sacred and intimate value. This act assures that the object transcends worldly constraints. In a similar fashion, in Part 3 of the biography, Christine proceeds to extricate the biography from the commissioning economy in which a book might constitute the alienable object inextricably linked to the patron. She redefines the biography as a sacrificial offering so as to reinvest writing with the intimacy crucial to her own nostalgic view of royal literary engagement. In the opening address to Part 3, Christine acknowledges the oddity of her intentions and prepares her readers for the conversion she envisions for her work. She explains in Part 3, chapter 2 that hereafter she will address her biography to Charles V: "me prent appetit de parler en sa personne en terme estrange, en maniere d'oroison, ainsi comme se ores fust vivant au monde" (I developed a desire to speak to him in an uncommon manner, in the manner of a speech as if he was still living) (*Charles V*, part 3, chap. 1; 2:8). Note Christine's insistence on her own desire. Similar to Deschamps, who took ownership of the "livre de memoire" to do as he wished, so Christine takes ownership of the biography. In the tradition of Machaut, who took pleasure in poeticizing the prince's nocturnal laments, so now Christine turns her gaze exclusively on the deceased royal subject, who had always been the true object of her pursuit, and she inserts herself into his *Sapientia* project; she performs as if one of his chosen writers, one who gives freely rather than produces on command.

Following the practice of Charles V's commissioned writers, Christine first confers on him the sobriquet of the Wise King: "*Charles le Sage* doyez estre appellez" (*Charles the Wise*, you must be called) (*Charles V*, part 3, chap. 1; 2:9, emphasis in original). She defines her work as service performed in his honour: "Soit doncques procedé à la louenge de sapience et de voz valereuses euvres" (Let us proceed to praise of wisdom and your worthy works) (*Charles V*, part 3, chap. 1; 2:9). Finally, Christine offers to labour on behalf of the Wise King: "Or me doint Dieux à tel fin exploitier que labeur face à gloire de vous, et la bienvueillence de voz amez en reviengne sur moy!" (May God use me so that my labour gives glory to you and that the goodwill of your loved ones falls to me)

(*Charles V*, part 3, chap. 1; 2:9). Here, Christine's readiness to serve the king's memory defines her text as a willing and unconditional gift – she writes for his glory, expecting nothing in return from him and hoping only that her gift will lead others to practise goodwill towards her. She imagines an intimacy with the deceased king that will generate loyalty, fidelity, and appreciation within a wider circle. In so doing, Christine effectively reconstitutes her audience as a closed community of intimates, a variation of the past learned sodality promoted by Charles V's commissioned writers. This new approach permanently silences the imaginary antagonistic audience that had threatened to overtake the work in Part 2.

The exchange dynamics introduced in Part 3 that make it possible to imagine anew a supportive community mark the return of the collective first-person plural pronoun. In this iteration of the speaking voice, unity derives from a shared belief system and a mutual desire to honour Charles V. Defining terms becomes an exercise that reinforces group cohesion: "Si est doncques ainsi que traittier nous convient particulierement de ce que nous disons en general sagece ... " (It is appropriate that we now address specifically what we mean generally by wisdom) (*Charles V*, part 3, chap. 1; 2:9). Group affiliation is further strengthened through reference to Charles V's status as a revered member of the community; that is, he is identified as "nostre sage roy Charles" (our wise king Charles) (*Charles V*, part 3, chap. 3; 2:12). Voices from this community contribute to the textual memorial with their own stories, including royal courtiers and chroniclers.[45] Christine inserts alongside their stories her own childhood memories of the royal court.[46] Generous use of direct citation to relate these memories even results in Charles V contributing to the text.[47]

When Christine brings to an end the biography, she makes a clear distinction between individual responsibility and collective goals:

> Retournerons à nostre premier objett, lequel, non obstant que neantplus que on pourroit espuisier une grant riviere, ne souffiroit mon sentement à souffisement en parler, est temps de terminer; mais, affin que emplies soient mes promesses, nous convient recueillir em briefves paroles les motifs de ceste oeuvre pris en un seul suppost qui est le sage roy Charles devant dit, duquel, en trois especiaulx dons avons declairié les vertus et bienfais assez au long, comme promis estoit. (*Charles V*, part 3, chap. 69; 2:178–9)
>
> (Let us return to our primary objective, of which, although one could draw from a bottomless river and although my intellectual capacities are not

> sufficient to speak of it, it is time to conclude. So as to satisfy my promises, it is appropriate that we briefly recall the purpose of this work undertaken with a single intention, which is the Wise King Charles of whom through reference to three special gifts, we have publicly spoken extensively of [his] virtues and good deeds at length, as promised.)

In closing, Christine recalls her binding responsibility as a commissioned writer and emphasizes that she has fulfilled her obligations or "promesses." Her reference to "three special/separate gifts" blurs the three traits assigned to Charles, those of courage, chivalry, and wisdom, with the three parts of the commissioned biography in which these qualities were treated separately. In this respect, the king's moral gifts blur with Christine's literary gifts, which she identified at the outset of the work as "don de Dieu et nature" (a gift from God and Nature) (*Charles V*, part 1, chap. 1; 1:5). Christine asserts that she has satisfied her worldly obligations, even as she redirects the biography from its initial ducal recipient to initiate a sacred ritual centred on incalculable giving. In this way, she frees the work from clientelistic obligations while avoiding the cynical conclusions reached by Machaut and Deschamps. Christine redefines the biography as her gift to give. This process had already begun to take shape in the prologue to Part 3, when she asserted her claim to the otherwise commissioned text through the triple appropriation of the work as "mon oeuvre ... mon volume ... ma ditte oeuvre" (my work ... my volume ... my said work) (*Charles V*, part 3, chap. 1; 2:7). This proprietorship differs markedly from her initial description of the work in the opening sections of Part 1, where she identified the work in relation to the duke's prescribed instructions. The conclusion to Part 3 asserts more fully her sole ownership of the biography when designating it as "ceste petite compillacion par moy traittée" (this little compilation that I have composed) (*Charles V*, part 3, chap. 72; 2:193). With this conversion of the commissioned object into the product of the author's labour, Christine leaves behind Duke Philip and turns to a princely audience, present and future, that is expected to read this work. She releases the work from its terrestrial bonds of exchange to ask that her future audience accept this book and the praise for them therein:

> Humblement suppliee tous les vivans tres haulz, excellens et redoubtez princes d'ycelle tres noble susditte royal lignée, dont ceste hystoire fait mencion, et à ceulz, qui d'eulx descendront à qui, es temps à venir, sera manifestée, que ilz veulent avoir à gré, plus mon desireux vouloir de exaucier leurs

> noms en louange veritable ..., et, après le terme de ma vie, mon ame leur soit recommandée. (*Charles V*, part 3, chap. 72; 2:193)

> (I humbly beseech all of the living very exalted, excellent, and great princes of this said noble lineage whom this story discusses and to those who will descend from them to whom, in the future, [this work] will be known, that they will willingly accept it and, in addition, my great wish to exalt their names through honest praise ... and, after my life ends, let my soul be recommended by them.)

In return she asks only for a deferred gift, that of their prayers after her passing. She concludes by recalling the genesis of this work, which began as a "digne commandement" (worthy commission) (*Charles V*, part 3, chap. 72; 2:193) that she accepted with pleasure, not in relation to the duke but because she fondly remembered her childhood at Charles V's court (*Charles V*, part 3, chap. 72; 2:193). Thus, in place of conceiving of the book as answering an obligation to Duke Philip, Christine presents it as a gift of gratitude offered the Wise King. In this final articulation of the work's purpose, Christine transforms the commission into an enterprise willingly undertaken by the writer and the finished product as a sacrificial offering presented to the illustrious king she had long sought to resuscitate.

When redirecting her biography to the Wise King and his descendants, Christine gave voice to Bataille's belief that the sacrificial gesture can restore a sense of intimacy to corrupted objects; "sacrifice is made of objects," he contends, "that could have been spirits, [...], but that have become things and that need to be restored to the immanence whence they came, to the vague sphere of lost intimacy."[48] Christine resuscitated the "spiritless" biography orphaned by Duke Philip that was then rejected by her imaginary antagonistic public by turning to the Wise King and offering him the fruits of her labour. In this manner she sought to revive the "lost intimacy" that she seems to have come to recognize as a truly nostalgic endeavour, for she had always desired the impossible – to play a part in Charles V's *Sapientia* project. Christine sought in the third and final part of the biography to restore an aura of intimacy to the work by seeking that relationship beyond the grave. Her ingenious repositioning of the biography triggered, however, another set of problems. For a sacrifice to be effective, as already stated, it must have observers, and herein resides the dilemma of relegating writing to the realm of sacrifice. Consideration of the material afterlife of *Charles V* exposes Christine's efforts to negotiate this dilemma.

Material Remains

The transformation of the biography into a sacrificial work might lead us to expect its removal from the literary economy. The evidence suggests otherwise. Christine appears to have immediately turned to presenting copies of the work to members of the Valois dynasty. Four extant manuscripts and one lost copy of the biography bear witness to Christine's oversight of a "series" of copies of this text produced in a limited one-year time frame.[49] At least two of these copies were likely offered as New Year's gifts to Valois princes one month after the text was completed. Inventory records indicate that linked to New Year's celebrations for 1405, Christine presented Duke John of Berry, the last living brother of Duke Philip and the Wise King, with a now-lost leather-bound copy of the biography.[50] In addition, BnF, MS fr. 10153 likely represents the presentation copy that Christine offered the new duke of Burgundy, John the Fearless, that same year. Burgundian records reference a "gift" (don) of 100 écus presented to Christine on 20 February 1405, "en recompensacion de deux livres qu'elle a presentéz a mon dit seigneur, dont l'un lui fu commandé a faire par feu mon seigneur le duc de bourgoingne, pere de mon dit seigneur" (in recompense for two books that she presented to my lord, of which one was commissioned from her by my late lord the duke of Burgundy, father of my said lord).[51] The book identified as having been commissioned by Duke Philip surely refers to the biography, and the second work referenced may very well be the *Mutacion*, for which Christine implied at the outset of the biography she had never received reward. The recipients of the remaining extant copies of *Charles V* remain uncertain, although, as Ouy and Reno remark, it is difficult to imagine that Charles V's direct descendants, Charles VI and Louis of Orléans, did not receive copies during the same time frame.[52] This evidence of Christine having assured the production and dissemination of manuscript copies of *Charles V* requires that we consider the manifest contradiction between the sacrificial gifting practices articulated in the final phase of the biography and real-life practices. The manuscript copies of the biography vividly capture this contradiction; for although inserted into court rituals focused on the distribution of gift items, these artefacts materially contest their potential status as luxury objects worthy of their noble recipients.

The four extant copies of *Charles V* stand out in the history of Christine's manuscript production because of their noticeably modest fabrication during a period when Christine invested heavily in the production of luxury manuscripts. James Laidlaw identifies two major phases distinguishing the manuscripts that Christine is believed to have supervised. The first phase resulted in modest copies with only rare illustrations during her early years of writing, whereas "by the end of 1403 [...] Christine's fortunes had improved sufficiently to allow her to commission copies [...] that are more elaborate than any of her previous productions."[53] Specifically, Laidlaw points to illustrations as the distinctive factor in books produced under authorial supervision after 1403: "Christine could ... afford to engage an artist who showed greater imagination and originality than any of the painters she had previously employed."[54] Laidlaw's study privileges complete-works collections, but copies of single works during this period are also relevant. Among single-text codices, Laidlaw follows Millard Meiss in recognizing copies of the *Mutacion*, including Duke Philip's copy, MS 9508, as marking "a new departure"[55] in Christine's manuscript activity. Laidlaw also reserves pride of place for earlier copies of the *Chemin*, including Duke Philip's likely copy, MS 10983, because he believes that the presentation frontispieces are "the first such examples commissioned by Christine."[56] Additional works composed and circulated as single texts following *Charles V* confirm Christine's sustained investment in producing luxury manuscripts. These include individual copies of the *Livre de la cité des dames*, the *Advision*, and the *Livre des trois vertus*, as well as the exquisite anthologies of her works, beginning with a complete-works collection containing 128 miniatures, which the duke of Berry purchased from her in 1408, followed by the queen's manuscript, to be discussed below.[57] In contrast, the four extant copies of *Charles V* produced during this "new departure" phase of manuscript activity identified by Laidlaw represent anomalies, given their lack of expected luxurious trappings.[58]

The four extant copies of *Charles V* share a near-identical format, evidenced from the first folios of the text. Each book opens with two columns of thirty-one to thirty-three lines that are framed by a delicate border similar to those found in the *Chemin* and the *Mutacion*. Each copy reserves at the head of the text ample space to accommodate rubrics, and even though none of the copies contain miniatures, this opening block provides room for small-scale illustration. Among the *Charles V* copies, BnF fr. 10153 merits particular attention since it is considered to be the earliest extant copy of the work and the presumed codex presented to Duke Philip's descendant, John the Fearless (Figure 6.2: BnF, MS fr. 10153, fol. 2r).

On one hand, this manuscript shows signs of great care given to its production. It opens within delicate tendrils of red, azure, and gold, followed by a floriated opening letter. On the other hand, while these decorative additions enrobe MS fr. 10153 in an aura of luxury, they also expose the

Figure 6.2: The *Livre des fais et bonnes meurs du sage roy Charles V*, Paris, Bibliothèque nationale de France, MS fr. 10153, fol. 2r.

sparseness of the open liminary block that was reserved at an early stage in production to receive future paratexual matter. This opening space in MS fr. 10153 is distinctive from other extant copies of the biography because it reserves a larger space for this matter; eight lines at the top of column A were cordoned off from the outset of manuscript production. Due to the relatively large size of this reserved block in comparison to other similarly structured books supervised by Christine, it is tempting to consider that it was initially intended to accommodate a miniature.[59] After all, some variation of a presentation scene would have been appropriate here, given that the biography stemmed from a commission, that Christine spoke of these origins at the outset of the work, that the work itself openly celebrated both Duke Philip and Charles V for their literary engagement, and that she identified several living princes as their worthy continuators, including Duke John of Burgundy, the recipient of this copy. Such was not the case, and in place of a miniature, rubric appears. Even more disconcerting is that this rubric stands as a poor substitute for a missing presentation scene. Beyond failing to provide expected information – it neither names the author nor the recipient[60] – it physically fails to occupy fully the reserved space. The text did not even require half of the eight available lines. To compensate for this shortage, the scribe opted to stretch out the text so as to occupy every other line in the cordoned-off space. This inability to fill entirely the empty space only draws the eye away from the luxurious excess pushing at the margins to meditate instead on this visual scene of scarcity.[61] And in so doing, the viewer discovers that where the opening rubric disappoints, a "back story" bleeds through the physical page to offer answers. From the verso side, we catch a vague glimpse of a different narrative in reverse. Turning the folio to read this "back story," we discover that column D of folio 2v records Christine's narrative of the actual commissioning event. Below is a transcription of the passage on folio 2v with the lines in bold that bleed through the parchment to fill the gaps left by the opening rubric on folio 2r:

> Janvier que nous disons le jour de l'an
> **lequel sa debonnaire humilite receupt**
> tres aimablement et a grant joye
> **me fut dit et raporte par la bouche de**
> monbertaut tresorier du dit seigne[ur]
> **que il lui plairoit que je compilas**
> se un traittie touchant certaine ma
> **tiere laquelle entierement ne me**
> **declairoit.**

(Bolded passages represent the lines that appear between the lines of the rubric on MS 10153, folio 2r.)

Folio 2r–2v could not have been more perfectly orchestrated if done deliberately. In the reserved space that might have accommodated a presentation or commissioning scene on folio 2r, we find only a haunting echo of the commission. This layout gives visual expression to the biography's removal from the sphere of luxury commodities and clientelistic arrangements at the same time that the overriding presence of a nostalgic account of exchange lingers in the interstices. For the observant reader of MS fr. 10153, this codex exposes its status as the remains of a collapsed commission.

Textual Traces: Rethinking Sacrificial Giving in the Queen's Manuscript and in the Dauphin's *Livre de Paix*

It is worth pursuing the traces of *Charles V* over the next decade since its memory lingered on in Christine's later writings and collections. In this closing section, two distinctive projects that brought the author, once again, into active pursuit of royal patronage will be considered. The first example relates to Queen Isabeau of Bavaria, wife of Charles VI. Christine declares in the dedicatory prologue heading British Library, MS Harley 4431 that the queen commissioned a copy of the author's collected works. Dating to approximately 1414, this manuscript is relevant to our discussion both because of the distinctive account of patronage it provides in its opening material and because of texts excluded from this collection, since they are precisely the works that would have provided the queen with models of the patronage relationship Christine desired. The second project to concern us here is the *Livre de Paix*, a work composed in phases from 1412 to 1414 and dedicated to the dauphin at the time, Louis of Guyenne. This last work marks a return to modelling the type of exchange Christine had long championed (even though she had, curiously, denied the queen access to this model in Harley 4431). That this model emerges in Louis's work through Christine's extensive auto-citation of *Charles V* adds even greater significance to the transaction.

In *The Life and Afterlife of Isabeau of Bavaria*, Tracy Adams argues that over the course of the first decade of the fifteenth century, Queen Isabeau's efforts to position herself in place of the mad king as the leader of France went beyond explicit political transactions to include interventions in contemporary literary events. Specifically, Adams explores the queen's possible leading role in the creation of the *cour amoureuse* as a means of "transcod[ing] the strife between the dukes [of Orléans and of Burgundy] into a setting of poetic competition."[62] Christine provides important evidence that the queen's literary pursuits went beyond this single courtly event. Writings that Christine dedicated to Isabeau prior to the production of MS Harley 4431 show clear awareness of the queen's efforts to appropriate for herself a leading role both culturally and politically. At the same time that the poet curried the favour of Louis of Orléans by addressing multiple works to him, she bolstered the queen's self-fashioning attempts. Christine addressed the queen directly in a dedicatory prologue to the *Epistres sur le débat du roman de la rose* (1401–2) and solicited her involvement in that debate.[63] Only after shifting attention away from Duke Louis did Christine lobby the queen in the *Epistre à Isabeau de Bavière* (1405) to assume a political role in the conflict dividing the dukes of Orléans and Burgundy.[64] In neither case, however, do we find Christine adopting the rhetoric she used with Valois princes that would suggest active pursuit of the queen's literary patronage. Instead, Christine presents herself as solely focused on urging Isabeau to intervene in conflicts that threatened the stability of the kingdom.

Given that there is no trace in Christine's earlier writings of her active pursuit of the queen's sponsorship, it is all the more surprising to read claims in the dedicatory prologue to MS Harley 4431 that the poet undertook this compendium of her collected works in response to the queen's commission ("Dès que vo command en recue"; "Once I received your order").[65] What further surprises is the distinctive model of patronage Christine sketches out for the queen, a model that breaks in important ways with the tradition that she had promoted in writings addressed to Duke Louis and Duke Philip. These discrepancies are on display in Harley 4431, which has been celebrated for its unparalleled portrayal of a female reading community and its detailed portrayal of Queen Isabeau.[66] Nonetheless, to recall the language of Aden Kumler in reference to identifying patron-figures, we "know patrons or owners when we see them because we've come to know their favorite haunts."[67] Countering expectations, the frontispiece and the dedicatory address in MS Harley 4431 offer a skewed depiction of patronage.[68] First, the liminary material reimagines the site and dynamics of literary exchange. Second, although Isabeau clearly figures as the recipient of the manuscript, the poet seems in doubt of the queen's ability to answer the conventional expectations associated with the role. In the frontispiece, Christine appears on bended knee offering an oversized codex to her queen.[69] The scene transpires in the queen's private royal chambers, where a gathering of ladies witnesses the event. Granted, this image stands out as a rare portrait of a queen receiving a book from an author; yet, this image deliberately denies Queen Isabeau access to the traditional seat of patronal authority. The queen does not sit on a throne in a royal setting, as Christine and her various artists had reserved for Duke Louis and Charles VI in miniatures heading Christine's *Deux amans*, the *Othéa*, and the *Chemin*. Nor does the queen assume the posture of someone who is about to take ownership of the codex. Instead, the queen sits in her private chambers with hands crossed on her lap while Christine presents the book to her. A lady-in-waiting behind the author points to the book, as if mediating the exchange between the two women. Finally, although presented as a collection commissioned by the queen, the book is placed at a physical remove from Queen Isabeau.

The dedicatory address only heightens the disconnect between traditional presentation scenes and this unconventional frontispiece. The ninety-six-line dedication makes clear Christine's careful reworking of the royal Valois tradition of textual commission to accommodate the particularities of her dealings with the queen as well as the role she expected Queen Isabeau to assume. Even though Christine will declare midway through her address that the queen commissioned the work (line 54), she opens her dedication by positioning her work as a gift-offering. She first adopts deferential language when presenting the book to the queen, then quickly shifts to self-promotion:

> Haulte dame, en qui sont tous biens,
> Et ma trés souvraine, je viens
> Vers vous, comme vo creature,
> Pour ce livre cy que je tiens
> Vous presenter ... ("Dédicace," lines 13–17)

> (High-ranking lady, in whom resides all goodness, and my very sovereign lady, I come before you, as your subject, to present to you this book here that I hold ...)

This book, she explains, took shape over an extended gifting cycle that began with her reception of a divine gift. Like Machaut, Christine designates, once again, her present gift as having resulted from literary gifts from God and nature ("des dons de Dieu et de nature," "Dédicace," line 22). In the third stanza, in the spirit of Charles V's commissioned writers,

Christine emphasizes the diversity of styles and the intellectual riches contained within the codex:

> Et sont ou volume compris
> Plusieurs livres es quieulx j'ay pris
> A parler en maintes manieres
> Differens, et pour ce l'empris
> Que on en devient plus appris
> D'oÿr de diverses matieres,
> Unes pesans, aultres legieres. ("Dédicace," lines 25–31)

> (And included in this volume are many books in which I undertook to speak in many different styles because one can learn more in hearing varied material, some profound, others light.)

Christine's language invites the queen to view the codex as a treasure trove in which intellectual wealth abounds. Christine then shifts to a defence of the value of her work. Whereas some may believe that Christine's courtly works are less valuable than her more learned ones, she claims that the diversity of her writings facilitates learning. The value of learning from books occupies Christine in the fourth stanza, where she informs the queen that wise men ("les sages," "Dédicace," line 37) have always valued reading because of the effect it has on its practitioners, adding for extra emphasis that wisdom is afforded to those who willingly read to chase away ignorance ("Dédicace," lines 38–41) and that there is no greater use of one's time than to learn ("Dédicace," lines 45–7). It is only after this explicit valorization of her literary "gift" and the actual "gift" produced with her talents that Christine acknowledges the queen's commission.

After having fully developed the magnitude of her gift, the subsequent stanza signals a competing value system that might have influenced the queen's request. It is suggested that rather than recognize Christine's gifts as an intellectual and literary treasure, the queen values more the luxury book-object. Christine explains that once she knew the work was destined for the queen, she understood that the collection must be well written and nicely illuminated ("le parfiner/ D'escripre et bien enluminer," "Dédicace," lines 52–3) and that the materials used must be of the finest quality ("il faloit des choses finer," "Dédicace," line 56) so as to "most richly enrich" the book ("bien richement l'affiner," "Dédicace," line 57). In the remaining lines, the author requests twice more that the queen accept her work ("Dédicace," line 62; line 90) and she further enhances the value of the codex by describing it as both the product of talents given by God and nature as well as the product "of [her] labour and many hours of work" ("de mon labour et lonc travail," "Dédicace," line 73). She concludes by reminding the queen that this codex is more than a luxury object, for it contains "big and difficult works" ("grant euvre et penible," "Dédicace," line 75). As the ultimate proof that the queen should value the writings more than the codex itself, Christine refers to the many "haulte gent" (high ranking people) who have willingly received these works from the author ("Dédicace," line 84). That these important people thereafter appear in several of the opening illuminations to individual works in MS Harley 4431 lends credence to Christine's claims and provides the queen with persuasive visual evidence that she should value the contents of this codex at least as much as the book object because others have apparently done so.[70]

If, as I have stated in the past, the queen's dedication touches on the conventions of patronage because Isabeau figures as "inspiration and judge" of the work,[71] it merits recognizing that the queen is also addressed as someone unfamiliar with this tradition. Herein lies the most striking difference between this address to the queen and Christine's previous engagement with members of the Valois dynasty. Christine does not position the queen alongside the learned leaders she has so often addressed and praised. First, the queen is physically removed from the typical space, as well as denied the ritualized gesture of the book presentation that would have visually confirmed her possession of the book. To repeat, the queen does not "take hold" of the book here. In the accompanying dedication, the queen is also not slotted into the expected rhetoric of patronage and is instead addressed as if in need of instruction regarding the value of books as tools of learning. Christine introduces the queen to this tradition when explaining that learning has always been valued by wise men, that study is a commendable use of one's time, that luxury books are mere vessels for the inestimable intellectual treasure contained within, and that both difficult and light reading contain a wealth of information. In case Christine's word is not enough, she further informs the queen that it is for these very reasons that "haulte gent" have acquired her books in the past. These "haulte gent," as already noted, appear throughout the queen's manuscript, where they are portrayed interacting with the poet, whether in opening miniatures in which they receive a copy of her work (e.g., the opening miniatures to the *Othéa* and the *Chemin*) or knowledge directly from her (e.g., the opening miniatures to the *Proverbes moraulx* or the *Enseignments moraulx*), or scenes in which they request works from her (e.g., the opening miniature to the *Livre du ducs des vrais amans*).[72] Strikingly absent from this lineup are those accounts of poet-prince relations in Christine's corpus in which the relationship is presented as intellectual exchange. Absent from the Harley manuscript are the *Rose*, in which Duke Louis was presented as the worthy subject of a text commissioned by the God of Love, and *Charles V*, in which a long line of Valois princes continued Charles V's learned tradition. A version of Duke Louis's *Prod'hommie* figures in the queen's collection under the title of *Livre de Prudence*, without, as already noted, the crucial framing account of Christine's dealings with the prince. While there are many reasons this material may have been excluded from Christine's corpus – including that these works testify to problematic literary dealings and remind readers of the ongoing civil war sparked by Duke Louis's assassination in 1407 – what is most striking about their absence is that it justifies Christine's rather pedantic instruction directed to the queen on what the patron-function entails. Christine implies that in spite of her gender, her foreign status, her damaged reputation, and even her presumed ignorance of or appreciation for this tradition, the queen might fill this function. Christine's careful repackaging of the patron-function to accommodate the queen, however, does not seem to have led to a sustained literary partnership, any more than earlier efforts had succeeded with the Valois princes. It may be for this reason that Christine returned to her initial strategies a few years later when writing her third and final work for the dauphin, Louis of Guyenne.

In contrast to the unconventional strategy used with the queen, Christine reverted to more common tactics for attracting a sponsor when addressing a few years later the *Paix* to Louis of Guyenne, who held the title of dauphin from 1401 until his death in 1415. Christine lists in the *Paix*, which was composed intermittently between 1412 and 1414, two earlier works that she had also gifted him: the *Livre de Policie* (registered in the dauphin's accounts of 1410) and the lost *Advision du coq* (said to have been presented to him during Lent 1413).[73] The third and final of Christine's work addressed to the dauphin treats at length the appropriate conduct expected of nobility, and when so doing, *Charles V* re-emerges as a key resource for this new composition. Claire Le Ninan recognizes Christine's decision to insert whole passages of *Charles V* into *Paix* as an effort to assure the posterity of the previous work.[74] It is also important to recognize the close ties between Louis of Guyenne and both the royal subject of the biography and the book's original patron. As Charles V's grandson and husband to Duke Philip's granddaughter Marguerite of Burgundy, Louis of Guyenne stood as the most promising candidate to assure the now shared legacy of his grandfather and great-uncle as a patron of learning.

Christine established clear connections between *Charles V* and *Paix* by linking the dauphin with his grandfather. The summary of Part 2 of the dauphin's book specifies that Christine will reference Charles V as a model when teaching the dauphin about the highest virtues ("en donnant exemples de son ayol le roy Charles quint"; "Examples are given from his forebearer, King Charles V").[75] Part 1, chapter 2 already alludes to this modelling when assigning the grandfather's distinctive qualities to his descendant. At this initial stage, Christine registers her wonderment that the dauphin behaves not like a child but "comme homme meur, tres sage et pesant, en euvre et en fait" (more like a grown man, most wise and thoughtful in deed and act) (*Peace*, 203, 61; translation altered). Having established that the young prince already possesses the fundamental qualities crucial to his grandfather's legacy, Christine states more deliberately five chapters later that the life of Charles V will provide specific examples of good princely conduct (*Peace*, 210, 70–1). She concedes that her examples derive directly from her earlier biography of the king, an acknowledgment that requires her to defend herself anew against accusations of self-plagiarism. Here, however, she provides a new defence:

> N'y voy meilleur preuve de t'aprendre a gouverner en tout le effect de la prudence qui t'est propice qu'encores dire de ton dit ayol ; duquel de tant que de sang descendus lui es plus prouchain, te doit embelir ouy de ses nobles faiz et t'y confourmer et prendre exemple; et de cestui quoy qu'en autre livre propre de ses fais en ay autre foiz plus a plain parlé, neantmoins, pour ce qu'il est expedient en ce present volume fait en ton singulier nom le ramentevoir, ne me soit reprouchié ne tenu a redicte.
>
> (I can find no better way to show you how to govern with the necessary prudence than to tell you again about your grandfather. Moreover, since you are directly and closely descended in blood, it must please you to hear of him and his noble feats, and to follow his example. In another work devoted to his deeds, I have spoken more fully about him; nevertheless it is useful in this present volume, written in your name alone, to recall this work, so let me not be reproached or be taken to be repetitive.) (*Peace*, 213, 73; translation altered)

Christine justifies recycling material drawn from her earlier still-unnamed work by insisting both on the blood relations of her newly privileged reader with the deceased king and on her efforts to reorganize the material so that it will relate to his unique case. This royal lineage joins with Christine's declaration that the present work is addressed solely to the dauphin to create a closed circuit in which Louis of Guyenne stands as the true inheritor of his grandfather's legacy and as recipient of Christine's literary and intellectual gifts.

Having thus justified literary borrowings from her earlier work, Christine strives to provide the dauphin with both a general model of good princely conduct and a model of a prince's appropriate engagement with the intellectual community. Christine returns to the history of the biography in Part 3, chapter 30 of *Paix* to justify her decision to offer only an abbreviated account of the Emperor Charles IV's visit at the royal court from 1377 to 1378. In addition to referring the dauphin to her earlier biography, Christine uses this moment to acknowledge Duke Philip's participation in the biography project:

> Si que autre fois ay parlé plus a plain de ceste matiere, qui plus au long de l'ordonnance de la dicte venue vouldra veoir ou livre que de ses fais et bonnes meurs fu par le commandement de tres noble prince le duc Philippe de Bourgongne dessus nommé, frere dudit roy, et par lequel rapport et memoires veritables qu'il m'en fist bailler sçay toutes ces choses.
>
> (I have spoken more fully about these matters elsewhere, so that anyone who wants can see more about the arrangements for this visit in the book of his deeds and good conduct that was made at the command of the most noble prince, Duke Philip of Burgundy, brother of the said King. It is from the account and truthful reports that he had given to me that I know all these things.) (*Peace*, 302, 174)

Although brief, this treatment of Duke Philip's role stresses that his request for the work resulted in his active contribution of resources. Here, Christine's dealings with Duke Philip strongly echo Denis Foulechat's testimony that Charles V provided him with crucial resources to complete his translation of the *Policraticus*.[76] Like Charles V, Duke Philip is remembered by Christine as an active intellectual collaborator.

Christine develops further the responsibilities of a patron when recalling Charles V's personal dealings with the intellectual community in Part 3 of *Paix*. Nine of the forty-eight chapters here are dedicated to retelling crucial aspects of Charles V's life and they draw heavily on the previous biography. In key cases, these new accounts become more explicit in communicating the purpose of the example. Nowhere is this more striking than in Christine's discussion of the Wise King's literary clientelism, since she provides far greater detail than anyone had done before – possibly because, as with his mother Queen Isabeau, she considered the dauphin to be unfamiliar with the details of royal literary engagement. She informs the dauphin that as a "droit philosophe et bon astrologien" (a real philosopher and a good astrologer) (*Peace,* 283, 153), Charles V is to be praised not only for his large collection of books but specifically for his determination to translate learned writings into French for the benefit of himself and "ses freres" (his brothers) (*Peace*, 283, 153). Christine's reference to the king's brothers breaks with the tradition, first articulated by his commissioned writers, that the king had these works produced for his people; in this way, she presents the king's literary activity as a family affair. Christine also emphasizes in this account the Wise King's economic support of intellectual activity. On two separate occasions, Charles V is described as having invested large sums of money in writers. In the first case, Christine qualifies the translators as "maistres a grans gaiges de ce continuellement occuppez" (highly paid masters who were fully occupied by [this work]) (*Peace*, 283, 153; translation altered). Later, she places the translators alongside architects as participants in "autres plusieurs cousteux ouvrages" (other costly projects) (*Peace*, 298, 171) that the king never failed to finance. This open acknowledgment of the financial underpinnings of literary clientelism is unprecedented in writers' accounts of Charles V's learned investments. Christine dares here to assert the financial obligations of the Valois dynasty to the learned community and the right of writers to receive "grans gaiges" for their services. Christine's treatment of the economic obligations of the king to writers may have resulted from years of delayed payments for her own works and repeated failure to secure sustained sponsorship or due to her lagging confidence in Louis of Guyenne.[77] This reference to the economic underpinnings of the textual commission, however, may also have sprung from Christine's growing realization that the royal model she celebrated was no longer common knowledge and that perhaps the euphemisms of her predecessors needed to be replaced with clearer statements about the financial details of a literary economy.

The dauphin's sudden death in December 1415 left no time for him to emerge as the sponsor Christine so desired. It is not even certain that Louis received a copy of *Paix* before his death. The only contemporary reference to Christine having circulated *Paix* dates to New Year's 1414, when, according to court records, she again chose to present a copy of her work to the duke of Berry.[78] Tania Van Hemelryck has further suggested that the only extant copy of the work, Brussels, Bibliothèque royale de Belgique, MS 10366, appears to have been produced for a Burgundian reader.[79] It is important to note that the opening miniature to MS 10366 depicts Christine alone in her study. Once again, a work intended to secure future sponsorship found itself orphaned, and in this instance, the illumination recycled the visual strategy used with the *Mutacion* by depicting Christine alone in her study and without obvious support, an image that I earlier suggested served to cultivate desire in readers.[80] The political turmoil building during this time in which the civil war escalated and the English finally took possession of the capital in 1418 left little hope of finding the ever-elusive Valois sponsor Christine so desired.

The paradox of *Charles V* and *Paix* is that these two works in which Christine celebrated the Wise King's support of intellectuals as among his greatest achievements stand as orphaned texts. Through the stumbling and stunted trajectory of the king's biography, we discover a work in constant transformation, reconstituting itself as it passed from reader to reader, a text that offered itself tentatively to the community but which was seemingly never enthusiastically appropriated by anyone. We begin to see clearly in the biography of *Charles V* that the late-medieval literary economy was fraught with tensions stemming from uncertainty about the economic as well as from interpersonal underpinnings of the enterprise. Did these works represent the fruits of intellectual exchange or did they function as luxury items? Were they intellectual gifts or commodities? Were they conduits of sycophancy or of wisdom? As for the writers themselves, did they consider themselves the prince's mouthpiece or were they communicating the beliefs of an intellectual community? At the apex of Christine's literary career, when she had achieved the greatest sign of her success in the form of a commission from a leading Valois prince to commemorate the figurehead of the dynasty, she discovered that the very fact of a work being in demand and produced on demand could be a curse. A decade later, when redirecting the contents of this work to the Wise King's grandson, she relived the same curse, which was triggered, once again, by sudden death. In this respect, while Bataille may celebrate sacrifice and the violent destruction it demands as restoring intimacy through the purest form of gifting, the history of *Charles V* offers a more tempered message; one that is anchored not in the ecstasy of freely giving but in the aftermath of loss and abandonment. *Charles V* haunts Christine's literary landscape, reappearing occasionally as a missed opportunity, a symbol of profound loss that was caused by Duke Philip's sudden death and, then, by the troubling obligation that required Christine to complete a work that she was then expected to abandon. The *Paix* marks Christine's final attempt to secure Valois sponsorship as well as the end of her personal crusade to revive the Wise King's practice of supporting intellectual activity at the royal court. A few years later she would flee Paris to enter a convent, re-emerging only once in that long exile to sing of Joan of Arc, whom she hoped might set the kingdom straight. By 1429, given her personal circumstances and, more importantly, the dire situation in France, Christine made no mention of Charles V's legacy. The time had passed for that revival. Of present concern was the reinstatement of a French king in Paris. It would be to later generations of writers to remind Valois leaders of the value and obligation to support intellectual activity.

Conclusion

This study has set out to examine an overlooked and yet foundational stage in the history of patronage linked to the rise of the Valois dynasty in France. While the reign of the direct Valois line spanned a 170-year period and included seven kings, I have concentrated on the reigns of the third and fourth Valois sovereigns because they inspired the literary community to think more critically about literary exchange dynamics and the importance of the intellectual community. This shift became especially apparent with the introduction of what I have referred to as Charles V's *Sapientia* project. I have maintained that more than the commissioning practices adopted by the Wise King, which reflected clientelistic ambitions, it was the literary and visual reworking of the royal commission as the writer's gift that profoundly influenced the literary economy. As manifestations of the patron's pleasure, books were material commodities that signalled the power and authority of the patron; as gifts, the knowledge contained within was confirmed as an incomparable treasure with transformative powers. As ordered works, texts celebrated the owner; as gifts, texts cultivated community.

Although this intellectual view of literary exchange spoke to the immediate and unique situation of Charles V's commissioned writers, who were celebrated intellectuals and masters of Latin culture, it would have a lasting impact on French vernacular literature. We see the effects of their claims for vernacular texts as gifts fit for a king refracted in the writings of their contemporaries Machaut and Deschamps, neither of whom could claim affiliation with this group of university intellectuals, but who, nonetheless, identified with the literary ambitions expressed in the group's vernacular learned works. In the case of Machaut, he expressed substantial doubt in the commissioned writers' premise that a secular ruler was ready and capable of recognizing vernacular writing as a treasure to be revered and coveted. Instead, Machaut imagined the ruling class as disrespectful, indifferent, or simply ill equipped to acknowledge the true worth of his poetry. In contrast, Deschamps's corpus invites us to think that he went well beyond the learned coterie of commissioned writers in attempting to influence the king's views about vernacular writing. Whereas the commissioned writers were focused on encouraging the king to recognize their work as an intellectual gift rather than a commodity, Deschamps very likely may have been engaged in efforts to convince Charles V of the even greater value of vernacular poetry. We find hints of Deschamps's attempts to influence royal views on poetry in writings addressed to Charles VI, but it is the tantalizing mystery surrounding the *Fragilité* that may represent the poet's earliest efforts to convince the ruling class that vernacular verse and its practitioners were invaluable to the kingdom.

As documented throughout this study, there is no evidence that Charles V reserved a serious role for vernacular poetry or its celebrated practitioners in his *Sapientia* project. Instead, it appears that his sudden death in 1380 augured unexpected opportunities for vernacular poets. These writers filled a void caused by the rapid disappearance of the intellectual community that had previously contributed to the *Sapientia* project. The young Charles VI's scant interest in the learning favoured by his father likely contributed to the exodus. Regardless of his proclivities, Charles VI was clearly in need of guidance, and several members of the court and the political community used their writing talents to address this issue. Both Deschamps and Christine loom large during Charles VI's reign as the most passionate and prolific members of this new *literati*, and their corpus allows us to track the extent to which the writing community was required to adjust the ideals of the past generation of learned writers to a sombre new reality. Each of these writers has allowed us to appreciate a second phase in the fashioning of Charles V as the quintessential patron, who was remembered as having taken seriously the role writers could play in society. This mythic remembrance of the Wise King, however, clashed with a clear unwillingness of contemporary princes to model themselves on this ideal. Writers became increasingly aware of the gaping disconnect between the ideal of literary exchange once championed by Charles V's commissioned writers and the continued arguments of the ruling elite who approached books as luxury items that served to reflect their power and wealth. Against this distortion of the past ideal, a writer such as Christine stands out for her astute manipulation of contemporary noble practices and ambitions to promote a nostalgic drive for intellectual and political partnership between writers and rulers.

In this regard, the prehistory of the patronage of arts and letters is anchored in a larger narrative about the relationship between the politically powerful and the writing community. It is a narrative focused on the production and promotion of learning by the intellectual class as a shared good that must not be identified as a commodity but as a rare gift in which all parties are deeply invested. Contrary to what medievalists have maintained, neither Christine nor her predecessors presented their works to members of the ruling class to acquire personal wealth or to enhance their fame. Thus, even when Christine openly speaks of the "high wages" that Charles V's commissioned writers garnered or when she prominently figures the Burgundian treasurer in the tale of a ducal commission, it is not because she identifies writing as a commodity to be bought and sold. Nor, however, were these medieval writers seeking *avant la lettre* a patronage relationship in which the powerful supported arts and letters in the name of aesthetic advancement or in honour of the writer's singularity, even though Machaut, Deschamps, and Christine were quick to identify their writing gifts as divine offerings. Based on its medieval heritage, today's definition of literary patronage ought to be recognized as having taken root in a philosophy that pushed against efforts to commodify knowledge and to favour instead a partnership between involved parties who shared the belief that knowledge must be preserved, promoted, and circulated in the name of social good.

This exploration of the prehistory of the modern concept of literary patronage casts a very different light on the development of set definitions of the terms later adopted to identify supporters of arts and letters. While it may be understandable that the patron is often cast as the dominant player in literary exchange dynamics given the labels used to identify this unique literary pact, awareness of late-medieval French vernacular writers' dealings with the Valois dynasty and the philosophy of exchange they promoted prepares us for a more critical assessment of later linguistic choices. French is especially important in this regard, given that a neologism was chosen early on to set apart the practice of sponsoring the arts and letters from all other forms of hieratic support.[1] In fact, while the coining of the term *mécénat* deliberately elides the medieval past to favour a Roman luminary, early definitions of this term reveal the enduring influence of late-medieval French ideals about literary exchange developed in the writings and books dedicated to the earlier Valois dynasty. That the term *mécène* to identify an individual who supported specifically writers only officially entered the language with Antoine Furetière's 1690 *Dictionnaire universel* is crucial to this story. Furetière's definition begins with reference to the real Mecenas, who "aimoit les gens de lettres, & les appuyoit de son credit, sur tout les Poëtes" (loved writers and who placed them under his care, especially poets). Furetière then defined modern usage of the term as serving "pour honorer tout les grands Seigneurs qui favorisent les sciences, & les Auteurs, & qui les protegent" (to honour all the great lords who favour the sciences and authors, and those who protect them). There is clear evidence that this lexicographer sought to present *mécène* as the sole title to confer on someone who supported knowledge and the learned community. In spite of the fact that here the first literary citation following the definition equates *patron* with *Mecenas*,[2] entries for *patron* and *patronage* do not list the support of letters among the recognized activities affiliated with these words. This early definition of *mécène* suggests that special honour ought to be conferred on those distinguished men interested in protecting knowledge and its producers. Later definitions reveal an even greater desire to reserve this honorific title for those rare individuals who held in high esteem creators of the arts and letters. By the eighteenth century, the definition of *mécène* established as a necessary quality for those who acquired this title an abiding admiration for thinkers and artists, and in so doing, the medieval ideal of literary exchange maintained its currency. As the 1762 *Dictionnaire de l'Académie française* testifies, the title of *mécène* was conferred on those who had great "estime pour ceux qui … cultivent" the arts and letters. This new definition of *mécène* signalled a shift from celebrating the protection of knowledge and authors to praising the respect extended to those who cultivated this knowledge. As such, this revised definition recalls the carefully crafted arguments of Charles V's commissioned writers that privileged intellectual labour as the basis of exchange. Likewise, this definition resurrects the philosophy put forth by the commissioned writers, and then promoted at the later court of Charles VI, that praise for aristocratic involvement in the transmission and preservation of knowledge was conferred in relation to the respect that the aristocracy showed to gifted artists and scholars in charge of the circulation of knowledge. In the late-medieval context, writers and artists had gone to great lengths to explain that inclusion in the exclusive partnership fostered by literary exchange required that partners share a mutual esteem for and commitment to the writer's gift. This obligation meant that to merit the role of addressee, one had to value the knowledge and the talents of the author, to be willing to support his or her work, and to recognize the end product as an inalienable good to be shared among like-minded individuals.

Were we to reclaim the medieval foundation for the patronage of arts and letters, it would demand serious reconsideration of current uses and practices associated with the term. It would require us, for example, to distinguish between collectors, who acquire works of art that are not shared with society, from patrons, who would be those individuals who support the preservation, production, and circulation of works of art. It would require us to reinvent the literary economy that is now almost exclusively dictated by buyer demand and that is increasingly viewed as part of the entertainment industry. To reclaim this medieval foundation and to reassert medieval concepts of literary partnerships forged between writers and the ruling elite, we would need to recognize medieval writers not as sycophants interested in their own fame and fortune, but as representing a far more altruistic drive than what has come to be celebrated in modern discussions of literary success. Moreover, to reclaim the medieval ideal of relations between the aristocracy and authors would mean challenging modern society to remove letters from the commercial sphere and to return to a philosophy that claimed for writing the status of an incomparable treasure expected to be shared in the name of the greater good. What would literature look like today were we to revive the medieval ideal of literary exchange? Would we see the resurgence of the *poète engagé* along with a public who turned to authors for access to knowledge and for the tools to address pressing social and political issues? Would we find our leaders turning to the intellectual community for support and guidance? Would there be a revalorization of learning?

Undoubtedly, the lofty ideals I have attributed to late-medieval writers will strike modern ears as quaint and impractical – even illusory and contrived – but they were repeatedly and passionately articulated by the coterie of writers and artists who had experienced firsthand a demand for books by the ruling class that was unmatched in living history. Inspired by a scholarly tradition that set knowledge apart from all other terrestrial goods as a treasure more worthy than a king's riches, to recall the words of Denis Foulechat, they took seriously their role as conveyers of this wealth and sometimes earnestly, sometimes ominously, they reminded their privileged recipients of the uniqueness of the gift first bestowed on authors themselves and only then freely offered in hopes of aiding the reader. Those who embraced the philosophy of the writer's gift claimed no affiliation with the wandering minstrel or the court entertainer of the vernacular tradition; instead, they claimed the roles of *orator*, *magister*, and counsellor. For this elite coterie of writers affiliated with the Valois royal court and satellite sites of Valois power, their work could not be converted to coin, nor did it represent a material good that could be reduced solely to evidence of the recipient's power and authority. Even those writers who faced a far less accommodating ruling class after Charles V's demise continued to argue this point. They continued to hope that the surviving Valois princes might take on the demanding role of intellectual partner and friend. Today, such ruminations surely seem impossible, maybe even ridiculous, in the sceptical world we now inhabit. Nonetheless, we ought to remember that a not-insignificant number of writers living in late-medieval France who endured political and social instability for most of their lives not only believed it was possible but even professed to have lived the experience. Perhaps we have worked so hard over the centuries to erase their story because of the challenge it puts before us. Perhaps it is time to revive the ideal even if we can't realize it and, in the process, to call on society to take seriously the gift writers present to us and to think less about turning to their works to simply satisfy our pleasures.

Notes

Introduction

1 Details taken from "Le livre d'heures de Jeanne de France est en ligne" on Blog BnF.
2 Quoted in Debeiesse, *Mécénat*, 29. Discussed in Fleury, *Cas Beaubourg*, 119–21. Throughout this study, English translation of quotations are mine, unless otherwise indicated.
3 Debeiesse, ibid., 28.
4 The law in question is loi n° 2003–709. For an overview of public patronage in France and related tax laws, see Gobin, *Mécénat*. It is important to recognize the uniqueness of the French state's efforts since the 1960s to reserve 1 per cent of its annual budget for the ministry of culture. As Françoise Benhamou notes, this ambition positions France "without an equal in the world" ("sans équivalent dans le monde"), *Économie de la culture*, 94).
5 *Raisons pratiques*, 149.
6 Signalling the importance of the religious theme developed in the image, *Le Figaro* observed that "dans un pays largement catholique comme la France, un livre de prières peut par ailleurs être considéré comme populaire, au bon sens du terme" ("in a predominantly Catholic country like France, a book of prayers can in fact be considered popular in the best sense of the term"): Claire Bommelaer, "Un trésor national pour la BnF," *Le Figaro*, 29 August 2012. As for the replacement of religion with art in post-Revolution France, one need only think of the transformation of the Egliste Sainte-Geneviève into the "Panthéon des grands hommes" in 1791.
7 Grégoire, "Rapport," 411.
8 So problematic is medieval sponsorship of the arts and letters in general that it is common practice in France to exclude the Middle Ages from discussions of

literary and artistic patronage. Consider the CAPES (certificat d'aptitude au professorat de l'enseignement du second degré) history exam topic for 2010. Although one of the three transhistoric topics proposed was "Le Prince et les Arts, du XIVème au XVIIIème siècle en France et en Italie," most preparation materials overlooked patronage prior to the Renaissance. In fact, Charles V was singled out only to be identified as an unviable example of patronage in Boucheron et al., *Prince et les arts. France*, 270; cf. Jansen, "Prince et les arts à la fin du Moyen Âge," 21–3 and 35–7.

9 Scholarship that honours the Valois dynasty for its formidable role in promoting French vernacular writing is vast. In addition to Delisle's *Recherches*, other consequential titles include Meiss, *French Painting*; Lusignan, *Parler vulgairement*; Taburet-Delahaye, *Création artistique* and *Paris 1400*; Avril and Lafaurie, *Librarie de Charles V*; and Avril et al., *Fastes du gothique*.

10 *Portraits of Charles V*.

11 In his touchstone work on literary patronage, Karl Julius Holznecht claimed that "patronage of letters, existing as a well-defined system, is not nationally restricted or dependent upon the spirit of any age but is the result rather of a few fairly obvious and universal social and economic conditions" (*Literary Patronage*, 1).

12 On the original coining of the neologism "mécénat" in sixteenth century France to distinguish artistic and literary patronage from other forms of sponsorship, see Petey-Girard, *Sceptre et la plume*, 15–32. On the English terminology, see McGrady, "Introduction," 146–7.

13 In the field of art history, in particular, scholars maintain that premodern patronage is hampered by the retroactive application of terminology and economies articulated in later periods. For an overview of the debate and the arguments, see Kent, *Cosimo de' Medici*, 8; Flora, "Patronage"; and the entry on literary patronage in Howatson, *Oxford Companion to Classical Literature*. For fresh reconsiderations of these issues, see Hourihane, *Patronage* (see esp. contributions by Kumler, "The Patron-Function," 307–8, and Schleif, "Seeking Patronage," 209–10). From a literary perspective, see Petey-Girard, *Sceptre et la plume*, 15–32.

14 Petey-Girard, ibid., 17–19, 22–3.

15 "Seeking Patronage," 206–7.

16 *Princely Court*, 255; cf. Warnke, *Court Artist*.

17 Early on, Holznecht concluded that medieval writers ingratiated themselves to the powerful through the obsequious and self-denigrating rhetoric that filled their dedications for personal gain, disdainfully adding that medieval society was "deal[ing] essentially with the economic phase of the literary profession" (*Literary Patronage*, 3). This view continues to dominate studies

of medieval literary patronage (see esp. Green, *Poets and Princepleasers*; Medeiros, "Pacte encomiastique"; Collet, "Littérature, histoire, pouvoir."

18 Poirion, *Poète et le prince*; Kelly, "Genius of the Patron"; Blanchard and Mühlethaler, *Ecriture et pouvoir*, esp. 7–32.

19 Scholarship on aristocratic women's involvement in literary culture and the arts is extensive. Here follow a few key works: Bell, "Medieval Women Book Owners"; Caviness, "Patron or Matron?"; McCash, "Cultural Patronage of Medieval Women"; Parsons, "Of Queens, Courts, and Books." Important work on the role of late-medieval aristocratic women in literature include Brown, *Queen's Library*, and "Mécénat d'Anne de Bretagne"; Brown and Legaré, *Femmes, l'art et la culture*; Legaré, *Livres et lectures de femmes*; Eichberger, Legaré, and Kusken, *Femmes à la cour*. See also Swift, "Circuits of Power"; McGrady, "Printing the Patron's Pleasure."

20 "Medieval Patronage," 29.

21 "Introduction," 5.

22 On the book-presentation scenes as anticipating a hoped-for acceptance of the book rather than serve as a testimony to lived events, see most recently, Erik Inglis, "A Book in Hand."

23 Scholars have tended to assign much later dates to the emergence of a "field of letters" or a "champ littéraire": Pierre Bourdieu proposes the nineteenth century (*Règles de l'art*), whereas Alain Viala dates it to the seventeenth century (*Naissance de l'écrivain*).

24 Although not addressed in this study, writers familiar with this tradition forged at the French royal court went further afoot and turned to more distant courts in an effort to persuade other rulers to take on the role of the enlightened royal patron modelled on Charles V. Richard II attracted particular attention both from Jean Froissart and Philippe de Mézières. Regarding Mézières, in 1395–6, he turned his attentions away from Charles VI to address a letter to the new king of England, Richard II (discussed briefly in Loomis, "Library of Richard II," 177).

25 As regards the investment in book culture by these important royal precursors, the reader is directed to several independent studies of these men, including Bullough, "Charlemagne's Court Library Revisited"; Smyth, *King Alfred the Great* (esp. chapters 9 and 18); Procter, *Alfonso X of Castile*; and Marquez-Villanueva, "Alfonso X of Castile." This last work is especially helpful in signalling the similarities and differences in the practices and intentions of the Spanish and French monarchs who would both be given epithets that celebrated their learning. See also George D. Greenie, "University Book Production," for treatment of how Alfonso X shaped his views on learning in light of a Parisian model.

26 On regional lords' investment in new vernacular writings, see Collet, "Littérature, histoire, pouvoir"; Spiegel, *Romancing the Past*. On Philippe le Bel's translation activity, see Lusignan, *Parler vulgairement*, 138, and Lusignan, "Culture écrite." A similar practice is found in England, where baronial investment in the literary arts continued well into the fifteenth century (Salter et al., *English and International*, 75–100).

27 Bibliothèque de l'Arsenal, MS 5107, fol. 2r–2v. For details on Vignay, see Beaune, *Naissance de la nation France*, 268, and Knowles, "Jean de Vignay."

28 For an overview of John the Good's literary patronage, see Delisle, *Recherches*, 1:326–36. In the specific case of the *Grandes chroniques*, see Hedeman, *Royal Image*, 61–73.

29 *Fastes du gothique*, 56.

30 On Philip IV's involvement in letters, see Lusignan, "Culture écrite." For a listing of Charles V's commissioned translators, see Delisle, *Recherches*, 1:82–119. Serge Lusignan added to this list new authors: see *Parler vulgairement*, 136–9.

31 It is noteworthy that those known to have authored earlier works had done so in Latin. For instance, Raoul de Presles reminds the king that he offered him a now-lost original work in Latin, *Musa* (*Cité*, 171), and Nicole Oresme was a well-established writer with more than a dozen Latin works when he began translating for the king (*Ethiques*, 28–33).

32 On their impact of these translations on the vernacular, see Lusignan, *Parler vulgairement*, 140–71.

33 Although the commissioned writers never claim that the king imposed prose over verse, the fact remains that not a single vernacular verse work figures among Charles V's recognized commissions. A possible exception to this may be Deschamps's *Double lay de la fragilité*. The curious circumstances surrounding this work are addressed in chapter 4 of this study.

34 Hedeman, *Royal Image*, xxi, and for further development, see 93–136.

35 Griggs and Dewick, *Coronation Book of Charles V*, ix; Sherman, "Queen"; O'Meara, *Monarchy and Consent*.

36 *Livre des fais et bonnes meurs du sage roy Charles V*, 2:42. Hereafter referred to as *Charles V*.

37 Within the francophone tradition, no one prior to Charles V can be confirmed as having used so extensively the commission to shape the literary field. Frequently cited precursors are Henri II of England, Eleanor of Aquitaine, and Marie de Champagne, but as Karen M. Broadhurst argues, few if any works linked to these figures can be labelled as certain commissions ("Patrons of Literature in French?"). Note also that Lusignan's list of thirty-one texts linked to Philip le Bel includes several titles that are not

identified as commissions but offerings ("Culture écrite," 32). This is not to suggest that unsolicited offerings to the king no longer transpired. Charles V's open valorization of books as treasures worthy of a king also inspired his entourage as well as his peers to offer him books during institutionalized giving events, such as New Year's, weddings, negotiations, and foreign visits. In these instances, foreign nobility, family members, and high-ranking clergy were just as likely to present Charles V with a book offering as court administrators, merchants, and writers of modest means. For a listing of individuals who offered books as gifts to Charles V, see Delisle, *Recherches*, 1:50–1. One of the earliest New Year's gift books on record in Charles V's collection was received the year prior to his coronation from Louis of Anjou (Van Praet, *L'Inventaire*, 41, entry 97).

38 "Circuits of Power," 222. See also Broadhurst, "Patrons of Literature in French?" 54.

39 Avril et al., *Fastes du gothique*, 89.

40 "Littérature autour de 1300," 74.

41 Compare for instance the 1363 inventory of the household possessions of the then Dauphin Charles (Gaborit-Chopin, *Inventaire du trésor du dauphin*) with the 1380 inventory (Van Praet, *Inventaire*). By the fifteenth century, the duke of Bedford would demand an inventory listing the price of each book (Douët-d'Arcq, *Inventaire de la bibliothèque du roi Charles*, xli–xlii). The commodity status of books was, of course, already manifested in the vibrant book trade in thirteenth-century Paris that is detailed by Richard Rouse and Mary A. Rouse in *Manuscripts and Their Makers.*

42 Other forms of literary exchange in medieval culture have been aligned with patronage, such as exchange between friends, monastic investment in the arts, as well as studies on group investment. For discussion of these variations, see, for example, Vines, "Rehabilitation of Patronage"; Knapp, *Bureaucratic Muse*; Luxford, "Construction of English Monastic Patronage"; Folda, *Art of the Crusader.*

43 *The Gift*, 3.

44 *Patronage System*, 1.

45 On Kent's dismissal of clientelism as a helpful paradigm for studying Renaissance patronage, see *Cosimo de' Medici*, 8 and 332. The use of clientelism by Renaissance scholars of patronage, has been hotly debated in the field. See Cooper, "*Mecenatismo* or *Clientelismo?*"; Viala, *Naissance de l'écrivain*, 51–5; Jouhaud and Merlin, "Mécènes, patrons et clients."

46 "Genius of the Patron."

47 *Princely Court*, 259.

48 "Seeking Patronage," 210.

49 *Medieval Market Economy*, 215. See also Vale, *Princely Court*, 247–78, and Buettner, "Past Presents." The consumer patterns of late-medieval patrons also merit being considered in the context of the much-debated concept of "bastard feudalism." See McFarlane, "Bastard Feudalism," for its early articulation; for the continued debate, see Coss, "Bastard Feudalism Revised," and Hicks, *Bastard Feudalism*.

50 See esp., Cassagnes, *D'Art et d'argent*; Cassagnes-Brouquet, "Étrangers à la cour"; Lindquist "'Will of a Princely Patron,'" "Accounting for the Status," and *Agency, Visuality and Society*; Buettner, "Past Presents." Further helpful reading in this vein includes Kaufmann, *Court, Cloister and City*; Vale, *Princely Court*; and Paviot, "Mécénat des princes Valois."

51 Gregory details this phenomenon in his study of objects exchanged among the colonized people of New Guinea who fused archaic gifting ideals with the consumption patterns introduced by the colonizers (*Gifts and Commodities*, 8 and 116).

52 Ibid., 10.

53 We can place a royal commission in J.L. Austin's category of commissives: that is, when a speaker commits to a cause or course of action. Such a speech act anticipates a "conventional procedure" that is already in place and known by involved parties (*How to Do Things with Words*, 14).

54 Eisenstadt, "Some Analytical Approaches," x.

55 *Patronage System*, viii.

56 On the contention that consumerism is not an eighteenth-century phenomenon but a medieval development, see Christopher Dyer, *An Age of Transition?* 128.

57 xi.

58 Sherman, *Portraits*.

59 To appreciate the extent to which new economic practices were of concern to the intellectual community, see Joel Kaye's discussion concerning the major shift in the "conceptual landscape" (*Economy and Nature in the Fourteenth Century*, 1) that resulted from the "rapid monetization" taking over Europe and changing intellectual views on mathematical issues (ibid., 2). On these ensuing intellectual shifts, see Le Goff, *Intellectuels*, and de Libera, *Penser au moyen âge*.

60 On this tradition of a learned sodality, see Post et al., "Medieval Heritage," and Lusignan, "*Vérité garde le roy*," 248–56.

61 Krueger, "Contracts and Constraints," 92–3. See also, Kellogg, *Medieval Artistry and Exchange*, 137–63, and Bossy, "Donnant, donnant."

62 Mauss, *Gift*, 3, 13.

63 Ibid., 3.

64 *Love for Sale*, 42–3, and for full development of this idea, ibid., 49–56. On the continuation of this tradition with the thirteenth-century poet Baudouin de Condé, see Foehr-Janssens, "Noblesse des lettres."
65 "Fullness and Emptiness," 233; see also Cerquiglini-Toulet, "Christine de Pizan," 208.
66 *Knowing Poetry*, 24.
67 Ibid., 14.
68 *Oeuvres poétiques*, 1:187–205.
69 This literary tradition continued with the *rhétoriqueurs* who deployed both gifting language and mercantile-inflected discourse to position their texts as valuable and desirable commodities. See Armstrong, *Virtuoso Circle*, and McGrady, "Printing the Patron's Pleasure."
70 The most important study in this arena is Davis, *The Gift* (see esp., 56–9). On the use of archaic gifting in a medieval context, see Krueger, "Contracts and Constraints"; Kellogg, *Medieval Artistry*; Frappier, "Motif du 'don contraignant'."
71 "Doing Things with Gifts," 18.
72 *Inalienable Possessions*, 6.
73 Ibid., 39.
74 *Sens pratique*, 167–89.
75 "Sacrifice."
76 Ibid.
77 *Charles V*, part 3, chap. 1; 2:7.

1 King Charles V's *Sapientia* Project: From the Construction of the Louvre Library to the Books He Commissioned

1 Debate surrounds the actual size of Charles V's book collection. My count follows Marie-Hélène Tesnière's assessment of the collection's contents ("Librairie modèle," 231). The actual inventories and extant royal books suggest a slightly smaller collection. Van Praet's edition of the Louvre inventory lists 910 entries (*Inventaire*, 1–146), which are supplemented by an additional 130 titles held elsewhere in the Louvre (ibid., 188–93 and 199–210) and at Vincennes (ibid., 194–8) for a total of 1,040 books (note that although the editor dates the inventory to 1375, 1380 is the accepted date). On the Vincennes collection, see also Avril, "Livres de Charles V."
2 Potin, "Recherche de la librairie," 34.
3 Lusignan, *Parler vulgairement*, esp. 129–71.
4 Monfrin, "Humanisme et traductions," 174–6 (although he acknowledges that the king's ambitions for these works were politically motivated rather than announcing a humanist interest, 176).

5 Sherman, *Portraits*. See also Plagnieux and Taburet-Delahaye, "Art et politique"; Pleybert, *Paris et Charles V*, especially Pleybert's contribution, "Art, pouvoir et politique"; and Mark Cruse, "Louvre of Charles V," regarding the central function of the Louvre library in the architectural articulation of royal identity (esp. 23–7).
6 Delisle, *Recherches*, 1:11.
7 Léopold Delisle originally listed twenty-five commissions linked to Charles V (*Recherches*, 1:82–119). Jacques Monfrin has since added four additional texts (*Questions sur les deux pouvoirs* by Raoul de Presles, a translation of Ptolemy's *Quadriparti* by Pelerin le Prusse and Robert Godefroy, and two works by Josèphe, *Les Antiquités Judaïques* and *Guerre des Juifs*, see "Humanisme et traductions," 174–5) and Serge Lusignan added two more titles (Evrart de Conti's translation of *Problemata* and Robert Godefroy's translation of *Liber novem judicum*, see *Parler vulgairement*, 136). Two other possible works to add to the list include St Augustine's *Soliloques*, which Christine de Pizan linked to the king (mentioned by Delisle, *Recherches*, 1:25) and Eustache Deschamps's *Fragilité* (to be discussed in chapter 4 of this study). On the king's influence on the *Grandes chroniques*, see Hedeman, who refers to the continuation as an "explicitly politicized vision of history" (*Royal Image*, xxi; a point more fully developed later in the study, 93–136). On evidence pointing to the *Livre du sacre de Charles V* as a commissioned text, see Griggs and Dewick, *Coronation Book*, ix; Sherman, "Queen"; and O'Meara, *Monarchy and Consent*.
8 *Recherches* 1:1.
9 "Littérature politique," 535.
10 See, for example, Daniel Poirion's passing remark on this matter (*Le Poète et le prince*, 26), as well as a similar brief acknowledgment by Jacques Krynen that Charles V's court inspired a great deal of political literature (*Idéal du prince*, 42).
11 E.g., Gilles de Rome, *Government des rois*, 66.
12 This is not to say that there were not crucial precursors to Valois interest in letters. See, for example, Delisle's discussion of St Louis's commissions in "Notice sur deux livres" and Patricia Stirneman's treatment of twelfth- and thirteenth-century princely libraries in "Bibliothèques princières."
13 Knowles, "Jean de Vignay."
14 Delisle, "Testament de Blanche de Navarre." For an analysis of Blanche's bequeathing of her books, see Buettner, "Système des objets."
15 On John the Good's dealings with illuminators, see François Avril, "Un moment méconnu"; Delisle, *Recherches*, 1:326–36; Hedeman, *Royal Image*, 53; and Rouse and Rouse, *Manuscripts and Their Makers*, 1:263–7.

16 See Rouse and Rouse, ibid., 1:261 and 1:267–8.
17 For details on John the Good's books, see Delisle, *Recherches*, 1:326–36. Gace de la Buigne recounts these events in his address to Duke Philip at the outset of the *Roman des deduis*.
18 On the presence of Jeanne d'Evreux's books in Charles V's collection, see Holladay, "Fourteenth-Century French Queens."
19 Ibid., 97 and notes 99–101.
20 "Littérature politique," 539.
21 Besançon Bibliothèque municipale, MS 434, 1r.
22 See, for example, depictions of nobility listening to clerics on folios 40r, 46r, 91v; nobility being read to on folios 197v and 255r; and receiving books from authors on folios 103r, 293r, and 377v. The manuscript is fully digitized on the BnF Gallica site.
23 Van Praet, *L'inventaire*, entries 142, 232, 369, 397, 505.
24 On reading Golein's prologue as part of the Mirrors tradition, see introduction to *Racional*, 31.
25 *Arts de gouverner*, 107; cf. Born, "The *specula principis*," 610.
26 *Idéal du prince*, 98.
27 *Charles V*, 106.
28 *Racional*, 66.
29 *Policratique*, 83.40. References are to page and line and are hereafter cited in text.
30 BnF, MS fr. 25287, fol. 105r–106v.
31 *Racional*, 655.
32 Ibid., 657. In their introduction to the edition, Golein's modern editors make clear that this nod to Charles V's activities is commonplace in his writings (ibid., 28 and 31).
33 *Vergier*, 1:6.13. References are to volume, page, and paragraph and are hereafter cited in text.
34 *Principis instructione*, 7.
35 *Li Livres*, 66.
36 Ibid.
37 Ibid., 69.
38 Ribémont, "Jean Corbechon," Appendix I, 15.
39 *Livre des fais et bonnes meurs du sage roy Charles V*, 2:37–41. Hereafter cited in text as *Charles V*.
40 *Paix*, 142.
41 Berty, *Topographie*, 1:124.
42 On Raymond du Temple, see Henwood, "Raymond du Temple." On his titles, see Chapelot, "Maître d'ouvrage," 365.

43 For a detailed description of the staircase, see Whitley, "Deux escaliers royaux," 144–50.
44 Whitley, "Deux escaliers royaux," 146.
45 Whitely's work is based largely on previous accounts by Henri Sauval who had access to now destroyed documents (for this earlier account, see Sauval, *Histoire et recherches*, 1:15–23).
46 "Louvre de Charles V," 66.
47 Ibid., 71n40.
48 Ibid., 66.
49 "Librairie modèle," 225
50 The following description of the library is based on these resources: Delisle, *Recherches*, 1:6–9; Sauval, *Histoire et recherches*, 1:15–23; Tesnière, ibid., 225–6; and Le Roux de Lincy, "Comptes des dépenses," 677–8.
51 Delisle, *Recherches*, 1:367.
52 Sauval, *Histoire et recherches*, 1:15.
53 Delisle, *Recherches*, 1:369–71.
54 On royal bookbindings, see Robin, "Luxe des collections."
55 Potin, "Recherche de la librairie," 35.
56 Van Praet, *Inventaire*, entries 6 and 7, respectively.
57 Ibid., entries 197 and 427, respectively.
58 Ibid., entry 33.
59 Ibid., entry 230.
60 Ibid., entries 17–20, 22, and 158.
61 Ibid., entries 142 and 14.
62 Ibid., entry 27.
63 Ibid., entries 26 and 262. The repurchased copy in question is BnF, n.a.f., 24541.
64 Ibid., entry 231 (Golein); entries 211, 233, 237, 244, 249 (works by Oresme); entry 228 (Foulechat); entry 193 (Presles); entry 242 (Hesdin); entries 245 and 246 (Evrart de Trémaugon's *Songe du Vergier* in French and Latin, respectively).
65 Ibid., entries 21 and 98, respectively.
66 Ribémont, "Jean Corbechon," Appendix 1, 15.
67 Kent would not agree with my linking of her concept of the "patron's oeuvre" with clientelism since she considers Renaissance scholars' use of modern economic terminology to understand premodern patronage as dangerous (*Cosimo de' Medici*, 8a) and anachronistic (ibid., 332b).
68 Burkolter, *Patronage System*, 1.
69 Delisle, *Recherches*, vol. 1, app. 6, 367–8.
70 Ibid., vol. 1, app. 7, 369–72.

71 Jean de Beauvais the elder filled this role from 1368–84. Rouse and Rouse take for granted that it would have been court practice to seek parchment from the royal parchmenter (see *Manuscripts and Their Makers*, 1:263). It is also, however, true that the court accounts register purchase of parchment for a Bible without naming the royal parchmenter (see Delisle, *Recherches*, vol. 1, app. 7, entry 4, 370 and entry 8, 372).

72 "Contrats de copistes," esp. 415 and 429–33. Note that Cottereau-Gabillet does not discuss Charles V's specific practices. For further study of this topic, see Peter Burke's earlier influential work (*Italian Renaissance*, 103–6) and the treatment of the French situation in Rouse and Rouse, *Manuscripts and Their Makers*, 1:267–83.

73 "Contrats des copistes," 432.

74 On Raoulet d'Orléans, see Delisle, *Recherches*, 1:70–9. On both scribes, see Rouse and Rouse, *Manuscripts and Their Makers*, 1:270–79, 2:51–2. New titles have been attributed to these scribes by Rouse and Rouse (ibid., 2:121–2) and Marie-Hélène de Tesnière, who identifies BnF, MSS fr. 22912–13 as the work of Raoulet d'Orléans on Gallica (http://archivesetmanuscrits.bnf.fr).

75 Delisle, ibid., 1:76. Claire Richter Sherman claims evidence of a record from the royal treasury for record of a single payment to Raoulet d'Orléans of 5 livres (*Imaging Aristotle*, 315). Rouse and Rouse observe that Raoulet d'Orléans frequently acted as *libraire*, "that is, directing the production of the book," and thus they posit that it is not out of the question that the production of the king's personal copy of the *Ethiques* was directed by Raoulet d'Orléans (*Manuscripts and Their Makers*, 1:275).

76 On documented payments to illuminators by John the Good and Charles V, see Meiss, *French Painting*, 1:22–3; Rouse and Rouse, *Manuscripts and Their Makers*, 1:268n34, 395n38, 395); Joubert, "Arts de la couleur," 174. On anonymous miniaturists believed to have been retained by the royal court, see Rouse and Rouse, ibid., 1:263–7 and Avril, "Parcours exemplaire." More generally, see Delisle, *Recherches*, 1:79–81.

77 Art historians have reached similar tentative conclusions regarding the king's influence on book aesthetics. See Kumler, "*Faire Translater*," 122, and Hedeman, *The Royal Image*, 95–133.

78 Taveau-Launay, "Raymond du Temple," 326.

79 What follows is a summary of the account of Malet's financial situation in Delisle, *Recherches*, 1:10–22.

80 Jean Golein's *Chroniques des Papes* from 1368 represents Charles V's first datable literary commission.

81 Delisle, *Recherches*, 1:104.

82 Ibid., 1:104.

83 Ibid., 1:105.
84 Ibid.
85 Ibid., 1:106.
86 Ibid., 1:109n1.
87 On the salaries of presidents of parliament, see Autrand, *Naissance d'un grand corps*, 33–4. For an additional comparison, see Taveau-Launay who identifies the salary of an officer of the Chambre de Comptes as 400 livres parisis per year ("Raymond du Temple," 326).
88 Delisle, *Recherches*, 1:109n2.
89 BnF MS fr. 22913, fol. 449r.
90 This term was coined by C.A. Gregory and is briefly discussed in relation to this project in the introduction to this study.
91 On Presles's family, see Lancelot, "Mémoire," 607, and for discussion and transcriptions of the king's legitimation letters, see Lombard-Jourdan, "Raoul de Presles," 199–205.
92 Bossuat, "Raoul de Presles," 124.
93 Laborde, *Manuscrits*, 1:36n1.
94 *Livre du ciel*, 730.
95 Neveux, "Nicole Oresme," 25. The missives in question are A.D. Seine-Maritime, G2115, 28 août 1372 and G2116, f. 67v.
96 Neveux, ibid., 21, 25–6.
97 Delisle, *Recherches*, 1:100.
98 Ribémont, "Jean Corbechon," Appendix 1, 15.
99 Delisle, *Anciennes traductions*, 294. On a possible interpretation of Daudin's comment, see Hamm, "Jean Daudin," 222.
100 Delisle, *Recherches*, 1: 53.
101 Ibid., 1:15.
102 Delisle, *Anciennes traductions*, 294.
103 Delisle, *Recherches*, 1:92.

2 The Writer's Work: Translating Charles V's Literary Clientelism into Learned Terms

1 On the debate surrounding the status of this manuscript as the king's personal copy, see Delisle, *Recherches*, 1: 60; *Policratique*, 24; and Tesnière, "Cas de censure," 273–4.
2 For other works linked to this master, see Avril, "Parcours exemplaire."
3 BnF, MS fr. 24287, fol. 2.
4 Holznecht claimed that "patronage of letters, existing as a well-defined system, is not nationally restricted or dependent upon the spirit of any

age but is the result rather of a few fairly obvious and universal social and economic conditions" (*Literary Patronage*, 1).

5 "Afterword," 371.

6 "Mécènes, patrons et clients," 47.

7 Miyazaki, "Gifts and Exchange," 253. The notion of approaching medieval book presentation scenes as "performances" is discussed in a complementary vein in Mahoney, "Courtly Presentation," 100.

8 Keane, "Value of Words," 606.

9 Important work on the vernacularisation of knowledge includes the seminal study by Jacques Le Goff, *Intellectuels* and elaborations on his work, Alain de Libera, *Penser au moyen âge*, and Jacques Verger, *Universités au moyen âge*. More recently, Marcia Colish has proposed new ways of addressing the issue in "Re-envisioning the Middle Ages." For the latest overview of the study of intellectual history, see Bose, "Intellectual History."

10 *Cité*, 163.2–3. Text references are to page and lines and are hereafter cited in text.

11 Delisle, 1:93. On record of Corbechon receiving remuneration, see ibid., 92.

12 "Value of Words," 606.

13 All three extant copies of Foulechat's *Policratique* bear material traces of these empty spaces that, in the case of MS fr. 24287, subsequently received the missing material. See Tesnière, "Cas de censure," 274–5; for a list of the additions in MS fr. 24287, see ibid., 275n14.

14 What little is known about Foulechat's sentencing by the university is covered in Brucker's introduction to his edition (*Policratique*, 22–3).

15 De Libera, *Penser au moyen âge*, 350.

16 Ibid., 12–13. In a similar vein, Jacques Le Goff had previously discussed the concept of an intellectual aristocracy ("Universities," 144–5), an argument further developed by Mariateresa Brocchieri, who posits that the 1,277 condemnations triggered "un singulier moment d'auto-conscience professionnelle" that resulted in the intellectual community breaking from university control ("L'intellectuel," 217). For an overview of these condemnations, see Tempier, "Condemnation of 219 Propositions."

17 *Penser au moyen âge*, 148.

18 *Universités*, 193–4.

19 In many regards, I see Charles V's commissioned writers as important precursors to men like Jean Gerson, who Daniel Hobbins identifies as a "public intellectual" (*Authorship and Publicity*, 16). Let me take this opportunity to acknowledge that my thinking about the important role the commissioned writers played in shaping discussions about literary exchange and their influence on subsequent vernacular poets reflects my own engagement with Hobbin's study of Gerson.

20 *Parler vulgairement*, 162–3.
21 In this regard, I disagree with Le Goff's claim that when intellectuals shifted their attention to the court in the fourteenth and fifteenth centuries, they orchestrated the demise of the intellectual movement (*Intellectuels*, 138–9).
22 The discussion of the commissioned writers that follows builds on the biographic information provided by Delisle, 1:82–119 and named entries in the *Dictionnaire du moyen âge*, unless otherwise indicated.
23 *Universités*, 198–9.
24 See Bossuat, "Raoul de Presles" for details on the translator's advances at court.
25 Nathalie Gorochov has debunked previous claims that Oresme also served as Grand Master (*Collège de Navarre*, 313–19).
26 Discussed in Delogu, *Allegorical Bodies*, 16 and 32–3.
27 Le Goff, *Intellectuels*, 54.
28 *Ethiques*, 99. Hereafter cited in text.
29 *Portraits*, 21.
30 Ibid., 23.
31 Ibid., 23.
32 Jean de Vignay is an important precursor as regards this practice. He often identified his translation work presented to the first Valois king and queen as an example of intellectual labour. In his prologue to the *Miroir historial*, he explained that having learned that the royal family desired a vernacular version of the text, he set himself to work on translating the text: "*si me sui mis a labourer* et ay commencie a descrire et a translater de latin en francois le mireoir des hystoires" (*I set myself to work* and began to describe and translate from Latin into French the *mireoir des hystoires*) (BnF, MS fr. 312, fol. 1v, emphasis added).
33 Two other works are identified by Presles as royal commissions: a translation of *La quastio inter clericum et militem* and *Rex pacificus*. The sole copy of the *quastio* translation, BnF, MS Latin 14617, opens with "Au commandement de tres hault et excellent prince Charles, par la grace de Dieu le Ve roy de France de ce nom, maistre Raoul de Praeles translata de latin en françois la question qui s'enssuit" (fol. 112r). The *Rex* translation closes with "Explicit Rex pacificus, translaté par cellui qui vous l'ordonnastes à translater" (Dainville, Archives départementales de Pas-de-Calais, Centre Machaut-d'Artois, 10, f. 1).
34 The canonists would eventually compromise and claim that masters with ecclesiastical benefices could accept payment from wealthy students. For treatment of the arguments surrounding these decisions, see Post, "Masters' Salaries" and the important follow-up article of Post et al., "Medieval Heritage."

35 For an overview of the early sources for positive views on labour in the twelfth century, see Nederman, "Virtues of Necessity," esp. 57–60.
36 Cited and discussed in Uebel and Robertson. "Conceptualizing Labor," 3. We hear important echoes with modern theories regarding "immaterial labor." See Knapp, "Poetic Work," for treatment of this concept in terms of changing late-medieval views on writing.
37 Aquinas, building on Aristotle, was most influential in this debate and he concluded that "docere artes liberales est actus spiritualis secundo modo; et ideo licet magistris atrium vendere labores suos sed non scientiam sive vertitatem quae spiritualis est" (IV. Sent. 25.3.2).
38 Discussed in Post et al., "Medieval Heritage," 222.
39 Ibid., 219.
40 Verger, *Universités*, 197–8.
41 *Recherches*, 1:86.
42 A digitized copy of this codex is available on BnF Gallica. Note that the author portrait heading John's prologue in the king's copy calls further attention to the word game announced in the manuscript's coda through the inscription of the first letters of the alphabet. While this coda also figures in BnF, MS fr. 1145, its first half, BnF, MS fr. 2692, does not contain the requisite highlighted letters making the instructions in the coda "fruitless" in this instance.
43 There are eighteen extant copies of the *Ethiques*, of which two are said to represent distinct early versions that Oresme presented to the king. Brussels, Bibliothèque royale, MSS 9505–6 (previously identified as MS 2902) is considered to be a copy of the earliest version of the *Ethiques* presentation codex offered to Charles V. This two-volume copy dated to 1372, thus two years after Oresme claimed to have completed the work in the "prohème," appeared in Gilles Malet's early inventory. The second version, Hague, Museum Meermanno-Westreenianum, MS 10 D-1, also figured in the king's collection, but appears to have been intended for private use. A colophon dates this copy to 1376. For complete listing and description of the extant copies, see *Ethiques*, 46–55. For a detailed study of these two copies, see Sherman, *Imaging Aristotle*, 45–59.
44 Gauthier, *Magnanimité*, 467.
45 Menut provides a concise bibliography of Oresme's writings in his introduction (*Ethiques*, 28–33).
46 See Bridrey, *Théorie*, 17–99.
47 *Ethiques*, 100n1 clarifies that in the Hague copy, "recommendacion" rather than "commendacion" was recorded in the rubric.
48 Lusignan arrives at a similar conclusion based on the *double entendre* of "bailler" that Oresme uses (*Parler vulgairement*, 165).

49 Ibid., 163.
50 *Imaging Aristotle*, 57. Sherman argues for Oresme's leading role in the illustrations (ibid., 32 and 55, and "A Second Instruction to the Reader").
51 *Portraits*, 2,1 and further developed in *Imaging Aristotle*, 55–7.
52 *Imaging Aristotle*, 55.
53 Ibid., 57.
54 *Portraits*, esp. 21–6, and *Imaging Aristotle*, 55–7.
55 *Parler vulgairement*, 162–3.
56 *Penser l'amitié*, 170–210.
57 *Nichomacean Ethics*, IX.1.6, and note of explanation, IX.1.7, p. 289. This issue is discussed below.
58 *Penser l'amitié*, 171. For original Aquinas citation, see *Commentary*, vol. 2, entry 1758.
59 *Nichomacean Ethics*, IX.1.6, and note of explanation, IX.1.7, p. 289.
60 *Commentary*, vol. 2, entry 1768.
61 Ibid.
62 *Penser l'amitié*, 171.
63 In fact, this prologue conjoined two translations by Oresme, the *Ethiques* with the *Politiques*, which were bundled together in the earliest copies presented to the king. On this bundling in the king's copy, see Delisle, "Les *Ethiques*, les *Politiques*," 257–82.
64 *Parler vulgairement*, 151.
65 Regarding the "commendacion," Lusignan remarks that "Oresme renverse ici l'ordre argumentative habituel des justifications de la tradition" (ibid., 166).

3 Guillaume de Machaut's Fictions of Engagement

1 Earp, *Guide to Research*, 25–6.
2 Ibid., 26–8.
3 Lawrence Earp considers the duke of Berry to be in clear possession of his first Machaut manuscript in the 1380s (Earp et al., *Ferrell-Vogüé*, 1:38), but he hypothesizes that Machaut had the codex produced in hopes of securing the duke's support (ibid., 1:43–4). Regarding King John's other children, Burgundian inventories suggest that the king's youngest son, Duke Philip, possessed a now-lost copy of Machaut's writings (Earp, *Guide to Research*, 102, entry 19; 104, entry 25, 105, entry 30), it has been posited that the *Dit de la marguerite* was composed to celebrate Philip's marriage to Marguerite of Flanders (Wimsatt, *The Marguerite Poetry*, 54–8), and Marie de France

possessed a Machaut manuscript before 1380 (Earp et al., *Ferrell-Vogüé*, 1:49). There is no trace of either Duke Louis of Anjou or Joan of France having taken an interest in Machaut, although it is noteworthy that Joan's spouse, King Charles of Navarre, figured as a judge in the *Navarre* and as the addressee of the *Confort*.

4 Reference first noted in Hoeppfner, ed., *Oeuvres de Guillaume de Machaut*, 1:xxv. For further details, see Earp, *Guide to Research*, 44.

5 *Voir dit*, line 3362. For treatment of Charles's presence in the *Voir dit*, see Earp, *Guide to Research*, 45–6.

6 *Prise*, line 802. Diana Tyson concludes from this reference that the work has ties to the king ("French Vernacular History Writers," 105).

7 In the *Voir dit*, the poet claims to write it for Toute Belle (line 12), and in the *Prise*, the intended recipient is evoked in line 813.

8 "Mass." Motet 22 is a second musical composition viewed as referring to Charles V, yet, once again, there is no evidence that it was presented to or commissioned by the king. (On the thematic link of this work to the king, see Earp, *Guide to Research*, 39 and 43.)

9 As for the conjecture that the king was involved partly in the production of two complete works manuscripts, see Earp et al., *Ferrell-Vogüé*, 31, for discussion of BnF, MS fr. 1586, and Perkinson, *Likeness of the King*, 226 and Roccati, "Guillaume de Machaut," for discussion of the tipped-in Prologue to BnF, MS fr. 1584.

10 On this now-lost manuscript that began with the opening line of Machaut's Lai 10, see Delisle, *Cabinet des manuscrits*, 2:199, entry 1233, and Earp, *Guide to Research*, 105, entry 29. Another luxury copy of music in an earlier inventory of Charles V's possessions has been linked to Machaut, again without overt reference to the author (Gaborit-Chopin, *Inventaire*, entry 577); Earp speculates that this reference may refer, in fact, to BnF, MS fr. 1586, the manuscript conjectured to have been undertaken for Charles V's mother and, following her death, to have been acquired by John the Good (*Ferrell-Vogüé Manuscript*, 31–20).

11 "Patron-Function," 311–12.

12 Line 2484. Hereafter cited in text, with English translations of Machaut's works from the same edition unless otherwise indicated in the text.

13 These anagrams are also famously unstable; on this subject, see Cerquiglini-Toulet, "*Un engin si soutil*," 235–8 and de Looze, "'Mon nom trouveras,'" and "Signing Off."

14 Line 32 and lines 7–8, respectively.

15 Kelly consistently describes the partnership along clientelistic lines: he claims that "[the patron] conceives the work" ("Genius of the Patron," 84), that "the writer puts into words the patron's thoughts or sentiments, and directs these toward an audience" (ibid., 87), and that when functioning as pupil, "the poet changes to fit the patron's thoughts" (ibid., 90).

16 E.g., the *Fonteinne* (lines 143–55) and mentioned in passing in the *Prise d'Alexandrie* (line 1055). The key exception is, of course, the *Jugement de roy de Behaigne* from the 1330s.

17 On the original coining of the neologism "mécénat" in sixteenth century France to distinguish artistic and literary patronage from other forms of sponsorship, see Petey-Girard, *Sceptre et la plume*, 15–32. On the English use of patronage, see McGrady, "Introduction," 146–7.

18 For a complementary treatment on questions of intimacy between author and privileged readers in the Navarre, see McGrady, "Textual Bodies," 9–17.

19 *The Gift*, 3.

20 Ibid., 12.

21 *Jugement dou roy de Navarre*, line 573. Hereafter identified as *Navarre* and cited in text, followed by English translation from the same edition unless otherwise indicated.

22 *Place of Thought*, 98.

23 Ibid., 99.

24 *Confort*, lines 1–5. Hereafter cited in text, with English translations from the same edition unless otherwise indicated.

25 *Confort*, ed. Palmer, xxxv.

26 One later edition of the text appears to revise the work to make it relevant to a more general audience. See Geer, "Devotional and Political Consolation."

27 Palmer speaks of vengeance (*Confort*, xxxii).

28 On Machaut's claims for imagination as a means of consolation, see Huot, "Consolation of Poetry."

29 On Machaut's presumed supervision of this codex, see Williams, "Author's Role," and cf. McGrady, *Controlling Readers*, 98.

30 Arsenal, MS 5203, fol. 91r. Digitized copy of manuscript available on Gallica. It is not out of the question that Charles's image was damaged as a direct response to his claims to be the rightful king of France.

31 It is worth noting that Ernst Hoepffner's claim that the anagram reveals John of Berry's name has been shown to be dubious (Ehrhart, "Machaut's *Dit*," 121–4).

32 *Fonteinne*, line 1. Hereafter cited in text, followed by English translation from the same edition unless otherwise indicated.

33 "Fullness and Emptiness," 231–2.

34 Ibid., 226.
35 Mauss, *The Gift*, 13.
36 *Judgment of the Trojan Prince*, 138. See also, Earhart, "Machaut and the Duties," 17.
37 "Tout son païs m'abandonna," 29. I want to take this opportunity to thank Yale University Press for giving permission to revisit here ideas first developed in this article. For discussion of the impact of the illustrations on this message, see my "Machaut and His Material Legacy," 364–70.
38 Image reproduced in McGrady, "Material Legacy," 385.
39 The Prologue in its entirety heads BnF, MSS fr. 1584 and fr. 22545. The first four ballades of the Prologue introduce BnF, MS fr. 9221. The Prologue is also found in a much later manuscript, Pierpont Morgan, M. 396, which contains works by Machaut mixed in with writings of other medieval writers.
40 Prologue in *Fonteinne*, 2, translation mine. Hereafter cited in text, with the translation from the same edition unless otherwise indicated in the text.
41 *Inalienable Possessions*, 39. See Introduction for further discussion of Weiner's importance to the medieval-patronage context.
42 François Avril links most of the collected works copies with the royal entourage, including Ferrell-Vogüé, which he refers to as "un exemplaire là encore destiné à quelque grand personnage lié à la cour, du temps du roi Charles V" ("Manuscrits enluminés,"124). Earp has pursued this line of thought and persuasively identifies the duke of Berry as an early owner of this codex (*Ferrell-Vogüé*, 1:35–46).
43 "Manuscrits enluminés," 127.
44 For an overview of work attributed to this master, see *Grove Encyclopedia*, 2: 389.
45 Ibid.
46 McGrady, "Guillaume de Machaut," 116.
47 "Regards sur le *Prologue*," 236. My translation.
48 See also McGrady, "Guillaume de Machaut," 116–18.
49 Earp identifies links to the Valois court in his individual descriptions of several of the codices (*Guide to Research*, 73–128). See esp. entries 1, 7, 8, 12 and note that entries 3, 4, 6 are now linked to the duke of Berry (Earp et al., *Ferrell-Vogüé*, 1:35–46).
50 Avril, "Manuscrits enluminés," 124, 128–30, and Earp et al., ibid., 1:38–46. What follows is a summary of Earp's account from *Ferrell-Vogüé*, vol 1.
51 Stephen Perkinson goes even further to speculate that Charles V played an active role in securing the decoration of this manuscript's tipped-in Prologue by one of his favoured artists (*Likeness of the King*, 226).
52 Earp et al., *Ferrell-Vogüé*, 1:35–46.

53 The identification of the owner of MSS 22545–6 was revealed by Yolanda Plumley and Uri Smilansky and first noted in print in Plumley, *Art of Grafted Song*, 417.
54 *French Painting*, 290. An important exception to this narrative concerns the duke's acquisition of a commissioned translation of the *Meditations Vitae Christi* in the 1380s (ibid., 289). Not mentioned by Meiss is the claim by the author of the *Melusine* romance that the duke commissioned the text before the turn of the century (Jean d'Arras, *Mélusine*, 110–13).
55 *Jean de Berry*, 439.
56 Ibid., 433.
57 See, for example Beauvoir, *Libraire de Jean duc de Berry*, entries 87, 93, and 100–7.
58 *French Painting*, 50.
59 Autrand discusses this reward in *Jean de Berry*, 472.
60 On Premierfait and his translations presented to the duke of Berry, see Hedeman, *Translating the Past*, 56–8, and ibid., app. 5, 239–48.
61 Ferrell-Vogüé, fol. 170 (see Earp et al, *Ferrell-Vogüé*, vol. 2, for reproduction), and MS fr. 22545, fol. 99 (see digitized copy on Gallica).
62 Ferrell-Vogüé, fol. 196v, see Earp et al, *Ferrell-Vogüé*, vol. 2, for reproduction.
63 Term coined by Nancy Regalado in "The *Chronique métrique*," 470.
64 For a discussion of the Ferrell-Vogüé illustration cycle of the *Fonteinne* and the ways in which it re-imagines the relationship between poet and prince in comparison to MS fr. 1584, see McGrady, "Machaut and His Material Legacy," 364–70.
65 "Manuscrits enluminés," 138. See also Avril's extended study of this master in "Parcours exemplaire."
66 BnF MS fr. 9221, fol. 1 (digitized copy available on Gallica). Note that in the remaining six images attributed to this master in MS fr. 9221, the author-figure is also depicted at the beginning of the *Dit dou vergier* genuflecting before the God of Love (fol. 18r). The first illustration in MS fr. 9221 placing the poet in a position of relative authority only appears with the miniature heading the *Jugement de Navarre*, which is attributed to the *Master of Policratique* (fol. 45r).
67 On Perrin Rémy (Rémiet) and MSS 22545-6, see Avril, "Manuscrits enluminés," 129. For Rémy's work on other manuscripts linked to Charles V, see Avril, "Trois manuscrits," 307–8 and 311–13. On the false identification of Rémy as the *Master of Death*, see Rouse and Rouse, *Manuscripts and Their Makers*, 2:216.
68 This background is first discussed by Avril, "Manuscrits enluminés," 129. On the identification of the emblem, see Plumley, *Art of Grafted Song*, 417.

69 *Portraits of Charles V*. See also the previous chapter of this study.
70 Ballade 123, l. 21 in *Oeuvres complètes*.

4 Eustache Deschamps on the Duties and Dues of Poetry

1 For an overview of the key political and social ideas that have preoccupied Deschamps scholars, see Becker, *Etat actuel*. Several collections of essays provide significant studies of Deschamps's treatment of contemporary issues, including edited volumes by Boudet and Millet, *Eustache Deschamps en son temps*; Buschinger, *Autour d'Eustache Deschamps*; Lassabatère and Lacassagne, *Témoin et modèle*; and Lacassagne and Lassabatère "*Dictez vertueulx.*" In addition, see the following insightful studies dedicated to Deschamps's politics: Becker, *Lyrisme d'Eustache Deschamps*; Dudash, "Eustache Deschamps"; Kendrick, "Art of Mastering Servitude"; Lassabatère, *Cité des hommes* and "Théorie et éthique de la guerre"; Minet-Mahy, *Esthétique et pouvoir*; and Poirion, *Le poète et le prince*. On the production of the posthumous manuscript by Raoul Tainguy, see Tesnière, "Manuscrits copiés."
2 The codex consists of 594 folios that record 1,501 works ascribed to Deschamps, ranging from discrete poems and lengthy *dits* to treatises and plays.
3 For an account of Deschamps's official affiliations with the royal courts of Charles V and Charles VI, see Deschamps, *Selected Poems*, 6–20, and Laurie, "Biography," 1–72. Note the unsubstantiated assumption that Deschamps's royal service represented a reward for his poetic activities (*Selected Poems*, 2).
4 *Oeuvres complètes*, B1125, lines 1–3. Deschamps's poetry is cited by genre, number, and verse from *d'Eustache Deschamps* and appears hereafter in text.
5 Cf. Gaston Raynaud, who believed (with no evidence) that the "livre de memoire" pointed to Deschamps's involvement in the *Grandes chroniques* (*Oeuvres complètes*, 9:327).
6 It is curious that only three of the king's sons are mentioned. It may be a reference to the three sons who were held captive in England along with their father while the dauphin Charles remained in France or it may be a discreet judgment on the king's second son, the duke of Anjou who broke his commitment and plotted a successful escape from his English captors, also in 1364. His unchivalrous behaviour required his father's return to England, where he would die only four months later.
7 But the earliest record of service to the extended Valois dynasty is his service beginning in 1375 as bailiff of Valois, thanks to Duke Philip of Orleans (Laurie, "Biography," 7).

8 For a definition of this genre, see Poirion, *Poète et le prince*, 101–11 and 121–7; and Thiry, "Poésie de circonstance," 125.
9 See also Ballade 222.
10 On Deschamps's self-effacement in works concerning Charles V, see Thiry, "Poésie de circonstance," 125–6.
11 *Master of Death*, 60.
12 The manuscript in question is Besançon, Bibliothèque municipale, MS 434, ff. 377v–400r.
13 Hasenohr, "Discours vernaculaire," 288–91, and Camille, *Master of Death*, 58, respectively. The codex can be viewed in full on Gallica.
14 Michon, "Édition manuscrite d'Eustache Deschamps," 30–1.
15 Camille, *Master of Death*, 58–60.
16 As a representative argument for the importance of careful scrutiny of the text-image relationship, see especially Camille's discussion of the illustration of Adam and Eve (*Master of Death*, 66–7). Note also that a fully digitized version of MS fr. 20029 is available on Gallica.
17 Ibid., 61.
18 *Oeuvres*, vol. 2, 362. Laura Kendrick is even more explicit on this matter in "Monument and the Margin," 855.
19 Camille, *Master of Death*, 62.
20 Ibid., 61.
21 See for example on Gallica, BnF, MS fr. 20029, folios 9v and 11v; as for other codices linked to the *Master of Death* that exhibit the same dimensions, see BnF, MS fr. 9106, fol. 358, and BnF, MS fr. 312, fol. 66v, both of which are reproduced in Camille, *Master of Death*, fig. 49, p. 90, and fig. 147, p. 201, respectively.
22 In fact, we have discussed two such cases already: the book presentation scene at the head of Charles V's copy of the *Songe du Vergier* (British Library, Royal MS 19 C IV; see Figure 3.4 of this study) and the opening miniature to Machaut's Prologue that decorates the duke of Berry's final copy of the poet's collected works (BnF, MS fr. 9221).
23 On this matter, see *Selected Poems*, 40n30, and Laurie, "Biography," 55n98.
24 *Songe du Vieil Pelerin*, 2:223.
25 "Cycle de l'avènement."
26 For a succinct and informative treatment of the different approaches to literary engagement by Charles V and Charles VI, see Hedeman, *Royal Image*, 138–40.
27 BnF, MS fr. 5749, fol. 1r. A digitized copy of this manuscript is available on Gallica.

28 Jean of Berry later commissioned Nicolas de Gonesse to continue Hesdin's work in 1401 (Millet, "Nouveaux documents").
29 Jackson, "*Traité du sacre*," 305–6. Another example is Bauchant, who authored the *Voies de Dieu* and whose name resurfaced in 1396 in Louis of Orléans's inventories when the duke purchased books from his estate (Le Roux de Lincy, *Bibliothèque de Charles d'Orléans*, 34–5).
30 *Oeuvres complètes*, 11:331.
31 Autrand, *Charles VI*, 75–119.
32 Titles listed in Delisle, *Recherches*, 1:131–2.
33 Autrand, *Charles VI*, 214–40.
34 Delisle, *Recherches*, 1:130–7.
35 Ibid., 1:135.
36 Ibid., 2, entries 912, 22, 1118, 251, respectively.
37 Ibid., 1:126.
38 Ibid., 1:126n1.
39 See ibid., 2, entries 330, 513, 667, 980. Also to be included is John the Good's Bible, which was confiscated by the English at the Battle of Poitiers, the return of which was credited to the then dauphin, Louis of Guyenne (ibid., 1:129).
40 Ibid., 2, entries 788 and 809.
41 Ibid., entries 1111, 616, 1212 and 1213.
42 *Idéal du prince*, 42. For a similar assessment, see Roux, "Charles V," 686.
43 "Introduction," 533.
44 For an overview of the writings produced in hopes of providing guidance to the young king, see Bourassa, *Counselling Charles VI*.
45 *Songe du Vieil Pelerin*, 1:101.
46 *Arbre des batailles*, 2.
47 Delisle, *Recherches*, 2, entries 1212 and 1213.
48 *Demandes faites*, 10.
49 *Of Counselors and Kings*, 9.
50 *Les demandes faites*, 5.
51 Ibid., 6.
52 "Cycle de l'avènement."
53 Note that the editor incorrectly numbered these lines, which should have been numbered as lines 230–5.
54 Internal evidence suggests that the "Lay de Franchise" dates to 1385, and Lassabatère locates the "Fiction" to the same period (*Cité des hommes*, 485).
55 Lacassagne incorrectly associates Beauté-sur-Marne with Charles VI, when in fact it was his father who had it restored in 1373 ("Lai de Franchise," 652–3).
56 "Interdépendances de forme," 43.

57 Raoul de Presles makes the comparison of Charles V to an eagle in his prologue to the *Cité* (165). Charles V's sceptre also depicted Charlemagne seated on a throne with eagles flanking each arm (Louvre, MS 83).
58 *Gift*, 58–9.
59 See Bliggenstorfer, "Poèmes de supplication," and Laidlaw, "Supplications de Deschamps."
60 Laidlaw, "Supplications de Deschamps," 81–3.
61 Four additional ballades reference this event: B835, B836, B845, and B864.
62 On this economy, see McFarlane, "Bastard Feudalism," and Hicks, *Bastard Feudalism*.
63 *Apparicion*, 58–63.
64 Gaston Raynaud floated the possibility that the duke of Burgundy was the intended recipient of the *Art de dictier* (*Oeuvres complètes*, 9:155). As concerns the *complainte*, Tainguy's closing rubric to the text in BnF, MS fr. 840 identified the translation as undertaken "au commandement de monseigneur de Bourgongne" (ibid., 7:311).
65 See *Oeuvres complètes*, 11:371.
66 *Oeuvres complètes*, 7:266. Hereafter, cited in text by volume and page.
67 The *Miroir de mariage* references a book by Deschamps that chronicles the events of the Valois dynasty that may also point to this abandoned project (*Oeuvres complètes*, 9:369–70, lines 11503–4).
68 Froissart's editor, Baron Kervyn de Lettenhove, imagined an encounter between Froissart and Deschamps (*Oeuvres de Froissart*, 1:413–15). The relevant passage in the *Chroniques* concerns book 4, chaps. 50–1. As for Pierre Salmon, he has little to say about the event itself, but he implies greater involvement in the process than either other writer (*Demandes faites*, 43–5).

5 The Pursuit of Patronage: From Chrisine de Pizan's Troubled Dealings with Louis of Orléans to Marketing Nostalgia

1 *Christine de Pizan*, 119–65.
2 *Cent ballades*, Ballade 1, lines 1–8 (*Oeuvres poétiques*, ed. Roy,1:1).
3 McGrady, "What Is a Patron?" 210–12; McGrady, "Authorship and Audience," 27.
4 "Autorité dans les traités," 21.
5 de Winter, *Bibliothèque de Philippe*, 19.
6 Quoted in Autrand, *Charles VI*, 304.
7 *Religieux*, 3:12. On contemporary statements on this matter, see Guenée, *Un Meurtre*, 158–9. For the most extensive recent treatment of Louis's positioning as second in command, see Adams, *Fight for France*.

8 Prior to 1389, there is evidence of Louis purchasing only one book of hours in 1388 (Laborde, *Ducs de Bourgogne*, vol. 3, entry 5441). Pierre Champion laments the paucity of information in the Blois archives concerning Louis's library (*Vie de Charles d'Orléans*, iv). Of course, this lack of information concerning Louis's possessions surely has to do with his assassination by his cousin Duke John of Burgundy in 1407. For a detailed and informed reconstruction of Louis's book holdings (totaling 128 titles), see Shultz, "Artistic and Literary Patronage," app. 2, 435–55. On the celebrated Burgundian library, see the inventory from 1404, which lists only sixty-seven manuscripts in Duke Philip's Paris hotel (de Winter, *Bibliothèque de Philippe le Hardi*, 121–42). When the duke of Berry's library was first inventoried in 1402, it contained 124 books (Beauvoir, *Librairie de Jean*). On this last collection, see Meiss, *French Painting*, 1:290–7.

9 On Louis's allowance, see Autrand, *Charles VI*, 203. On Valentina Visconti's books, see Laborde, *Ducs de Bourgogne*, vol. 3, entries 5462–3 and 5465–8.

10 Regarding the purchase of his great-aunt's books, see Shultz, "Artistic and Literary Patronage," 193. Louis also is on record for having purchased *Échecs amoureux* and "autres romans" (other romances) from a Parisian *libraire* and a "livre de chants" (book of music) from his sommelier (Laborde, *Ducs de Bourgogne*, vol. 3, entries 5626 and 5567, respectively).

11 "Artistic and Literary Patronage," 194.

12 Ibid., 301–5.

13 On copies of the *Miroir*, see Laborde, *Ducs de Bourgogne*, vol. 3, entries 5682, 5709, 5725; for the *Cité*, see ibid., entry 5703; and on Oresme's translations, see ibid., entries 5703, 5762.

14 Ibid., entries 5800, 5672, and 5650, respectively.

15 On the Lord of Chantilly's book-gift in relation to New Year's celebrations in 1401, see ibid., entry 5946; and on Philip's 1403 gift of a copy of Hayton's work, see Champion, *Vie de Charles d'Orléans*, xii.

16 Laborde, *Ducs de Bourgogne*, vol. 3, entry 5598. The presence of Froissart's *Meliador* in Charles d'Orléans's 1417 inventory may signal a second gift-text received by Louis from Froissart (Delisle, *Cabinet des manuscrits*, vol. 1, entry 14). Concerning Deschamps, a now-lost copy of his poetry figured among Valentine Visconti's books, inventoried after her death in 1408 (Laborde, *Ducs de Bourgogne*, vol. 3, entry 6132).

17 Laborde, *Ducs de Bourgogne*, vol. 3, entry 5864.

18 Ibid., entry 5797. See also ibid., entries 5372 (misdated, see Laborde, ibid., 1: xxxviii), 5783, 5820, 5828, 5829, 5836, 5856, 5868.

19 Delisle, *Recherches*, 1:14.

20 Laborde, *Ducs de Bourgogne*, vol. 3, entry 5805.

21 Jean le Seneschal, *Cent ballades*, 205, and Deschamps, *Oeuvres complètes*, B1378.
22 *Apparicion*, 60 –1. Translation from this edition unless otherwise indicated in text. Hereafter cited in text.
23 *Archiloge Sophie*, 25. Hereafter cited in text.
24 *Oeuvres complètes*, 7:311.
25 See *Apparicion*, 8n20, 25–7 and 233–49.
26 This point has been surmised based on two later incomplete copies (BnF, MS fr. 143 and MS fr. 1508), see *Archiloge Sophie*, 11 and 52–7. The author later dedicated his *Livre de bonnes meurs* to the duke of Berry in 1409, hence two years after Louis's assassination, even though we believe an early version to have been completed in 1404 (*Archiloge Sophie*, 299).
27 This study excludes from the list of manuscripts produced for Duke Louis the complete-works manuscript purchased by the duke of Berry in 1408 (BnF, MSS fr. 835, 606, 836, 605, 607) that Millard Meiss and Sharon Off hypothesized was originally intended for Louis of Orléans ("Bookkeeping of Robinet d'Estampes, 228). No evidence has since been provided to confirm this popular speculation.
28 Vatican, Biblioteca Apostolica Vaticana, Reg. Lat. 1238, folio 1v. Hereafter cited in text.
29 "*Livre de la Prod'hommie*," 386.
30 *Livre du corps de policie*, xix. On the debate regarding the dating of this work, see Solente, *Christine de Pisan*, 57–9; Picherit, "*Livre de la Prod'hommie*"; Reno, "*Livre de Prudence*."
31 On Bovet, see *Apparicion*, 4–9, and regarding Legrand, see Beltran, "Jacques Legrand prédicateur" and "Jacques Legrand O.E.S.A."
32 *Débat de deux amans* in Altmann, ed., *Love Debate Poems*, line 1. Hereafter cited in text as *Deux amans*.
33 Altmann proposes Machaut as Christine's source in "Reopening the Case."
34 *Epistre Othéa*, ed. Gabriella Parussa, lines 12–15. Hereafter cited in text as *Othéa*.
35 My reading is supported by Adams's contention that the prologue and the presentation miniatures reinforce the idea that "Louis … is the rightful regent of the kingdom" (*Fight for France*, 76).
36 Hindman, *Christine de Pizan's "Epistre Othéa,"* 38–9, and Adams, *Fight for France*, 75.
37 Hindman considered this codex to have been presented by Christine to the duke (ibid., 43). Cf. Ouy et al. *Album Christine*, 349). For an overview of Christine's involvement in manuscript production, see Laidlaw, "Christine and the Manuscript Tradition." More recently, it has been argued that

Christine's hand appears in fifty-four of her manuscripts (Ouy et al., *Album Christine*; cf. Parussa and Trachsler, "*Or sus, alons*," and Lefevre, "*Manu Propria*," 635–40).
38 BnF, MS fr. 848, fols. 1v and 2r. Access to digitized copy available on Gallica.
39 *Christine de Pizan's "Epistre Othéa,"* 43.
40 Ibid., 43–51.
41 This reading is bolstered by Rosalind Brown-Grant's claims that Christine both de-sexualized and allegorized female characters to establish them as models for male readers (*Moral Defence of Women*, 80–7).
42 "Dit de la Rose," lines 41–9 (*Oeuvres poétiques*, ed. Roy, 2:29–48). Hereafter cited in text as *Rose*.
43 Christine details her familiarity with Charles V's library in *Charles V*, 2:42–6. For discussion of the influence of the commissioned translations on Christine, see Lefevre, "Aristote Oresmien"; Hicks, "Mirror for Misogynists"; Lechat, "Utilisation"; and Walters, "Biographe royale."
44 On these copies, see Ouy et al., *Album Christine*, 357–77, and Altmann, ed., *Love Debate Poems*, 36–58 and 81–152.
45 *Album Christine*, 361 and 92, respectively.
46 Ibid., 122–9.
47 "Past Presents," 619. For a complementary study of the queen's politics of royal New Year's giving, see Adams, "Isabeau de Bavière, le don."
48 Chattaway, *Order of the Golden Tree*, 9.
49 "Past Presents," 619.
50 McGrady, "What Is a Patron?" 205.
51 On Valentine traditions in the late Middle Ages, see Henry Ansgar Kelly, *Cult of Saint Valentine*.
52 *Fight for France*, 52–7.
53 On these collections, see Ouy et al. *Album Christine*, 228–93 and 316–43.
54 "*Livre de la Prod'hommie*," 381.
55 Christine presents this excuse for her celebrity in *Advision*, 111.
56 Laennec, "'Christine Antygraphe.'"
57 Ouy et al., *Album Christine*, 627.
58 "Genius of the Patron," 79.
59 Laborde, *Ducs de Bourgogne*, vol. 3, entry 6129.
60 Louis is, for example, referenced in *Oroison Nostre Dame* (1402–3) (*Oeuvres poétiques*, 3:4, line 91) and in the *Charles V* (1405) (1:169–76).
61 For discussion of this offering, see Ouy et al., *Album Christine*, 367–8.
62 Reproduction of the two dedication scenes are provided in ibid., 367.
63 *Love Debate Poems*, ed. Altmann, 39.
64 Ibid., pp. 37–8, lines 21–8. Hereafter cited in text as "Albret Dedication."

65 Of the seven manuscripts containing the *Deux amans*, only one additional manuscript includes observers, BnF, MS fr. 835, but in this copy, they frame the duke and gaze on the transaction. Note also that BnF, MS fr. 12779 is missing the presentation scene and the first fifty-one lines due to vandalism. For further details, see Ouy et al., *Album Christine*, 357–71.
66 On the significance of the baton for identifying court members, see Louis Alexandre Expilly, *Dictionnaire géographique*, 2:449–50.
67 Our only records of these alternative prologues to the *Othéa* that name someone other than Louis as the privileged recipient are from copies produced outside of Christine's control. For discussion of these manuscript copies, see comments on the work by its most recent editor Parussa (*Othéa*, 81–6). Note that following previous scholarly hypotheses, Parussa points out that the Burgundian dedication may have been rewritten by Jean Mélior who reworked Christine's text (ibid., 84). As for Henry IV as the king identified in the alternative dedication, James Laidlaw persuasively overturned previous speculation that the dedication was addressed to Charles VI to argue that the unnamed king is Henry IV (see "Earl of Salisbury" for his full argument on the matter). Parussa provides a transcription of these alternative dedications in a series of (unnumbered) appendices (*Othéa*, ed. Parussa, 501–6). These dedications are cited as *Othéa*, followed by page and line.
68 Compare *Othéa*, p. 501, line 5; p. 504, lines 5–9; and p. 507, lines 5–9.
69 Louis is replaced by the Duke of Berry in Oxford, Bodleian Library, laud. Misc. 570. In Brussels, Bibliothèque royale de Belgique, MS 9392, the frontispiece replaces both Duke Louis and Christine with the Duke of Burgundy and the redactor Jean Miélot.
70 Christine discusses this matter in *Advision*, 112–13.
71 This dating of the queen's copy of Christine's works reflects the most recent work by Laidlaw; see "Date of the Queen's MS."
72 Christine Reno details the differences between the two works in "*Livre de Prudence*," 27–8. Picherit also provides a comparative analysis of these two works in "*Livre de la Prod'hommie*."
73 British Library, Harley 4431, fol. 287v.
74 "*Livre de Prudence*," 31.
75 *Chemin de longue étude*, lines 9–12. Hereafter cited in text as *Chemin*.
76 See Andrea Tarnowski's comment on this issue in her introduction to ibid., 39–40.
77 John of Berry's copy (BnF, MS fr. 1188) is documented as having been presented by the author on March 1403 in the duke's inventories (Guiffrey, *Inventaires de Jean*, vol. 1, entry 932). Philip of Burgundy received his copy (Bibliothèque royale de Belgique, MS 10983) before his death in 1404 (de

Winter, *Bibliothèque de Philippe*, entry 63). BnF, MS fr. 1643 points to the duke of Orléans ownership since it is one of his secretaries who produced this copy dated to 1403 and according to Ouy et al., it includes signature evidence of Christine's involvement in the transcription (*Album Christine*, 383 and 409).

78 Hobsbawm cited in Frow, *Time and Commodity*, 77; Boym, *Future of Nostalgia*, xiii; Bakhtin quoted and discussed in Hutcheon and Valdés, "Irony, Nostalgia," 20, respectively.

6 The Curse of the Commission: Christine de Pizan on Sacrificing Charles V's Biography

1 McGrady, "What Is a Patron?" 203–6, and "Authorship and Audience," 30–2.

2 Two other possible contemporary commissions of vernacular original works by Valois princes that might have preceded Christine's biography are Deschamps's 1393 *Art de dictier*, which he declares to have been commissioned by an unnamed prince (possibly Louis himself), and *Mélusine* by Jean d'Arras, who claims that the duke of Berry commissioned the work (*Mélusine*, 112–13).

3 Lindquist, "Will of a Princely Patron," 47.

4 *Charles V*, 1:xxix.

5 *Advision*, 114. Hereafter cited in text.

6 On these events, see Cockshaw, "Mentions d'auteurs," 133–4, no. 46; de Winter, *Bibliothèque de Philippe*, 67; Lowden, *Making of the "Bibles Moralisées"*, 1:251–84, and notes on pp. 329–32; and Lowden, "Beauty or Truth?" 202–8.

7 Lowden, *Making of the "Bibles Moralisées,"* 1:279–82.

8 I borrow this view of the biography from Zimmermann, "Mémoire – tradition," 171.

9 *Livre des faits*, Part 2, chap. 1; 1:111. Hereafter cited in text as *Charles V*, followed by part and chapter; volume and page.

10 "Sacrifice," 212–13.

11 *Bibliothèque de Philippe*, 3, 10, respectively.

12 Ibid., 56.

13 Ibid., 58–9.

14 Ibid., 222–3.

15 Ibid., 58–9. Lowden believes this *Bible moralisée* to be BnF, MS fr. 167, which ultimately served as the model for the Limbourgs when they were illustrating BnF, MS fr. 166 for Duke Philip ("Beauty or Truth?" 205).

16 *Oeuvres complètes*, 7:311.

17 de Winter, *Bibliothèque de Philippe*, 17–21 and 24–6.
18 Schultz, "Artistic and Literary Patronage," 194. This point is discussed in the previous chapter of this study.
19 de Winter, *Bibliothèque de Philippe*, 133, entry 37; 131–2, entry 35; 136, entry 49; 133, entry 38; 30–1, entry 34, respectively. Transcriptions of inventory record of payment to the Rapondis for these works are provided in ibid., 196–7, 206, 209. On the frequent use by the Valois dynasty of the Rapondi brothers to acquire books, see ibid., 3, 29.
20 Ibid., 196, 206, 209.
21 Ibid., 218.
22 The second manuscript is Brussels, Bibliothèque royale, MS 10982. On the debate surrounding these two manuscripts, see Willard, "Autograph Manuscript"; de Winter, *Bibliothèque de Philippe*, 219; Laidlaw, "How Long," 85; and Ouy et al., *Album Christine*, 40).
23 Gilbert Ouy and Christine Reno identify in the three copies the presence of "Hand X," which they hypothesize to be Christine's own hand (ibid., 390, 396, 431).
24 For a complete description of these manuscripts, see Ouy et al., *Album Christine*, 377–400, 427–36.
25 "Introduction," 38.
26 On conspicuous consumption in medieval book culture, see Alexander, *Medieval Illuminators*, 138, and Robin, "Luxe des collections," as well as discussion of this issue in the Introduction to this study.
27 Strengthening this point is the lack of any record of the *Chemin* entering the royal library, whereas there is evidence that the dukes of Orléans, Berry, and Burgundy all acquired copies in 1403 (Ouy et al., *Album*, 379–84).
28 "How Long," 87.
29 Ouy and Reno, in fact, identify three of the extant copies of the *Mutacion* from 1404 as presentation copies directed to the dukes of Burgundy, Berry, and Orléans; they also provide reproductions of the opening folios of these manuscripts (*Album Christine*, 427–66).
30 Christine argues for the distinctiveness of her tale based on the unique suffering she has endured at the hands of Fortune (*Mutacion*, lines 29–32).
31 "Past Presents," 619.
32 Ibid., 600.
33 In "'Will of a Princely Patron,'" Sherry Lindquist analyses the treatment of gift exchange in Burgundian court records, where gifting language most often identifies the transaction. Lindquist suggests that this terminology ("don," "contredon," "recompensacion," and "offres") was deliberately used

to disguise mercantilism as expressions of archaic gifting. While Lindquist's analysis centres on the use of this terminology by nobility to disguise economic realities, her argument has served here to illuminate how an astute writer such as Christine would be conscious of these efforts to disguise personal desire through reference to gifting and to then use this knowledge to her advantage.

34 Benveniste, *Indo-European Language*, 79.

35 See entry 3a of the online definition in *DMF*.

36 See Part 1, chaps. 5 (1:12), 9 (1:22), 10 (1:24), 13 (1:33), 14 (1:36), 22 (1:59), 23 (1:62), 28 (1:79).

37 Daisy Delogu briefly discusses Christine's acknowledgment of her detractors as a means of acquiring greater authority for herself (*Theorizing the Ideal Sovereign*, 163–6). I agree with Delogu that these defences serve to strengthen Christine's status as a writer, although I believe Christine sought to highlight her isolation in these passages.

38 *Prison amoureuse*, lines 327–36. For discussion of this remark, see McGrady, *Controlling Readers*, 175–6.

39 *Imagination and the Erotic Life*, xiv.

40 *Songe du Vieil Pelerin*, 2:223.

41 On Christine's claims of familiarity with Charles V's library, see *Charles V*, 3:42–6.

42 See entry 3a of the online definition in *DMF*.

43 Frow, *Time and Commodity*, 77.

44 "Sacrifice," 210.

45 Part 3, chap. 31 (2:82) and chap. 49 (2:131), respectively.

46 Part 3, chap. 31 (2:85).

47 See especially Part 3, chaps. 18–40 (2:57–111) and chap. 71 (2:182–92) for multiple examples of direct citations of the king's words.

48 "Sacrifice," 213.

49 For a complete description of these manuscripts, see Ouy and Reno, "Manuscrits copiés en série," and Ouy et al., *Album Christine*, 477–515.

50 Guiffrey, *Inventaires de Jean*, vol. 1, 9, number 943, and Ouy and Reno, *Album Christine*, 477n8.

51 Cited in Cockshaw, "Mentions d'auteurs," 137–8, entry 64.

52 *Album Christine*, 408.

53 "Manuscript Tradition," 237. Note that Laidlaw's use of commission here serves to identify a market transaction in which Christine seeks out clients skilled in bookmaking.

54 Ibid., 237.

55 "Publisher's Progress," 35. See also Laidlaw, "Manuscript Tradition," 237.
56 "Manuscript Tradition," 236.
57 These collections are now housed at the Bibliothèque nationale de France and the British Library. The duke's codex includes the following volumes: BnF, MSS fr. 835, 606, 836, 605, 607. On the duke's purchase of this collection, see Guiffrey, *Inventaires de Jean*, 1:252–3, entry 959. The queen's manuscript is British Library, MS Harley 4431.
58 "Publisher's Progress," 35. In fact, these copies join with a number of undecorated single-text copies to be produced between 1405 and 1407. Examples include the first two early copies of the *Cité des dames* (BnF, fr. 24293 and Arsenal 2686) and copies of the *Livre du corps de policie* (Chantilly, Bibliothèque du château, 294; Arsenal 2681; BnF, Fr. 1197; Besançon, BM, 423). Reproductions of the opening folios of these codices provided in Ouy et al. *Album Christine*, 530, 536, 636, 650, 642, and 656.
59 It is helpful to compare this copy of the biography with extant copies of the *Corps de policie*, Paris, Bibliothèque de l'Arsenal 2681, and Besançon, Bibliothèque municipale, 423, fabricated between 1406 and 1407. Both manuscripts display a similar layout and elucidate its flexibility. Into the allotted space of the Arsenal copy, a small copy of the iconic image of Christine writing is inserted, whereas the contemporary Besançon copy relies on rubric to fill the void (reproductions of folios are provided in Ouy et al., *Album Christine*, 650, 656, respectively).
60 A reader of a Vatican copy addressed this absence by underlining Christine and Duke Philip's names in the body of the text. Image provided in Ouy et al., *Album Christine*, 510.
61 Cf. ibid., 246.
62 *Life and Afterlife*, 160.
63 McGrady, "Onneur et louenge."
64 Adams, "*Moyennerresse de traictié de paix.*"
65 "Dédicace à la reine Isabelle," line 54. Full text transcribed in *Oeuvres Poétiques*, 1: xiv–xvii. Hereafter cited in text as "Dédicace."
66 Hindman, "Iconography," 102 and 110.
67 "Patron-Function," 311–12.
68 The present reading revisits my arguments detailed in "What Is a Patron?"
69 A reproduction of the frontispiece is provided in ibid., 196.
70 Cf. ibid., 203–6.
71 "What Is a Patron," 195.
72 Reproductions of these images and analysis provided in ibid., 203–12.
73 Christine furnishes these details in *Paix* (*Book of Peace*, 293).
74 "Christine de Pizan à la recherche."

75 *Book of Peace*, 200 and 58. Cited hereafter as *Peace*, followed by pagination for original and then the English translation.
76 Discussed in chapter 2 of this study.
77 Green, "Introduction," 20.
78 Van Hemelryck, "Description of the Manuscripts," 48.
79 Ibid., 42–9.
80 For discussion of the presentation miniatures of this copy and later copies, see ibid., 51.

Conclusion

1 Note, however, that the term *mécénat* only entered the *Dictionnaire de l'Académie française* with the ongoing ninth edition, where the entry dates its existence only to the nineteenth century.
2 The citation provided is as follows: "Où chercher un Patron dans le siècle où nous sommes?/ Il est de grans espris, il est de savans hommes;/ Mais il n'est plus de Mecenas."

Bibliography

Manuscripts

Besançon, France, Bibliothèque municipale, MS 434.
Brussels, Bibliothèque royale de Belgique, MS 9392.
– MSS 9505–6.
– MS 9508.
– MS 10366.
– MS 10982.
– MS 10983.
– MS 11034.
Cambridge, Corpus Christi College, Parker Library, MS Vg.
Chantilly, Bibliothèque du château, MSS 492–3.
The Hague, Museum Meermanno-Westreenianum, MS 10 D-1.
London, British Library, MS Harley 4431.
– Royal MS 19 C IV.
Paris, Bibliothèque de l'Arsenal, MS 5107.
– MS 5203.
Paris, Bibliothèque nationale de France, MS fr. 143.
– MS fr. 166.
– MS fr. 167.
– MS fr. 312.
– MS fr. 434.
– MSS fr. 605–7.
– MSS fr. 835–6.
– MS fr. 840.
– MS fr. 848.
– MS fr. 1145.

– MS fr. 1188.
– MS fr. 1508.
– MS fr. 1584.
– MS fr. 1585.
– MS fr. 1586.
– MS fr. 1643.
– MS fr. 1740.
– MS fr. 1950.
– MS fr. 2692.
– MS fr. 2813.
– MS fr. 5749.
– MS fr. 9221.
– MS fr. 10153.
– MS fr. 12420.
– MS fr. 12779
– MS fr. 2002.
– MS fr. 24287.
– MSS fr. 22545–6
– MSS fr. 22912–13.
– MS fr. 25287.
– MS Latin 14617.
Vatican, MS Reg. Lat. 1238.

Primary Works

Aquinas, Thomas. *Commentary on the Nicomachean Ethics by Thomas Aquinas.* Translated by C.I. Litzinger, O.P. 2 vols. Chicago: Henry Regnery Company, 1964.

– *Commento alle sentenze di Pietro Lombardo e testo integrale di Pietro Lombardo. Libro quarto. Distinzioni 24–42. L'Ordine, il Matrimonio*. Bologna: PDUL Edizioni Studio Domenicano, 2001.

Aristotle. *Nicomachean Ethics.* Translated by Terence Irwin. Indianapolis: Hackett Publishing, 1999.

Bovet, Honorat. *L'arbre des batailles d'Honoré Bonet*. Edited by Ernest Nys. Brussels and Leipzig: Muquardt, 1883.

– *Medieval Muslims, Christians, and Jews in Dialogue. The "Apparicion Maistre Jehan de Meun" of Honorat Bovet: A Critical Edition with English Translation.* Edited and translated by Michael Hanly. Arizona: Arizona Center for Medieval and Renaissance Studies, 2005.

Budé, Guillaume. *De l'institution du prince*. Patis: Nicole Patis, 1547.

Christine de Pizan. *Le chemin de longue étude*. Edited and translated by Andrea Tarnowski. Paris: Livre de Poche, 2000.

– *Epistre Othéa*. Edited by Gabriella Parussa. Geneva: Droz, 1999.

– *Le livre de l'advision Cristine*. Edited by Christine Reno and Liliane Dulac. Paris: Honoré Champion, 2001.

– *Le livre de la Mutacion de la Fortune*. Edited by Suzanne Solente. Paris: SATF, 1959.

– *Livre de Paix. The Book of Peace by Christine de Pizan*. Edited by Karen Green, Constant J. Mews and J. Pinder. University Park, PA: Pennsylvania State University Press, 2008.

– *Le livre des fais et bonnes meurs du sage roy Charles V*. Edited by Suzanne Solente. 3 vols. Paris: Honoré Champion, 1936.

– *Le livre du corps de policie*. Edited by Angus J. Kennedy. Paris: Honoré Champion, 1998.

– *The Love Debate Poems of Christine de Pizan. Le livre du débat de deux amans, le livre des trois jugemens, le livre du dit de Poissy*. Edited and translated by Barbara K. Altmann. Gainesville: University of Florida Press, 1998.

– *Oeuvres poétiques de Christine de Pisan*. Edited by Maurice Roy. 3 vols. Paris: 1886; rpt., New York: Johnson Reprint, 1965.

– *The Selected Writings of Christine de Pizan*. Edited by Renate Blumenfeld-Kosinski. Translated by Renate Blumenfeld-Kosinski and Kevin Brownlee. New York and London: W.W. Norton, 1997.

Chronique du religieux de Saint-Denys: Contenant le règne de Charles VI, de 1380 à 1422. Edited by M.L. Belleaguet. 6 vols. Paris: Impr. de Crapelet, 1839–42.

Deschamps, Eustache. *Eustache Deschamps: Selected Poems*. Edited by Ian S. Laurie and Deborah M. Sinnreich-Levi. Translated by David Curzon and Jeffrey Fiskin. New York and London: Routledge, 2003.

– *Oeuvres complètes d'Eustache Deschamps*. Edited by le Marquis de Queux de Saint-Hilaire and Gaston Raynaud. 11 vols. 1888–1903.

Evrart de Trémaugon. *Songe du Vergier: Edité d'après le manuscript royal 19 CIV de la British Library*. Edited by Marion Schnerb-Lièvre. 2 vols. Paris: Editions du CNRS, 1982.

Ferrière, Henri de. *Le livres du roy modus et de la royne ratio*. Edited by Gunnar Tilander. 2 vols. Paris: Société des anciens textes français, 1932.

Foulechat, Denis. *Le policratique de Jean de Salisbury (1372), Livres I–III*. Edited by Charles Brucker. Geneva: Droz, 1994.

Froissart, Jean. *Jean Froissart: La prison amoureuse (The Prison of Love)*. Edited and translated by Laurence de Looze. New York: Garland, 1994.

– *Oeuvres complètes de Froissart*. Edited by Baron Kervyn de Lettenhove. 28 vols. Brussels: Librairie de Victon Devaux, 1870–3.
– *Oeuvres de Froissart. Poésies*. Edited by Auguste Scheler. 2 vols. Brussels: Devaux, 1870–2; rpt., Geneva: Slatkine, 1977.
Gace de la Buigne. *Le roman des deduis. Édition critique d'après tous les manuscrits*. Studia romanica holmiensa 3. Edited by Åke Blomquist. Stockholm: Almquist and Wiksells; Paris: Librairie J. Thiébaud, 1951.
Gerald of Wales. *De principis instructione liber*. In *Giraldi Cambrensis Opera*. Edited by J.S. Brewer. Vol. 8. Nendeln: Kraus Reprint, 1964–6.
Gilles de Rome. *Li livres duo gouvernement des rois: A XIIIth Century French Version of Egidio Colonna's Treatise "De regimine principum."* Edited by S.P. Molenaer. London: Macmillan & Company, Ltd., 1899.
Golein, Jean. *Le "racional des divins offices" de Guillaume Durand, Livre IV*. Edited by Charles Brucker and Pierre Demarolle. Geneva: Droz, 2010.
Guibert de Tournai. *Le Traité* Eruditio regum et principum *de Guibert de Tournai, O.F.M.* Edited by A. de Poorter. Louvain: Institut Supérieur de Philosophie, 1914.
Guillaume de Machaut. *Le Confort d'ami (Comfort for a Friend)*. Edited and translated by R. Barton Palmer. New York and London: Garland, 1992.
– *The Fountain of Love (La Fonteinne amoureuse) and Two Other Love Vision Poems*. Edited and translated by R. Barton Palmer. New York and London: Garland, 1993.
– *Le jugement dou roy de Navarre*. Edited and translated by R. Barton Palmer. New York and London: Garland, 1988.
– *Le livre du voir dit*. Edited and translated by Jacqueline Cerquiglini-Toulet. Paris: Livre de Poche, 1999.
– *The Marguerite Poetry of Guillaume de Machaut*. Edited by James I. Wimsatt. Chapel Hill: University of North Carolina Press, 1970.
– *Oeuvres de Guillaume de Machaut*. Edited by Ernest Hoeppfner. 3 vols. Paris: Librairie de Firmin-Didot etc., 1908–21.
– *La prise d'Alixandre (The Taking of Alexandria)*. Edited and translated by R. Barton Palmer. New York and London: Garland, 2002.
Jean d'Arras. *Mélusine ou la noble histoire de Lusignan*. Edited by Jean-Jacques Vincensini. Paris: Livre de Poche. Lettres Gothiques, 2003.
Jean de Brie. *The Medieval Shepherd: Jean de Brie's "Le bon berger" (1379)*. Edited by Carleton W. Carroll and Lois Hawley Wilson. Tempe, Arizona Center for Medieval and Renaissance Studies, 2012.
Jean de Condé. *Dits et contes de Baudouin de Condé et de son fils Jean, d'après les manuscrits de Bruxelles, Turin, Rome, Paris et Vienne*. Edited by Auguste Scheler. 3 vols. Bruxelles: Devaux, 1866–7.

Jean le Seneschal. *Les cent ballades: Poème du XIVe siècle composé par Jean le Seneschal avec la collaboration de Philippe d'Artois, comte d'Eu, de Boucicaut le jeune et de Jean de Crésecque*. Edited by Gaston Raynaud. Paris: Firmin-Didot, 1905.

Laurière, Marquis de, ed. *Recueil des ordonnances des roys de France de la 3ème race*. 22 vols. Paris: Imprimerie Nationale, 1723–1869.

Legrand, Jacques. *Archiloge Sophie et livre de bonnes meurs*. Edited by Evencio Beltran. Geneva and Paris: Slatkine, 1986.

Moranvillé, Henri, ed. *Le songe veritable: Pamphlet politique d'un parisien du 15e siècle*. Paris, 1891.

Oresme, Nicole. *Le livre du ciel et du monde*. Edited by Albert Douglas Menut and Alexander Joseph Denomy. Translated by Albert Douglas Menut. Madison: University of Wisconsin Press, 1968.

– *Le livre de Ethiques d'Aristote*. Edited by Albert Douglas Menut. New York: G.E. Stechert & Co., Publishers, 1940.

– *Traitié de la première invention des monnoies de Nicole Oresme, textes français et latin d'après les mss de la Bibliothèque Impériale*. Edited by L. Wolkowski. Paris: Librairie Guillaumin, 1864.

Philippe de Mézières. *Le songe du Vieil Pelerin*. Edited by G.W. Coopland. 2 vols. Cambridge: Cambridge University Press, 1969.

Raoul de Presles. *"La cité de Dieu" de saint Augustin traduite par Raoul de Presle (1371–1375), Livres I à III. Edition du manuscrit BnF, fr. 22912*. Edited by Oliver Bertrand. 2 vols. Geneva: Slatkine, 2013.

Salmon, Pierre. *Les demandes faites par le roi Charles VI, et les réponses de son secrétaire et familier Pierre Salmon*. Edited by Georges-Adrien Crapelet. Paris: Imprimerie de Crapelet, 1833.

Tempier, Etienne. "Condemnation of 219 Propositions." Translated by Ernest L. Fortin and Peter D. O'Neill. In *Medieval Political Philosophy: A Sourcebook*, edited by Ralph Lerner and Mhusin Mahdi, 337–54. New York: Free Press, 1963.

Vincent of Beauvais. *Vincent of Beauvais. De erudition filiorum nobelium*. Edited by Arpad Steiner. The Medieval Academy of America, Publication 32. Wisconsin: George Banta Publishing Company, 1938.

Secondary Works

Adams, Tracy. *Christine de Pizan and the Fight for France*. Pennsylvania: Pennsylvania State University Press, 2014.

– "Isabeau de Bavière, le don et la politique de mécénat." *Le Moyen Age* 117 (2011): 475–86.

– *The Life and Afterlife of Isabeau of Bavaria*. Baltimore: Johns Hopkins Press, 2010.

– "*Moyennerresse de traictié de paix*: Christine de Pizan's Mediators." In *Healing the Body Politic: The Political Thought of Christine de Pizan*, edited by Karen Green and Constant J. Mews, 177–200. Turnhout, Belgium: Brepols, 2005.

Alexander, J.J.G. *Medieval Illuminators and Their Methods of Work*. New Haven and London: Yale University Press, 1994.

Algazi, Gadi. "Introduction: Doing Things with Gifts." In *Negotiating the Gift: Pre-Modern Figurations of Exchange*, edited by Gadi Algazi, Galentin Groebner, and Bernhard Jussen, 9–28. Göttingen: Vandenhoeck and Ruprecht, 2003.

Algazi, Gadi, Galentin Groebner, and Bernhard Jussen, eds. *Negotiating the Gift: Pre-Modern Figurations of Exchange*. Göttingen: Vandenhoeck and Ruprecht, 2003.

Altmann, Barbara K. "Reopening the Case: Machaut's *Jugement* Poems as Source in Christine de Pizan." In *Reinterpreting Christine de Pizan*, edited by Earl Jeffrey Richards, 137–56. Athens and London: University of Georgia Press, 1992.

Appadurai, Arjun. "Introduction: Commodities and the Politics of Value." In *The Social Life of Things: Commodities in Cultural Perspective*, edited by Arjun Appadurai, 3–63. Cambridge: Cambridge University Press, 1988.

Armstrong, Adrian. *The Virtuoso Circle: Competition, Collaboration, and Complexity in Late Medieval French Poetry*. Tempe, Arizona: Arizona Center for Medieval and Renaissance Studies, 2012.

Armstrong, Adrian, and Sarah Kay. *Knowing Poetry: Verse in Medieval France from the "Rose" to the "Rhétoriqueurs."* New York: Cornell University, 2011.

Austin, J.L. *How to Do Things with Words*. 2nd ed. Edited by J.O. Urmson and M. Sbisá. Cambridge, MA: Harvard University Press, 1962.

Autrand, Françoise. *Charles V le Sage*. Paris: Fayard, 1994.

– *Charles VI: La folie du roi*. Paris: Fayard, 1986.

– *Christine de Pizan*. Paris: Fayard, 2009.

– *Jean de Berry: L'art et le pouvoir.* Paris: Fayard, 2000.

– *Naissance d'un grand corps de l'état: Les gens du Parlement de Paris, 1345–1454*. Paris: Publications de la Sorbonne, 1981.

Avril, François. "Les livres de Charles V au château de Vincennes." In *Vincennes et la naissance de l'État modern*, edited by J. Chapelot and E. Lalou, 329–40. Paris: Presse de l'Ecole normale supérieure, 1996.

– "Les manuscrits enluminés de Guillaume de Machaut." In *Guillaume de Machaut: Poète et compositeur. Actes et colloques. Reims (19–22 avril 1978)*, 117–33. Paris: Éditions Klincksieck, 1982.

– "Un moment méconnu de l'enluminure française: Le règne de Jean le Bon." *Archeologia* 162 (1982): 24–31.

– "Parcours exemplaire d'un enlumineur parisien à la fin du XIVe siècle: La carrière et l'oeuvre du maître du policratique de Charles V." In *De la sainteté à l'hagiographie: Genèse et usage de la Légende dorée*, edited by Barbara Fleith and Franco Morenzoni, 265–82. Geneva: Droz, 2001.

– "Trois manuscrits napolitains des collections de Charles V et de Jean de Berry." *Bibliothèque de l'école de Chartes* 127, no. 2 (1969): 291–328.

Avril, François, Françoise Baron, and Danielle Gaborit-Chopin. *Les fastes du gothique: Le siècle de Charles V*. Paris: Réunion des musées nationaux, 1981.

Avril, François, and Jean Lafaurie. *La librairie de Charles V*. Paris: Bibliothèque nationale, 1968.

Bataille, Georges. "Sacrifice, the Festival and the Principles of the Sacred World." In *The Bataille Reader*, edited by Fred Bottin and Scott Wilson, 210–20. Oxford: Blackwell, 1997.

Baxandall, Michael. *Painting and Experience in Fifteenth Century Florence*. Oxford: Oxford University Press, 1972.

Beaune, Colette. *Naissance de la nation France*. Paris: Bibliothèque des histoires, 1985.

Beauvoir, Alfred Hiver de. *La librairie de Jean duc de Berry au château de Mehun-sur-Yevre, 1416. Publiée en enitère pour la première fois d'après les inventaires et avec des notes par Hiver de Beauvoir*. Paris, 1860.

Becker, Karin. *Eustache Deschamps: État actuel de la recherché*. Paris: Paradigme, 2000.

– *Le lyrisme d'Eustache Deschamps: Entre poésie et pragmatisme*. Paris: Classiques Garnier. 2012.

Bell, Dora M. *L'idéale éthique de royauté en France au Moyen Âge*. Geneva: Droz, 1962.

Bell, Susan Groag. "Medieval Women Book Owners: Arbiters of Lay Piety and Ambassadors of Culture." *Signs* 7 (1982): 746–68.

Beltran, Evencio. "Jacques Legrand O.E.S.A.: Sa vie et son oeuvre." *Augustiniana* 24 (1974): 132–60 and 387–414.

– "Jacques Legrand prédicateur." *Analecta Augustiniana* 30 (1967): 148–209.

Benhamou, Françoise. *L'économie de la culture*. 7th ed. Paris: La Découverte, 2011.

Benveniste, Émile. "Gift and Exchange in the Indo-European Vocabulary." In *The Logic of the Gift: Toward an Ethic of Generosity*, edited by Alan D. Schrift, 33–42. New York and London: Routledge, 1997.

– *Indo-European Language and Society*. Translated by E. Palmer. London: Faber and Faber, 1973.

Berty, Adolphe. *Topographie historique du vieux Paris*. 6 vols. Paris: Imprimerie imperial, 1885.

Blanchard, Joël, and Jean-Claude Mühlethaler. *Ecriture et pouvoir à l'aube des temps modernes*. Paris: Presse Universitaire de France, 2002.

Bliggenstorfer, Susanna. "Interdépendances de forme et de contenu dans l'oeuvre d'Eustache Deschamps." In Lacassagne and Lassabatère, *Les "Dictez vertueulx" d'Eustache Deschamps*, 27–42.

– "Les poèmes de supplication d'Eustache Deschamps." In *Les niveaux de vie au Moyen Âge: Mesures, perceptions et representations. Actes du Colloque international de Spa (21–25 octobre 1998)*, edited by Jean-Pierre Sosson et al., 49–75. Louvain-la-Neuvre: Academia-Bruylant, 1999.

Blog BnF. "Le livre d'heures de Jeanne de France est en ligne," 2013. http://blog.bnf.fr/gallica/index.php/2013/03/15/le-livre-dheures-de-jeanne-de-france-est-en-ligne/.

Born, Lester. "The Perfect Prince: A Study in Thirteenth and Fourteenth Century Ideals." *Speculum* 4 (1928): 470–504.

– "The *specula principis* of the Carolingian Renaissance." *Revue belge de philologie d'histoire* 12 (1933): 583–612.

Bose, Mishtooni. "The Intellectual History of the Middle Ages." In *Intellectual History*, edited by Richard Whatmore and Brian Young, 92–108. Hampshire and New York: Palgrave Macmillan, 2006.

Bossuat, Robert. "Raoul de Presles." *Histoire littéraire de la France* 40 (1974): 113–86.

Bossy, Michel-André. "Donnant, donnant: Les échanges entre Froissart et ses interlocuteurs à la cour de Gaston Phébus." In *Courtly Literature and Clerical Culture*, edited by Christophe Huber and Henrike Lähnemann, 29–38. Tubingen: Attempto Verlag, 2002.

Boucheron, Patrick, Pascal Brioist, and Delphine Carrangeot, eds. *Le Prince et les arts. France, Italie, XIVe–XVIIIe siècles.* Quetigny, Burgundy: Atlande, 2010.

Boudet, Jean-Pierre, and Hélène Millet, eds. *Eustache Deschamps en son temps.* Paris: Publications de la Sorbonne, 1997.

Bourassa, Kristin Leigh Erika. *Counselling Charles VI of France: Christine de Pizan, Honorat Bovet, Philippe de Mézières, and Pierre Salmon.* PhD diss., University of York, 2014.

Bourdieu, Pierre. *Raisons pratiques: Sur la théorie de l'action*. Paris: Editions du Seuil, 1994.

– *Les règles de l'art: Genèse et structure du champ littéraire*. Paris: Seuil, 1992.

– *Le sens pratique*. Paris: Edition de Minuit, 1980.

Boym, Svetlana. *The Future of Nostalgia*. New York: Basic Books, 2001.

Bridrey, Emile. *La théorie de la monnaie au XIVe siècle: Nicole Oresme*. Geneva: Slatkine Reprints, 1978.

Broadhurst, Karen M. "Henry II of England and Eleanor of Aquitaine: Patrons of Literature in French?" *Viator* 27 (1996): 53–84.

Brocchieri, Mariateresa Fumagalli Beonio. "L'intellectuel." In *L'homme médiéval*, edited by Jacques Le Goff, 201–32. Paris: Editions du Seuil, 1989.

Brown, Cynthia J. "Le mécénat d'Anne de Bretagne et la politique du livre." In *Patronnes et mécènes en France à la Renaissance*, edited by Kathleen Wilson-Chevalier, 195–224. Saint-Étienne: Publications de l'Université de Saint-Étienne, 2007.

– *Poets, Patrons, and Printers: Crisis of Authority in Late Medieval France*. Ithaca: Cornell University Press, 1995.

– *The Queen's Library: Image-Making at the Court of Anne of Brittany, 1477–1514*. Philadelphia: University of Pennsylvania Press, 2010.

Brown, Cynthia J., and Anne-Marie Legaré, eds. *Les femmes, l'art et la culture en Europe entre Moyen Âge et Renaissance / Women, Art and Culture in Medieval and Renaissance Europe*. Turnhout, Belgium: Brepols, 2016.

Brown-Grant, Rosalind. *Christine de Pizan and the Moral Defence of Women: Reading beyond Gender*. Cambridge: Cambridge University Press, 1999.

Bruni, G. "Il *De regimine principum* di Egidio Romano, Studio bibliografico." *Aevum* 6 (1932): 339–72.

Buettner, Brigitte. "Past Presents: New Year's Gifts at the Valois Courts, ca. 1400." *Art Bulletin* 83, no. 4 (2001): 598–625.

– "Le système des objets dans le testament de Blanche de Navarre." *Clio. Femmes, Genre, Histoire* 19 (2004), http://journals.openedition.org/clio/644.

Bullough, Donald A. "Charlemagne's Court Library Revisited." *Early Medieval Europe* 12 (2003): 339–63.

Burgwinkle, William E. *Love for Sale: Materialist Readings of the Troubadour Razo Corpus*. New York: Garland, 1997.

Burke, Peter. *The Italian Renaissance: Culture and Society in Italy*. Rev. ed. Princeton: Princeton University Press, 1986.

Burkolter, Verena. *The Patronage System: Theoretical Remarks*. Basel: Graphische Betriebe Coop Schweiz, 1976.

Buschinger, Danielle, ed. *Autour d'Eustache Deschamps: Actes du Colloque du Centre d'Études Médiévales de l'Université de Picardie-Jules Verne Amiens, 5–8 novembre 1998*. Amiens: Presses du Centre d'Études Médiévales, 1999.

Camille, Michael. *Master of Death*. New Haven, CT: Yale University Press, 1996.

Caskey, Jill. "Medieval Patronage and Its Potentialities." In Hourihane, *Patronage: Power and Agency in Medieval Art*, 3–30.

Cassagnes, Sophie. *D'art et d'argent: Les artistes et leurs clients dans l'Europe du Nord, XIVe–XVe siècles*. Rennes: Presses Universitaires de Rennes, 2001.

Cassagnes-Brouquet, Sophie. "Des étrangers à la cour: Les artistes et les échanges culturels en Europe au temps du gothique international." In *L'étranger au moyen âge. XXXe Congrès de la SHMES (Göttingen, juin 1999)*, 165–77. Paris: Publications de la Sorbonne, 2000.

Caviness, Madeline. "Patron or Matron? A Capetian Bride and a Vade Mecum for Her Marriage Bed." *Speculum* 68 (1996): 333–62.

Cerquiglini-Toulet, Jacqueline. "Christine de Pizan et les arts." In *Création artistique en France autour de 1400*, edited by Taburet-Delahaye, 207–18. Paris: La Documentation française, 2006.

– *"Un engin si soutil": Guillaume de Machaut et l'écriture au XIVe siècle*. Paris: Honoré Champion, 2001.

– "Fullness and Emptiness: Shortages and Storehouses of Lyric Treasures in the Fourteenth and Fifteenth Centuries." In "Contexts: Style and Values in Medieval Art and Literature," edited by Nancy Regalado and Daniel Poirion. Special edition, *Yale French Studies* (1991): 224–39.

Champion, Pierre. *Vie de Charles d'Orléans, avec un album de fac-similés*. Paris: Honoré Champion, 1910.

Chapelot, Jean. "Charles V, maître d'ouvrage: A propos de la construction du donjon de Vincennes et de quelques chantiers contemporains." In *Du projet au chantier: Maîtres d'ouvrage et maîtres d'oeuvre aux XIVe et XVIe siècles*, edited by Odette Chapelot, 339–404. Paris: Editions de l'Ecole des Hautes Etudes en Sciences Sociales, 2001.

Chattaway, Carol M. *The Order of the Golden Tree: The Gift-Giving Objectives of Duke Philip the Bold of Burgundy*. Turnhout, Belgium: Brepols, 2006.

Cockshaw, Pierre. "Mentions d'auteurs, de copistes, d'enlumineurs et de libraires dans les comptes généraux de l'état Bourguignon (1384–1419)." *Scriptorium* 23 (1969): 122–44.

Colish, Marcia. "Re-envisioning the Middle Ages: A View from Intellectual History." In *The Future of the Middle Ages and the Renaissance: Problems, Trends and Opportunities for Research*, edited by Roger Dahood, 19–26. Turnhout, Belgium: Brepols, 1998.

Collet, Olivier. "Littérature, histoire, pouvoir et mécénat: La cour de Flandre au XIIIe siècle." *Médiévales* 38 (2000): 87–110.

Cooper, T. "*Mecenatismo* or *Clientelismo*? The Character of Renaissance Patronage." In *The Search for a Patron in the Middle Ages and Renaissance*, edited by D. Wilkins and R. Wilkins, 19–32. New York: E. Mellen Press, 1996.

Coss, P.R. "Bastard Feudalism Revised." *Past & Present* 125 (1989): 27–64.

Cottereau-Gabillet, Emilie. "Les contrats de copistes en France aux XIVe et XVe siècles et l'influence des formules notariales bolonaises." *Mélanges de l'école française de Rome moyen âge* 119 (2007): 415–45.

Cruse, Mark. "The Louvre of Charles V: Legitimacy, Renewal, and Royal Presence in Fourteenth-Century Paris." *Esprit créateur* 54 (2014): 19–32.

Dauphant, Clotilde. "Le cycle de l'avènement de Charles VI dans le manuscrit des *Oeuvres complètes d'Eustache Deschamps* (pieces 164 à 172)." In Lassabatère and Lacassagne, *Eustache Deschamps, témoin et modèle*, 49–68.

Davis, Natalie Zemon. *The Gift in Sixteenth-Century France.* Madison: University of Wisconsin Press, 2000.

Day, John. *The Medieval Market Economy.* Oxford: Basil Blackwell Publishing, 1987.

Debeiesse, François. *Le mécénat.* Paris: Presse universitaire de France, 2007.

Delaborde, Henri-François. "La vraie chronique du Religieux de St-Denis." *Bibliothèque de l'Ecole des Chartes* 51 (1890): 93–110.

de Libera, Alain. *Penser au moyen âge.* Paris: Editions du Seuil, 1991.

Delisle, Léopold. *Anciennes traductions françaises du traité de Petrarque sur les remèdes de l'une et d'autre Fortune.* Lille: Librairie C. Klincksiek, 1881.

– *Le cabinet des manuscrits de la Bibliothèque impériale: Etude sur la formation de ce dépôt comprenant les éléments d'une histoire de la calligraphie de la miniature, de la reliure, et du commerce des livres à Paris avant l'invention de l'imprimerie.* 3 vols. Paris: Imprimerie impériale, 1868–81.

– "Les *Ethiques*, les *Politiques* et les *Economiques* d'Aristote traduites et copiées pour le roi Charles V." In *Mélanges de paléographie et de bibliographie* by Léopold Delisle, 257–82. Paris: Champion, 1880.

– "Notice sur deux livres ayant appartenu au roi Charles V." *Notices et extraits des manuscrits* 31, no. 1 (1884): 1–16.

– *Recherches sur la librairie de Charles V.* 2 vols. Paris: Honoré Champion, 1907.

– "Testament de Blanche de Navarre, Reine de France." *Mémoires de l'Histoire de Paris et de l'Île-de-France* 12 (1885): 1–64.

Delogu, Daisy. *Allegorical Bodies: Power and Gender in Late Medieval France.* Toronto: University of Toronto Press, 2015.

– "Reinventing the Ideal Sovereign in Christine de Pizan's *Livre des fais et bonne meurs du sage roy Charles VI.*" *Medievalia et Humanistica* 31 (2005): 41–58.

– *Theorizing the Ideal Sovereign: The Rise of the French Vernacular Royal Biography.* Toronto: University of Toronto Press, 2008.

de Looze, Laurence. "'Mon nom trouveras': A New Look at the Anagrams of Guillaume de Machaut – The Enigmas, Responses, and Solutions." *Romanic Review* 79, no. 4 (1988): 537–57.

– "Signing off in the Middle Ages: Medieval Textuality and Strategies of Authorial Self-Naming." In *Vox Intexta: Orality and Textuality in the Middle Ages*, edited by Alger N. Doane and Carol Braun Pasternack, 162–78. Madison, WI: University of Wisconsin Press, 1991.

DMF: *Dictionnaire du Moyen Français*, version 2015 (DMF 2015). ATILF-CNRS & Université de Lorraine. Site internet: http://www.atilf.fr/dmf.

Devaux, Jean. "Images des guerres de Flandre chez Eustache Deschamps et Jean Froissart." In Buschinger, *Autour d'Eustache Deschamps*, 57–72.

– "Introduction. Littérature politique sous les premiers Valois." *Le Moyen Âge* 116 (2010/13): 533–43.

de Winter, Patrick M. *La Bibliothèque de Philippe le Hardi, duc de Bourgogne (1364–1404): Etude sur les manuscrits à peintures d'une collection princière à l'époque du "style gothique international."* Paris: CNRS, 1985.

Douët-d'Arcq, Louis Claude. *Inventaire de la bibliothèque du roi Charles VI, fait au Louvre en 1423 par ordre du régent duc de Bedford*. Paris: Société des bibliophiles, 1867.

Douglas, Mary. "Foreword." In *The Gift: The Form and Reason for Exchange in Archaic Societies*, by Marcel Mauss, vii–xviii. New York and London: W.W. Norton, 1990.

Dudash, Susan. "Eustache Deschamps: Poète et commentateur politique." In Lassabatère and Lacassagne, *Eustache Deschamps, témoin et modèle*, 147–62.

Dulac, Liliane. "L'autorité dans les traités en prose de Christine de Pizan: Discours d'écrivain, parole de prince." In *Une femme de lettres au Moyen Age: Études autour de Christine de Pizan*, edited by Liliane Dulac and Bernard Ribémont, 15–24. Orléans: Paradigmes, 1995.

Dyer, Christopher. *An Age of Transition? Economy and Society in the Later Middle Ages*. Oxford and New York: Oxford University Press, 2005.

Earp, Lawrence. *Guillaume de Machaut: A Guide to Research*. New York and London: Garland Publishing, Inc., 1995.

Earp, Lawrence, Domenic Leo, and Carla Shapreau. *The Ferrell-Vogüé Machaut Manuscript: Facsimile and Introductory Study*. Preface by Christopher de Hamel. 2 vols. Oxford: DIAMM Publications, 2014.

Ehrhart, Margaret. *The Judgment of the Trojan Prince Paris in Medieval Literature*. Philadelphia: University of Pennsylvania Press, 1987.

– "Machaut and the Duties of Rulers Tradition." *French Forum* 17 (1992): 5–22.

– "Machaut's *Dit de la fonteinne amoureuse*, the Choice of Paris, and the Duties of Rulers." *Philological Quarterly* 59 (1980): 119–39.

Eichberger, Dagmar, Anne-Marie Legaré, and Wim Kusken. *Femmes à la cour de Bourgogne. Présence et influence, actes du colloque à Malines du 26 au 27 novembre 2005*. Turnhout: Brepols, 2010.

Eisenstadt, Shmuel N. "Some Analytical Approaches to the Study of Patronage." Preface to *The Patronage System: Theoretical Remarks*, by Verena Burkolter, i–x. Basel: Graphische Betriebe Coop Schweiz, 1976.

Eisenstadt, Shmuel N., and Luis Roniger. "The Study of Patron-Client Relations and Recent Developments in Sociological Theory." In *Political Clientelism, Patronage and Development*, edited by Shmuel N. Eisenstadt and René Lemarchand, 271–96. Beverly Hills and London: SAGE Publications, 1981.

Epstein, Steven A. *An Economic and Social History of Later Medieval Europe, 1000–1500*. Cambridge: Cambridge University Press, 2009.

Evans, Ruth. "An Afterword on the Prologue." In *The Idea of the Vernacular: An Anthology of Middle English Literary Theory, 1280–1520*, edited by Jocelyn Wogan-Browne, Nicholas Watson, Ruth Evans, Andrew Taylor, 371–8. University Park, PA: Pennsylvania State University Press, 1999.

Expilly, Louis Alexandre. *Dictionnaire géographique, historique et politique des Gaules et de la France*. 6 vols. Paris: Chez Desaint & Salliant, 1762–70.

Fabienne, Joubert. "Les arts de la couleur." In Pleybert, *Paris et Charles V*, 166–85.

Famiglietti, Richard C. "Laurent de Premierfait: The Career of a Humanist in Early Fifteenth-Century Paris." In *Un traducteur et un humaniste de l'époque de Charles VI, Laurent de Premierfait*, edited by Carla Bozzzolo and Ezio Ornato, 31–51. Paris: Publication de la Sorbonne, 2004.

Ferrand, Françoise. "Regards sur le *Prologue* de Guillaume de Machaut." In *Guillaume de Machaut: Poète et compositeur. Actes et colloques. Reims (19–22 avril 1978)*, 235–9. Paris: Éditions Klincksieck, 1982.

Fleury, Laurent. *Le cas Beaubourg. Mécénat d'état et démocratisation de la culture*. Paris: Armand Colin, 2007.

Flora, Holly. "Patronage." *Studies in Iconography* 33 (2012): 207–18.

Foehr-Janssens, Yasmina. "La noblesse des lettres autour de 1300 (Badouin de Condé et Dante)." In *La moisson des lettres: L'invention littéraire autour de 1300*, edited by Hélène Bellon-Méguelle, Olivier Collet, Yasmina Foehr-Janssens, and Ludivine Jaquiéry, 213–32. Turnhout: Brepols Publishers, 2011.

Folda, Jaroslav. *The Art of the Crusader in the Holy Land, 1098–1187*. Cambridge: Cambridge University Press, 1995.

Frappier, Jean. "Le motif du 'don contraignant' dans la littérature du Moyen Âge." In *Amour courtois et table ronde*, 223–64. Geneva: Droz, 1973.

Frow, John. *Time and Commodity: Essays on Cultural Theory and Postmodernism*. Oxford: Clarendon Press; New York: Oxford University Press, 1997.

Gaborit-Chopin, Danielle. *L'inventaire du trésor du dauphin futur Charles V, 1363: Les débuts d'un grand collectioneur*. Nogent-le-Roi: Jacques Laget, 1996.

Gauthier, R.A., O.P. *Magnanimité: L'idéal de la grandeur dans la philosophie païenne et dans la théologie chrétienne*. Paris: Librairie Philosophique J. Vrin, 1951.

Geer, Rachel. "Devotional and Political Consolation in Manuscript BnF fr. 994." *Digital Philology: A Journal of Medieval Cultures* 5, no. 1 (2016): 104–15.

Gellner, Ernest. "Patrons and Clients." In *Patrons and Clients in Mediterranean Societies*, edited by Ernest Gellner and John Waterbury, 1–6. London: Duckworth, 1977.

Gobin, Alain. *Le mécénat: Histoire – droit – fiscalité*. Paris: Entreprise Moderne d'édition, 1987.

Goldthwaite, Richard. *Wealth and the Demand for Art in Italy, 1300–1600*. Baltimore: Johns Hopkins University Press, 1995.

Gorochov, Nathalie. *Le collège de Navarre de sa fondation (1305) au début du XVe siècle (1418): Histoire de l'institution de sa vie intellectuelle et de son recrutement*. Paris: Honoré Champion, 1997.

Grabar, Oleg. "The Shared Culture of Objects." In *Byzantine Court Culture from 829 to 1204*, edited by Henry Maguire, 115–30. Harvard University Press, 1997.

Graziano, Luigi. "A Conceptual Framework for the Study of Clientelistic Behavior." *European Journal of Political Research* 4, no. 2 (1976): 149–74.

Green, Karen. "Introduction." In Christine de Pizan, *Livre de Paix*, edited by Green, Mews and Pinder, 1–31.

Green, Richard Firth. *Poets and Princepleasers: Literature and the English Court in the Late Middle Ages*. Toronto: Toronto University Press, 1980.

Greenie, George D. "University Book Production and Courtly Patronage in Thirteenth-Century France and Spain." In *Medieval Iberia: Essays on the History & Literature of Medieval Spain*, edited by Donald J. Kagay and Josheph T. Snow, 103–28. New York: Peter Lang, 1997.

Grégoire, Abbé. "Rapport de Grégoire à la Convention nationale sur le vandalisme révolutionaire." *Bulletin du bibliophile* 9 (1843): 399–421.

Gregory, C.A. *Gifts and Commodities*. London and New York: Academic Press, 1982.

Griggs, William, and E.S. Dewick. *The Coronation Book of Charles V of France*. London: Harrison and sons, 1899.

Groag, Susan Bell. "Medieval Women Book Owners: Arbiters of Lay Piety and Ambassadors of Culture." *Signs* 7, no. 4 (1982): 742–68.

Guenée, Bernard. *Un meurtre, une société: L'assassinat du duc d'Orléans 23 novembre 1407*. Paris: Gallimard, 1992.

Guérout, Jean. *Le Palais de la Cité à Paris des origines à 1417: Essai topographique et Archéologique*, Paris, 1953.

Guiffrey, Jules. *Inventaires de Jean, duc de Berry (1401–1416)*. 2 vols. Paris: Ernest Leroux, 1894.

Gundersheimer, W.L. "Patronage in the Renaissance: An Exploratory Approach." In *Patronage in the Renaissance*, edited by G.F. Lytle and S. Orgel, 3–23. Princeton: Princeton University Press, 1981.

Hamm, Frédérique. "Jean Daudin, chanoine, traducteur et moraliste." *Romania* 116 (1998): 215–38.

Hasenohr, Geneviève. "Discours vernaculaire et autorités latines." In *Mise en page et mise en texte du livre manuscrit*, edited by Henri Martin and Jean Vezin, 288–91. Paris: Promodis, 1980.

Hedeman, Anne D. "Constructing Memories: Scenes of Conversation and Presentation in Pierre Salmon's *Dialogues*." *The Journal of the Walters Art Gallery* 54 (1996): 119–34.

– *Of Counselors and Kings: The Three Versions of Pierre Salmon's "Dialogues."* Urbana and Chicago: University of Illinois Press, 2001.

– *The Royal Image: Illustrations of the* Grandes chroniques de France, *1274–1422*. Berkeley: University of California Press, 1991.

– *Translating the Past: Laurent de Premierfait and Boccaccio's "De Casibus."* Los Angeles: J. Paul Getty Museum, 2008.

Heers, Jacques. *L'occident aux XIVe et XVe siècles. Aspects économiques et sociaux*. Paris: Presse Universitaire de France, 1970.

Heidenreich Findley, Brooke. *Poet Heroines in Medieval French Narrative: Gender and Fictions of Literary Creation*. New York: Palgrave, 2012.

Henwood, Philippe. "Raymond du Temple, maître d'oeuvre des rois Charles V et Charles VI." *Bulletin de la société de l'histoire de Paris et de l'Ile-de-France* 105 (1978): 55–74.

Hicks, Eric. "A Mirror for Misogynists: John of Salisbury's *Policraticus* (8.11) in the Translation of Denis Foulechat (1372)." In *Reinterpreting Christine de Pizan*, edited by Earl Jeffrey Richards with Joan Williamson, Nadia Margolis, and Christine Reno, 7–110. Athens and London: University of Georgia Press, 1992.

– ed. *Au champ des escriptures: IIIe Colloque international sur Christine de Pizan (Lausanne, 18–22 juillet 1998)*. With the assistance of Diego Gonzalez and Philippe Simon. Paris: Honoré Champion, 2000.

Hicks, Michael. *Bastard Feudalism*. London and New York: Routledge, 1995.

Hindman, Sandra L. *Christine de Pizan's "Epistre Othéa": Painting and Politics at the Court of Charles VI*. Toronto: Pontifical Institute of Mediaeval Studies, 1986.

– "The Iconography of Queen Isabeau de Bavière (1410–1415): An Essay in Method." *Gazette des Beaux Arts* 102 (1983): 102–10.

Hobbins, Daniel. *Authorship and Publicity before Print: Jean Gerson and the Transformation of Late Medieval Learning*. Pennsylvania: University of Pennsylvania Press, 2009.

Holladay, Joan A. "Fourteenth-Century French Queens as Collectors and Readers of Books: Jeanne d'Evreux and Her Contemporaries." *Journal of Medieval History*, 32 (2006): 69–100.

Holznecht, Karl Julius. *Literary Patronage in the Middle Ages*. New York: Octagon Books, Inc., 1966.

Hourihane, Colum. *The Grove Encyclopedia of Medieval Art and Architecture*. 6 vols. Oxford: Oxford University Press, 2012.

– ed. *Patronage: Power and Agency in Medieval Art*. University Park, PA: Pennsylvania State University Press, 2013.

Howatson, M.C., ed. *Oxford Companion to Classical Literature*. Oxford University Press, 2011.

Huot, Sylvia. "A Book Made for a Queen: The Shaping of a Late Medieval Anthology Manuscript (B.N. fr. 24429)." In *The Whole Book: Cultural Perspectives on the Medieval Miscellany*, edited by Stephen G. Nichols and Siegfried Wenzel, 123–43. Ann Arbor: University of Michigan Press, 1996.

– "Guillaume de Machaut and the Consolation of Poetry." *Modern Philology* 100 (2002): 169–95.

Hutcheon, Linda, and Mario J. Valdés. "Irony, Nostalgia, and the Postmodern. A Dialogue." *Poligrafías. Revista de Literatura Comparada* 3 (1998): 18–41.

Hyde, Lewis. *The Gift: Imagination and the Erotic Life of Property*. New York: Vintage Books, 1983.

Inglis, Erik. "A Book in Hand: Some Late Medieval Accounts of Manuscript Presentations." *Journal of the Early Book Society for the Study of Manuscripts and Printing History* 5 (2002): 67–71.

Jackson, Richard A. "The *Traité du sacre* of Jean Golein." *Proceedings of the American Philosophical Society* 113 (1969): 305–24.

Jansen, Philippe. "Le prince et les arts à la fin du Moyen Âge (ca. 1300–ca. 1520)." In *Le Prince et les arts en France et en Italie, XIVe–XVIIIe siècles*, edited by Michel Figeac, Olivier Chaline, Philippe Jansen, Jérémie Koering, and Géraud Poumarède, 11–74. Paris: Sedes, 2010.

Jeannot, Delphine. *Le mécénat bibliophilique de Jean sans Peur et de Marguerite de Bavière (1404–1424)*. Turnhout: Brepols, 2012.

Joubert, Fabienne. "Les arts de la couleur." In Pleybert, *Paris et Charles V*, 166–85.

Jouhaud, Christian, and Hélène Merlin. "Mécènes, patrons et clients: Les médiations textuelles comme pratiques clientélaires au XVIIe siècle." *Revue terrain* 21 (1993): 47–62.

Kaufmann, Thomas DaCosta. *Court, Cloister, and City: The Art and Culture of Central Europe, 1450–1800*. Chicago: University of Chicago Press, 1995.

Kay, Sarah. *The Place of Thought: The Complexity of One in Late Medieval French Didactic Poetry*. Philadelphia: University of Pennsylvania Press, 2007.

Kaye, Joel. *Economy and Nature in the Fourteenth Century*. Cambridge: Cambridge University Press, 1998.

Keane, Webb. *Ku War: Language and Segmentary Politics in the Western Nebilyer Valley, Papua New Guinea*. Cambridge: Cambridge University Press, 1991.

– "The Value of Words and the Meaning of Things in Eastern Indonesian Exchange." *Man* 29, no. 3 (1994): 605–29.

Kellogg, Judith. *Medieval Artistry and Exchange: Economic Institutions, Society, and Literary Form in Old French Narrative*. New York: P. Lang, 1989.

Kelly, Douglas. "The Genius of the Patron: The Prince, the Poet and 14th-Century Invention." *Studies in the Literary Imagination* 20 (1987): 77–97.

Kelly, Henry Ansgar. *Chaucer and the Cult of Saint Valentine*. Leiden: E.J. Brill, 1986.

Kendrick, Laura. "The Art of Mastering Servitude: Eustache Deschamps's Deployment of Courtly Love." *Romanistische Zeitschrift für Literaturgeschichte* 16 (1992): 30–45.

– "The Monument and the Margin." *South Atlantic Quarterly* 91 (1992): 835–64.

Kent, Dale. *Cosimo de' Medici and the Florentine Renaissance: The Patron's Oeuvre*. New Haven and London: Yale University Press, 2000.

Kent, F.W., Patricia Simons, and J.C. Eade. *Patronage, Art and Society in Renaissance Italy*. Oxford, 1987.

Kibler, William. "Poet and Patron: Froissart's *Prison amoureuse*." *Esprit Créateur* 18, no. 1 (1978): 32–46.

Knapp, Ethan. *The Bureaucratic Muse: Thomas Hoccleve and the Literature of Late Medieval England*. University Park, PA: Pennsylvania State University Press, 2001.

– "Poetic Work and Scribal Labor in Hoccleve and Langland." In *The Middle Ages at Work*, edited by Kellie Robertston and Michael Uebel, 209–28. New York: Palgrave Macmillan, 2004.

Knecht, R.J. *Renaissance Warrior and Patron: The Reign of François Premier*. Cambridge and New York: Cambridge University Press, 1994.

Knowles, Christine. "Jean de Vignay: Un traducteur du XIVe siècle." *Romania* 75 (1954): 353–83.

Krueger, Roberta L. "Contracts and Constraints: Courtly Performance in *Yvain* and the *Charrette*." In *The Medieval Court in Europe*, edited by Edward E. Haymes, 92–104. Munich: Wilhelm Fink Verlag, 1986.

Krynen, Jacques. *Idéal du prince et pouvoir royal en France à la fin du Moyen Age (1380–1440)*. Paris: Picard, 1981.

Kumler, Aden. "*Faire Translater, Faire Historier*: Charles V's *Bible Historiale* and the Visual Rhetoric of Vernacular *Sapience*." *Studies in Iconography* 29 (2008): 90–135.

– "The Patron-Function." In Hourihane, *Patronage: Power and Agency in Medieval Art*, 297–319.

Laborde, Marquis Léon de. *Ducs de Bourgogne. Etudes sur les lettres, les arts et l'industrie pendant le XVe siècle*. 3 vols. Paris: Plon frères éditeurs, 1849–52.

– *Les manuscrits à peintures de la "Cité de Dieu" de Saint Augustin*. 2 vols. Paris: Société des bibliophiles François, 1909.

Lacassagne, Miren. "Le lai de franchise d'Eustache Deschamps ou de l'autre côté du miroir." *Le Moyen Age* 116 (2010/13): 645–56.

Lacassagne, Miren, and Thierry Lassabatère, eds. *Les "Dictez vertueulx" d'Eustache Deschamps: Forme poétique et discours engagé à la fin du Moyen Âge*. Paris: Presses de l'Université Paris-Sorbonne, 2005.

Laennec, Christine Moneera. "'Christine Antygraphe': Authorial Ambivalence in the Works of Christine de Pizan." In *Anxious Power: Reading, Writing, and Ambivalence in Narrative by Women*, edited by Carol J. Singley and Susan Elizabeth Sweeney, 35–50. New York: SUNY Press, 1993.

Laidlaw, James. "Christine and the Manuscript Tradition." In *Christine de Pizan: A Casebook*, edited by Barbara Altmann and Deborah McGrady, 231–50. New York and London: Routledge, 2003.

– "Christine de Pizan – An Author's Progress." *Modern Language Review* 78 (1983): 532–50.

– "Christine de Pizan – A Publisher's Progress." *Modern Language Review* 82 (1987): 37–75.

– "Christine de Pizan, the Earl of Salisbury and Henry IV." *French Studies* 36 (1982): 129–43.

– "The Date of the Queen's MS (London, British Library, Harley MS 4431)," 2005. http://www.pizan.lib.ed.ac.uk/harley4431date.pdf.

– "How Long Is the *Chemin de longue estude*?" In *The Editor and the Text*, edited by Phillip E. Bennett and Graham A. Runnells, 83–95. Scotland: Edinburgh University Press, 1990.

– "Les supplications de Deschamps – le pouvoir de persuasion." In Lacassagne and Lassabatère, *Les "Dictez vertueulx" d'Eustache Deschamps*, 73–84.

Lancelot, A. "Mémoire sur la vie et les ouvrages de Raoul de Presles." *Mémoires de littératures, tirez des registres de l'Académie royale des inscriptions et belles-lettres* 13 (1740): 607–13, 617–65.

Lassabatère, Thierry. *La cité des hommes: Eustache Deschamps, expression poétique et vision politique*. Paris: Honoré Champion, 2011.

– "Théorie et éthique de la guerre dans l'oeuvre d'Eustache Deschamps." In *Fondations et oeuvres charitables au Moyen Âge. Actes du 121e congrès national des sociétés historiques et scientifiques, Section d'histoire médiévale et philologie, Nice, 26–31 octobre 1996*, edited by Jean Dufour and Henri Platelle, 129–41. Paris: Éditions du CTHS, 1999.

Lassabatère, Thierry, and Miren Lacassagne, eds. *Eustache Deschamps, témoin et modèle: Littérature et société politique (XIVe–XVIe siècles)*. Paris: Presses de l'Université Paris-Sorbonne, 2008.

Laurie, Ian S. "Biography." In *Eustache Deschamps, French Courtier-Poet: His Work and His World*, edited by Deborah M. Sinnreich-Levi, 1–72. New York: AMS Press, 1998.

– "Introduction." In Deschamps, *Eustache Deschamps: Selected Poems*, 1–46.

Lechat, Didier. "L'utilisation par Christine de Pizan de la traduction de Valère Maxime par Simon de Hesdin et Nicolas de Goness dans *Le livre du chemin de long estude*." In Hicks, *Au champ des escriptures*, 175–97.

Lecoq, Anne-Marie. *François 1er imaginaire: Symbolique et politique à l'aube de la Renaissance française*. Paris: Macula, 1987.

Lefevre, Sylvie. "Christine de Pizan et l'Aristote Oresmien." In Hicks, *Au champ des escriptures*, 231–50.

– "*Manu Propria.* Les enjeux de l'écriture autographique." *Comptes rendus de l'Académie des Inscriptions et Belles-Lettres* 2014, no. 2 (April–June, 2014): 611–40.

Legaré, Anne-Marie, ed. *Livres et lectures de femmes en Europe entre Moyen Âge et Renaissance*. Turnhout: Brepols, 2007.

Le Goff, Jacques. *Les intellectuels au Moyen Âge*. Paris: Editions du Seuil, 1957.

– "Les universités et le pouvoir public au moyen âge et à la Renaissance." In *Pour un autre moyen âge. Temps, travail et culture en Occident: 18 essais*, 198–219. Paris: Editions Gallimard, 1977.

– "The Universities and the Public Authorities in the Middle Ages and the Renaissance." In *Time, Work and Culture in the Middle Ages*, translated by Arthur Goldhammer, 135–49. Chicago: Chicago University Press, 1980.

Le Ninan, Claire. "Christine de Pizan à la recherche d'une postérité littéraire." In *Christine de Pizan: Une femme de science, une femme de lettres*, edited by Juliette Dor and Marie-Elisabeth Henneau, with the collaboration of Bernard Ribémont, 159–69. Paris: Honoré Champion, 2008.

Le Roux de Lincy, Antoine. *La bibliothèque de Charles d'Orléans à son château de Blois en 1427*. Paris: Firmin-Didot frères, 1843.

– "Comptes des dépenses faites par Charles dans le château du Louvre des années 1364–1368." *Revue archéologique* 8 (1850–1): 670–91 and 760–72.

Lièvre, Marion. "Note sur les sources du *Somnium viridarii* et du *Songe du vergier*." *Romania* 81 (1960): 483–91.

Lindquist, Sherry C.M. "Accounting for the Status of Artists at the Chartreuse de Champmol." *Gesta* 41, no. 1 (2002): 15–28.

– *Agency, Visuality and Society at the Chartreuse de Champmol*. Farnham, England: Ashgate, 2008.

– "'The Will of a Princely Patron' and Artists at the Burgundian Court." In *Artists at Court: Image-Making and Identity, 1300–1550*, edited by Stephen J. Campbell, 46–56. Chicago: University of Chicago Press, 2004.

Lombard-Jourdan, Anne. "A propos de Raoul de Presles, documents sur l'homme." *Bibliothèque de l'école de Chartres* 139, no. 2 (1981): 191–207.

Loomis, Roger Sherman. "Library of Richard II." In *Studies in Language, Literature, and Culture of the Middle Ages and Later*, edited by E. Bagby Atwood and Archibald A. Hill, 173–8. Austin: University of Texas at Austin, 1969.

Lowden, John. "Beauty or Truth? Making a *Bible moralisée* in Paris around 1400." In *Patrons, Authors and Workshops: Books and Book Production in Paris around 1400*, edited by Godfried Croenen and Peter Ainsworth, 197–222. Louvain, Paris, and Dudley, MA: Peeters, 2006.

– *The Making of the "Bibles Moralisées."* University Park, PA: Pennsylvania State University, 2000.

Lusignan, Serge. "Culture écrite et langue française à la cour de Philippe le Bel." In *La moisson des lettres: L'invention littéraire autour de 1300*, edited by Hélène Bellon-Méguelle, Olivier Collet, Yasmina Foehr-Janssens, and Ludivine Jaquiéry, 31–48. Turnhout: Brepols Publishers, 2011.

– *Parler vulgairement: Les intellectuels et la langue française aux XIIIe et XIVe siècles*. Montreal: Les Presses de l'Université de Montréal, 1986.

– *"Vérité garde le roy": La construction d'une identité universitare en France (XIIIe–XVe siècle)*. Paris: Publications de la Sorbonne, 1999.

Luxford, Julian M. "The Construction of English Monastic Patronage." In Hourihane, *Patronage: Power and Agency in Medieval Art*, 31–52.

Mahoney, Dhira B. "Courtly Presentation and Authorial Self-Fashioning: Frontispiece Miniatures in Late Medieval French and English Manuscripts." *Mediaevalia* 21 (1996): 97–160.

Marquez-Villaneuva, Francisco. "The Alfonsine Cultural Concept." In *Alfonso X of Castile: The Learned King (1221–1284). An International Symposium, Harvard University, 17 November 1984*, edited by Francisco Marquez-Villaneuva and Carlos Alberto Vega, 6–109. Cambridge, MA: Department of Romance Languages and Literatures of Harvard University, 1990.

Mauss, Marcel. *The Gift: The Form and Reason for Exchange in Archaic Societies*. Translated by W.D. Halls. Foreword by Mary Douglas. New York, London: W.W. Norton Press, 1990.

McCabe, Richard. "*Ungainefull Arte": Poetry, Patronage, and Print in the Early Modern Era*. Oxford: Oxford University Press, 2016.

McCash, June Hall. "The Cultural Patronage of Medieval Women: An Overview." In *The Cultural Patronage of Medieval Women*, edited by June Hall McCash, 1–49. Athens, GA: University of Georgia Press, 1996.

McFarlane, Kenneth Bruce. "Bastard Feudalism." In *England in the Fifteenth Century: Collected Essays*, 23–44. London: Hambledon, 1981.

McGovern, John F. "The Rise of New Economic Attitudes – Economic Humanism, Economic Nationalism – During the Late Middle Ages and the Renaissance, A.D. 1200–1550." *Traditio* 26 (1970): 217–53.

McGrady, Deborah. "Authorship and Audience in the Prologues to Christine de Pizan's Commissioned Poetry." In Hicks, *Au champ des escriptures*, 25–40.

– *Controlling Readers: Guillaume de Machaut and His Late Medieval Audience*. Toronto: University of Toronto Press, 2006.

– "De 'l'onneur et louenge des femmes': Les dédicaces épistolaire du *Débat sur le* Roman de la Rose et la réconfiguration du champ littéraire." Special issue, *Etudes françaises* 47, no. 3 (2011): 11–28.

– "Guillaume de Machaut." In *The Cambridge Companion to Medieval French Literature*, edited by Sarah Kay and Simon Gaunt, 109–22. Cambridge University Press, 2008.

– "Introduction: Rethinking the Boundaries of Patronage." Special issue, *Digital Philology: A Journal of Medieval Cultures* 2, no. 2 (2013): 145–54.

– "Machaut and His Material Legacy." In *A Companion to Guillaume de Machaut*, edited by Deborah McGrady and Jennifer Bain, 361–85. Leiden and Boston: Brill, 2012.

– "Printing the Patron's Pleasure for Profit: The Case of the *Épîtres de l'Amant Vert*." *Journal of the Early Book Society* 2 (1999): 89–112.

– "Textual Bodies, the Digital Surrogate, and Desire: Guillaume de Machaut's Judgment Cycle and his Protean Corpus." Special issue, *Digital Philology* 5, no. 1 (2016): 8–27.

– "'Tout son païs m'abandonna': Reinventing Patronage in Machaut's *Fonteinne amoureuse*." *Yale French Studies* 110 (December 2007): 19–31.

– "What is a Patron? Benefactors and Authorship in MS Harley 4431, Christine de Pizan's Collected Works." In *Christine de Pizan and the Categories of Difference*, edited by Marilynn Desmond, 195–214. Minnesota: Minnesota University Press, 1998.

Medeiros, Marie-Thérèse de. "Le pacte encomiastique: Froissart, ses *Chroniques* et ses mécènes." *Le moyen âge. Revue d'histoire et de philologie* 94 (1988). 237–55.

Meikle, Scott. *Aristotle's Economic Thought*. Oxford: Clarendon Press/New York: Oxford University Press, 1995.

Meiss, Millard. *French Painting in the Time of Jean de Berry: The Late Fourteenth Century and the Patronage of the Duke*. 2 vols. New York: Phaidon, 1967.

Meiss, Millard, and Sharon Off. "The Bookkeeping of Robinet d'Estampes and Chronology of Jean de Berry's Manuscripts." *Art Bulletin* 53 (1971): 225–35.

Michon, Patricia. "Une édition manuscrite d'Eustache Deschamps: Le *Double lay de la fragilité humaine*." *Travaux de littérature* 14 (2001): 27–41.

Millet, Hélène. "Nouveaux documents sur Nicolas de Gonesse, traducteur de Valère Maxime." *Romania* 102 (1981): 110–14.

Minet-Mahy, Virginie. *Esthétique et pouvoir de l'œuvre allégorique à l'époque de Charles VI: Imaginaires et discours*. Paris: Champion, 2005.

Minois, Georges. *La guerre de cent ans: Naissance de deux nations*. Paris: Perrin, 2008.

Miyazaki, Hirokazu. "Gifts and Exchange." In *The Oxford Handbook of Material Culture Studies*, edited by Dan Hicks and Mary C. Beaudry, 246–64. Oxford: Oxford University Press, 2010.

Monfrin, Jacques. "Humanisme et traductions au moyen âge." *Journal des savants* 3 (1963): 161–90.

– "Les traducteurs et leur public en France au moyen âge." *Journal des savants* 4 (1964): 5–20.

Nederman, Cary J. "The Virtues of Necessity: Labor, Money, and Corruption in John of Salisbury's Thought." *Viator* 33 (2002): 54–68.

Neveux, François. "Nicole Oresme et le clergé normand du XIVe siècle." In *Autour de Nicole Oresme, Actes du colloque oresme organisé à l'université de Paris XII*, edited by Jeannine Quillet, 9–36. Paris: Libraire philosophique J. Vrin, 1990.

O'Meara, Carra Ferguson. *Monarchy and Consent: The Coronation Book of Charles V of France*. London: Harvey Miller Publishers, 2000.

Ouy, Gilbert, and Christine Reno. "Manuscrits copiés en série: Les quatre témoins contemporains du *Livre des fais et bonnes meurs du sage roy Charles Ve d'icelluy nom*." *Cahiers de recherches médiévales* 16 (2008): 239–52.

Ouy, Gilbert, Christine Reno, and Inès Villela-Petit. *Album Christine de Pizan*. Brussels: Brepols, 2012.

Parsons, John Carmi. "Of Queens, Courts, and Books: Reflections on the Literary Patronage of Thirteenth-Century Plantagenet Queens." In *The Cultural Patronage of Medieval Women*, edited by June Hall McCash, 175–201. Athens, Georgia: University of Georgia Press, 1996.

Parussa, Gabriella. "Autographes et orthographe. Quelques considération sur l'orthographe de Christine de Pizan." *Romania* 117 (1999): 143–59.

Parussa, Gabriella, and Richard Trachsler. "*Or sus, alons ou champ des escripturs.* Encore sur l'orthographe de Christine de Pizan: L'Intérêt des grands corpus." In *Contexts and Continuities*, edited by Angus Kennedy, Rosalind Brown-Grant, James C. Laidlaw, and Catherine M. Müller, vol. 3, 621–41. Glasgow: Glasgow University Press, 2002.

Paviot, Jacques. "Le mécénat des princes Valois vers 1400." In *Création artistique en France autour de 1400*, edited by Elisabeth Taburet-Delahaye, 19–24. Paris: La Documentation française, 2006.

Payen, Jean-Charles. "Littérature et chrétienté sous le règne de Saint Louis: Equilibres et malaises." In *Septième Centenaire de la mort de Saint Louis (Actes des colloques de Royaumont et Paris, 1970)*, edited by L. Carolus-Barré, 331–44. Paris: Académie de Belles Lettres, 1976.

Perkinson, Stephen. *Likeness of the King: A Prehistory of Portraiture in Late Medieval France*. Chicago: University of Chicago Press, 2009.

Petey-Girard, Bruno. *Le sceptre et la plume. Images du prince protecteur des Lettres de la Renaissance au Grand Siècle*. Geneva: Droz, 2010.

Picherit, Jean-Louis. "*Le livre de la Prod'hommie de l'homme* et *Le livre de Prudence* de Christine de Pizan: Chronologie, structure et composition." *Le Moyen Âge* 40 (1985): 381–413.

Plagnieux, Philippe, and Elisabeth Taburet-Delahaye. "Art et politique au temps des princes des fleurs de lys." *Histoire de l'art: Bulletin d'information de l'institut national d'histoire de l'art* 55 (2004): 19–21.

Pleybert, Frédéric. "Art, pouvoir et politique." In Pleybert, *Paris et Charles V*, 49–58.

– ed. *Paris et Charles V: Arts et Architecture*. Paris: Action artistique de la ville de Paris, 2001.

Plumley, Yolanda. *The Art of Grafted Song: Citation and Illusion in the Age of Machaut*. Oxford: Oxford University Press, 2013.

Poirion, Daniel. *Littérature française: Le Moyen Âge 1300–1480*. Paris: Arthaud, 1971.

– *Le poète et le prince: L'évolution du lyrisme courtois de Guillaume de Machaut à Charles d'Orléans*. Paris, 1965.

Post, Gaines. "Masters' Salaries and Student-Fees in the Mediaeval Universities." *Speculum* 7 (1932): 181–98.

Post, Gaines, Kimon Giocarinis, and Richard Kay. "The Medieval Heritage of a Humanistic Ideal: *Scientia donum Dei est, unde vendi non potest.*" *Traditio* 11 (1955) 195–234.

Potin, Yann. "A la recherche de la librairie du Louvre: Le témoignage du manuscrit français 2700." *Gazette du livre medieval* 34 (1999): 25–36.

Procter, Evelyn Stefanos. *Alfonso X of Castile: Patron of Literature and Learning*. Oxford: Clarendon Press, 1951.

Quillet, Jeannine. *Charles V, le roi lettré: Essai sur la pensée politique d'un règne*. Paris: Perrin, 1984.

Regalado, Nancy. "The *Chronique métrique* and the Moral Design of BN fr. 146: Feasts of Good and Evil." In *Fauvel Studies: Allegory, Chronicle, Music, and Image in Paris, Bibliothèque nationale de France, MS français 146*, edited by M. Bent and A. Wathey, 469–94. Oxford and New York: Clarendon Press and Oxford University Press, 1998.

Reno, Christine. "Le *Livre de Prudence/ Livre de la Prod'hommie de l'homme*: Nouvelles perspectives." In *Une Femme de lettres au Moyen Age: Etudes autour de Christine de Pizan*, edited by Liliane Dulac and Bernard Ribémont, 25–37. Orléans: Paradigme, 1995.

– "Les *nota bene* dans trois manuscrits de présentation de la *Mutacion de Fortune*." In Hicks, *Au champ des escriptures*, 780–87.

Ribémont, Bernard. "Jean Corbechon, un traducteur encyclopédiste au XIVe siècle." *Cahiers de recherches médiévales et humanistes* 6 (1999): 2–16.

Robertson, Anne W. "The Mass of Guillaume de Machaut in the Cathedral of Reims." In *Plainsong in the Age of Polyphony*, edited by Thomas Forrest Kelly, 100–39. Cambridge: Cambridge University Press, 1992.

Robin, Françoise. "Le luxe des collections aux XIVe et XVe siècles." In Vernet, *Les bibliothèques médiévales: VIe siècle–1530*, 193–214.

Roccati, G. Matteo. "Guillaume de Machaut, 'Prologue' aux oeuvres: La disposition du texte dans le MS. A (Paris, B.N.F., fr. 1584)." *Studi Francesi* 11 (2000): 535–400.

Rouse, Richard H., and Mary A. Rouse. *Illiterati et uxorati: Manuscripts and Their Makers. Commercial Book Producers in Medieval Paris, 1200–1500*. 2 vols. London: Harvey Miller Publishers, 2000.

Roux, Brigitte. "Charles V et Charles VI en miroir(s)." *Le Moyen Age* 116 (2010): 679–95.

Rubin, David Lee. *The Sun King: The Ascendancy of French Culture during the Reign of Louis XIV*. Washington: Folger Shakespeare Library; London: Associated University Presses, 1992.

Salter, Elizabeth, Derek Pearsall, Nicolette Zeeman, eds. *English and International: Studies in the Literature, Art, and Patronage of Medieval England*. Cambridge and New York: Cambridge University Press, 1988.

Sauval, Henri. *Histoire et recherches des antiquités de la ville de Paris*. 3 vols. Reprint. Franborough: Gregg International Publishers, 1969.

Schleif, Corine. "Seeking Patronage: Patrons and Matrons in Language, Art, and Historiography." In Hourihane, *Patronage: Power and Agency in Medieval Art*, 206–32.

Schrift, Alan D., ed. "Introduction: Why Gift?" In Schrift, *The Logic of the Gift*, 1–22.

– *The Logic of the Gift: Toward an Ethic of Generosity*. New York: Routledge 1997.

Sennelart Michel. *Les arts de gouverner. Du regimen médiéval au concept de gouvernement*. Paris: Seuil, 1995.

Sère, Bénédicte. *Penser l'amitié au Moyen Âge*. Turnhout, Belgium: Brepols, 2007.

Sherman, Claire Richter. *Imaging Aristotle: Verbal and Visual Representation in Fourteenth-Century France*. Berkeley: University of California Press, 1995.

– *The Portraits of Charles V of France, 1338–1380*. New York: New York University Press, 1969.

– "The Queen in Charles V's 'Coronation Book': Jeanne de Bourbon and the 'Ordo ad Reginam Benedicendam'." *Viator* 8 (1977): 255–310.

– "A Second Instruction to the Reader from Nicole Oresme, Translator of Aristotle's *Politics* and *Economics*." *Art Bulletin* 61 (1979): 468–9.

Shultz, Christopher R. "The Artistic and Literary Patronage of Louis of Orléans and His Wife, Valentine Visconti, 1389–1408." PhD diss., Emory University, 1977.

Smith, Sharon Dunlap. "Illustrations of Raoul de Praelles' Translations of St. Augustine's *City of God* between 1375 and 1420." 2 vols. PhD diss., New York University, 1974.

– "New Themes for the *City of God* around 1400: The Illustrations of Raoul de Presles' Translation." *Scriptorium* 36, no. 1 (1982): 68–82.

Smyth, Alfred P. *King Alfred the Great*. Oxford: Oxford University Press, 1996.

Solente, Suzanne. *Christine de Pisan. Histoire littéraire de la France*. Vol. 40. Paris: Klincksieck, 1969.

Spiegel, Gabrielle. *The Chronicle Tradition of St Denis*. Brookline, MA: Leyden, 1978.

– *Romancing the Past: The Rise of Vernacular Historiography in Thirteenth-Century France*. California: University of California Press, 1995.

Spufford, Peter. *Handbook of Medieval Exchange*. Royal Historical Guides and Handbooks 13. With the assistance of Wendy Wilkinson and Sarah Tolley. London: Royal Historical Society, 1986.

Stirneman, Patricia. "Les bibliothèques princières et privées aux XIIe et XIIIe siècles." In Vernet, *Les bibliothèques médiévales: VIe siècle–1530*, 173–92.

Swift, Helen. "Circuits of Power: A Model for Rereading Poet-Patron Relations in Late-Medieval Defences of Women." Special issue, *Digital Philology: A Journal of Medieval Cultures* 2, no. 2 (2013): 222–42.

Taburet-Delahaye, Elisabeth, ed. *Création artistique en France autour de 1400.* Paris: Ecole du Louvre, 2006.

– ed. *Paris 1400: Les arts sous Charles VI*. Paris: Fayard, 2004.

Taveau-Launay, Isabelle. "Raymond du Temple, maître d'oeuvre des rois de France et des princes." In *Du projet au chantier*, edited by Odette Chapelot, 323–38. Paris: Editions de l'Ecole des Hautes Etudes en Sciences Sociales, 2001.

Tesnière, Marie-Hélène. "Un cas de censure dans la Librairie du Louvre." *Cultura neolatina* 65 (2005): 271–85.

– "La librairie modèle." In Pleybert, *Paris et Charles V*, 225–33.

– "La littérature autour de 1300 dans la librairie du Louvre: Recherches." In *La moisson des lettres: L'invention littéraire autour de 1300*, edited by Hélène Bellon-Méguelle, Olivier Collet, Yasmina Foehr-Janssens, and Ludivine Jaquiéry, 49–80. Turnhout: Brepols Publishers, 2011.

– "Les manuscrits copiés par Raoul Tainguy: Un aspect de la culture des grands officiers royaux au début du XVe siècle." *Romania* 107 (1986): 282–368.

Thiry, Claude. "Poésie de circonstance." In *Grundriss der romanischen literature des Mittelalters*, edited by Hans-Robert Jauss and Erich Köhler; vol. 8, *La littérature française aux XIVe et XVe siècles*, edited by Daniel Poirion, 111–38. Heidelburg: Carl Winter, 1988.

Tyson, Diana B. "French Vernacular History Writers and Their Patrons in the 14th Century." *Medievalia et Humanistica* 14 (1986): 103–24.

Uebel, Michael, and Kellie Robertson. "Introduction: Conceptualizing Labor in the Middle Ages." In the *Middle Ages at Work: Practicing Labor in Late Medieval England*, edited by Kellie Robertson and Michael Uebel, 1–16. New York: Palgrave, 2004.

Vale, Malcolm. *The Princely Court: Medieval Courts and Culture in North-West Europe, 1270–1380*. Oxford: Oxford University Press, 2001.

Van Den Hoven, Birgit. *Work in Ancient and Medieval Thought: Ancient Philosophers, Medieval Monks and Theologians and their Concept of Work, Occupations and Technology*. Amsterdam: J.C. Giveben, Publisher, 1996.

Van Hemelryck, Tania. "Description of the Manuscripts." In Christine de Pizan, *Livre de Paix*, 41–52.

Van Praet, Joseph Basile Bernard. *L'inventaire ou catalogue des livres de l'ancienne bibliothèque du Louvre fait en l'année 1375 par Gilles Mallet*. Paris: De Bure frères, 1836.

Vaughan, Richard. *John the Fearless: The Growth of Burgundian Power*. Woodbridge, UK: Boydell Press, 2002.

Verger, Jacques. *Les universités au moyen âge*. Paris: Presses universitaires de France, 1973.

Vernet, André, ed. *Les bibliothèques médievales, du VIès siècle à 1530*. Vol. 1. In *Histoire des bibliothèques françaises*, edited by Pascal Fouche. 4 vols. Paris: Promodis, 1988.

Viala, Alain. *Naissance de l'écrivain*. Paris: Les Éditions de Minuit, 1985.

Vidal, Denis. "Le prix de la confiance: Les Renaissances du clientélisme." *Revue terrain* 21 (1993): 9–32.

Vines, Amy N. "Fictions of Patronage: The Romance Heroine as Sponsor in John Metham's *Amoryus and Cleopes*." *Journal of the Early Book Society for the Study of Manuscripts and Printing History* 13 (2010): 139–68.

– "The Rehabilitation of Patronage in Hoccleve's *Series*." Special issue, *Digital Philology: A Journal of Medieval Cultures* 2, no. 2 (2013): 201–21.

Walters, Lori. "Christine de Pizan comme biographe royale." In *Le passé à l'épreuve du présent: Appropriations et usages du passé du Moyen Âge à la Renaissance*, edited by P. Chastang, 223–36. Paris: Presses universitaires de Paris-Sorbonne, 2008.

– "The Royal Vernacular: Poet and Patron in Christine de Pizan's *Charles V* and the *Sept psaumes allégorisés*." In *The Vernacular Spirit: Essays on Medieval Religious Literature*, edited by Renate Blumenfeld-Kosinski, Duncan Robertson, and Nancy Bradley Warren, 145–82. New York: Palgrave, 2002.

Warnke, Martin. *The Court Artist: On the Ancestry of the Modern Artist*. Translated by David McLintock. Cambridge and New York: Cambridge University Press, 1993.

Weiner, Annette. *Inalienable Possessions: The Paradox of Keeping-while-Giving*. Berkeley: University of California Press, 1992.

Whitely, Mary. "Deux escaliers royaux du XIVe siècle: Les 'grands degrez' du Palais de la Cité et la 'Grande Viz' du Louvre," translated by Monique Chatenet. *Bulletin Monumental* 147, no. 2 (1989): 133–54.

– "Le Louvre de Charles V: Dispositions et fonctions d'une residence royale," translated by Monique Chatenet. *Revue de l'art* 97 (1992): 60–71.

Wilkins, Nigel. "A Pattern of Patronage: Machaut, Froissart and the Houses of Luxembourg and Bohemia in the Fourteenth Century." *French Studies* 37, no. 3 (1983): 257–81.

Willard, Charity Cannon. "An Autograph Manuscript of Christine?" *Studi Francesi* 27 (1965): 452–7.

– *Christine de Pizan: Her Life and Works*. New York: Persea Books, 1984.

Williams, Sarah J. "An Author's Role in Fourteenth-Century Book Production: Guillaume de Machaut's 'livre où je met toutes mes choses'." *Romania* 90 (1969): 433–54.

Winn, Mary Beth. "Louise de Savoie, ses enfants et ses livres: Du pouvoir familial au pouvoir d'état." In *Patronnes et mécènes en France à la Renaissance*, edited by Kathleen Wilson-Chevalier, 251–81. Saint-Étienne: Publications de l'Université de Saint-Étienne, 2007.

Zimmermann, Margarete. "Mémoire – tradition – historiographie: Christine de Pizan et son *Livre des fais et bonnes meurs du sage roy Charles V*." In *The City of Scholars: New Approaches to Christine de Pizan*, edited by Margarete Zimmermann and Dina de Rentiis, 158–73. Berlin: Walter de Gruyter & Co., 1994.

Zingesser, Eliza. "The Value of Verse: Storytelling as Accounting in Froissart's *Dit du florin*." *Modern Language Notes* 125 (2010): 861–72.

Index